AGGRESSIVE WAR
AN INTERNATIONAL CRIME

AGGRESSIVE WAR
AN INTERNATIONAL CRIME

PROEFSCHRIFT

TER VERKRIJGING VAN DE GRAAD VAN DOCTOR IN DE RECHTSGELEERDHEID AAN DE RIJKSUNIVERSITEIT TE UTRECHT, OP GEZAG VAN DE RECTOR MAGNIFICUS, Dr V. J. KONINGSBERGER, HOOGLERAAR IN DE FACULTEIT DER WIS- EN NATUURKUNDE, VOLGENS BESLUIT VAN DE SENAAT DER UNIVERSITEIT TEGEN DE BEDENKINGEN VAN DE FACULTEIT DER RECHTSGELEERDHEID TE VERDEDIGEN OP WOENSDAG 14 JANUARI 1953 DES NAMIDDAGS TE 4 UUR

DOOR

CORNELIS ARNOLD POMPE
GEBOREN TE NIJMEGEN

's-GRAVENHAGE
MARTINUS NIJHOFF
1953

Promotor: Prof. Dr J. H. W. VERZIJL

ISBN 978-94-011-8177-8 ISBN 978-94-011-8821-0 (eBook)
DOI 10.1007/978-94-011-8821-0

AAN MIJN VADER EN MOEDER
AAN MÁIRE

Terugziende over de jaren van mijn academische studie, gaan mijn gedachten op de eerste plaats naar hem, die mij al op prille leeftijd rechtskundige lessen gaf en die, als hoogleraar, aan mij zoals aan zijn andere studenten zijn vaderlijke leiding, zorg en belangstelling heeft gegeven. Bij alles wat ik hem en mijn moeder dank en wat niet op deze plaats en niet in woorden kan worden uitgedrukt, denk ik hier bijzonder aan de zorg, die zij voor mijn studie hebben gedragen, en aan de vorming en het voorbeeld, die zij mij daarbij hebben gegeven.

Hooggeleerde Verzijl, hooggeachte promotor, het is een groot voorrecht zich Uw leerling te mogen noemen, te behoren tot hen, voor wie Gij de wereld van het volkenrecht hebt ontsloten en in dienst van wier vorming Gij Uw grote bekwaamheden hebt gesteld. Met grote dankbaarheid denk ik aan de jaren van mijn assistentschap, aan het geregelde contact, dat ik met U heb kunnen onderhouden, en aan Uw nooit aflatende belangstelling en critische zorg, ook voor de ontwikkeliing van inzichten, die niet geheel met de Uwe stroken.

Dankbare herinneringen bewaar ik aan het onderricht, dat ik van U, Hoogleraren en Oud-Hoogleraren van de Juridische Faculteit, heb mogen ontvangen.

Met vreugde en dankbaarheid denk ik aan het Collegium Studiosorum Veritas en aan de vorming en vriendschap, die ik in het Collegium gevonden heb.

Velen in binnen- en buitenland hebben mij bij het werk aan mijn proefschrift hun belangstelling en hulp gegeven. Hun allen, en met name aan de heer Edward Hallam Tuck, die mij hielp bij de revisie van de juridische terminologie, zeg ik hierbij mijn hartelijke dank.

Men heeft het probleem van de definitie van aggressie wel trachten te verhelderen met een verwijzing naar het probleem van de definitie van een lief meisje. Nog onoplosbaarder is voor mij het probleem hoe onder woorden te brengen wat mijn vrouw – niet alleen door het reviseren van de Engelse tekst – voor de totstandkoming van mijn proefschrift heeft betekend.

CONTENTS

"pacis causa perpetua"

INTRODUCTION

Six years after the rendering of the Nuremberg Judgment world conditions are not such as to encourage a study on what constituted its principal innovation in the legal field: the punishment of the authors of aggressive war.

The war alliance against the Axis Powers which was the political basis of the Nuremberg Trial and of the United Nations Organisation has broken up. Mutual fear, threats and accusations and a gigantic armament race are the dominating factors in international life during the cold war period, and the minds of statesmen, military men and lawyers alike are more preoccupied with the problem of how to win a possible third world war than with that of preventing its occurrence and avoiding responsibility for its outbreak. While the survival of their freedom and civilization is at stake, the nations seem more intent on preparing for what is vaguely and equivocally called 'self-defence' than on accepting and assuring the reign of law. The strain of the protracted struggle in Korea, moreover, seems to turn the first experiment with military sanctions against an aggressor into a classic game of power politics.

It is not surprising that in such circumstances little energy is displayed in efforts to implement the principles to which the United Nations pledged themselves in Nuremberg, and that many statesmen and lawyers seem prepared to abandon, at least for the near future, the precedent of the time of alliance, expression of confidence in the victory of law over force. There is a tendency to justify, or at least to excuse, the former enemy leaders for their aggressive actions and to judge the cases submitted in Nuremberg and Tokyo in the light of the past and present conduct of some of the prosecuting Powers and of to-day's political conditions which ask for political freedom and not for strict legal rules. According to this view it would be wise to give way to thc insistence of the defeated on the revisal of the Judgments and to recognize the unfairness of the proceedings, thus undoing some of the harm this 'victor's justice' has caused.

This view is certainly more logical than that of those who approve the judgments as the politically justifiable elimination of dangerous elements but deny the desirability of drawing any general consequences from the principles proclaimed. It is asserted that the acts relating to war and peace are of such magnitude that they cannot give rise to individual criminal responsibility. Wars arise from history, they are movements of peoples rather than of men. Reference can here be made to Tolstoy who, in his 'War and Peace', compares Napoleon leading his troops through Russia to a traveller who, pushing against the inner side of his coach, imagines that it is he who is making the carriage move. On much the same lines it is contended that punishment of the authors of a war cannot have any preventive effect as nations go to war in the idea that they will win it and not because they think they will remain unpunished. In addition to these arguments it is alleged that the law proclaimed in Nuremberg would render whole categories of soldiers and public servants liable to punishment for the fulfilment of their duties in the preparation and waging of a war. The uncertainty of the concepts 'aggression' and 'defence' would, moreover, always allow a victor to eliminate whole categories of enemy persons by judicial proceedings.

The basic question of international relations is whether law can rule over power politics. Though every epoch has known its idealists and its pessimists, a Vitoria and a Macchiavelli, a Grotius and a Thomas Hobbes, some periods have been strongly affected by the attempts to establish world order, while during others mankind seemed to have resigned itself to international chaos and the rule of force.

This century has on the whole been a period of legal construction in the international field, twice interrupted but also greatly stimulated by the occurrence of the catastrophe of a world war. The post-war trials together with the adoption of the United Nations Charter were, after the Second World War, the powerful confirmation of the world's faith in justice as the foundation of peace. The immediate development of a new crisis has shattered this faith but not destoyed it. Objective factors like the total interdependence of nations and the unimaginable increase of destructive power through atomic weapons have made the creation of a just legal order not only desirable but imperative, the only way of saving freedom and civilization which can no more be entrusted to the power of single sovereign nations.

This study has been written on grounds of the conviction that the efforts to create an international legal order, of which criminal justice is an essential part, must and will be continued and that there exist objective standards of international conduct which criminal justice can help to enforce upon individual statesmen and nations. It is not the purpose of this study to argue the desirability of the punishment for aggressive war but only to give a legal justification of the relevant part of the post-war Judgments and to elucidate, as precisely as possible, their legal impacts.

These Judgments and the execution of the sentences imposed by the tribunals are facts which are sealed by the express and solemn approval of the majority of civilized nations and which can no more be undone. And what the nations instituted, adhered to and approved were not extra-ordinary political proceedings but the administration of justice, what they recognized and reaffirmed were not principles of political action but principles of law which they solemnly pledged to apply to themselves as well as to their former enemies.

Though before Nuremberg no rule existed making aggressive war a crime for which individuals could be punished, there was nothing unlawful or unjust in the punishment of the Nazi leaders who launched the Second World War. Resort to aggressive war had been forbidden and condemned in a basic and unequivocal rule of international law. And the Nuremberg Tribunal established beyond any doubt that aggressive war had been resorted to not as a sudden national reaction on international events, not in any mistaken interpretation of the right of self-defence, but after years of careful and deliberate planning and preparation. The Tribunal, recognizing this grave violation of the fundamental rule of international law as having all the essentials of criminality, was justified in punishing its authors in the name of the offended world community, thus establishing a law-making precedent in a field where no criminal law had existed before.

The step making aggressive war an international crime has, thus, been taken. The question of the desirability of such a step is no more a basic issue and the theoretical arguments against holding the authors of an aggressive war individually responsible are refuted by the clear proof of the personal guilt of the Nazi leaders who brought about the war. The penal rule developed in the Nuremberg case can be invoked by any tribunal called upon to judge the authors of an aggressive war and the great task facing the United Nations is to incorporate this rule in a system of international penal law and to institute an international criminal jurisdiction to apply it. A failure to execute this task would be a breach of a heavy moral obligation, but it would not invalidate the established substantial law.

While elaborating this view of the foundation and significance of the post-war Judgments with respect to the criminality of aggressive war, this study presents an attempt to determine the content and limits of the rule developed by the Nuremberg and subsequent tribunals. In view of the far-reaching and exaggerated conclusions which some opponents as well as some supporters of the Nuremberg Judgment have drawn from its *dicta,* the state of international law in this field should be carefully defined. The Nuremberg law remains embodied in the concrete judicial decisions, and in drawing abstract conclusions one continuously runs the danger of overlooking the circumstances of the case in which these decisions were given and the conditions of today's international society.

The first two chapters of this book are concerned with the determination of the state of international public law with regard to the concepts of war and aggression. The last two chapters concern aggressive war as a crime under international penal law and contain an analysis and interpretation of the post-war judgments in the light of preparatory works and subsequent literature, as well as of the steps taken so far for implementing the Nuremberg principles. Between these two parts the third chapter traces the idea of criminal war to the history of international law preceding Nuremberg and contains a survey of the development of the legal concept of war in theory and practice.

Every study dealing with such vital and topical subjects as the definition of aggression and the criminality of war runs the risk of being immediately rendered out of date by the fast-moving international events, by the continuing discussions in the United Nations and by the constant flow of new literature. With the knowledge that effords to be complete and to present definite conclusions on the legal situation are vain, research on the subject has been closed in October 1952.

In this legal study political and philosophical considerations have been discarded as far as possible. But when dealing with a revolutionary development like that which led to the establishment of aggressive war as an international crime, one cannot avoid touching the deeper grounds where law and other sciences find their common origin. No attempt has therefore been made to abstain from expressing convictions which underly every conception and interpretation of law.

ABBREVIATIONS

A.J.I.L.: American Journal of International Law.
B.Y.I.L.: British Yearbook of International Law.
I.M.T.: International Military Tribunal (Nuremberg Tribunal).
L.o.N.: League of Nations.

De Martens, R., N.R., N.S., N.R.G.: Successive parts of de Martens, Recueil de Traités.

R.d.C. (A.D.I.): Recueil des Cours de l'Académie de Droit International.
R.D.I.: Revue de Droit International, de Sciences Diplomatiques, Politiques et Sociales (Genève).
R.G.D.I.P.: Revue Générale de Droit International Public.
U.N.C.I.O.: United Nations Conference on International Organisation (San Francisco 1945).
U.N.W.C.C.: United Nations War Crimes Commission.

CHAPTER I

WAR

SECTION 1. INTRODUCTORY

From the beginning of history until the present day war as a reality and as a problem has influenced the life of man and occupied his mind. In to-day's shrunken world there are few phenomena, events and actions which have no connection with the consequences of a past, or the threat of a new war.

Yet, or perhaps because of this, it was only the accidentals of war, a matter so real in the life of mankind, that were considered in the science of international law. Legal authors have for many centuries had the most widely differing views of the nature of war and have till recently mostly considered the matter as being not strictly relevant in law.

Since Grotius, who defined war as a status [1]), the legal consequences of war – the special rules applicable between belligerents and, in a later period, those applicable between belligerents and neutrals – have been described and developed in a consistent way. But the acts of starting and waging war, and the juridical qualifications to be attached to these acts, which for Grotius and his time were the essentials of the matter, lost more and more of their significance for what is known as 'classic' international law.

The question of war *in se* was ignored by many as it was considered to have no legal significance, and was left to philosophical

---

1) De Jure Belli ac Pacis, Liber I, caput I, section ii, par. 1, (editio Molhuysen, p. 21): „Cicero dixit bellum certationem per vim. Sed usus obtinuit, ut non actio, sed status eo nomine indicatur, ita ut sit Bellum status per vim certantium qua tales sunt".

and meta-juridical speculation [1]. Other writers have emphatically affirmed the right to wage war inherent in sovereignty, and have regarded war as a procedure, a legal remedy, a means for solving international disputes [2], or as a corrective of the static character of international society, a means – the principal and necessary means – of international development [3]. Most writers, however, considered war as a fact, a phenomenon, which legal science could only record but on the occurrence of which law could never have any influence [4].

The Covenant of the League of Nations which prohibited resort to war under most circumstances, and the subsequent treaties and declarations which branded war as an international crime, compelled even the most positivistic author to consider the launching of war again as a responsible act of legal subjects.

It is from the latter point of view, the only relevant point of view for international criminal law, that aggressive war, war as a criminal act, must be determined. But this determination must necessarily be preceded by an examination of the limits of the classic concept of war, as it has been developed in international law prior to, and during the attempts to regulate and abolish the right to resort to war. Only with and on the basis of the technical, objective concept of the state of war can the act of aggression, of the initiating of a war of aggression, be defined through a determination of the responsibility for this situation.

Which then are the criteria on which the application of the

---

1) D. Anzilotti, Corso di Diritto Internazionale, Vol. III, (Roma 1915), p. 185; J. Westlake, International Law, Vol. II, 2nd ed., (1913), p. 3; F. von Liszt, Das Völkerrecht, 12th ed. (Berlin, 1925), p. 446. See further, also with regard to notes 2)–4) hereunder, Chapter III, p. 138 ff. below.

2) R. Phillimore, Commentaries upon International Law, Vol. III (London 1885), p. 77; Wheaton's International Law, Vol. II, 7th English ed. (London 1944), p. 99; Fauchille–Bonfils, Traité de Droit International Public, Tome II, 8me éd. (Paris 1921), p. 7; P. Guggenheim, Lehrbuch des Volkerrechts (Basel 1951), p. 591. See further authors quoted in Quincy Wright, Changes in the concept of war, A.J.I.L. 1924, p. 755 ff., notes 15 and 46. According to Kelsen war is always an international sanction (see p. 146 below).

3) Bluntschli, Le Droit International Codifié (Paris 1895), p. 11, and particularly the German authors quoted there. Oppenheim–Lauterpacht, International Law, Vol. II, 7th ed. (London 1952), pp. 277 ff., speaks of two contradictory functions of war, as a legal remedy and as a means of change. On the alleged 'legality' of war, see Chapter IV, p. 301.

4) Karl Strupp, Elements de Droit International Public (Paris 1927), p. 332, and authors quoted there.

law of war depends and with which the state of war can be distinguished from other forms in which force is used or threatened? It appears that on three sides war must be marked out with respect to contiguous situations. First, war as combat between States must be distinguished from internal military struggle, insurgence or civil war. Secondly war must be distinguished from the interstate use of armed force which does not give rise to a state of war but, according to some authors, to a 'status mixtus'; in this category are peaceful blokades, reprisals, interventions, peaceful occupations, 'incidents', 'armed conflicts' and whatever other forms and terms have been designed to cover warlike acts and situations occurring more and more frequently in recent history. And finally it is an open question whether a military action against a State, pursuant to a decision or recommendation of a collective organ responsible for the maintenance of peace and security and common to the majority of States, creates indeed the normal belligerent relations and the relations of neutrality as between the fighting powers and possible outsiders [1]).

The first as well as the last distinction concerns the legal position of the fighting parties. When for the purpose of these distinctions the parties to a war can provisionally be indicated as individual, recognized States, modern state-practice and international law traditionally based on the alternative of peace and war are faced with the more complicated question: which objective conditions or situations determine whether a use of armed force between States is to be qualified as war?

The great majority of civilized States determined in the third Hague Convention of 1907 – 'relative to the opening of hostilities' [2]) – that hostilities between them should only take place when preceded by a declaration of war 'giving reasons' or by the passing of a time limit announced in an ultimatum. Three characteristics of the position of war in international law appear from the text of this Convention.

First of all the remarkable quasi-legality of the breach of the law of peace by giving the use of force the frame of war. The

1) See below, p. 36.
2) Convention relative to the Opening of Hostilities, text in The Hague Conventions and Declarations of 1899 and 1907, edited by J. B. Scott, 3d ed. (1918), pp. 96 ff..

breach of existing treaties, the violation of the most fundamental obligations which the international law of peace imposes on the States with respect to each other, the continued use of the utmost force intended to bring about the realisation of real or pretended claims or of purely political aspirations, all these acts cease to be illegal and are quasi-legalised by a declaration of war by the State committing them.

For hostilities and declarations of war do not, in general, come from both sides at the same time, and it is therefore in the power of any State to bring about the state of war with any other State. This is the second conclusion to be drawn from this convention the drafters of which demonstrated by their careful description of this circumstance a certain dislike of international anarchy.

And, finally, it follows from this convention that the state of war can also come about without a declaration or ultimatum. The contracting parties bind themselves to the use of a certain procedure; they do not make the use of this procedure a condition precedent to a state of war. This is apparent from the second article of the Convention where it is stated with respect to neutrals that they cannot refer to the absence of a notification of the outbreak of a war – which the belligerents are bound to give – "if it is clearly established that they were in fact aware of the existence of a state of war". It was precisely to avoid the initiation of a state of war by the mere opening of hostilities and to avoid the consequent uncertainty concerning the transition from peace to war, especially embarrassing for neutrals, that this convention was concluded.

There was also, certainly, a more ambitious motive behind the conclusion of this Convention. While the direct efforts to limit the competence to resort to war had failed at the Second Hague Conference, this Convention could make a definite contribution towards the efforts directed at lessening the possibility of war by making its commencement more formal and therefore more difficult.

Armed force is also used outside the state of war, notably in interventions and reprisals. For this reason some legal writers require for the establishment of a state of war, in addition to a condition of fact which is the use of military force, an element of intent, the *animus belligerendi* [1]). This latter condition is, however, more easily accepted in theory than in practice. Proof of such an *animus belligerendi* can be sought in the informal declarations by the initiator of the hostilities to the effect that it seeks the complete military defeat of its opponent, or by the attacked State to the effect that it considers the military acts directed against it as the beginning of a war.

Concerning both these declarations, doctrine and practice agree that they bring about a state of war. But, in the absence of more or less clear statements from one or other of the contending parties, can evidence of the *animus* also be gathered from the nature and circumstances of the acts which they commit with respect to each other? Range and intensity of the military operations or preparations, like a general mobilisation, the rupture of diplomatic and consular relations, the State's prohibition of traffic and intercourse with the 'enemy' nationals, the declaration of a blockade or the seizure of prize, can indeed be unambiguous indications of the existence of an *animus belligerendi.*

It has been rightly remarked [2]) that in these cases it is the nature of these acts themselves rather than the possible intent behind them which leads States to use their right to declare that a war exists with regard to which they intend to remain neutral. The state of war not only establishes special relations, different from those applying in peace-time, between the belligerents but also between these and the other powers. And these relations have become even more important since the creation of an interstate organisation for the maintenance of collective security. The collective interest in the maintenance of international peace, first of the League of Nations, and now of the United Nations, weighs more heavily than the legal, political and commercial interests involved in a foreign war, on the part of individual States.

War was never a matter for the belligerents only, and in the

---

1) Arnold McNair, The legal Meaning of War, and the Relation of War to Reprisals, Grotius Society Transactions, Vol. 11 (1926) pp. 29 ff., p. 45; Quincy Wright (When Does War Exist?, A.J.I.L. 1932, pp. 362 ff., p. 365) states: "An act of war starts a state of war only if there is a real intent to create a state of war".

2) Clyde Eagleton, The Attempt to Define War, International Conciliation (Carnegie Endowment for International Peace), No. 291, 1933, pp. 235 ff., p. 270.

present world, characterized as it is by a far-reaching interdependence it can be said that it is not even primarily so. This is the main objection against the very vague doctrine of *animus belligerendi* which makes the existence of a state of war, even in the absence of a pertinent declaration of belligerency, completely dependent on the willingness of the parties to demonstrate their intention, however their acts may disturb the international order.

If the doctrine ever had any value it was definitely eliminated by Article 11 of the Covenant of the League of Nations which declared "any war or threat of war, whether immediately affecting any of the Members of the League or not, ... a matter of concern to the whole League". Even clearer in this respect is Article 39 of the United Nations Charter which, though not using the term 'war', leaves to the Security Council the determination of "any threat to the peace, breach of the peace or act of aggression". Objective criteria, or at any rate considerations independent from the mere intention of the parties concerned, must be applied in defining the concept of war.

It follows from what has been said before that a state of war always comes into force, with all its consequences for the relations between the belligerents and with respect to neutrals, through a formal declaration of war, or what is equivalent to that, by a State, even if the existence of a war is denied by the opponent or by the other States. The same applies to an act of armed force against another State, when the State committing that act, or the State which is victim of it, makes it clearly known that it considers that act as an act of war.

The situation is different when neither of the States using armed force against the other is prepared to recognize the existence of a state of war. In that case, however, every other State is entitled to give a declaration of neutrality, and a competent collective organ of the States is, *a fortiori,* qualified to declare that it holds that the conflict nevertheless constitutes a war.

The cloud of confusion which has laid itself round the concept of war, especially since the last century, results from the fact that in the latter cases, because of the nature of the international society, special relations are established only between the declaring State, or States, or the collective organ, on the one hand, and both the belligerent parties on the other. Neither the relations between the latter nor their relations with other States are influenced by such declarations of neutrality.

To clarify these statements some examples may be given from the practice of States before and after the efforts to eliminate war, which efforts have considerably increased the tendency to mask war and to conduct vast international military operations under pacific names.

SECTION 2. RELATIVITY OF THE STATE OF WAR

In the last century especially the cases of pacific blockade demonstrated the relativity of the state of war. In the beginning of the century British, French and Russian squadrons blockaded the Turkish coast to prevent Egypt from assisting Turkey against the Greek insurgents. The blockade resulted in the sea-battle of Navarino, 1927, where the Turkish-Egyptian navy was utterly routed and thousands lost their lives. But no war was declared by either of the parties and the ambassadors of the blockading powers remained in Constantinople [1]. No third State seems to have applied the rules of neutrality with respect to this situation.

That, however, is what happened in one of the last cases of pacific blockade, when in 1902 England, Germany and Italy sent battle-ships to blockade Venezuela in order to compel this State to fulfil its financial obligations towards their subjects. The United States of America, resenting the use of force by European states on the American continent, declared that it considered the proceeding as an act of war [2]. And though the process of this blockade was less violent than in the case mentioned above, Great Britain afterwards renewed a number of its treaties with Venezuela "inasmuch that it may be contended that the establishment of a blockade of a Venezuelan port by the British naval forces has, *ipso facto,* created a state of war between Britain and Venezuela and that any treaty existing between the two countries has been thereby abrogated" [3]. This case was the motive for the

1) McNair, l.c., p. 37. Grant-Temperly, Europe in the Nineteenth and Twentieth Century, 6th ed. (London 1952), p. 204 nt. 1), quotes the official qualification of the battle by the Allied Governments as 'an untoward event'. See also R. Redslob, Histoire des Grands Principes du Droit des Gens (Paris 1923), p. 371.

2) Wright, l.c., p. 364.

3) Protocol of 13 February 1903 between the United Kingdom and the United States of Venezuela, Article VIII, de Martens, N.R.G., 3me série, Vol. I, p. 30.

so-called Porter Convention of 1907, respecting the limitation of the employment of force for the recovery of contract-debts, whereby the States agreed to abstain from recourse to arms for this purpose except when the debtor State would refuse a pacific settlement of the conflict by arbitration [1]).

From a comparison of these two cases it is clear that the success of the design of the blockading powers, that is to impose their will on the blockaded State, is dependent on their military and political supremacy. And only in the case where such a supremacy existed would third powers be satisfied with 'the pacific character' of the blockade. The power of the three European States on the American hemisphere in 1902 was considerably less than that of the European Concert in the Medditeranean, and the resulting situations were in accordance with these different conditions. When, in 1884, Formosa was blockaded by one State only, France, England declared that in view of the hostilities which had occurred, it took the notice of the blockade to mean that a war was going on.

Also due to the consequences for third States, the pacific blockade was the most dangerous form of 'hostilities short of war', whether it be in the form of reprisals – acts illicit in themselves to which States resort in order to redress a wrong – or in the form of intervention – "dictatorial interference by a State in the affairs of another State for the purpose of maintaining or altering the actual conditions of things" [2]). Yet only in five out of many cases has such blockade in the last century led to a State of war [3]).

During the First World War the Convention relative to the opening of hostilities was observed by nearly all parties [4]). After

1) Convention respecting the Limitation of the Employment of Armed Force for the Recovery of Contract-debts, Article I, The Hague Conventions, o.c., p. 89.

2) Oppenheim–Lauterpacht, o.c., Vol. I, 7th ed. (London 1948), p. 272. The difference from reprisals is not very strict, as the interfering State will most times hold or allege that 'the actual condition of things' which it wishes to alter constitutes a wrong.

3) McNair, ibidem, and, quoted by him, Howard, Pacific Blockade (1908), pp. 73–76. See on the Allied blockade against Greece in 1916, J. H. W. Verzijl, Le Droit des Prises (Leyde 1924), p. 950, par. 545.

4) Turkey which attacked the Allied forces without a previous declaration was no party to the Convention of 1907.

the war a period opened which was characterised not only by continuous attempts to restrict and abolish the right to wage war, but also by the frequent occurence of acts of force which were justified as 'reprisals' or covered by various 'legal' terms which had never been used before. Between 1919 and 1939 war was declared only in one case, namely by Paraguay in 1934, in its dispute with Bolivia over the Chaco-Boreal. In the years immediately after the Peace-Treaties of 1919 some of the newly established or re-established States in East and Central Europe resorted repeatedly to the use of force in order to obtain territorial advantages. In all these cases the state of war was avoided and the purpose of the enterprise for the greater part achieved.

Italy occupied and kept Fiume, Poland in the same way obtained Wilna, the capital of Lithuania, while the latter in its turn took the East-Prussian Memel-territory. By the use of force Poland managed to improve its position in Upper-Silesia, and the renewed occupation of the Austrian Burgenland by Hungary finally brought it the city of Oedenburg. All this happened at a time of peace. The temporary supremacy of the acting States was in all these cases the condition of their successes, which were more or less sanctioned by the League of Nations [1]).

A more classic case was the bombing, followed by the occupation, of the Greek Island of Corfu by Italy as a reprisal for the murder of Italian state-officials on Greek territory 1923). In the course of the following dispute in which Italy completely achieved its purpose, the Council of the League of Nations appointed a Committee of Jurists to report to it on the legal aspects of the matter. The Commission reported its opinion to the effect that "coercive measures which are not intended to constitute acts of war may or may not be inconsistent with the provisions of Articles 12 to 15 of the Covenant" and that the Council of the League had to decide whether or not these measures are to be maintained [2]).

The Articles referred to above prohibit 'resort to war' without previous exhaustion of the methods of peaceful settlement prescribed therein. Though the conclusion of the Committee has been

---

1) See on these cases, Gathorne-Hardy, A short History of International Affairs, 1920–1939, 4th ed., (London 1951), pp. 83–101.

2) Opinion of the Commission of Jurists on the Janina-Corfu Affair, Quincy Wright, Changes in the Conception of War, A.J.I.L., 1924, pp. 536–544, p. 541.

severely criticised on account of its ambiguity [1]) it clearly enunciates the thesis advanced above according to which the intention of the States using force is not the decive criterion in deciding whether or not 'resort to war' has taken place. The Report of the Jurists affirms unequivocally that the international organism concerned has the competence to answer this question even contrary to the declared will of the parties [2]).

The fact that the Council of the League never used this right may be called a proof of political wisdom in the Corfu-case, and a proof of offensive political weakness in the later Japanese 'incidents' in China, but that did not alter the aforesaid competence of the Council which was necessary for the effectiveness of the system of collective security.

Greece, victim of violence in 1923, itself invaded Bulgaria in 1925, following a border-incident. Because of the withdrawal of Bulgarian troops and because of the speedy action of the League-Council the conflict was settled and the *status quo ante* was restored. This first succesful action of the League was based on conciliation; neither between the parties, nor in the League procedure was there any question of war [3]). The Greeks appealed to the right of legitimate self-defence.

In the period separating this incident from that of Mukden – on the consequences of which the problems of the boundary between peace and war have been centred – many supplementary treaties and resolutions were proposed and adopted for the purpose of making the system of maintaining peace and settling disputes firmer and more coherent than it was in the Covenant. It is remarkable that the treaties designing procedures and sanctions for the organisation of peace – the Draft Treaty of Mutual Guarantee (1928) [4]), the Protocol of Geneva (1924) [5]),

---

1) McNair, l.c., p. 45; Eagleton, l.c., pp. 247–250 and authors quoted by him.

2) H. Lauterpacht, 'Resort to War' and the Interpretation of the Covenant during the Manchurian Dispute, A.J.I.L., 1934, pp. 43 ff., p. 54.

3) League of Nations, Official Journal, 1925, pp. 1696–1718.

4) Articles 1–4, L.o.N. Official Journal, 1923, pp. 1521 ff.

5) Protocol for the Pacific settlement of International Disputes, adopted by the league Assembly of 1924, but never ratified, Articles 2, 9, 10 and 11. Text in International Legislation, a collection of the texts of multipartite international instruments of general interest, edited by Manley O. Hudson, (Carnegie Endowment for International Peace), Vol. II, 1922–1924 (Washington 1931), pp. 1378 ff.

the Locarno Treaties (1925) [1]) and the General Act of Geneva (1928) [2]) – use the terms 'aggression' and 'attack' which had been used in treaties of alliance since 1815, and put them on the same level with 'war', 'aggressive war' or 'resort to war', as used in the Covenant. The more succinct resolutions of the Sixth and Eigth League Assembly [3]) and the Briand-Kellogg Pact [4]) address their incriminations, so far in harmony with the Covenant, exclusively against war, and thus ignore the growing doubt as to the meaning of this term, which was replaced in bilateral non-aggression and alliance treaties by the more material definition of 'hostile acts [5]).

The Japanese action consequent to the 'incident' in Manchuria in 1931 has rightly been said to constitute a resort to war in violation of the Covenant "in the only sense intelligible to the ordinary man", which "only escaped the charge through an open conspiracy not to define it so" [6]). The political history of this struggle clearly demonstrates both the weakness of the great powers and the reason for an attacked State's not resorting to a declaration establishing a state of war. The refusal of the League of Nations Council to recognize the practical existence of a state of war and the League Members' fear of the consequences of a formal war would have annihilated the possibility, however small, of effective help for China, if it itself had proclaimed such a war [7]).

The League Assembly in 1933 adopted the passage from the report of the Lytton-Commission in which it was declared that "the present case is not that of a country which has declared war on another country without previously exhausting the opportuni-

1) Treaty of Mutual Guarantee, Locarno 16 October 1925, Article 2. Text in International Legislation, o.c. Vol. III, pp. 1689 ff.

2) General Act for the Pacific Settlement of Disputes, International Legislation, Vol. IV, pp. 2529 ff..

3) Assembly Resolution of 25 Sept. 1925, L.o.N. Off. Journal, Special Supplement No. 33, 1925, p. 130. Assembly Resolution of 24 September 1927, Off. Journal, Special Supplement No. 54, 1927, p. 155.

4) See below p. 55.

5) See also Article 2 of the (unratified) General Convention to Improve the Means of Preventing War, 1931, (International Legislation, o.c., Vol. IV., pp. 2529 ff.) providing for measures of evacuation of troops to be ordered by the Council "if in circumstances which, in the Council's opinion, do not create a state of war between the Powers at issue which are parties to the present Convention, the forces of one of these powers enter the territory of the other...".

6) Gathorne Hardy, o.c., p. 324.

7) Wright, l.c., pp. 365–6; Eagleton, l.c., pp. 255–6; Lauterpacht, l.c., p. 47.

ties for conciliation provided in the Covenant of the League of Nations". The Assembly thus pronounced that it did not consider that Article 12 had been violated insofar as this Article prohibited 'resort to war'. But the Assembly, following the report, held also "that no question of Chinese responsibility can arise for the development of events since September 18th 1931", and it gave recommendations for the withdrawal of Japanese troops from Manchuria, etc. [1]). These decisions were Japan's reasons for denouncing its membership of the League.

It can be argued, as by Lauterpacht, that these decisions, which were intended to avoid the application of Article 16 prescribing sanctions in case of war, were not literally in violation of the Covenant, at least insofar as Articles 12—15 were concerned [2]). The freedom of the organs of the League not to consider as war hostilities which do not create the state of war between the parties, is also in harmony with the pronunciation of the Committee of Jurists quoted before. But the consequence of the use of this discretionary power in this first Chino-Japanese conflict as well as in the second, following on the Lukouchiao-incident of 1937, was at least, to deprive the terms 'war' and 'resort to war' of 'the only sense intelligible to the ordinary man' and to make the clear opposition between peace and war upon which international law was based, and upon which the system of the Covenant was built, a legal fiction. In the Chaco conflict between Bolivia and Paraguay and during the Italian conquest of Abyssinia the League organs were compelled by the conduct of Paraguay and Abyssinia respectively to recognize the existence of a war, as they were by Finland's reaction to the Soviet-invasion in 1939.

The Charter of the United Nations has in this respect profitted from the League experience and no longer uses the concept of war as a condition of the application of its provisions. The term no longer occurs in the Charter, except in the Preamble and the Articles referring to the Second World War (Artt. 53, 77 and 107). It has been replaced by the terms 'aggression' and 'use of force' introduced long ago in particular treaties, and by the concepts

---

1) L.o.N. Off. Journal, Special Supplement No. 112, 1933, pp. 56—76 and l.c. p. 73 ff..

2) Lauterpacht, l.c., p. 55. Article 10 was certainly disregarded by the Council and the Members of the League, ibidem note 25.

'breach of the peace' and 'threat to the peace' (Artt. 2, par. 4, and 39)[1]).

After the Second World War there are, therefore, no examples of international discussions on the question whether a certain armed conflict amounts to war, but so many more questions have arisen concerning another boundary of the concept of war, that of insurgence or civil war. In fact the question concerns the status of the parties using force.

In the present world divided into organised States the distinction between *bellum publicum* and *bellum privatum* no longer constitutes the same problem as it did in the feudal ages. The former requirement of the *auctoritas principis* on the part of the belligerents in a *bellum justum* (*justa contentio publicorum armorum*) was transformed in classic international law into the rule that every sovereign State was competent to enter into a state of war with any other sovereign State. As such, it no longer constitutes a problem for the individual member of international society. But here the possibility of recognition of belligerency in case of insurgence against the established government of a State, has determined a development which, under an aspect other than the one discussed before, gives even more frequent examples of the relativity of the state of war.

The consequences of an attribution by foreign States of belligerent rights to fighting insurgents are entirely analogous to the consequences of a declaration by foreign States of neutrality in case of hostilities considered as 'short of war' by the parties involved. The non-recognition of the existence of war by the lawful government, that is the attacked party, is in a civil war precisely the characteristic element of the situation. Recognition of the belligerency of the rebellious party, even if given by all other States, cannot by itself alter this, no more than the declarations of the one State can have consequences for the relations between third States and the combatting parties in the case of hostilities short of war.

The essential difference between a declaration of neutrality in case of hostilities and the recognition of belligerency lies

---

1) See below Chapter II, p. 97.

naturally in the fact that the latter does not establish interstate relations between the belligerent insurgents and the neutral State. Recognition of belligerency does not contain the normal international recognition of a State. The analogy between the two recognitions is, however, the inverse application of that suggested above [1]. While declarations of neutrality in the case of hostilities short of war belong to a rather recent period, recognition of belligerency has frequently occured in former centuries and has often given rise to a war between the recognizing State and the State involved in civil war. It was one of the chief purposes of the Holy Alliance to safeguard the established governments against outside interference in civil wars [2].

The situation created by a recognition of belligerency has by itself little importance in view of the penalisation of aggressive war. Whatever the influence of foreign interference on the development, whatever international consequences an insurgence may have, the responsibility for its domestic beginning will not easily become relevant in international penal law. But the great interest which such situations have received in the short history of the United Nations, although regarded as domestic matters by one of the conflicting parties, necessitates a brief survey of these cases.

The Spanish civil war between 1936 and 1939 and the legal positions of the parties involved were the subject of such conflicting opinions between the European governments that, with the imminent danger of an open international conflict, a great confusion arose as to the boundary between war and peace and as to what acts were permitted in the latter situation. The ambiguous concept of 'non-belligerency' was presented as a legal ground for the observance of a qualified neutrality and covered the perpetration of far-reaching military and economic actions at a time of peace.

While the League of Nations did not intervene in the situation arising from the Spanish civil war, the domestic conflicts after the Second World War derived their international interest precisely from the active interference by United Nations organs. First

---

1) Wright l.c., p. 367.
2) Holy Alliance of 26 September 1815. Text in Colliard, Droit International et Histoire Diplomatique, (Paris 1950), pp. 407 ff.

of all it must be noted that in the system of this organisation the competence of which to take measures is not conditioned by the occurrence of a resort to war, there are far more possibilities for international intervention than under the rule of the Covenant. Article 10 of the latter which brought 'external aggression' within the sphere of competence of the League Council was less integrated into the practical system than the following Articles concerned with war only [1]).

It is, further, interesting to note that neither in Article 34 and those following – authorising investigations and recommendations by the Security Council relative to "any dispute, or any situation which might lead to international friction or give rise to a dispute" – nor in Article 39 and those following – prescribing active interference with regard to "any threat to the peace, breach of the peace, or act of aggression" – is it stipulated that the situation, that the threat to the peace, must have been created by the action of a recognized State. And the reservation of the domestic jurisdiction of Member States in Article 2, paragraph 7 does not limit the application of enforcement measures and is, besides, in every concrete situation, subject to a decision of the competent organ of the U.N..

These provisions enabled the United Nations General Assembly to deal with the Greek guerilla war and to investigate the situation through a special committee without previously determining whether the insurgents were assisted by foreign States. Once the fact of this foreign assistance was established, the conduct of these States did not need to be qualified in terms of peace and war to justify orders being given to them [2]).

Situations in colonies were traditionally a welcome opportunity for intervention of third States in internal matters, for example by a declaration of neutrality. The wide discretionary power of the Security Council made it possible that under Article 40 cease-fire orders were given to the Governments of the Netherlands and the Republic of Indonesia, although the latter had not been recognized as a State and although the Dutch sovereignty over Indonesian territory was not questioned [3]).

---

1) See Memorandum Rutgers, quoted below p. 44.

2) General Assembly Resolution 109 (II) of 21 October 1947.

3) Security Council Resolutions S/459, of 1 August 1947, and S/1150, of 24 December 1948.

From this point of view a very interesting situation arose when England had finished the exercise of her mandate over Palestine and when, subsequently, the State of Israël was proclaimed over part of the territory thus left and the new 'State' was attacked by the surrounding Arab States. Though Israël had only been recognized by a few States the Security Council repeatedly applied Article 40 when dealing with the situation. The summons for a prevention of the use of armed force or for a cease-fire was first addressed to 'the Arab and Jewish communities of Palestine' and subsequently to the Arab High Committee and 'the Jewish Agency for Palestine', which, in a later phase, was called 'the provisional Government of Israël' [1]).

Once the State of Israël had been recognized by a great number of States and its condition consolidated, and once hostilities had more or less ceased, negotiations on the conclusion of peace-treaties began, notably between Israël and Jordan which had no more than the other Arab States recognized Israël *de facto* or *de jure*. A peace-treaty ends a state of war. It has happened before that it embodies at the same time the recognition of the State with which it is concluded, for example when it was a peace-treaty between the former mother-country and an emancipated colony, like in 1783 between England and the United States of America.

But the legal judgment of what in U.N. terminology has always carefully been called 'the situation in Palestine' will, after the conclusion of peace-treaties which will end neither a war nor a civil war nor insurgence, become obscured by politico-juridical mists.

The situation consequent to the attack by the People's Republic of North Korea on its twin-sister, the Republic of Korea, also presents a special case. The Republic of Korea, created under the auspices of the United Nations and recognized by the majority of its Members, is ignored by Russia and its Allies which give full recognition to the People's Republic of the North, established in the former zone of Russian occupation. The majority of the United Nations, in their turn, withhold recognition of the

---

1) Security Council Resolutions S/714 (L), of 1 April 1948, and S/902, of 15 July 1948, the latter even more evasively addressing itself to 'the Governments and authorities concerned' with their 'military and para-military forces'

latter. On both sides the respective governments are referred to as puppet-regimes.

Here also, the first activation of the United Nations machinery of enforcement action in application of Article 42 must not be-regarded as recognition of a situation of war. Apart from other problems involved in characterizing the conflict in Korea, it is permissible to assume that as regards the status of the original opponents the intervention of the United Nations and the appeals to the conflicting parties may no more than in the Palestine-conflict, and no more than during actions in Indonesia be considered as recognition of an international status of the North Korean Republic.

There was an 'armed attack' determined to constitute 'a breach of the peace'; a cease-fire was ordered and 'the North Korean authorities' were requested to withdraw their armed forces to the 38th parallel [1]). The use of this phrase, compared with the corresponding reference to the Republic of Korea, indicates a conception of the North Korean Government as an extra-legal, actual power to which, exclusively *ad hoc,* in view of its illegal proceedings, warnings, orders and a collective military force have been adressed.

The position of the North Korean authorities has more in common with that of a pirate than that of an 'outlaw' which term has been suggested with regard to Germany during the Second World War [2]). For the concept of 'outlaw' supposes a previous legal existence. The foregoing consideration may be supported by a reference to the proceedings of the U.N. Commission for Korea and of the U.N. Supreme Commander who at the end of 1950 when the U.N. troops had conquered nearly all of North Korea, completely ignored the previously existing state organisation and announced elections for the whole of Korea as a unified State.

The recognition of that state organisation by a number of States including the People's Republic of China, whose government is also recognized by only a minority of States and which has already offered hospitality to the 'exiled government' of North Korea, makes any qualification of the situation according to general

1) Security Council Resolution S/1501, of 25 June, 1950.

2) See Georg Schwarzenberger, International Law and Totalitarian Lawlessness, (London 1943).

international law extremely relative. The opinion of the U.S.S.R. that the collective action of the United Nations amounts to "unauthorised interference in a civil war" testifies to the deficiency of the traditional terminology in view of modern international situations.

SECTION 3. 'CONSTRUCTIVE' STATE OF WAR

Even a relative concept of war not dependent on the intention of the conflicting parties but on the declarations of outsiders, primarily on those of the organ of the community of States for the maintenance of collective security, seems no longer to have a place in the most recent developments and in the framework of the United Nations. The concept of war seems to have disappeared from the practice of international law.

The question arises as to what international organs are authorised independently to qualify a situation as a war, and as to what limits are set to their freedom of qualification. The question must be considered specifically in view of the competence of the international military tribunals of Nuremberg and Tokyo to determine whether acts constituting 'planning, preparation, imitiation or waging of a war of aggression' had been committed [1]. Is an international judicial organ authorised to carry the 'constuction' of the concept of war further than was done by international governmental organs at the time of the perpetration of such acts?

Before the relevant judicial decisions are examined, further consideration and analysis of what Lauterpacht calls the 'constructive state of war' and of the relation between this concept and that of the classic, legal state of war may be useful. As said before, in the course of legal history there have occurred instances in which a third State declared itself neutral with regard to the relations between two States which, notwithstanding reciprocal acts of violence, considered themselves to be in a state of technical peace with each other. As was the case with recognition of the belligerency of a rebellious movement in another State, the object of the third State was to safeguard its own security, its trade and economic relations, while sometimes a more political motive was involved. The attitude of the U.S. with regard to the

---

1) See below p. 20.

blockade of Venezuela was, for example, evidently inspired by the Monroe-doctrine.

Since the existence of the League of Nations, more specifically since the Janina-Corfu case, the power of its Council and Assembly independently to qualify as a resort to war acts of armed force on the part of a State, whether or not a Member of the League, was generally recognized. None of these organs, however, ever made use of this competence when the existence of a state of war was not admitted by the belligerents. In all these cases a state of war would be called into existence in a very limited sense; it could be said that such a state of war was a derivative of the classic state of war. A state of war would exist in view of certain limited consequences only, be it the establishment of neutrality relations between a third State and the conflicting parties or the application of certain Articles of the Covenant and the it the application of certain Articles of the Covenant and the obligation of Member-States to fulfil the duties incumbent on them in virtue of these Articles. The war existing in the latter case is a concept proper to a particular 'international legal milieu' which, though it was meant to be universal, did not extend to the society of States ruled by international customary law.

This derived concept of war was characterized by its dependence on an actual decision of the competent organ to the effect that one of the Articles 12, 13 or 15 had been violated by a resort to war or that Article 16 had become applicable. In the same way the government of a third State could 'construct' a state of war by declaring that it wanted to remain neutral in an armed conflict, or by a similar declaration. From this dependence on actual decisions it follows that for the 'constructed' state of war the intention of the parties to the conflict is irrelevant.

Common sense demands a limit to the competence to 'construct' a state of war, *id est* the occurence of extended and continued use of armed force between two States. In fact the concept stands between the legal state of war between belligerents and the absence of the use of force in international relations. Schwarzenberger [1])

---

1) Georg Schwarzenberger, Jus Pacis ac Belli, A.J.I.L., Vol. 37, 1943, pp. 460 ff., pp. 470–1. In Power Politics, 2nd ed. (London 1951), p. 196, the same author refers to the 'three states of international law' without, however, indicating what rules apply in that intermediary state.

has termed the state between these two conditions the *status mixtus,* a sociological characterization rather than a legal, as no juridical elements of this status are indicated, though the occurrence of hostilities short of war may be said to determine the existence of this status.

But it is precisely the absence of legal criteria and of a general legal regulation in this state of twilight between war and peace, where the lights have been intentionally obscured in the course of the last decades, which created the necessity for a concept of war, which was to be established by decisions of competent government organs. Due to the practices of the League of Nations this concept was not developed outside the sphere of abstract commission reports and discussions of legal experts.

It is worth while to examine what concept of war has been developed through the judicial decisions of the postwar military tribunals.

SECTION 4. 'WAR' IN NUREMBERG AND TOKYO

Notwithstanding the new terminology of the U.N. Charter the concept of war was included in the definitions of 'crimes against peace' in the Nuremberg and Tokyo Charters because these latter instruments were largely based on the Briand Kellogg Pact [1]). The acts of which the Tribunals had to take cognizance had been committed while this Pact banning 'war as an instrument of national policy' had been binding on about 60 states, including Germany and Japan. The Charter for the establishment of an International Military Tribunal in Nuremberg defined as 'crimes against peace'; "planning, preparation, initiation or waging of a war of aggression, or a war in violation of international treaties, agreements or assurances ..." [2]). The different individual crimes against peace must, thus, have for their object a war, be it an aggressive war or one in violation of treaties etc..

So far as appears from the Report on the International Confer-

---

1) See below Chapter IV, sections 2 and 3.

2) Charter of the International Military Tribunal, Article 6 (a), in Report of Robert H. Jackson, United States Representative to the International Conference on Military Trials, London 1945 (Department of State Publication 3080, released February 1949), p. 423.

ence on Military Trials, held in London from July to August 1945 between representatives of the Four Powers, the limitation of the 'crimes against peace' to individual acts relating to *war* has not been the subject of much discussion once the proposal to declare individuals responsible for specific wars or aggressions liable to punishment had been accepted. The mainly French proposal was aimed at bringing only the general *policy* of aggression against, and of domination over other peoples, within the sphere of the Tribunal's competence, because the legal position of war and aggression was deemed to be ambiguous.

Till the end of the Conference the draft definitions of crimes included, apart from war, also 'aggression', 'invasion', 'threat of invasion' and 'armed attack'. The final limitation to war only may be presumed to have been mainly the consequence of the wish of the American delegation to found the criminality of the crimes against peace on the pre-war treaties and resolutions for the prohibition and condemnation of war, notably the Kellogg Pact of 1928 [1]).

No more than the Charter did the Prosecution or the Tribunal try to define the concepts of war, aggressive war or war in violation of treaties, etc.. The Tribunal decided that certain of the defendants had planned and waged wars of aggression against a number of countries and that it was therefore unnecessary "to discuss the matter in further detail" [2]). 'Aggressive acts' were proved to have been committed against Austria and Czechoslovakia. But in both these cases the Nazi-leaders had reached their goal without the use of armed force: internal subversive actions and the immediate threat of extreme violence assured in these cases the 'peaceful co-operation' of the governments concerned. The Judgment referred to these acts only as parts of the 'common plan or conspiracy', they were "premeditated aggressive steps in furthering the plan to wage aggressive war against other countries" and such a war would have been waged against these

---

1) See below, p. 198.

2) Judicial Decision of the International Military Tribunal, in Trial of the Major War Criminals before the International Military Tribunal, Nuremberg, 14 November 1945–1 October 1946, published at Nuremberg, Germany, Vol. 22, p. 459. Same in A.J.I.L., Vol. 41, 1947, pp. 172–333.

countries too if their 'co-operation' could not have been assured by intimidation only [1]).

Though the terminology used in the Judgment lends here and there to uncertainty [2]), the distinction between these aggressive acts, only mentioned as evidence to substantiate the conspiracy charge, and the aggressive wars, for which he responsible defendants were punished, was on the whole strictly maintained by the Tribunal. This is especially evident from the individual convictions. Determining that Schacht's part in the occupation of Austria and in that of Sudetenland is too small to make him a participant in the common plan, the Tribunal adds that both these acts were not charged as aggressive wars. And of von Papen, also found not-guilty under the conspiracy-charge, it is said: "there is no evidence that he was a party to the plan under which the occupation of Austria was a step in the direction of furthering aggressive action, or even that he participated in plans to occupy Austria by aggressive war, if necessary" [3]). Even for behaviour so far removed from the time of action as conspiracy, the Tribunal held the element of war to constitute a necessary element of criminality.

The exclusion of these acts from the field of aggressive war does not, however, throw much light on the concept of war which the judges of Nuremberg had in mind. So far the delimitation of war from other military acts has been discussed, but it must be admitted that opposite the concept of hostilities short of war, there is also the possibility of war short of hostilities. The Bulgarian withdrawal before the Rumanian troops in the second Balkan War created such a situation, and this was obviously also the case with the declarations of war by some South-American governments in the First World War, and with those by some South-American and Arab States in the last months of the Second.

---

1) L.c., pp. 435 ff.

2) The Judgment, l.c. p. 459, refers to 'aggressive wars against twelve nations'. As the wars which England and France declared upon Germany could not be considered as aggressive wars on the part of the latter, it must be the actions against Austria and Czechoslovakia which, though otherwise defined as only 'acts of aggression', are here comprised in the twelve aggressive wars.

3) On Schacht, l.c., p. 555, on von Papen, l.c., p. 573. In the later case of the United States vs. Weiszaecker, the 'invasions' in Austria and Czechoslovakia were, however, found to constitute 'crimes against peace' in conformity to the provisions of Control Council Law No. 10, below p. 232.

Without excluding the possibility that an international tribunal 'constructs' a 'pacific occupation' as an act of war, the forementioned decisions of the Nuremberg Tribunal seem to be founded less on the non-military [1]) than on the conventional character of the German occupations in Central Europe during 1938 and 1939. Even apart from the acquiescent attitude of the other European powers at the time, the 'consent' of the governments of Austria and Czechoslovakia in the German proceedings – though purely formal, and revocable because extorted – make it difficult to qualify these proceedings as acts of war.

The only case which can serve as a test for the Tribunal's opinion of war is the German occupation of Denmark, with that of Norway qualified as 'invasion' and 'act of aggressive war'. For Denmark is the only country in the series of Germany's victims since September 1939 whose relations with Germany were ambiguous. All the others of the ten aggressive wars which Germany launched are not subject to doubt. Poland, Norway, the Netherlands, Belgium, Luxemburg, Greece, Yugoslavia and the U.S.S.R. made it clear, by their declarations and by their continued resistance against the invader, that they were engaged in a war, while, after Pearl Harbour, Germany declared war on the U.S.A.. England and France themselves declared war on Germany after its attack on Poland, and Germany's wars with these two countries were, therefore, no subject for the Tribunal [2]).

Denmark stands apart. Shortly after the German troops had crossed the Danish frontier on the 9th of April 1940, the resistance which had been put up by detached units of the Danish army was stopped on an order of the King. The German 'protection' was accepted by the King and by the government, and the Danish administration remained, with small changes, intact, notwithstanding the resistance movements, increasing in the course of the following years, and the repeated strikes. Elections were normally held under the German occupation.

But decisive on this point is the maintenance of foreign relations by the Danish government. In 1944 the King protested

---

1) As suggested in the Memorandum of the U.N. Secretariat on Charter and Judgment of the Nuremberg Trial, Doc A/CN 4/5 U.N. Publ. 1949. V. 7, p. 49.

2) Judgment, l.c., pp. 435–459. See Rowland Kenney, The Northern Tangle, London 1946, pp. 156–178.

against the declaration of independence by Iceland, occupied by the American army. And still stronger evidence is given by Denmark's adherence in 1941, under pressure of course, to the Anti-Komintern Pact. These facts exclude the simultaneous existence of a state of war with the occupying power, also a party to the same Pact. Denmark's position can perhaps best be compared with that of Iran under Anglo-Russian occupation during the second part of the war.

Denmark's occupation – a 'pacific occupation' according to classic international law – has been 'constructed' as an act of war by the Tribunal. On the one hand there was Hacha's signature under the treaty establishing the Czech protectorate, extracted, under the irresistible threat of an air-bombing of Prague, *before* the entrance of the German troops. On the other hand there was King Christian's acceptance of the 'protection' *after* the entrance of German troops and some skirmishing. Between these two situations the Nuremberg Tribunal drew the line within which it deemed the crime of aggressive *war* committed, even though there was no question of a legal state of war and not even of its usual material appearance.

Much wider limits were set to the concept of war by the International Military Tribunal for the Far East in the case against Tojo *cum suis* [1]). In East AsiaJapan had executed its imperialist projects with much more variation than Germany could do in Europe, divided by much stricter frontiers and much more anxiously watched by the big powers. The central part of the Japanese policy was the 'China-incident' by neither the League of Nations nor by any government considered as a war, although only its second phase, from the incident on the Marco Polo bridge in 1937 to 1941, when after Pearl Harbour China finally declared war on Japan, cost China 3.000.000 men and Japan 100.000.

Round this 'pièce de résistance' of modern war-disguising stand the 'pacific occupations' of Thailand and French Indo-China in

---

1) Judgment of the International Military Tribunal for the Far East, in mimeographed Record of Proceedings of the I.M.T. for the Far East, pp. 48. 445–49. 858. There exists also a separate transcript of the Judgment Parts A–C with annexes. No publication has been given to the Judgment either as a whole or to parts of it, or to any other documents of the Tokyo-Trial, except for the Charter, the Indictment and the Opening Statement of the Chief Prosecutor (see p. 25, note 2).

1941, accomplished after the consent of the governments concerned – in the latter case that of Vichy – had been extracted with threats, and two more incidental skirmishes, one at Lake Khasan on the Russian frontier in 1938 and one in the territory of the Khackhin-Gol river, at the frontier of the 'Mongolian People's Republic', in 1939. Both the latter incidents, which, moreover, had more the character of border-incidents in distant, insufficiently demarcated territories, ended after a very short time with mutual agreement.

Only in three of the 'aggressive wars' on grounds of which a number of the defendants was convicted had there existed legal states of war [1]). After the Japanese attacks on Pearl Harbour and Kota Baru on the 8th of December 1941, declarations of war were exchanged between Japan on the one hand and the United States of America and the British Commonwealth of Nations on the other. The Netherlands, not being attacked but acting in self-defence, as the Tribunal determined, declared war on Japan at the same time, before even the forementioned Powers had done so.

In the light of these circumstances the insertion of the words 'declared or undeclared' before 'war of aggression' in the definition of crimes against peace of the Charter of the Tokyo Tribunal, otherwise adopted from the London Charter, is quite explicable though by no means clear [2]). 'Declared' can only refer to a formal declaration of war or, anyway, to an initiation of war in conformity with the third Hague Convention of 1907. This, as has been said, is only one of the ways in which a state of war can be created. Such a state can also be brought about by the mere opening of hostillities when the attacked power makes it clear that in consequence of this action it considers itself in state of war with the attacker, or also when, at a later stage of the conflict, the latter shows in an informal way its warlike intention.

Both these latter cases should then be covered by the concept of 'undeclared war', as 'war', once considered in connection with

---

1) The number may be brought to four insofar as, after Pearl Harbour, the Republic of China declared war on Japan, and so transformed, after ten years of fighting, the 'hostilities' into formal war.

2) The Charter is, together with Indictment and Opening Statement, published in Trial of the Japanese War Criminals, Department of State Publication, No. 2613, Far Eastern Series 12 (Washington 1946).

'declaration', must necessarily refer to the legal state of war. And it is apparent from Indictment and Judgment that 'declared war' must be taken in this formal sense as at every mention of the Japanese attacks on the Soviet Union on China, on the U.S. and on the Commonwealth it is emphasized that they took place 'without declaration of war', 'without declaring war', 'as undeclared war'. In fact, Japan did not initiate any 'declared war'. Japan entered in a state of war, only in consequence of a formal declaration of war by another State – the Netherlands – or of a Japanese attack followed by a formal declaration on the part of the attacked power – as was the case with the United States and the British Commonwealth.

The intention of the drafters of the Tokyo-Charter was undoubtedly to give the Tribunal, by explicit provision, the competence which has been discussed before, *id est* to determine that a certain act or series of acts constituted war, even if the parties involved had not admitted that at the time of the conflict [1]). As the Tribunal, following the Indictment, used that competence and declared all the aforementioned incidents and actions against other States except that against Thailand to constitute 'aggressive wars', the definition of the crimes against peace in the Charter can only be interpreted, contrary to the text, by linking the term 'war' not to the technical but to the 'constructed' concept of war.

Instead of 'declared or undeclared war of aggression' could have been said 'war of aggression whether or not entailing a legal state of war', which phrase would at least not have been contradictory, though as useless as the first. For since the drafters of the Charter did not say by positive definition what was an 'undeclared war', properly said a war in the non-technical sense, and since it was decided not to define the concept of aggressive war but to leave its interpretation to the Tribunal, which no

1) In History of the United War Crimes Commission, and the Development of the Laws of War (London, His Majesty's Stationery Office, 1948), p. 257, it is, on the contrary, alleged that the effect of the provision added in Tokyo was "to make it expressly clear that to precede the initiation of war by its formal declaration did not deprive such a war of its criminal nature if it is aggressive". But why should the drafters of the Tokyo Charter have incorporated a provision to that effect while the criminality of resort to formal war was so clearly established in Nuremberg, and while, moreover, the Japanese never preceded their wars by such a declaration?

more tried to define it, the original text as drafted in London was for all purposes sufficient.

Already at the time of the League of Nations some authors interpreted 'resort to war' as including every use of military force between States [1]). The ban on all use of force not provoked by other use of force, whether or not termed as resort to war, is indeed the only solid fundament for an effective world-organisation, though such a ban was certainly not in force at the time of the League: Wilson's proposal to that effect was rejected in Versailles and the whole practice of the League, as recalled before, excludes any such interdiction.

Though the Tokyo Tribunal branded all instances of Japanese use of force as 'aggressive wars', it appears from an analysis of its Judgment that there was another than the purely material criterion which led it to that decision. Even more than in Nuremberg the emphasis was laid on the 'common plan': Count One of the Indictment charging the defendants with a conspiracy to dominate East-Asia and the territories around the adjacent oceans, if necessary by means of war, in fact absorbs the greater part of all the other more specific counts of the Indictment. 'Planning and preparation' of the separate aggressive wars were seen as parts of the over-all common plan while, apart from that, as far as the crimes against peace are concerned, only the 'waging' — wherein the 'initiation' was deemed to be included — of a number of wars was considered a separate crime [2]).

But also while determining what *in concreto* were aggressive wars, what was the execution, the materialization of the common plan, the Tribunal attached primary importance to the element of intention. The impression is made that the Tribunal did not consider it so much its task to attribute responsibility for acts committed in international life, as to disclose the existence of a criminal design directed towards such acts. It would seem that not the accomplishment of aggressive wars but the general policy of which these wars were expression was the ground of the punishments.

---

1) Sir John Fischer Williams, The Covenant of the League of Nations and War, Cambridge Law Journal, 1933, p. 14.

2) See Judgment l.c. 48. 448, below p. 255, and S. Horwitz, The Tokyo Trial, International Conciliation, No. 465, 1950, p. 499.

Leaving aside the more penal aspects which will be discussed later [1]), it must be stated that this subjectivity did not help to clarify the international legal concepts used. This is most sharply demonstrated by the Tribunal's dealing with the hostilities which took place from 31 July till 11 August 1938 between Japanse and Russian border troops at Lake Khasan.

There was a border incident typical for these regions, there were contradictory witnesses concerning the crossing of the frontier by the other party and there was a certain preparation in Tokyo and certain reinforcements of the Japanese troops in this territory. None the less these troops, according to the Tribunal, had been "defeated and practically wiped out" when on the 10th of August 1938 Shigemitsu and Molotov agreed on a settlement of the boundary dispute.

But the Tribunal then concludes [2]): "though the force employed was not very large, the purpose above mentioned" (the restoration of the frontier according to the Japanese wishes) "and the result if the attack had been succesful" (this result is not specified) "are sufficient in the opinion of the Tribunal to justify describing the hostilities as a war". The material elements of this war, its extent and duration, being weak as they are, the whole qualification as such hangs on the silk thread of the intention, the 'animus', of certain ministers in Tokyo who knew about the hostilities.

Different again was the situation in the second Russo-Japanese conflict, at the border of Russia's vassal or satelite, the later People's Republic of Mongolia. Outer Mongolia was at that time occupied by Russian troops in virtue of an agreement with the Mongolian 'government'. In May 1939 Japanese reconnaissance troops attacked Russian-Mongolian border reinforcements and in the combats carried on for four months, over a front of 50 by 25 kilometers, the Japanese were again, according to the Judgment, utterly defeated leaving 50.000 men behind on the battlefield while Soviet troops lost only 9.000.

Though the extent of the hostilities was here much greater than the previous year at Lake Khasan, the initiative for this action, again motivated by an unsettled border dispute, was taken by

---

1) See below, pp. 251–252.

2) Judgment, l.c., p. 49. 395.

the local commander alone and Tokyo was only informed in the course of the fighting. The boundary dispute was only settled long after the fighting had ceased by a mutual withdrawal of the troops. On the 9th of June 1940 the Togo-Molotov agreement was signed and was later confirmed in the Japanese-Russian treaty of neutrality of 1941.

Against the Defence argument that this was only a border incident begun even without the consent of the government, the Tribunal determined the warlike character of the hostilities at the Khackhin Gol river on the grounds of their careful preparation and of the "intention to exterminate the enemy troops" [1]). Preparation and intention could only, however, be attributed to the local military authorities; at the other Russo-Japanese frontiers there was no question of 'enemies'. The generals concerned were among the accused in Tokyo but from the point of view of international law 'war' begun and carried on by subordinate authorities in a restricted region is a concept difficult to imagine. And to that must be added that the principle of condonation should have prevented the Tribunal from punishing the accused for acts the effects of which had already been subject to settlement with the 'victim' [2]).

Also a dubious case was the relation existing with France in consequence of the Japanese occupation of Indo-China. The consent to this occupation had finally, after different other concessions, by an ultimatum been extracted from the Vichy government, under concurring pressure from Italy and Germany. The Tribunal did not quite follow the Prosecution which had charged this occupation as an aggressive war right from the beginning, and specified the existence of a war with France: "The occupation by Japanese troops of portions of French Indo-China, which Japan had forced France to accept, did not remain peaceful". For in March 1945 a Japanese ultimatum demanding the command over all local French troops and the control of the military means of communication, was refused by the French Governor, whereupon fighting broke out in different places. These ended after a month with the suppression of French resistance [3]).

---

1) L.c., p. 49. 402.
2) Dissenting Opinion of Mr. Justice Röling, separate transcript, p. 10.
3) Judgment, l.c., p. 49. 583 ff..

In this case also, though on the other side, the highest authorities of the State were not involved in the decision, but the situation is complicated by the fact that in the mother country the government of 'Free France', which had already declared war against Japan after Pearl Harbour, had in the meantime replaced the Vichy government. The Tribunal, however, does not pay any attention to this circumstance.

The march through Thailand by Japanese troops and the partial occupation of this country which lasted till 1945 is for three reasons not qualified by the Tribunal as a war. There had been in the years preceding 8 December 1941 (the date of Japan's occupation of Thailand) "a position of complicity and confidence" between both countries. At the same time there were already, when the Japanese crossed the border, negotiations going on about a treaty of alliance which the two countries in fact concluded two weeks afterwards and in which the military situation was regulated. And finally the Tribunal mentions as the most important point that "no witness on behalf of Thailand has complained of Japan's actions as being acts of aggression" [1]).

Here also primary importance is given to intentional elements and a decision is based upon the atmosphere of the situation rather than on its objective and material characteristics. When one considers that no hostilities at all took place between Japanese and Siamese troops and that this circumstance is hardly mentioned in the Judgment, it must be concluded that the concept of war of the Tokyo Tribunal has only the name in common with the legal concept of war and with the material common sense notion of war. In reality it was the warlike intention for which the Tribunal was looking and every military demonstration of that intention in a situation of international conflict was declared to constitute a war.

Though the Tribunal did not try to give a definition of war, the Judgment declares of the attacks launched on 8 December 1941 against the British Empire and the United States: "They were unprovoked attacks, prompted by the desire to seize the possessions of these nations. Whatever may be the difficulty of stating a comprehensive definition of 'war of aggression', attacks

---

1) L.c., p. 49. 589.

made with the above motive cannot but be characterised as wars of aggression" [1]). It was certainly not the intention to clarify by this statement the concept of war, but precisely because all attention is given to the aggressive intention, the reduncancy of the addition 'war' in the conception of the Tribunal can be deduced from it.

An attack for the motive of territorial ambitions has always in resolutions and treaties been qualified as 'an act of aggression', or just 'aggression'. The lack of any indication regarding the extent, in space and in time, of 'possessions' and 'attack' in the quoted statement of the Tokyo Tribunal, and its failure to indicate the authority from which the 'attack' must proceed, demonstrate, in view of the application of the concept so defined to the incidents with Russia and those in Indo-China, the meaninglessness of the term 'war'.

As will be argued later [2]) the Tribunals in Nuremberg and Tokyo could only, in the absence of a generally accepted definition of aggression, determine the perpetration of aggression with reference to the aggressive planning, the criminal intent of the accused. But the quoted statement of the Tokyo Tribunal which establishes a relation of identity and not one of causality between 'attack' and 'war', clearly proves the unavowed transition from the concept of bilateral war, qualified by objective characteristics, to that of unilateral aggression, characterized by the intention of its agent. If 'war' still has any significance, it was not an element of the crime against peace as conceived by the Tokyo Tribunal.

It appears from the Judgment that this Tribunal certainly had a bad conscience concerning its very extensive interpretation of aggressive war. Only in concluding its dealing with the forementioned incidents does the Judgment speak of 'wars', while even the headings of the specific sections concerned read 'offensive operations', 'attack', 'aggressive action', etc.. With respect to the 'China incident' which the Tribunal, here in complete conformity with the contemporary judgment, characterizes as a war beginning in 1931, the Judgment contains a remarkable expression: "From 1937 onwards" – the Tribunal says of the defendants – "they *continued* their aggressive war against China on a vast

1) L.c., p. 49. 584.
2) Below p. 251, and Chapter IV. Section 5.

scale" [1]), herewith indicating that there was neither an incidental attack, which cannot be 'continued', nor a proper situation of war, which one party, after unilateral interruption, can no more 'continue'.

While "for the sake of technical accuracy" the alleged "aggressive war against the Philippines" – at the time still part of the United States – was counted as part of the war against the latter State [2]), the Tribunal did not demonstrate the same care for accuracy in its use of the concept 'state of war'. When the American ambassador in Tokyo left Togo's department at 00.30 in the carly morning of 8th December 1941, the Tribunal says, "the two countries were at war as the (Japanese) Naval Operations Order already referred to fixed 00.00 hours of the 8th December (Tokyo time) as the time at which 'a state of war' will exist" [3]). The attack on Kota Baru only followed at 1.25 hours, that on Pearl Harbour two hours later, and the following day only did the Japanese Privy Council begin to deliberate on a declaration of war against America [4]). The Tribunal, thus, links the existence of the international state of war to the internal proclamation of such a state for the national fleet. It would be interesting to know what the Tribunal would have decided if this proclamation had not been followed by attacks.

By a similar construction the Tribunal determined Japan's aggressive war against the Netherlands notwithstanding the fact that the Dutch declared war against Japan six weeks before Japan did so and actually attacked the Dutch Indies. Also this country was in the forementioned Naval order indicated as 'expected enemy', with whom there would be a state of war from midnight 8 December onwards. Says the Court: "recognising the existence of a state of war and faced by the imminent threat of invasion of her Far Eastern territories, which the conspirators had long planned and were now about to execute, the Netherlands in self-defence declared war on Japan" [5]). That the Tribunal was conscious of the difference between a Japanese military 'state of war' and an international one, is evident from the mention of the

---

1) Judgment, l.c., p. 49. 766. Italics supplied.
2) L.c., p. 49. 591.
3) L.c., pp. 49. 568–9.
4) L.c., pp. 49. 568 and 49. 579.
5) L.c., p. 49. 768.

threat to Dutch territory and from the addition of the words 'in self-defence'. The two arguments are contradictory. If there was indeed an international state of war between Japan and the Netherlands, the latter, by its declaration, acted in the same way as England and the United States, and did not, then, begin a war 'in self-defence'. For the declaration of war by a country which is attacked does not begin a war, but recognizes its existence. What the Netherlands actually did was to start a preventive war, by the circumstances justified as self-defence, or, more properly speaking perhaps, a war in assistance of its Allies.

That Japan' decisions on the *non*-existence of a state of war were otherwise irrelevant was decided by the Tribunal with respect to the action in Indo-China in 1945.

SECTION 5. DISAPPEARANCE OF THE CONCEPT OF WAR

Juridical terminology has the function of establishing the certainty without which no legal order can exist. This applies more than in any other field to penal law and especially to the definition of criminal acts.

By its extension, unprecedented in international practice and legal literature, of the concept of war, and by the inconsistent use of this concept in its Judgment, the Tokyo Tribunal turned 'war' into a useless and deceiving element of the crimes against peace, this quite apart from the Tribunal's hardly impartial dealing with the facts of the Japanese-Russian incidents [1]).

This concept of war has no longer any resemblance to the original concept of war in international law, from which it was deduced. There was certainly always a double use of this term [2]): as indicating something bilateral, a relationship between States, and, in connection with epitheta like defensive, aggressive, just, as

---

1) It is even harder to apply the notion of impartiality to the Tribunal's dealing with Togo's defence that due to his efforts the *casus quo* of the anti-Komintern Pact had been restricted to the case of an *unprovoked* attack on the part of Soviet Russia. The Tribunal stated that as no proof had been introduced of aggressive intentions of the U.S.S.R. with respect to Japan and Germany "the conclusion of the Pact against the eventuality of an unprovoked attack on the part of the U.S.S.R. would appear to have had no justification" (l.c., p. 49. 341).

2) See below Chapter II, section 1, and cf. Wright, Changes in the Conception of War, l.c., pp. 761 ff.

referring to the unilateral conduct or to the intention of one of the parties. But both concepts were connected, they indicated two aspects of the same thing.

The three elements which served till now to distinguish war from other armed proceedings [1]) have disappeared or have become irrecognizable in the Tokyo Judgment.

The material element, that of fact, – a certain extent and duration of the hostilities and their general effect on the relations between the parties involved – has no more significance, as every act of military force, even if strictly localized and immediately stopped, as every extra-territorial use of force, seems to constitute war. The element of intention, as evidenced by declarations or acts of the parties, has lost much of its significance because, for the determination of war, merely a warlike mentality of one of the parties, even if not openly expressed, seems to be sufficient evidence. And finally the element of the *auctoritas principis* has been abandoned as the existence of a war can be determined on the grounds of the action and intention of local military officers.

The only conclusion that can be drawn from the Tokyo Judgment is that in case of a mere threat of force or in the absence of all signs of resistance or disapproval on the part of the government in whose territory the troops have entered, there can be no question of war.

It would not have been necessary to deal at such length with the Tokyo Judgment if the confusion and vagueness of the concept of 'war' appearing from it had not to be deemed symptomatic for the dead end to which this concept has come in international life. Certainly, concepts of penal law have their independent characteristics. Even if 'war' were a living concept in the international society and in international organisation, this concept could have another meaning for the international judge than the one it has for the international governmental organ which has to deal with recent situations, which necessarily disposes of less information and documents and for which the intention and responsibility of the acting agent are not the over-riding criteria.

---

1) Eagleton discusses four elements: that of force, that of intention, the qualification of force, and the status of the parties to war (l.c., respectively pp. 262 ff., 265 ff., 275 ff. and 281 ff.)

But war is no longer a living concept in the practice of international law. In the Charter on the basis of which the nations have formally been united the term is only used in relation to the past. For the present and the future it has been replaced by the purely material concepts – 'threat or use of force' – or by 'threat to the peace, breach of the peace or act of aggression' which in practice are assimilated to the first. As will be shown later the precise meaning of these terms is also not quite clear but they are at least the workable concepts of the new organisation for international security.

Already long in use in international treaties these concepts gradually superseded the concept of war which, precisely because of the *chantage* to which it has been subjected by warlike States and especially by Japan, has now nearly completely disappeared from treaty terminology [1]. The concept became obsolete through a system of paper promises and legalistic shortsightedness, which proves how a legal system is doomed to decay when it is not based on the reality of an executive power or on voluntary observance by subjects sharing the same legal convictions.

It has been called "the most striking result" of the Kellogg Pact "that signatories who wanted to violate it, have merely adopted the simple device of going to war without a declaration, so that we have really relapsed into the primitive age before 'civilised' warfare existed" [2]. Though somewhat unhistorical – the majority of the wars of former centuries were not declared though not denied either [3] – the statement contains a grain of truth with respect to the recent past.

For the maintenance of peace and order the concept of war has anyway lost its distinguishing function, and therewith the importance of a determination of a *status mixtus* has disappeared also, as, apart from resort to formal war, every other use of armed force is prohibited too.

1) It must be noted that the Sino-Soviet Treat of Friendship, Alliance and Mutual Assistance, concluded in Moscow 14 February 1950, restricts, in its Article I, the *casus quo* to "the event of one of the High Contracting Parties being attacked by Japan or States allied with it, and thus becoming involved in a state of war" (text in Aitchen K. Wu, China and the Soviet Union (London 1950), Appendix D, p. 415). The reference to this generally abandoned notion is especially curious in the light of China's recent history!

2) Gathorne-Hardy, o.c., p. 184, note 2.

3) See survey in Quincy Wright, A Study of War, 2 vols. (Chicago 1944), Vol. I, appendices.

There is, however, a still more fundamental reason why the traditional legal notion of war, and with that the law of war and neutrality, has to lose its significance since the right to resort to war has become subject to restrictive regulations by world organisations tending to universality. In the beginning of this chapter the question was raised as to whether a collective military action, ordered or authorized by the international organ for the maintenance of peace and security, could still be called a war.

The question presents interest for the relations between the State which is object of the action and the other States whether or not participating in it. Are the traditional rules of war and neutrality applicable to these relations? If the proceeding States are considered as bound by an alliance the answer must be yes. But if the collective organ is seen as a general international legal institution with universal jurisdiction it is no. Once there is a universal, or universality-enforcing, security-organisation which regulates or prohibits the right to resort to war and to force, and which determines whether or not a specific use of force is lawful, there is no longer any question of the traditional essentials of the state of war, the juridical equality of the contending parties and the general rights and obligations of neutral States based on that equality. Then it is a matter of lawfully and unlawfully contending parties and of the general obligation for all the others to assist and support the former [1].

Strictly this was already the consequence of the Covenant of the League of Nations though it left – in law – some gaps for a 'neutral', legally unqualified war and though the organisation did not in fact apply the relevant provisions and did not, moreover, attain or enforce universality [2].

The situation is, however, different under the regime of the United Nations. The Charter prohibits all use of force and imposes on the Member States the duty to participate in, or anyway to support, a collective action against a violator of this prohibi-

1) An attempt to draw the general legal consequences of this new situation with regard to the position of outsider states is made in the Draft Treaty on Rights and Duties of States in Case of Aggression, of the Harvard Research on International Law (A.J.I.L., vol. 33, 1939, Supplement, pp. 819–909. See also, E. Borchard, Effects of War on Law, A.J.I.L., vol. 40, 1946, pp. 620 ff.

2) See below, p. 155.

tion. And the Organisation has, besides, some important reasons for considering itself universal. It has far more members than the League ever had. As is evident from their requests all outside States desire to possess membership. And what is even more important, the collective action against North Korea has also, apart from constituting the first international enforcement action against an aggressor, set a precedent as an application of Article 2, paragraph 6, as it is directed against the non-member North Korea and is in assistance to the South Korean Republic also not belonging to the United Nations.

Putting aside the ambiguous status of North Korea in international relations, it can be argued that with respect to the fighting in Korea there is no question of war and neutrality. The rules and customs of military warfare stand apart, because they must be applied in all cases of hostilities, as is evident from the provisions of the Geneva Conventions of 1949 [1]).

There remains, of course, the possibility of an armed conflict with respect to which the Security Council or the General Assembly [2]) would not take or recommend any measures, which would not be qualified, by an international decision, in terms of aggression and legitimate defence, and which could, in consequence, retain the characteristics of traditional 'neutral' war. But it could be argued, on the basis of Article 51 giving all the States the right of individual and collective self-defence [3]), that even in such cases the old legal equality of the belligerents would not exist and that there would be no place for traditional neutrality.

It must be concluded that the legal concept of war has no place anymore in international society under the rule of the United Nations Charter. The concept became obscured from the moment an international institute was given the competence to discriminate between 'lawful' and 'unlawful' war. The 'state of war' dates from the time that the right to resort to war was held to constitute the inalienable privilege of sovereignty, and that unrestricted sovereign equality imposed on third States the duty to respect

---

1) Article 2 of each of the four Geneva Conventions of 1949, see Joyce A. C. Gutteridge, The Geneva Conventions of 1949, B.Y.I.L. 1949, pp. 294—326, p. 297.

2) In pursuance of the Resolution Uniting for Peace, see below, p. 42.

3) See below, Chapter II, section 3.

the exercise of this privilege [1]). The 'state of war' disappeared the moment a higher instance received the competence to decide that a given resort to war was an illegal act.

The traditional concept of war was bilateral; the same juridical concept cannot be used to indicate simultaneously a lawful and an illegal proceeding. To-day 'war' is either a sanction or a crime and therefore 'war' does no more exist [2]).

---

1) See below, Chapter III, section 4.

2) Cf, Carl Schmitt, Die Wendung zum diskriminierenden Kriegsbegriffs, Schriften der Akademie für Deutsches Recht (München 1938).

CHAPTER II

WAR OF AGGRESSION

SECTION 1. WAR AS A STATUS AND WAR OF AGGRESSION

Once it is agreed that the concept of war is of little help in elucidating the extent of the crimes against peace as defined in the charters of the post-war tribunals, all the emphasis in that definition falls on the qualification 'of aggression'. Even apart from this the element of aggression constitutes the penal element of the phrase. If war as such still has any meaning it is principally that of a certain *situation* which, however regrettable, cannot by itself be the object of penal law. The addition 'of aggression' or 'aggressive' lifts the concept of war from the neutral field of pure fact and indicates an action and a responsible actor. In connection with aggression, 'war' does not stand for a certain situation of international relations or a certain form of military combat, but for the unilateral conduct of one of the States involved in the conflict.

'War' has the same meaning in the opposite term, 'defensive war' or 'war of defence'. It indicates the legal or moral position of one of the parties in the pre-classic terminology of just and unjust war, and it indicates likewise the intention of the attacking party in the terms 'colonial war', 'war of expansion', etc..

As noted in the first chapter, the two meanings of war are related to the same fact, the same event, of which each give a different aspect. A State can be said to be involved in a war, and a State can plan, prepare and launch a war, just as individuals can be said to be engaged in a fight or to have started a fight. In the first case the relation or situation in which States or individuals are engaged is considered in itself, apart from those involved; in the second case attention is paid to the actions, or the motives behind actions, which have led to the situation, or to the legal qualification which the conduct of each party deserves.

It is very important to realize this double use of the term 'war' which can be summarized in the generally applicable [1]) statement that in case of 'war' between two States the one State will wage a 'war' of aggression, the other a 'war' of defence. The consideration of war exclusively as a legal condition giving rise to the application of special rules was characteristic of the 'classic' period of international law which came to an end in the last decades. So long as international law was considered only as a law of co-ordination between completely independent States, the sovereign acts and decisions of which had the final force of law and could not be invalidated by an appeal to a higher instance, this law could only, with the free co-operation of its subjects, create some order with regard to certain consequences of the wars arbitrarily initiated by them.

Only after 1919 did the notion of 'aggressive war' become of significance in *general* international law. Before that it had been used restrictedly in particular conventions of non-aggression, alliance and guarantee [2]). The international community first restricted and then completely prohibited the freedom of resort to war. Its organs were given the competence to qualify the conduct of the parties leading up to a war, to determine the aggressor in a war unlawfully resorted to, to prescribe diplomatic, economic and military action against him, to exclude him from international relations [3]), and finally to bring the government leaders responsible for the war to trial.

Though after the trials of Nuremberg and Tokyo and after the military proceedings of the United Nations in Korea, precedents have now been created for all these types of action by the

---

1) See, however, below Section 3 of this chapter.

2) See a survey of these conventions in Wilhelm Steinlein, Der Begriff des nicht herausgeforderten Angriffs in Bündnisverträgen seit 1870 und insbesondere im Locarnovertrag, dissertation Frankfurt (Leipzig 1927), p. 133, and especially in Enrico Serra, L'Aggressione Internazionale, Milano 1946, pp. 25—30. For the treaties after 1919, see ibidem pp. 129—174 and Draft Convention, with comment, prepared by the research in international law of the Harvard Law School, A.J.I.L., Supplement 1939, (further quoted as Harvard Research) pp. 847 ff., comment on Article 1 (c).

3) G. Schwarzenberger, International Law and Totalitarian Lawlessness, London 1945.

international community, the period from 1919 till to-day still has the character of a transitory period in which both the old and the new notion of war, though the actual term 'war' is hardly used any more, play a role. In the matter of war and aggression, the observation made by Giraud in his study on *La théorie de la légitime défense* of 1934 [1]) still holds good: "S'en tient-on aux conceptions traditionnelles, c'est à dire aux conceptions de droit antérieur à la Société des nations, on raisonne en fonction d'un passé qui n'est plus. Tient-on pour acquises l'organisation internationale et la solidarité active des Etats, on anticipe sur l'avenir".

Even though the international organisation has now been invested with the competence to determine the aggressor and prescribe a collective action against him, international practice has followed the tendency to consider war or armed conflict as a *situation* to which the collective security-organ should try to put an end by mediation and conciliation, leaving aside the question of responsibility for its origin. In the records of the League organs and even in those of the United Nations the principal role appears to be attributed to "the type of war which is charitably called accidental war, the war which is the 'inevitable' result of a 'regrettable' incident", and not the intended result of a policy.

Only in some flagrant cases when moreover the political circumstances happened to be favorable, as at the time of the Italian attack on Ethiopia in 1935, the Russian invasion in Finland in 1939 and the Korean aggression in 1950, did the international organ make use of its competence to determine the aggressor and to prescribe a more or less far-reaching action.

The continued use of both these concepts of war – or 'international conflict' which for the present purpose amounts to the same – in the practice of international organisations, is evidenced by the adoption, during the Fifth Session of the General Assembly of the United Nations, of the two resolutions 'Uniting for Peace' and 'Duties of States in the event of the outbreak of hostilities [2]).

1) Emile Giraud, La théorie de la légitime défense, R.d.C.A.D.I. 1934 (Vol. 49), p. 691.

2) Resolutions 377 (V), of 3 November 1950, and 378 (V), of 17 November 1950.

The former resolution – adopted in consequence of the aggression in Korea – provides for the case in which the Security Council, because of lack of unanimity of the permanent Members, "fails to exercise its primary responsibility – in any case where there appears a threat to the peace, breach of the peace, or act of aggression". Provision is made for immediate consideration ot the matter by the General Assembly, if necessary by the calling of an emergency special session, "with a view to making appropriate recommendations to Members for collective measures, including in the case of a breach of the peace or act of aggression the use of armed force when necessary . . .". In addition, a Peace Observation Commission and a Collective Measures Committee are established to help set in motion the machinery of the United Nations blocked by a veto in the forementioned circumstances [1]).

The point of departure of this resolution is thus the same as that of Articles 39 ff. of the Charter, notably the occurrence of an act of aggression, that is the illegal use of force on the part of a State, against whom the international organ will, if necessary, recommend a collective armed action.

The second resolution which the General Assembly adopted shortly after 'Uniting for Peace', provides for the case in which "a State *becomes engaged in armed conflict* with another State or States . . ." and imposes on this State the duty to proclaim immediately its readiness, on the condition of reciprocity, to cease fire and to withdraw all its military forces [2]). The definition of the *casus* clearly recalls the undifferentiated conception of war in which a State becomes 'engaged', heedless of the causes and the origin of the 'armed conflict' and of the responsibility for it.

In the original Yugoslav draft resolution this tendency was particularly evident: the State, 'engaged in hostilities', which would not proclaim its readiness to discontinue the military operations and withdraw its troops, or which would not give effect to such a declaration, would be considered as aggressor, and held responsible for the conflict, before the international forum, regardless of who launched the original attack[3]). In the

---

1) Res. 377 A (V), sections A, B and D.
2) Res. 378 A (V), par. 1 (a) and (b) (italics supplied).
3) United Nations Document A/C. 1/604, of 30 October 1950, p. 2.

final form this provision was mitigated to the recommendation under (e): "that the conduct of the States concerned in relation to the matters covered by the foregoing recommendations be taken into account *in any determination of responsibility* for the breach of the peace or act of aggression" [1]).

Yet the vagueness of the italicized words still demonstrates the tendency to obscure the responsibility for the conflict itself – a tendency which grew out of the experience of endless difficulties in determining that responsibility with regard to any conflict, and of the unwillingness of the Member States to brand as such an obvious aggressor. The discussion on the Yugoslav proposal in the First Committee of the General Assembly shows, however, that most States are prepared, in principle at least, to recognize and to solve the question of responsibility for an international conflict, and no longer regard a war or an armed combat as a situation in which the States involved "are placed on the same footing" [2]).

Also in the system of the League of Nations there was this difference between Article 11 which declared any war or threat of war "a matter of concern to the whole League" which had to take "any action that may be deemed wise and effectual to safeguard the peace of nations", and, on the other hand, Articles 10, 12, 13, 15 and 16, embodying strict prohibitions and prescribing actions for the case of their violation. By Article 10 the Members of the League undertook "to respect and preserve as against external aggression the territorial integrity and existing political independence of all Members". Articles 12, 13 and 15 severely restricted the freedom of the States to go to war for the solution of international disputes, and Article 16 sanctioned these prohibitions by providing for diplomatic, economic and military mea-

---

1) Italics supplied.

2) See the records of these discussions held in the First Committee Meetings from 4th till 10th November, U.N. Doc. A/C. 1/SR. 384 till A/C. 1/SR. 390, pp. 247 till 290, and especially the observations presented by the United Kingdom Representative (p. 250), by the U.S.S.R. Representative (p. 256), by the U.S.A. Representative (p. 261) and Canadian Representative (p. 264). The Colombian Representative, Urrutia, resumed the main objection against the Yugoslav proposal as follows: "An automatic method of suspending hostilities might have its merits in situations involving minor incidents between two States neither of which had any aggressive intentions ... but not in case of real aggression", p. 254, par. 13.

sures to be taken against any Member who would "resort to war in disregard of its covenants under Articles 12, 13 or 15 . . .".

On the one side there is the conciliatory, or otherwise peaceful approach to a situation of war in which two States have become involved, in whatever manner it may be. On the other side there is the police proceeding against a State which, in breach of its obligations, has started a war and which, therefore, "shall *ipso facto* be deemed to have committed an act of war against all other Members of the League . . ." (Article 16).

It is a remarkable fact that in the Charter of the United Nations all operative articles relative to the elimination of the use of force speak only of recommendations, measures and action "to maintain or restore international peace and security", that there is no provision to the effect that the action of the Security Council must be directed against the aggressor State, and that, unless implicit in the terms 'breach of the peace' and 'act of aggression', no single reference is made to the responsibility for the outbreak of a conflict. And it is characteristic for the development of international organisation that still, under the regime of this Charter, the willingness to take the second road, the new road against war, is greater than at any time in the League of Nations, as is apparent from the collective action in Korea and from the resolution 'Uniting for Peace'.

From the very first session of the League Assembly in 1920, when Canada put forward its proposal to delete Article 10, there was a constant tendency to consider war and the use of force a situation to be eliminated by procedures of discussion and conciliation in the organs of the League, by virtue of Article 11, with disregard of Art. 16, of the question of responsibility and of 'war' as an action imputable to a State. The amendments to Article 16, adopted in 1921, weakening the 'automatic' obligations imposed by that article, were not ratified by the Members but were kept as 'directives' and applied in practice [1]).

This tendency culminated at the end of the twenties when Rutgers wrote his well known memorandum [2]). His central theme

---

1) See these amendments in International Legislation, Vol. I, pp. 29—35.

2) Memorandum on Articles 10, 11 and 16 of the Covenant by J. Rutgers, L.O.N. Documents of the Preparatory Commission for the Disarmament Conference, Series VI, C. 165. M. 50, 1928. Series IX, pp. 142—158.

was that there was no sense in emphasizing an article which, however necessary for a future international legal order, was not in harmony with political reality and with the views of the Member States in whose hands lay the decision whether action would be taken under Articles 10 and 16 or not. Even if the doctrine of the resolutions of 1921 were not generally accepted, "the Council could not invoke a text or apply a sanction to oblige a Member to obey a decision of the Council in virtue of Article 16 which that Member did not consider to be well founded".

"If ever the question of the application of Article 16 arose, the decisions of the different countries would not depend on interpretations, however authoritative, or on the deductions of lawyers; the great question would be whether the principle of Article 16 was of was not a living reality" [1]).

On the other hand: "Article 11 is the essential expression of the principle of the League, and is designed to protect the interests of all. It does not impose upon Members of the League any obligations which can be rigidly specified; the Council's action under this Article is political rather than legal. It is in Article 11 that the moral factors and the solidarity of the Members of the League are most clearly brought out" [2]).

No more than in the system of the United Nations was there in the League of Nations an organ competent to maintain and apply the provisions of the Covenant independent of the will of the Member States bound by those provisions. Also with regard to the interpretation of the constitutions of international organisations should it be born in mind that, as was said of the League, it would be what its Members made it. In the interpretation of these political documents primary consideration should be given to contemporary political practice.

Under the League that political reality was the lack of world wide solidarity against any aggressor and therefore a decisive preference for the application of Article 11 over that of Article 16. War was considered as an unhappily arising situation to be prevented by deliberation and to be remedied by mediation and conciliation rather than a conscious act whose author should be called

---

1) Ibidem pars. 164 and 165.
2) Ibidem par. 128.

to account and should be fought by common action if he refused to cede way.

The action against the aggressor in Korea, started under favourable circumstances by a dominating Member of the United Nations and till now hesitatingly followed by some ten others, has perhaps changed the practice of the consideration of war on the part of the United Nations. But with regard to the handling by the U.N. of other conflicts, as for example that between Israël and its neighbour States, the conclusion reached in 1935 by the League's Commission on the Chaco-dispute between Bolivia and Paraguay is still valid: "No enquiry into the question of responsibility for the war as long as there is any possibility of peaceful settlement. An enquiry would only be in place if all such possibilities had vanished" [1]).

This conclusion applies for the whole period of transition from international anarchy to world-order, begun in 1919 and lasting till to-day. Only when this order has been established can the demands of justice get the priority they deserve. Until then the requirements of political opportunism will continue to force political practice towards the neutral consideration of war as a situation, a consideration essentially the same as that accepted and approved in the foregoing period of unrestricted disorderly sovereignty.

It was only after the Axis Powers had forced the reality of an aggressive war upon a great number of States that the other concept of war triumphed in world society producing legal consequences including the trials of Nuremberg and Tokyo. The following pages will deal with this concept of war qualified by law, which has long since received a place in doctrine and in particular treaties, and which has recently been introduced in the practice of general international law.

SECTION 2. AGGRESSIVE WAR AND AGGRESSION

The obscuring of wars, described in Chapter I, was the main

---

[1]) Conclusion No. 1 of Chapter IV, "On the question of the enquiry into the responsibility for the war" of the Commission's Report, See A.J.I.L., 1934, Supplement, pp. 198—202.

reason for the increasing employment of the term 'aggression' instead of, or in addition to, 'war' and 'aggressive war' which latter terms no more occur in the Charter of the United Nations.

Already in 1815, in the Secret Treaty of Defensive Alliance concluded in Vienna between England, France and Austria, the term 'aggression' was used to indicate the *casus foederis:* "Si les possessions d'aucune d'Elles (les Hautes Parties Contractantes) étaient attaquées, alors et dans ce cas, Elles s'engagent et s'obligent á se tenir pour attaquées toutes trois ... pour repousser une telle aggression" [1]. The apparent identity established here between aggression and military attack, obviously on the part of a State [2], is a constant feature of treaties of mutual assistance and non-aggression of the nineteenth and early twentieth century [3].

To this element yet another characteristic of aggression must be added. To constitute a case of aggression the attack must be of such a nature and of such magnitude as to force the victim State to use its military forces to repel the attack and undo its consequences [4]. This qualification may appear to be self-evident in the context of the treaties of alliance but in view of the later development of the notion of aggression which will be discussed below it is necessary to consider this characteristic separately.

In line with the very restrictive conditions with which the *casus foederis* was surrounded – as, for example, the absence of

---

1) De Martens, Nouveau Recueil, Nouvelle Série, Vol. I, p. 368. The term "bellum aggressivum" is already used by Vittoria ("De Iure Belli", quaestio 2, propositio I, no. 2) and Suarez ("De Bello", sectio I, no. 5). See Chapter III, section 3.

2) Steinlein, o.c., pp. 5–15, argues this point extensively to show the distinction between the observance of treaties of alliance with their international *casus foederis* and the interventionist policy of the Concert of Europe. The interference of the Security Council with internal conflicts has weakened also this element of aggression, see above, p. 15.

3) See the surveys referred to in note 2, p. 40.

4) Compare Steinlein's definition of the concept 'Angriff': "das gewaltsame Vorgehen völkerrechtlich berufener (legitimierter) Staatsorgane durch Verletzung eines Rechtes oder Gutes eines Staates, das bei der Art und dem Umfang des Vorgehens geeignet ist, für den Staat, gegen den sich die feindliche Masznahme richtet, eine Lage zu schaffen, aus der er sich nur durch militärische (kriegerische) Gegenmasznahmen befreien kann", o.c., conclusion of Kapitel I. The indication of the so-called "Angriffsobjekte" (third line from above) is superfluous as every military action against a State is necessarily a violation of a right of that State unless the action is in self defence or assistance. See below, p. 109 ff..

'provocation directe' on the part of the ally [1]) and the limitation to aggression on the part of one or more specified States [2]) – the term aggression could only have the narrow meaning of a hostile action leaving the attacked State no choice but to defend itself with all its forces. The nature of the alliance treaty which entailed for the partner pledged to assistance the unavoidable consequence of becoming involved in a war once the *casus foederis* became evident, required that only in the forementioned extreme case could the partner be considered obliged to render assistance.

Moreover the indiscriminate interchange, in otherwise similar alliance treaties, of the terms 'serait attaquée' (to which 'aggression' and 'aggression' referred) and 'se trouverait en guerre' clearly indicates the close connection between attack or aggression and war [3]). It proves what may be called the war-producing nature of aggression.

This second element of the concept of aggression as understood before 1919 – that is the fact that it *necessitated* self-defence on a warlike scale, by which reaction the state of war was usually created – can in modern conditions, in which the freedom to resort to force is restricted, be described by the requirement that

---

1) Article II of First Tripartite Alliance, of 20 May 1882, N.R.G., 3me série, vol. X, p. 17; "sans provocation aucune", Article II of the Treaty of Alliance between Austria-Hungary and Rumania, of 30 October 1883, N.R.G., l.c., p. 22; "unprovoked attack or aggressive action", Article II of the English–Japanese Alliance of 12 August 1905, N.R.G., 2me série, vol. XXXV, p. 402.

A more recent example of the use of the term "aggression non provoquée" is given by Article 2 of the French–Russian Pact of 2 May 1935, N.R.G., 3me série, vol. XXXI, p. 645, where it is still reinforced by the phrase: "malgré les intentions pacifiques des deux pays". The Inter-American Treaty of Reciprocal Assistance, Petropolis, 2 September 1947, lists in its Article 9 as aggression: "(a) Unprovoked armed attack by a State against the territory, the people, or the land, sea or air forces of another State". Quoted in A.J.I.L., 1947, p. 863.

2) The Treaty Alliance between England and Japan quoted in note 1 is one of the few applicable in case of aggression "wherever arising, on the part of any other power or powers".

3) The connection between aggression, or attack, and war, as cause and necessary consequence, is very clear, for example, in Article 1 of the ""Reassurance"-treaty of 1887 in which Germany and Russia undertook to maintain a benevolent neutrality towards each other "dans le cas où l'une des hautes parties se trouverait en guerre avec une troisième puissance". But "Cette disposition ne s'appliquerait pas à une guerre contre l'Autriche ou la France dans le cas où cette guerre résulterait d'une attaque dirigée contre l'une de ces deux dernières puissances par l'une des hautes parties contractantes".

aggression gives the *right* of legitimate self-defence. For though the notion of an 'inherent right' of self-defence is long since admitted, a positive *right* of self-defence can only exist in a legal order in which the freedom to resort to force for political ends is abolished or restricted, that is only since 1919.

Considered as a military action on the part of the authorities of a State necessitating that the victim State reacts with military measures on war-level, aggression differs from aggressive war only insofar as it is a different stage of the same process. Both concepts are in the same line since an act of aggression may from another point of view, that of its consequences, be called an act of aggressive war. The latter notion also includes bilateral military combat, which is the practical consequence, the nearly certain, immediate development to which the unilateral military action of aggression gives rise [1]). Aggressive war is aggression answered.

The point of departure for this concept of aggression is the existence of an armed conflict, and the crucial problem of the definition of aggression is, therefore, one of defining the specific military acts the first author of which must be considered as the initiator of the conflict, as the aggressor responsible for the war. But in a society of States which did not know any rule for the regulation of the competence to resort to force and for which war was the only efficient means to enforce its rights, the suffering of an armed attack and the claim to receive assistance on account of that could not be linked under all circumstances.

In most of the treaties of assistance, therefore, the *casus foederis* was not attack as such but the 'unprovoked attack' (*attaque sans provocation, nicht-herausgeforderter Angriff*). And even if this or a similar condition [2]) were not added to the concept of attack (*aggression, Angriff*), the previous conduct of the attacked party could never be considered irrelevant to the determination

---

1) Cf. the Report of the Belgian Delegate, de Brouckère, for the Preparatory Commission of the Disarmament Conference, (Doc. C. 740, M. 279, 1926, series IX, p. 100). Also according to Steinlein (o.c., Kapitel I, sub IV) war is the attack plus the counter-attack.

2) For example Article I of the First Alliance between Austria—Hungary and Germany, of 24 September 1879, N.R.G., 3me série, vol. X, p. 6: "weder Verhoffen und gegen den aufrichtigen Wunsch der beiden hohen Kontraken-ten".

of the *casus foederis* [1]). This conclusion follows even from the defensive character of alliances in general. The military element was qualified by the moral element of responsibility.

Before 'aggression' in this sense became a current concept in treaty law, it had, as a political and popular term, become associated with the notion of responsibility for a war in the broadest possible sense, so as to comprise not only military actions, but also non-violent breaches of law and purely political acts against another State, if only grave enough to justify the latter's resort to armed force. An historian of international law summarizes as follows the theories on the matter from the first period of the French Revolution: "L'agresseur n'est point celui qui accomplit le premier fait d'armes ou qui franchit le premier la frontière ennemie. L'agresseur est l'état qui commet un empiètement tel sur la souveraineté d'autrui, que l'adversaire est reduit à la lutte armée comme à un dernier moyen de salut. Peu importe que l'empiètement revête telle forme ou telle autre ... pourvu qu'il soit assez grave pour motiver le recours à la force" [2]).

This broader notion of aggression remains, like the strict strategical concept discussed before, within the field of war or military conflict, indicating the responsibility for it, or the first act. Of course it is possible that aggression remains unanswered. The attacked or gravely offended party can surrender without resistance, as the Danes did in 1940 [3]), it can withdraw its troops to avoid the contact with the invading forces, as Bulgaria did before the Rumanian invasion in the second Balkan war, or it can accept without resistance the grave prejudice to its independence or the loss of a part of its territory.

But the essence of traditional 'aggression' was not that it was always followed by a war, but that, as in the two historical cases quoted, an armed reaction would have been unavoidable for the attacked State if its independence or the integrity of its territory were to be preserved against the aggressor. The qualification of an action against a foreign State with the term 'aggression' in

---

1) It was on arguments borrowed from the previous conduct of Germany and Austria–Hungary that Italy, in 1915, refused to observe its obligations of assistance under the Tripartite Alliance.

2) R. Redslob, Histoire des grands principes du droit des gens, Paris 1923, p. 282.

3) See before, p. 23.

its traditional sense does not, therefore, depend on the *fact* of the subsequent reaction on the part of the latter but on the necessity to react in military self-defence. And this necessity cannot be said to exist in every case of military measures, peaceful blockade [1]) or peaceful occupation [2]).

But when, after 1919, the concept of 'aggression' was transferred from the field of particular treaties of alliance or neutrality to that of universal or multitaleral covenants in which the rights and obligations of the associated States were defined in general, the term was further loosened from its close association with war or armed conflict. Aggression then became every extra-territorial use of force of whatever extent, whether or not it creates for the 'attacked' State the necessity to react on war level.

A clear example of this isolated use of the term 'aggression' is given in Article 2, (par. 2 sub 1°) of the Treaty of Locarno which provides that a violation, on the part of Germany, of Articles 42 or 43 of the Peace Treaty of Versailles in virtue of which the left bank of the Rhine was demilitarised, shall constitute *un acte non provoqué d'aggression* against the other parties [3]). In the terminology of the organs of the League, and still more in that of the United Nations in the Charter of which the term 'war' does not occur, the identity between 'aggression' and 'use of armed force' has become firmly established.

In its new meaning the term 'aggression' comprises every extra-territorial use of force and the question of the definition of aggression is now not only that of the attribution of responsibility for a conflict but also, and primarily, that of specification of the obligation of the States to abstain from that use of force.

The concept 'aggression' was extended furthest during the last decades with the use of the 'economic', 'financial' and 'ideological aggression', which no longer has any connection with a military conflict or even with unilateral military acts directed against another State. The military element — the *nucleus* of the concept

---

1) Listed as aggression in the Convention for the Definition of Aggression, of July 1933. Article II, sub 4, International Legislation, Vol. VI, pp. 410–419.

2) Like that of the Greek Island Corfu on the part of Italy, above p. 9.

3) Treaty of Mutual Guarantee (Locarno Pact), of 16 October 1925. Article II, par. 2, sub 1, N.R.G., 3me série, vol. XVI, p. 3. By express provision the other contracting parties had the right of military reaction against this 'aggression'.

of aggression – has been completely lost here and the term has begun to indicate all sorts of interstate acts – prohibited by international law, by *comitas* or by international morality – from which a State suffers some prejudice in one field or another [1]).

In so far as the 'aggression' – in the second meaning mentioned (above p. 50) – was also applied to purely political acts, these acts were seen from the angle of the ensuing war which they caused and there remained, thus, a connection between 'aggression' and military force. Once taken out of the framework of military conflicts the concept 'aggression' can, in principle, be used for any act of a State which effectively harms an essential interest of another State.

Among the new forms of aggression there is one, however, which on account of the acute danger it presents to the 'attacked' State, or, more properly said, government, deserves special attention: the so-called 'internal aggression', the 'fomenting of civil strife' [2]). The overthrow of a foreign government or regime by a State which does not, with its own armed forces, encroach upon the foreign territory concerned had, in a specific form, already been declared a case of aggression in the Litvinof Convention of 1933 [3]). The help given by a State to armed bands formed on its territory which invade foreign territory, would under this Convention automatically qualify the first State as the aggressor in a subsequent international conflict between the two States concerned. In this context, therefore, the indirect aggression remained

---

1) The Delegate of Ecuador observed during the discussions referred to on p. 43, note 2 that "some States might not be prepared to include the consideration of economic or financial aggression. In the opinion of some other States, however, the financial strangulation of one State by another did represent a type of aggression", l.c., p. 280, par. 15. The term 'economic aggression' was introduced by Litvinof, on other occasions a protagonist of strict criteria for aggression, at the Economic World Conference in London, 1932.

2) See General Assembly Resolution, 380 (V) of 17 November 1950, "Peace through deeds" which speaks of "aggression, whether committed openly, or by fomenting civil strife in the interest of a foreign Power, or otherwise . . .".

3) L.c., Article II, sub 5 (see text quoted below, p. 91). The omission of this form of aggression in the Soviet Proposal of 1950, for the rest in conformance with the Litvinof definition, aroused an understandable distrust on the part of the other delegates in the First Committee. The Greek Delegate remarked that "such an omission might lead to the disastrous conclusion that that type of aggression was implicitly legal", l.c., p. 265, par. 5. The main objection against the Soviet definition, the Canadian Delegate said, was „that it did not deal with indirect aggression, which, at the present time, was proving far more dangerous than aggression of the old type", l.c., p. 263, par. 49.

within the framework of an international armed conflict.

Since that time, however, the world had the experience of the way in which the 'Anschlusz' of Austria was brought about in 1938, of the *coup d'état* which, in 1948, established a communist regime in Czechoslovakia, of the assistance given between 1946 and 1949 to the Greek communist rebels by Greece's northern neighbours, and of the activity of 'fifth columns' threatening the existence of many still independent States. Through indirect action, via secret agents or internal groups supported by outside propaganda (the 'ideological' aggression), money, arms, and, at the critical moment of the disturbances, by direct intimidation and political pressure, a State can put an end to the independent existence of another as effectively as with the classical, external, military aggression. Especially because of its complex character and because of the many varying forms in which this action can be carried through, its formal prohibition, and defence, guarantees and assistance against this form of aggression are at the present moment considered of primary importance.

Four categories of aggression can, thus, be distinguished depending whether or not aggression is seen in direct connection with war and whether or not aggression is considered as an exclusively military action. The first, original concept indicates the military beginning of a war, the second includes an aggressive policy which causes a war. A further extension of 'aggression' comprises, in principle, every (illicit) use of armed force against another State, including the threat of armed force. And finally there is the last category, since at one time or another all sorts of either illegal, or merely unfriendly acts harmful to other States have in the course of the last years been named 'aggression'. The notion of internal or indirect aggression combines elements of the last category with a final internal, but internationally determined use of force.

The Charters of Nuremberg and Tokyo do not speak of aggression but only of war of aggression. Therefore, in that context, only the first two categories of aggression are relevant, that is the aggression which is identical with the beginning of a war of aggression. The planning, preparation and perpetration of such aggression is identical with the 'planning, preparation and initiation' of aggressive war.

Due to the present and future development of international criminal law, insofar as the 'crimes against peace' are concerned, (see Chapter V), it is, however, opportune to pay attention to the other categories of aggression also. Materially the distinction between the former and the latter two categories cannot always be made, as the distinction lies in what follows upon them rather than in the acts themselves: *id est* in both former cases a military reaction of the victim, which creates a situation of general armed conflict between the two States. With regard to the definitions of Tokyo and Nuremberg, the occurrence of war can be called an additional element of the criminal act which has to be present apart from the elements of which the *act* of aggression will appear to consist [1]). If the victim does not react with warlike action there can be no war of aggression, but, it would seem, only aggression in the third sense indicated above, more often referred to as 'aggressive acts' or 'aggressive action'. However, in view of the cases (referred to on p. 50) of full military attacks which necessitated the attacked State to defend its territory and independence with armed force (which gave the right of self-defence) but which were not, in the case, followed by warlike action, the element of war in 'aggression' in the original sense should be considered as a potential, a juridical element rather than one of fact. Aggression in the original sense is then qualified not by the fact that war followed, but by the characteristic that it normally follows, that it can reasonably be expected, and, if a *duty* of self-defence is assumed [2]), that it *has to* follow.

Whether aggression, in the classical sense, is considered to be dependent on the actual beginning of a war, as the initiatior or the cause of it, or whether it is seen as an independent act likely to produce a war, in both cases one is confronted with what formerly was called the necessity, and what is now called the *right* of self-defence.

---

[1]) See on the concept of additional elements of the criminal act ("bijkomende voorwaarden van strafbaarheid") W. P. J. Pompe, Handboek van het Nederlandse Strafrecht, 3rd ed., Zwolle 1950, p. 67. The crime of aggressive war could also be formulated as a materially defined crime, *id est,* as the causing of an effect, which is a war, l.c., p. 66. See further, Chapter V, section 3.

[2]) As is done by many scholastic writers and by Grotius, see below, p. 123. In the same sense Montesquieu, quoted by Fauchille, l.c., p. 9.

SECTION 3. AGGRESSION AND DEFENCE

When the existence of a war or an armed conflict is the starting point for the determination of both these concepts, the question arises whether in every international armed conflict aggression and defence are each other's complement; that is to say, with regard to the parties, whether the State which is not the aggressor is always acting in a state of self-defence, and with regard to the facts, whether the acts which do not constitute aggression are always acts of self-defence. In case of an affirmative answer both concepts would, *in abstracto* and *in concreto,* determine each other.

This is indeed the general view among statesmen and authors, in harmony with the ordinary use of language in which attack and defence are each other's counterpart. Thus in his famous address of 28 April 1928 to the American Society of International Law, Kellogg said, with reference to the draft of the treaty later named after him: "Express definition by treaty of this inalienable right" (of self-defence), "however, gives rise to the same difficulty, encountered in any effort to define aggression. It is the identical question approached from the other side" [1]). From the fact that Kellog's address was joined to the American notes inviting the Powers to conclude that treaty and that not one of them protested against the demonstrated concept of 'the natural right of self-defence' it may be concluded that this concept was generally accepted in the practice of States. And as the wording of Article 51 of the United Nations Charter closely follows the terminology used by Kellogg, it may moreover be assumed that that conclusion still holds good for the present.

If aggression is taken in the original, narrow sense, as the military operation which creates the necessity, or gives the right to the attacked State to react with acts of war, aggression and defence are by definition complementary; only one State can strike the first blow. If, in line with the Litvinof definition, the first author of any of a number of defined acts will in case of war be considered the aggressor, there is, even when an aggressive policy is followed, and frontier incidents have

---

1) Quoted by A. N. Mandelstam, L'Interprétation du Pacte Briand-Kellogg par les gouvernements et les parlements des Etats signataires, Paris 1934, p. 9.

occurred on both sides, finally only one military action which causes war. The other party is, thus, in a state of self-defence.

Instead of a military action it can, naturally, also be a declaration of war which puts the opponent in a position of defence. On the latter ground, for example, was Paraguay, which at the time of its declaration of war upon Bolivia in 1934 had for three years been in a situation of hostilities with this State, declared to be guilty of a breach of the Covenant. The embargo on arms initially directed against both States was henceforward suspended with regard to Bolivia [1]). After the Greco-Bulgarian conflict of 1925 had been suppressed through timely action of the League Council, Greece was ordered to pay an indemnity to Bulgaria for having invaded that country with its armed forces, notwithstanding the previous attack on a Greek border unit by Bulgarian soldiers. The latter action could not be considered to constitute aggression and the inadequate reaction was, therefore, not self-defence but itself aggression.

A limitative definition of acts constituting aggression makes it, therefore, possible to distinguish in every conflict an attacker and a defender. A case of simultaneous mutual attacks seems in practice hardly possible, although the expectation and the threat of aggression play a most important role among the causes and the responsibilities for a conflict, so that two States may both resort to war out of sincere *considerations* of self-defence. But from a purely military and objective point of view there must always be one which first steps across the limit separating preparations, and perhaps frontier-incidents, and actual aggression.

As soon as acts and situations not consisting in the immediate use of military force against another State are taken into consideration, the narrow concept of aggression is given up and aggression and defence are no longer clear-cut concepts complementing each other. Such acts and situations can consist in a general mobilisation, in military intimidation, in a policy of economic boycott, in warlike propaganda in the press, and also in a fear of aggression on the part of the military attacker.

---

1) Cf. the resolution of the League Assembly of 24 November 1934, and L. H. Woolsey, The Chaco Dispute, A.J.I.L., 1934, pp. 724–729.

2) See Official Journal of the League of Nations, Special Supplement No. 44, pp. 179 ff..

It is clear that once the forementioned broad concept of aggression is adopted, one which includes also non-military, political, economic or financial measures taken by the one State against the other, aggression and defence are no longer in every conflict counterparts. For a war will often be found to have been preceded by such political acts on both sides.

But these acts can also be taken into consideration in the concept of aggression not as positive, constituent, but as negative, excluding elements of aggression, *id est* insofar as in the form of 'provocation' they prevent the occurrence of the *casus foederis* defined as *aggression non-provoquée* or keep the attack of a provoked State outside the range of a rule of interdiction conceived in those terms. Because the treaties employing this terminology consider only *aggression non-provoquée* and not the 'provocation' itself, there cannot, in the systems established by these treaties, be any question of a distinction between an aggressor State and one acting in self-defence in the case of *aggression provoquée.* But these treaties are the inheritance of a century which did not concern itself with this discriminating distinction in a universal way. They were not intended to establish a multilateral system but only to delimit certain bilateral obligations and rights.

As the provocation or the absence of provocation qualifies the military aggression it is evident that provocation itself can never consist in a military attack [1]): the provoking State acts, therefore, from a strict, military point of view in self-defence, but the provoked State has on the other hand, under a non-aggression treaty formulated in these terms, not violated its obligations. This mixture of military and non-military criteria makes the problem of the determination of the aggressor in case of provoked aggression equal to that of the finding of a *Zirkelquadratur* to which Bismarck reduced the whole problem of aggression in a war [2]).

---

1) W. G. Hertz, Le problème de l'aggression en droit international, Revue internationale de la théorie du droit, 1935, pp. 203 ff., rightly qualifies the identification established by some authors between the aggressor and the 'provocateur' as 'une violence au langage'.

2) "...eine Zirkelquadratur, definitiv nicht klar zu stellen und durch keinen Vertragstext theoretisch lösbar, sobald man nicht der bona fides des Verbündeten mehr vertraut als dem Wortlaut der Klauseln". From Die grosze Politik der europäischen Kabinette 1871—1914, edited by Lepsius, Mendelsohn-Bartholdy and Thimme, Band VI, p. 81. As a rejection of an abstract rule

If, therefore, the question is not to be restricted to that of direct responsibility for the military conflict and if, either by the introduction of the broad concept of aggression or by adding the qualification 'unprovoked' to the narrow one, further removed causes and acts are to be taken into consideration, aggression and defence cease to constitute pure contrasts. In that case there is no longer a clear criterion for the distinction between an aggressor and a defender in a war and a definition of aggression as entailing the responsibility for a war can no longer be given. The question of the determination of the aggressor *in concreto* becomes that of balancing the responsibilities on both sides, with, in principle, no limit either to the field over which the investigation as to the conduct of the parties which finally became involved in a war can be extended, or to the period which this investigation will cover. It is clear, therefore, that the quoted observation of Kellogg concerning the complementary character of aggression and defence fits only into the mainly Continental European conception of strict military criteria for aggression. And it does not fit into the conception of Kellogg himself who, as appears from his address [1]), shares the broad and indefinable notion of

---

defining aggression this statement forms a curious counterpart to that of Chamberlain, quoted below p. 59. The German Commission of Experts for the Protocol of Geneva gave as its opinion that the aggressor could only be determined after the conflict and after "the disclosure of all sources, the opening of all archives, the hearing of witnesses and experts and the forwarding of all other evidence", Steinlein, o.c., p. 1. In the same sense MacDonald in the Sixth Session of the League Assembly, Off. Journal, Spec. Suppl. No. 23, p. 43.

Though all this kind of material is of great importance for the judge, and was indeed, to a certain extent, used in Nuremberg and Tokyo, the quoted conceptions of 'aggressor' have nothing to do with law, but only with pure fact and history. No legal rule can be drafted which counts with 'all circumstances'.

1) "Nobody would construe the treaty (*id est* the proposed Pact of 1928) as prohibiting self-defence. The right of self-defence is not limited in the continental United States for example. It means that this government has right to take such measures for the defence of the country or to prevent things that might endanger the country; but the United States must be the judge of that; and it is answerable to the public opinion of the world if it is not an honest defence; that is all", Kellogg before the Committee on Foreign Relations of the American Senate, from Mandelstam, o.c., p. 37, note 60. While the Senate restated in its approval of the treaty that "the right of self-protection may extend beyond the limits of the territorial jurisduction of the State exercising it" (ibidem p. 13), Great Britain stated that there existed "certain regions of the world the welfare and integrity of which constitute a special and vital interest" to the peace and safety of Great Britain, and the protection from attack of which must be regarded as a measure of self-defence (Ibidem p. 13, and Oppenheim-Lauterpacht, Vol. II, p. 187, note 1.

aggression of Anglo-American political practice as expressed by statesmen and legal authors.

Perhaps the objection will be raised that also non-military criteria for aggression can be specified in a list of precisely defined acts the military reaction to which will automatically have the character of self-defence. This is, in fact, an abstract speculation, for the broad conception of self-defence as Kellogg formulated it following the one time British Foreign Secretary, Sir Austen Chamberlain, is always closely linked with the rejection of a definition of aggression which would turn out to be "a trap for the innocent and a signpost for the guilty" [1]). Even an enumeration of cases of aggression which could constitute an auxiliary means for the international organ competent to determine the aggressor in an international conflict was on these and similar grounds rejected.

But, it is doubtful whether, even on theoretical grounds, political, economic and propagandistic acts could ever be included in a precise definition of aggression in such a way that resort to war or armed force against these acts would *per definitionem* deserve the qualification 'self-defence'. Apart from the possibility, indicated above (p. 46), that such acts, be it in various ways, will mostly be found to have taken place on both sides before one of the parties has recourse to arms, the difficulty lies in the protean character of those non-military acts. The element of intention and other modalities withheld from observation largely determine the nature of such acts, while, even with the modern technical development, the acts of military force, being concretely perceptible, can still be rather precisely defined.

Here it is only the question of the relation between aggression and defence, complementary when taken in the strict, strategical sense but more or less disconnected in the broader conception. The subject of a later section will be the criteria determining

---

1) Sir Austen Chamberlain in his Memorandum for the Subcommittee on Security of the Preparatory Commission for the Disarmament Conference, quoted approvingly by Kellogg who added: "It is difficult for me to see how a definition could be agreed upon which would not be open to abuse", See Foreign Affairs, Vol. VI, no. 3, Special Supplement, p. viii. The same argument dominated the discussions on definition of aggression held in 1950 and 1951 in the General Assembly of the U.N..

aggression in the present phase of international law, and in the actually existing treaty systems. But what can already be concluded from the foregoing is that the question of responsibility for a war, in which aspect the question of aggression is here considered, can always be susceptible of solution within a strict system, provided there exists an impartial organ of observation. In the broad system the responsibilities in different fields must be weighed and divided, and the possibility remains that both States must be considered to have committed aggression or, on the contrary, both to have acted in self-defence, so that a *non-liquet* will follow on the question of culpability.

It was the acceptance of the latter conception of aggression, that is the admission of all possible criteria and all sorts of historical and political considerations in the determination of the aggressor, which was the main support of the forementioned neutral conception of war in the practice of the world organs for the maintenance of peace and security. The vagueness of the concept of aggression amply provided the Council and the Members of the League with reasons and pretexts for not deeming aggression to have been committed, in the sense of Articles 10 and 16 of the Covenant, in such clear cases of military aggression as the Japanese actions in Manchuria and later in China itself.

The uncertainty of the concept of aggression was caused however, not only by the unwillingness of most States to practice international solidarity, but also by the uncertainty existing at this time concerning the obligations which the States had accepted to abstain from the use of force. The concept of aggression used heretofore only in bilateral treaties, was, after 1919, seen as a corollary of the illegality of 'resort to war', still limited in the Covenant but proclaimed without restrictions in Assembly Resolutions and, particularly, in the Kellogg–Briand Pact. 'Aggression' in the penal sense, as constituting an element of the 'crimes against peace' defined in the Charters of Nuremberg and Tokyo and punished in the post-war trials, must therefore be interpreted with reference to those pre-war instruments upon which the Charters and Trials were founded.

If the meaning and the extent of the concept of aggression is thus seen as a corollary of the obligations to abstain from the use of military force on war level, it can be said that wherever these obligations are violated aggression is committed. In this sense an identity can be established between the perpetration of aggression (or the 'initiation of a war of aggression' [1]) and the 'resort to war in disregard of (the) covenants under Articles 12, 13 or 15', of Article 16 of the League Covenant. Resort to war, initiation of a war, perpetration of aggression, to be aggressor in a war, all these expressions signify: committing an act which causes a general military conflict, an act which may be answered with acts of war by the State against which it is directed.

It follows from this connection between the concept of aggression and the prohibition of resort to war that the narrow, military concept of aggression must be held to prevail whenever in international law or in a special system there is a rule that a State may only resort to acts of war in defence against a military attack [2]). If, on the other hand, a State also has the freedom to resort to acts of war in consequence and on account of actions which do not have the character of a military attack, the broad concept of aggression, not susceptible of precise definition, must be assumed.

When the term 'causing war' is used here and when the question of aggression is called a question of causality, it must be understood that reference is made to acts on account of which international law or treaty law attributes – in virtue of a prohibition of the use of force – the responsibility for an ensuing war to the State which first commits them. If these acts coincide with the military initiation of the war, the strict concept of aggression prevails. If also acts committed before that initiation are included it is the broad conception of aggression which is being applied. The question is as to what acts in the process of events leading up to a war are given legal relevance.

Before an attempt is made to answer this question with regard to positive international law the conclusions drawn above concerning the concepts of aggression and defence must be pursued a little further. The close relation which has been established since 1919 between aggression and the unlawfulness of all or certain

---

1) See above, p. 47 ff..

2) As is provided by Article 51 of the Charter of the United Nations. The present interpretations of the Charter, do not, however, take this strict line, see below, p. 199.

use of armed force, has led many authors to consider unlawfulness an essential element of the concept of aggression. Aggressive war is defined as illegal war, aggression as the illegal use of force.

Quincy Wright, for example, states: "A State which is under an obligation not to resort to force, which is employing force against another State, and which refuses to accept an armistice proposed in accordance with a procedure which it has accepted to implement its no-force obligation, is an aggressor..." [1]). And the Harvard Research Draft Convention on the Rights and Duties of States contains, for the use of the Convention, the definition: "Aggression is a resort to armed force by a State when such resort has been duly determined, by a means which this State is bound to accept, to constitute a violation of an obligation" [2]). Though this is not meant to be a doctrinary definition it follows that the authors of this draft held that, apart from the element of armed force and that of act of State, aggression can only formally be characterized, namely by reference to the concrete decision of a duly qualified organ. Such an interpretation of the term 'aggression' deprives it of a proper meaning and must therefore be rejected. It denies, moreover, in line with several strictly positivistic authors, the existence of a concept of aggression in general international law, for, according to these interpretations, an act can only constitute aggression in virtue of a specific obligation assumed by the States [3]).

---

1) Quincy Wright, The concept of aggression in international law, A.J.I.L., 1935, p. 373 ff.. The inserted clause concerning the acceptance of an armistice was one *de lege ferenda* at the time, but has now become a rule in the system of the League of Nations. Cf. Articles 39 and 40 of the Charter, and see below, p. 78.

2) Harvard Research, l.c., p. 847, Article 1 (c).

3) Hertz, l.c.: "L'illégalité en droit international ne crée pas l'aggression, mais elle s'ajoute à la notion pour constituer l'aggression illégale". Hertz points out that international law can still demand other requirements before it attaches legal consequences to aggression — like the existence of a state of war or the absence of provocation. The latter is a typical example as here the supposition that aggression is *per se* illegal runs counter to the text of the treaty concerned. Hertz brings erroneously, however, the violation of 'engagements' in this category of other elements. This element coincides with the illegality unless the latter is seen as a norm of general international law in addition to which the treaty would still attach other 'conséquences juridiques' to the violation of its provision through aggression. But this is not the case, as a general interdiction of aggression can only be constructed on the basis of the treaties declaring aggression to be illegal and by which practically all States are bound now

From the survey given below it will appear that aggression was prohibited and declared illegal, first, with certain restrictions, by Article 10 of the Covenant, and later, without any qualification, by certain treaties, official pronouncements and resolutions of the League Assembly. But the very fact of the interdiction of 'aggression', and of the renunciation and condemnation of 'recourse to war', as pronounced in the Kellogg Pact, clarifies the illegality of aggression as a qualification added by these treaties and pronouncements to *an already existing concept of aggression*. If aggression itself is reduced to this illegality, the declaration by said international instruments that aggression or aggressive war is illegal, would become a tautology. These conceptions have, indeed, a close connection with the opinion that aggression cannot be defined, that is the so-called broad conception of aggression.

Clarification is also necessary with regard to the term 'self-defence'. Sometimes the term 'defensive war' is used and the Tokyo Judgment stated that the Netherlands 'in self-defence declared war upon Japan', referring not to a 'declaratory' declaration of war in answer to a military attack but to a war initiated out of considerations of self-defence (see page 33 above). It is clear that such terminology supposes the acceptance of the large concept of aggression. For when aggression is considered to coincide with the initiation of hostilities (whether or not preceded by a declaration of war on the part of the attacker), the perpetration of aggression means the initiation of war, and vice versa. The aggressor creates the *casus belli,* the situation in which the attacked State can only save itself by resorting, in its turn, to acts of war. But also when just by this military reaction the (undeclared) war becomes a fact, even then the State acting in self-defence does not initiate the war: it acts in a state of self-defence, that is in a situation in which it has been put by the aggressor [1]).

Only in the broad conception of aggression is there reason to speak of self-defence as an express exception to the general interdiction of resort to war as was done in the exchange of notes preceding the conclusion of the Kellogg Pact [2]). In the strict con-

---

1) See Hans Wehberg, The Outlawry of War, New York 1931, p. 21.

2) Though on Kellogg's insistence, contrary to the original French proposal, no express exception for the right of self-defence was inserted in the treaty,

ception it is actually redundant to speak of 'resort to aggressive war, and the phrase 'initiation of a war of aggression' would certainly be the same if it appeared that the drafters of the London and Tokyo Charters who had used this phrase adhered to the strict concept of aggression [1]).

It would appear that the concept of aggression has lost much of its importance with regard to the definition of the rights and obligations of States, since the United Nations Charter prohibits, in Article 2 (4) all 'threat or use of force'. The question is now that of the distinction between unlawful and lawful use of force, the latter including the exercise of 'the inherent right of individual and collective self-defence' which is no more determined by the ambiguous concept of aggression but by the unequivocal 'armed attack'. As will appear, however, from the recent Assembly discussions (see below, section 6), the majority of States does not accept this strict limitation of the right of self-defence. More than ever before is it the concept of aggression, loaded with contradictory meanings on the part of the different States, which is the central problem in the search for a reliable system of peace and security.

Apart from the prohibition of the use of force there is another factor in modern international law which has changed the position of aggression, as it has more or less rendered obsolete the traditional notions connected with war. The question concerns the qualification of the position of those intervening in a war or military

---

the only reason for this was that if the declaration of renunciation of war as an instrument of national policy would be accompanied by definitions of the term 'aggression' "and by exceptions and qualifications stipulating when nations would be justified in going to war, its effect would be very greatly weakened and its positive value as a guarantee of peace virtually destroyed". See the annex of Karl Strupp, Der Kellogg-Pact im Rahmen des Kriegsvorbeugungsrechts, Leipzig 1928, p. 37. The other powers did not, in their favorable answers to the invitation to participate in the conclusion of the treaty, forget expressly to stipulate this 'inherent, inalienable right', Strupp, l.c., passim. Curiously enough, the Protocol of Geneva, conceived as a system of strict criteria, provides for the 'resistance to aggression' as an exception to the interdiction of resort to war (Article 2). Jean Diamandesco, Le problème de l'aggression, Paris 1935, p. 11, speaks, more logically, of an action in self-defence as "une résistance consécutive à l'aggression' and adds that "dans le Droit International nouveau, le mot guerre, fût-elle défensive, est un terme impropre et qu'il n'est plus bon d'employer quand il s'agit d'une action de légitime défence".

1) See below Chapter IV, section 2.

conflict. In the foregoing argument with respect to the complementary character of aggression and defence only bilateral situations were considered. Now however the question arises as to whether third States share the qualification of the party whose side they take. If not are they then always aggressors or is their position not susceptible of qualification in terms of aggression and defence?

In the time of the alliances when 'aggression' was mainly a technical term to indicate the first transgression of the frontier *pour quelque motif que ce soit,* military operations against a State in execution of the obligations of the alliance were referred to as *agression* or *attaque*[1]). But since the 'outlawry' of war has loaded the concept of aggression with the notion of illegality and criminality, assistance and recourse to armed force on the side of the attacked State can no longer be qualified as aggression[2]).

This was already evident in the League system, and the action against the People's Republic of North Korea which had been declared the aggressor is a practical example of large scale military proceedings whose authors are not the aggressors, though they are not in a state of self-defence either. On the other hand there is the Assembly declaration of 1 February 1951 against the People's Republic of China which constitutes, in the system of collective security, the first example of a State being declared an aggressor on account of its intervention on the side of the original aggressor State[3]).

But in which position are those fighting with the victim of aggression? The term 'collective self-defence' — as appears from Article 51 of the U.N. Charter — is only applicable to the military

---

1) See Article 2 of the First Tripartite Alliance, N.R.C., l.c., and Article 1 of the Accord Franco-Russe, concluded between 1891 and 1893: "Si la France est attaquée par l'Allemagne... la Russie emploiera toutes ses forces disponibles pour *attaquer* l'Allemagne" (italics supplied), Colliard, p. 415.

2) Most recent definitions of aggression expressly excluded assistance to an attacked State, that is the right of 'collective self-defence, see below, section 6 of this chapter. When in the First Committee discussion the Canadian Delegate objected against the Russian definition that, under its provisions, France and England would have been aggressors in 1939, when declaring war upon Germany, Zarubin rightly answered that Germany had attacked Poland "before England and France *entered* the war", l.c., p. 264, par. 249, and p. 266, par. 18.

3) General Assembly Resolution 498 (V), Doc. A (1771).

assistance to the attacked State as long as the Security Council has not taken measures for the maintenance of international peace and security [1]. Moreover, Kelsen has rightly pointed out the defectiveness of this term: the right to assist another State against armed attack – a right which is considered to be of the same 'inherent' nature as the right of self-defence – is perhaps a right of collective defence but never one of *self*-defence [2]. And collective defence it can only be insofar as there existed a specific collectivity, *id est* a previous alliance, while according to general opinion [3] and practice – compare the immediate military assistance of the United States to the attacked Republic of Korea – Article 51 gives, or recognizes, the right of every State – also in the absence of a specific alliance – to succour any attacked State.

If, as was argued before (p. 37), the system of the United Nations Charter for the maintenance of peace and security is held to have universal legal validity, the participation in a collective action against an aggressor, in pursuance of Article 42, cannot be regarded as resort to war nor as aggression, nor as defence if the latter term is to retain its authentic meaning.

In the process of the establishment of world order the concepts of aggression and defence will gradually give way to those of illegal use of force and repressive police action; the United Nations Charter anticipates this development by omitting the term 'war', by restricting the use of the concept of aggression to cases in which collective measures can be taken, and by defining the obligations of the States in terms of use of force. But as long as self-defence is given a narrow meaning, dependent on aggression, the latter concept, which indicates a particularly serious form of the use of force – which in Nuremberg, moreover, was called 'the supreme crime' – will remain of decisive importance in the system of peace and security.

SECTION 4. THE FUNCTION OF A DEFINITION OF AGGRESSION

An investigation into the limits of the concept of 'aggression' or aggressive war, brought within the compass of international

1) See Goodrich and Hambro, The Charter of the United Nations, 2nd ed., Boston 1949, p. 304.
2) Hans Kelsen, The Law of the United Nations, London 1950, p. 792.
3) Goodrich and Hambro, l.c., p. 302; Kelsen, o.c., p. 796.

criminal law by the Charter of London, provokes the question whether among the numberless variations in which this concept appears in the various treaties, let alone the vast literature, there exists a general concept of aggression. A recent author concludes an exhaustive study of the relevant texts convinced of 'the non-existence of a customary rule (defining aggression) and, thus, of aggression itself as an institution of international law' [1]). For there is neither a repeated use nor an *opinio juris vel necessitatis* regarding the limits of aggression. And even with respect to the U.N. Charter the author quotes, in agreement, the words of Eden that aggression is a concept 'without a precise and accepted meaning' [2]).

Apart from more detailed criticism, serious objections can be raised against this method of putting the question. First of all every investigation of international legal concepts must count with the peculiar nature of international law, the development of which is completely and the interpretation of which is nearly completely in the hands of its subjects which conclude treaties and which act in international practice, while not recognizing above them a legal authority which may other than with their special consent correct their interpretations. With the method here applied to the concept of aggression Anzilotti reached the conclusion that the international protectorate does not exist as an institution and that there are only mutually divergent treaties establishing certain restrictions to the exercise of sovereignty of certain States designated by the common term international protectorates [3]). But mutual divergencies are not an absolute obstacle for the recognition of an international legal concept which in its main features is sufficiently distinguished from adjacent concepts.

The second objection is of a more specific nature and has an essential impact on the consideration of the concept of aggression. It is the dependence of the nature and limits of 'aggression' on the

---

1) Serra, o.c., p. 173: "L'inesistenza di una norma consuetudinaria e quindi dell' aggressione come instituto di diritto internazionale è un risultato che si può considerare ... come definitivo".

2) L.c., p. 196.

3) D. Anzilotti, Cours de Droit International Public, 3me éd., traduit par G. Gidel, Paris 1929, pp. 226 ff..

framework in which it is used and on the function it fulfils therein.

When the four stages were indicated in the development of the concept of aggression (see above pp. 51 and 53) attention was drawn to the difference existing between a concept which is linked with 'war' and refers to the act whose first author will be considered responsible for the ensuing military conflict, and a substantial concept intimating acts which the States are bound not to commit. 'Aggression' in the treaties of alliance, in the Protocol of Geneva (Articles 2 and 10), in the Convention for the Definition of Aggression of 1933 [1]), in short, wherever 'aggression' is *casus foederis* or guide for the decisions of an international organ qualified to attribute the responsibility for international conflicts, means: the launching of a war or conflict. In bilateral or multilateral treaties of non-aggression, in Article 10 of the League Covenant, in Articles 8 and 9 of the Protocol of Geneva, in Article 2 (1) of the Treaty of Locarno, and wherever a general prohibition of 'aggression' is given, it has a substantive meaning.

The 'aggression' which is the condition of an obligation to render military assistance will most probably be a narrower concept comprising fewer cases than the 'aggression' to which the States, in a non-aggression treaty or in a general declaration of renunciation, undertake not to resort in their mutual relations. The concept of aggression which develops from the 'jurisprudence' of the international organs for the maintenance of peace may well, in its turn, prove narrower than the forementioned and not comprise all cases of forbidden 'aggression', on account of the far reaching consequences which every determination of aggression and every designation of the aggressor by such an organ entails for the whole international society.

Finally the international penal concept of aggression may tend to be more specific itself because the requirements of criminal justice where the life of the individual is at stake are different and more precise than those of the maintenance of political order.

Such a distinction is not meant to constitute a dogmatic point for the interpretation of the mostly undefined concept of aggression. But it may explain differences between divergent definitions

---

1) Concluded on 3 July 1933 between Russia and its neighbour States, International Legislation, o.c., Vol. VI, pp. 410—419.

in treaties and doctrine and divergent interpretations in international practice. It may, thus, demonstrate certain constant and general features of the otherwise differentiated concept of aggression.

The difference between 'aggression' as the initiation of aggressive war and 'aggression' as embracing every use of armed force, and even some non-military acts, can, to a certain extent, be explained in the light of the difference between rules and measures with a repressive and those with a preventive function. Obligations to render military assistance to an ally, the right of legitimate self-defence, Article 16 of the Covenant and Articles 39 ff. of the Charter all provide for the 'repression' of armed force, they become applicable, that is: 'aggression' according to these rules, will be declared to exist, only when the acts of the aggressor have directly lead to a military conflict or threaten to lead to that immediately.

Rules of prohibition not threatening the violators with sanctions or serious consequences will, generally speaking, cover a wider field and include every use of armed force whether or not it compels the victim to resort to acts of war in order to preserve its territorial integrity or political independence. This is the case with Article 2 of the Kellogg Pact, which by prescribing the use of pacific means forbids, in addition to war, also every use of armed force for the solution of international disputes. The same applies to Article 2 (4) of the Charter, and, in general, to non-aggression treaties. The latter, moreover, demonstrate the tendency to include non-military acts harmful for the other party. In practice as the recent Assembly discussions fully confirm, the difference between the two functions of aggression is demonstrated by the fact that many States are as zealous to bring every possible unfriendly act under the scope of a *déclaration gratuite* of non-aggression as they are scrupulous to delimit the concept when it comes to accepting precise obligations or when the determination of a case of aggression would have any practical consequences for them.

But also among the rules providing for an effective repression of 'aggression' a distinction must be made between rules of criminal law and those of the world organisation. Determination of aggression in the framework of the latter entails, apart from the application of sanctions, the right to resort to armed force in self-defence. Determiniation of a case of aggression by a competent tribunal entails the punishment of the responsible authors. The consequence of war is very serious, and there will be many acts included in some definitions of aggression but not amounting to 'aggression' in the narrow sense which deserve punishment. But, on the other hand, the authors of an act which the Security Council has declared to constitute an act of aggression might not, in view of the uncertainty of the relevant rules, be held to have committed the criminal act of aggression though their conduct was so dangerous for international peace and security that military sanctions had to be taken.

The different functions of the rules embodying the element of aggression must especially be borne in mind as long as there is no unambiguous and generally accepted definition of aggression. For in the absence of such a definition the limits of 'aggression' will depend on the practice of States and, before all, on the concrete decisions of the Security Council. It would be rather objectionable, from a point of view of criminal law, to let a political organ decide *in casu* whether a certain act is to be regarded as a crime, the crime of aggression. The inclusion of aggression in the list of crimes of international law would then amount to the rule that the individual whose acts are considered as aggression by the Security Council, is liable to punishment.

As long as 'aggression' is not defined but only determined *in casu,* the difference in function between criminal and public law makes it necessary that a tribunal determines in every case, independently of possible previous decisions by a political organ, whether 'aggression' has been committed. This is, from a point of view of international criminal law, the significance of the much discussed question whether the definition of aggression is a political or a legal question. Insofar as 'aggression' has not been precisely defined it remains a predominantly political concept. When it was brought within the compass of criminal law the competent Tribunals had to determine *in concreto* wheter culpable aggression had been committed.

While the Charter of London relied upon the prohibitions contained in the Kellogg and Locarno Pacts and in resolutions of the League Assembly, the Tribunal benefitted from another inheritance of the League of Nations – not a definition of aggression but "the principle that an international organisation should determine the existence of acts of aggression [1]".

SECTION 5. THE DETERMINATION OF THE AGGRESSOR

In a study devoted to the international crime of aggressive war or aggression, the question of the determination of the aggressor State is of great importance. The determination of aggression by international organs prepared the way for the punishment of individuals for aggression or aggressive war and was, juridically, the condition for it.

Even were it proved impossible to specify the characteristics of 'aggression' under general international law as the forequoted authors contend [2], their conclusion to the effect that such a concept is non-existent would be wrong. For the concept of aggression wás transferred from the field of particular conventions to that of general international law at the moment an international organ was given the power to designate a State as aggressor, with legal consequences for the whole society of States.

The fact that a State resorted to war, that it committed an attack or aggression, had, before, only moral and political significance except for the State which had undertaken a specific obligation not to commit such action, or to render assistance to a State victim of aggression. Sometimes public opinion reacted and compelled a non-attacked State to intervene. Even when such an attack constituted a violation of an obligation towards the victim the consequences were limited strictly to that bilateral relationship. As it is rightly stated in the Harvard Draft on rights and duties of States in case of aggression: "in 1890 it would not have been possible to characterize a State which went to war as an 'aggressor' in the instant sense of that term, no matter what legal obligation that State had violated" [3].

The Harvard commentary, in line with many authors, contends that 'aggression' received that general legal sense in virtue of its prohibition contained in Article 10 of the Covenant, in virtue of the 'outlawry of war' in the Kellogg Pact and of the numerous

---

1) The Colombian Delegate, Urrutia, in the First Committee discussion of 1950, l.c., p. 254, par. 13.

2) Above, p. 67 ff..

3) Harvard Research, o.c., p. 857.

declarations, preambles and treaties which branded aggression as a crime. But because of the vagueness of the concept and the absence of a general definition, the existence of 'aggression' as a concept of positive international law could not be affirmed as long as the question whether or not a given action constituted aggression was left entirely to the discretion of the individual States. And the American note, accepted by all parties as the official interpretation of the Kellogg Pact, stated expressly that: "Every nation is free at all times and regardless of treaty provisions to defend its territory from attack or invasion and it alone is competent to decide whether circumstances require recourse to war in self-defence" [1]).

It has been a subject of long and ardent discussions whether any Article of the Covenant conferred on the Council the right to determine the aggressor State in an obligatory way. At the Conference of Versailles the question was brought forward by the Dutch Delegate, Mr Loder, but his proposal providing for an impartial, permanent organ for the determination of violations of the Covenant was not accepted [2]).

The opponents of the principle of international competence for the determination of the aggressor appealed to Articles 10 and 16 (1) and to the resolutions accepted in 1921 for the amendment of Article 16 which, though not ratified, constituted an important guide for the interpretation of that Article. The fourth resolution, notably, says: "It is the duty of each Member of the League to decide *for itself* whether a breach of the Covenant has been committed. The fulfilment of their duties under Article 16 is required from Members of the League by the express terms of the Covenant and they cannot neglect them without breach of their obligations under Article 16".

Under these resolutions the Council could only give an opinion on the question whether or not a breach of the Covenant had taken place. And it could, eventually, co-ordinate the measures which the States might take against the violator [3]). The authorit-

---

1) Text in Strupp, o.c., p. 61. See also Mandelstam, o.c., p. 20, and Diamandesco, o.c., p. 186 ff..

2) Documentation Internationale II, Conférence de la Paix et la Société des Nations, p. 287, quoted by Diamandesco, p. 180.

3) For the text of these amendments, see International Legislation, o.c., Vol. I, pp. 29—35. Italics supplied.

ative reports of de Brouckère and Rutgers [1]) state the case in the same way.

The opposite arguments relied upon the second phrase of Article 10 and on Article 16 (2) which conferred on the Council the power to make recommendations with regard to the measures by which the States could fulfil their obligations, on Article 11 which declared every war or threat of war a matter of concern for the whole League and, particularly, on Article 4 (4) which made the Council competent to deal with "any matter within the sphere of action of the League or affecting the peace of the world". The majority held that only by analogy and implication were these Articles indications of the competence of the Council to put Articles 10 and 16 into operation. They were not considered strong enough to remove the dogmatic prejudice in favour of unrestricted sovereignty.

Even if this interpretation of the Covenant were correct, it must not be forgotten that an 'avis' recommending measures against a State upon which the responsibility for a war or military conflict is laid, really constitutes a pronouncement, though not a binding one, of the principal organ of the society of States. Such pronouncements were given, by implication, against Greece (Demi-Kapour conflict of 1925) and Japan (actions in Manchuria in 1931 and in China during later years), and, expressly, against Paraguay (Gran Chaco conflict, 1934), Italy (war against Ethiopia, 1935) and Soviet Russia (war against Finland, 1939).

These pronouncements have created precedents for the rule of international competence in the matter of determining the aggressor. The pronouncement of the Council against Italy particularly – those against Japan and Paraguay were given by the Assembly under Article 15 (9) – has been of great importance in this respect because apart from the sanction taken, "at the twenty fifth hour", against Russia, it has lead to the only application of Article 16 [2]).

---

1) Rutgers, o.c., quoted above, p. 35. Report de Brouckère, Documents of the Preparatory Commission for the Disarmament Conference, C. 740. M. 279, 1926 series IX, pp. 93–105, p. 98. De Brouckère, however, points out that under Article 16 (4) sanctions can be taken against the State which either does not act in case of obvious aggression or falsely alleges that another State is aggressor and itself commits aggression under Article 16.

2) See for an analysis of the cases previous to the Abyssinian War, Giraud, o.c., p. 816 ff.. For the latter case, Q. Wright A.J.I.L., 1936, pp. 45–6.

Another development in favour of international determination of the aggressor appears from the numerous treaties and draft treaties concluded or proposed in the League period which, within a restricted legal sphere, conferred upon the Council the authority to decide the existence of aggression and to determine the aggressor. The draft Treaty of Mutual Assistance of 1923 contained already, in Article 4, a provision to that effect [1]). The Geneva Protocol left, for the case in which its automatic system of legal presumptions would not work, the determination of the aggressor to a unanimous decision of the Council [2]).

Article 4 (1 and 2) of the Locarno Rhine Pact became of practical importance conferring the determination of the aggressor on the Council except in the case of *aggression flagrante* in which the States could and should act without awaiting the Council's decision. The Franco-Russian treaty of mutual assistance of 1935 bound the parties in case of *aggression non-provoquée* against the other, to obey the recommendations which the Council might take in virtue of Article 16 of the Covenant [3]). Also the Treaty for Financial Assistance to the victim of aggression, of 1930 [4]), and that for the development of the means to prevent war, of 1931 [5]), neither of which ever came into force, provided for determination of the aggressor by the Council, the former by implication, the latter indirectly (Article 7 juncto Article 5 (2)).

The tendency which appears from these instruments and which was effectuated by decisions of the League organs mainly during the thirties, was directed towards an extension of international competence in the matter of declaring the existence of aggression and determining the aggressor. Great freedom remained, however, with the individual States which did not need to bother about the decisions of the Council and which retained, even in the strictest systems devised for the strengthening of the League, free discretion in case of *aggression flagrante* and in case of existence of the agreed legal presumptions for aggression.

This freedom was further restricted, in favour of international

---

1) See Diamandesco, o.c., p. 195.
2) L.c., Article 10.
3) L.c., Article 3 juncto Protocol I.
4) Text in Official Journal of the L.O.N., spec. suppl. No. 84, p. 503.
5) See above, p. 11, note 5.

competence, by the Charter of the United Nations. Article 39 provides that the Security Council *determines* the existence of "a breach of the peace, threat to the peace, or act of aggression" and the freedom of the individual States to assist each other against an armed attack, and even that of the attacked State to resort to force in self-defence, is strictly limited to the period in which the Security Council has not yet taken its measures (Article 51) [1]).

'Aggression' in the Charter is *primarily* a matter of international concern and is only secondarily an act on which the individual States may react — within certain limits and under the control of the Security Council.

Apart from the individual State and the international organ for the maintenance of peace and security there is a third authority which could determine, and has in the past determined, the existence of aggression and the aggressor: an international judicial instance. It has often been proposed *de jure constituendo;* more than once has expression been given to the need for an organ more impartial than the political League Council, one the pronouncements of which as a rule of conduct for the States and even for the League organs themselves, would have more authority and would more readily be followed [2]).

The Dutch proposal in San Francisco to leave decisions on the violation of the Charter to a body of eminent, impartial persons, can be seen as a politico-juridical solution on the same lines. But in view of the consequences of a determination of the existence of aggression, it can hardly be imagined that within a foreseeable period he States would be willing to leave the decision on war

---

1) Since, in virtue of the resolution 'Uniting for Peace', the General Assembly has assumed the authority to make, in case of aggression, appropriate recommendations to the Member States for collective measures, including the use of armed force, the international competence to determine the existence of aggression has become wider. By majority decisions the Assembly can pronounce, negatively or positively, on all cases even those in which a big power is involved.

2) See N. Politis, The New Aspects of International Law, Washington 1928, p. 35, who mentions an American proposal to this effect dating from 1924. See also M. Caloyanni, L'Organisation de la Cour Permanente et son avenir, in R.d.C. de l'Acad. de Droit International, vol. 38 (1931, IV), p. 706 ff., Komarnicki, L'intégrité territoriale dans le Pacte de la Société des Nations, p. 158, Wehberg, o.c., p. 118, and Diamandesco, o.c., p. 207 ff.. See, however, Giraud, o.c., pp. 839—841.

or peace – these terms taken in their current, non-juridical sense – to an organ in which they would have no voice [1]).

Quite a different way of international judicial determination of the existence of aggression and of the aggressor is that of international criminal jurisdiction, as exercised by the Tribunals of Nuremberg and Tokyo over the major war criminals. Acts which were submitted to their jurisdiction were qualified by these Tribunals as aggressive wars and the international and individual responsibility for these wars was determined after a prolonged investigation. Leaving aside the circumstance that in this examination of the facts no attention was paid to the possible responsibilities of States other than those of the accused and the fact that the archives of those other States were not at the disposal of the Tribunal [2]), it can, in principle, be said that the Tribunals exercised the competence to determine the aggressor in conflicts on which – apart from the Japanese invasions in Manchuria and China – no international organ had yet pronounced itself. By what way the Tribunals came to their decision is related in Chapter IV while in the last Chapter this matter is discussed with regard to the projects for the future to which the post-war trials have given rise.

In the beginning of this section attention was drawn to the connection between international determination of the aggressor State and international punishment of the responsible individuals. The question of the competence to determine the aggressor would not deserve so much attention if the elements of which 'aggression' consists were sufficiently established and generally agreed upon. The refusal of many States, and of many authors, to accept "hard and fast" criteria of aggression, and the absence, in general international law and in the Charter of the United Nations, of a clear definition of the concept makes the chief characteristic of 'aggression under international law' a purely formal one: for the world-organisation that State is aggressor which by the Security Council, *casu quo* the General Assembly, is designated as such.

If this were all that could be said of aggression – and some States and authors deny indeed any further substantial element – 'aggres-

1) See J. H. W. Verzijl, De aanwijzing van den aanvaller bij internationale conflicten, Weekblad voor het Recht, 1933, Nos. 12644 en 12645.

2) See below, p. 246.

sion' would be non-existent as a legal concept. It would only be a question of political decisions, from which even in the long run no 'jurisprudential' concept could be derived, as every obligatory force of previous decisions would, under this conception, be contrary to the political requirements of the maintenance of peace. Only under a legal doctrine such as that of Kelsen who considers rules of competence as the essence of law would such a conception of aggression still have a legal character.

The other extreme is the conception underlying the enumerative definition of aggression proposed by Litvinoff at the Disarmament Conference of 1933, included in the Convention for the Definition of Aggression of 1933, and in different other treaties between Soviet Russia and its neighbours [1]), and again introduced by the Russian Delegate to the General Assembly of 1950 [2]). Under this conception the part of the organ qualified to determine aggression is reduced to the minimum; it has just to determine the facts and apply the definition to them: the aggressor in an international conflict is the State which is the first to commit any of the five precisely-defined actions. As the definition was adopted by neither the Disarmament Conference nor, up till now, by the General Assembly, it was only in operation in virtue of the Litvinof-conventions which left its application to the individual States.

This circumstance can hardly be called accidental. To leave the appreciation of the facts to the States was to take back with one hand the freedom given with the other in accepting the strict definition. The clear substantial rule which, as mostly in domestic law, qualified the facts and distinguished the actions constituting aggression from other illegal and improper acts, separately listed [3]), which did not deserve that qualification, would really only have

---

1) Litvinof's proposal was elaborated by the Commission on Security Questions of the Disarmament Conference in the Politis Report (see below p. 80, note 1). It was not adopted by the Conference but laid down in the Convention of 3 July 1933 (above p. 68, note 1) which was open to all States and in two other conventions of 5 and 6 July 1933, International Legislation, Vol. VI, pp. 410—419.

2) Compare the remark of the Dutch Delegate, Prof. Röling, in the Sixth Committee of 1951, to the effect that history did not recommend this definition as "of the eleven States which had signed the Treaty of London of 1933 with the U.S.S.R. three had become part of the U.S.S.R. and three now belonged to the Soviet block", Doc. A/C. 6/SR. 289, p. 12.

3) See Article II of the Convention of 3 July 1933, l.c..

contributed to world order if the determination of the facts had been left to an international authority.

Between these two extremes – arbitrary decisions of an all-deciding authority and automatic operation of an exact rule – there are many conceptions, definitions and treaty clauses which in proportion to their nature, precision and range leave more or less freedom of decision to the organ entrusted with the concrete determination of aggression and of the aggressor – be it the individual State, an international authority or a judicial body. Most nearly related to the enumerative definition is the system of legal presumptions embodied in the Geneva Protocol (Article 10) and in the General Convention for the prevention of war (Article 5 (2)).

Instead of giving material definitions of acts constituting aggression, this system formalises the concept of aggression insofar as it connects aggression with the violation of an obligation, as is done in the Harvard definition and in that of Quincy Wright discussed above (p. 62), and also in the Yugoslav proposals of 1950 (above p. 42). In a military conflict the aggressor will be considered to be that State which has not submitted the underlying dispute to a procedure of pacific settlement, which has not conformed to a report of the Council, or to an arbitral or judicial award, which has not accepted the provisional measures of the Council, which has not accepted or observed an imposed armistice, or which has violated the statute of a demilitarised zone [1]). And these automatic criteria will apply, according to the Geneva Protocol, *sauf décision contraire du Conseil prise à l'unanimité.*

The part played by the authority designated to determine the aggressor is in two respects larger than would have been the case under the Litvinof definition if its application had been conferred upon an international authority. The Council indirectly determines the aggressor by imposing measures, or an armistice, the violator of which will be held responsible for an eventual conflict [2]). And, secondly, the Council can by a unanimous decision suspend the legal presumption – *praesumptio juris tantum* [3]).

---

1) Article 10 of the Geneva Protocol.

2) This system has become the practice of the League of Nations as well as of the United Nations. The procedure of provisional measures has for the latter been laid down in Article 40 of the Charter.

3) Georges Scelle, in his Memorandum on the question of the definition

On the other hand, the automatic system could be considered stricter than the enumerative definition insofar as the refusal of arbitration, of an armistice, etc., is a fact more evident and more easily determined than the first shot or the first crossing of the border which launches a military conflict. From this point of view, the competent authority has under the enumerative system a greater freedom of decision and a greater influence on the determination of the aggressor. More strictly bound in law it is freer in appreciation of the facts.

The latter circumstance is perhaps also an explanation of the fact hat the automatic system never came into force, contrary to the enumerative definition which apparently was considered less binding. It certainly was a juster obligation; the method of legal presumptions entirely leaves aside the question of the original responsibility for the conflict and only takes into account the secondary reactions of the parties. The recent attempt to introduce an automatic criterion for aggression – the readiness to accept, and the observance of, a cease fire order – into the system of the United Nations, was as strongly opposed by the majority of States as was, in its time, the Geneva Protocol on the part of England and other States.

The essence of both systems does not, however, lie in the criteria they choose but in what they have in common: the binding character of these criteria. As rules of conduct both kinds of criteria – those of fact and those of procedure – have always guided the authority qualified to determine the aggressor. Paraguay was considered responsible for the development of the Gran Chaco conflict on account of its non-acceptance of the recommendations of the League Council and its subsequent declaration of war. Italy was declared the aggressor after it had invaded Ethiopia and refused to follow the recommendation of the Council to withdraw its troops, and the same was the case with the 'North Korean authorities'.

But what is required more than anything else in the prevailing practice – which may be called that of the 'elastic criteria' – is the complete freedom of decision for the deciding authority. On no account does it want to be compelled, by previously deter-

of aggression, submitted to the I.L.C., speaks, none the less, of 'praesumptio juris et de jure'. Doc. A/CN. 4/L. 19, p. 3.

mined rules, to brand a certain State as the aggressor in a case in which it would deem that unjust or politically undesirable. And, inversely, it is feared that such rules might prevent the competent authority determinating as aggressor a State which circumstances not foreseen by the definition point to as such. A definition delimits; it makes certain actions decisive and excludes other actions and circumstances. And it is exactly those circumstances, all aspects of the case – strategical and political, juridical and economic, the state of international relations as well as the previous history – which the prevailing doctrine and practice want to take into consideration in any determination of what, in a concrete case, constitutes aggression and of which State the aggressor [1]).

The discussion on the Russian draft definition of aggression in the First Committee of the General Assembly of 1950, the study of the question of defining aggression which, on demand of the Assembly, was subsequently made by the International Law Commission [2]) and the discussion which followed thereupon in the Assembly Session of 1951, this time in the Sixth (juridical) Committee [3]), amply demonstrate that among the States the en-

1) Cf. the summing up of this opinion in the Politis Report of 1933, Doc. of the Disarmament Conference DC/CG 108, in Documents de la Conférence, Vol. II, Genève 1935, pp. 679 ff., par. 8: "Certains membres du Comité... ont marqué leur préférence pour une définition souple de l'aggression, qui permettrait aux organismes internationaux de tenir compte de toutes les circonstances, évitant ainsi les inconvénients de l'application de définitions rigides qui pourraient, dans certains cas, ne pas s'adapter à la réalité des faits. Ce qui serait essentiel dans cette conception, c'est que les parties en conflict consentissent à soumettre l'appréciation des faits dans les cas d'agression prétendue à un organisme international". Rutgers, l.c., par. 118, and the Commission of Jurists in the Corfu question (above p. 9) voiced the same opinion.

2) See Report of the special rapporteur, Mr. J. Spiropoulos, on 'The possibility and desirability of a definition of aggression', Doc. A/CN. 4/44, Chapter II; further, the memoranda of the members Amado (A/CN. 4/L. 6), Alfaro (A/CN. 4/L. 8), Scelle (l.c.), the drafts of the members Yepes (A/CN. 4/L. 7, later replaced by A/CN. 4/L. 12), Cordova (A/CN. 4/L. 10), Shuhsi Hsu (A/CN. 4/L. 11) and the tentative definition of the Commission (A/CN. 4/L. 13). See Chapter III of the Report of the Commission on the work of its third session, Doc. A/1858 and further below, p. 97.

3) See records of these discussions, held between 5 and 23 January 1952, in Documents A/C. 6/SR. 278–295 (provisional). Particularly to be noted are the observations of the Russian Delegate (A/C. 6/SR. 279, pp. 7 ff.), the Greek Delegate (A/C. 6/SR. 279, pp. 2 ff.), the Delegates of the United Kingdom (A/C. 6/SR. 281, pp. 4 ff.), Israël (A/C. 6/SR. 282, pp. 7 ff.) and the Netherlands (A/C. 6/SR. 289, pp. 9 ff.).

thusiasm for 'hard-and-fast' rules concerning aggression has not increased since 1933. The last discussion resulted in the adoption of an Assembly Resolution recognizing the possibility and desirability of a definition of agression "by reference to the elements constituting it", and the advantage of formulating "directives... for the future guidance of such international bodies as may be called upon to determine the aggressor" [1]). It is clear that this does not envisage a strict, enumerative definition.

If during its Seventh Session the Assembly arrives at a definition of aggression this will most probably not be one having for consequence what was in the mind of the authors of the 1933 definition: that "States would thus be definitely informed in advance of what they could not do without being regarded as aggressors" [2]). Even those who in 1950 proposed a definition on the lines of that of 1933 did not have in mind "a precise definition which these bodies" (called upon to determine in fact the aggressor in a given conflict) "would have to apply" – "determining acts of aggression in a definite, practical and direct manner" and "putting an end to doubts and controversies on the point whether States which resort to force have committed aggression or not" [3]). They stated that it was necessary to define aggression "in order to give *some guidance* to the organs (concerned)", and that it would serve "as a basis" [4]).

The same definition was, thus, no longer proposed as a legally binding rule, in all circumstances strictly to be applied, but rather as an auxiliary means to be used at the discretion of the organs concerned.

Bolivia and the Philippines which at the San Francisco Conference proposed to include in the Charter an enumerative definition of aggression "did not claim" – as the report on Chapter VIII (B) of Dumbarton Oaks proposal states [5]) – "to specify all cases of aggression. They proposed a list of eventualities in which intervention by the Council would be automatic. At the same

---

1) Resolution 599 (VI), of 31 January 1952.
2) Politis Report, l.c. par. 2.
3) Ibidem par. 3.
4) The Delegate of the Soviet-Union and that of the Byelorussian S.S.R. in the First Committee, 1950, (1. c.p. 283 and p. 260).
5) United Nations Conference on International Organisation, Commission III, Committee 3 (on enforcement measures), Doc. 881, III/3/3, May 9th, 1945.

time they would have left to the Council the power to determine the other cases in which it would likewise intervene".

But even a definition with such modalities as to, in fact, make it contradictory and without any practical consequence [1]), could not receive the approbation of the majority of States which opposed the old argument: "a list of cases being necessarily incomplete, the Council would have a tendency to consider of less importance the acts not mentioned therein; those omissions would encourage the aggressor to distort the definition or might delay action by the Council" [2]).

All these and similar efforts to lay down rules for the exercise of the competence and procedure of the Security Council stranded in San Francisco on the predominant tendency of Dumbarton Oaks and of the Big Powers mainly concerned to give "only latitude to enable the Security Council to decide in the best interest of maintaining peace according to the situation with which it is faced" [3]). It was this spirit of "avoiding legalities" [4]) which sat at the cradle of the United Nations and inspired the young organisation in its conduct towards the post-war conflicts with which it became faced.

All systems and doctrines which reject fixed rules for the determination of what *in concreto* constitutes aggression – be it in the form of procedural, automatic criteria or in that of an enumeration of the manifestations of aggression – agree on one point: that the determination of the aggressor must from case to case be left to the complete, or nearly complete freedom of decision of the qualified authority [5]). That authority is, as is now generally recognized on the ground of Article 39 of the Charter, the Security

---

1) See below, pp. 90–92.

2) L.c., p. 80, note 5. Compare Kellogg's statement: "It is far too easy for the unscrupulous to mould events to accord with an agreed definition", Mandelstam, o.c., p. 9, note 17.

3) Paul-Boncour in his opening statement for the said Committee, U.N.C.I.O., Doc. 134, III/3/3, May 9th, 1945.

4) See conclusion of Kelsen. quoting the words of the Chinese Delegate to the Security Council, in his survey of the Security Council's dealings with the first Dutch police-action in Indonesia, summer 1947. The Law of the United Nations (London 1950), pp. 438–443, notes 8 and 9.

5) In the words of the U.N.C.I.O. Committee: „The Committee, therefore, decided to adhere to the text drawn up at Dumbarton oaks and to leave to the Council the entire decision as to what constituted a threat to the peace, a breach of the peace or an act of aggression", ibidem, note 2.

Council [1]), and no more the individual State, as was the case under the system of the Kellogg Pact and, partially, of the Covenant of the League of Nations.

A distinction must certainly be made, however, between those who do not want to recognize any substantial element of aggression, and those who, either in a list of *indices* for aggression or in a general, abstract definition, want to indicate certain main lines or put certain limits to the concept.

In the first category comes the Permanent Consultative Commission of the League of Nations which in 1923 drafted a list of a number of actions – more or less covering those listed sub (2) and (3) in the definition of 1933 – which, according to the Commission. "dans bien de circonstances constituent une agression". A second list was added containing actions which "peuvent servir comme elements d'appréciation pour la détermination de l'agresseur" [2]).

Rutgers speaks of "un certain nombre de faits qui, selon les circonstances, peuvent servir d'indices pour la constatation de l'agression" [3]).

The attempt to solve the problem of aggression by an abstract definition which would contain the necessary elements of every aggression has received much emphasis in the Third Session (of 1951) of the International Law Commission, a Commission established as a subsidiary organ of the General Assembly which has for its object "the promotion of the progressive development of international law and its codification" [4]). The remarkable feature of this attempt is its practical purpose though this, as will appear, is not well specified. For most authors of manuals of international

---

1) And since the adoption of Resolution 377 (V), 'Uniting for Peace', of 3 November 1950, also the General Assembly, whose competence in this regard has been based on Articles 10 and 11(2) of the Charter, restricted only by the provision of Article 12(1). Though no express competence 'to determine the existence of any . . . act of aggression' has been given to the Assembly, the latter, by the recommendation and organisation of collective measures against a State, can attach important consequences to its decision that a certain State has committed aggression. The Assembly can in this way, 'outlaw' an aggressor.

2) Rapport de la Commission Permanente Consultative, 4me Assemblée, Doc. A/35/1923, IX.

3) Rutgers, l.c., par. 113. The double reservation with the phrase 'selon les circonstances' evidences the concern to avoid everything that bore the slightest likeness to a rule.

4) Article I of the Statute of the International Law Commission, Gen. Ass. Resolution, 174 (II) of 21 November 1947.

law and of monographs on the subject have given abstract definitions of aggression from a theoretical and systematic point of view. The idea that the international organisation, the individual States or international tribunals would draw practical advantage from such a definition is relatively new.

The efforts of the International Law Commission, however, and also those of the General Assembly so far, have failed, and the forementioned system of *indices* has never been adopted in a treaty or been accepted by an international authority. In these circumstances the conclusion seems justified that, as in 1919, the desire to specify the obligations of the States by a rule defining aggression is still squarely confronted with the conviction that it must be left entirely with the competent organ to determine that certain conduct falls in the given circumstances under this notion — a notion in principle indefinite and illimited. A middle way between legal rule and political freedom has not yet been found [1]).

The first attempts to give a strict definition of aggression date from a time when the decision whether certain conduct constituted aggression was still left entirely to the individual States. A definition such as that of 1933 was intended mainly to fill the gap in the individualistic system of the Kellogg Pact [2]). The definition would bind the States which are not bound by decisions of a higher instance, to a legal rule. Only when such a rule is accepted can there be a difference between definition and decision, between *définition de l'aggression* and *détermination de l'agresseur* [3]).

Now that the decision, the determination, by an international authority has received binding force under the system of the United Nations the problem has changed but the definition of aggression has not lost its essential importance. It alone can add legal security and justice to the political authority conferred upon the Security- Council by Article 39 of the Charter. It is, there fore, worth while considering further the different aspects of

1) Article 9 of the Inter-American Treaty of Mutual Assistance of 1947 is but an apparent compromise between these two approaches, see below, p. 91.

2) "L'acte définissant l'agresseur est conçu comme le prolongement du Pacte de Paris", Politis quoted by Giraud, l.c., p. 779.

3) See Diamandesco, o.c., pp. 52—55.

such a definition and attempting to specify the elements of aggression.

SECTION 6. DEFINITION OF AGGRESSION

In the Assembly discussion of 1950 there was a sharp controversy on the question whether definition of aggression is a political or a legal matter. Apart from the Delegates of the Soviet-bloc who, with a justified appeal to the past in which the question had always been discussed in political bodies, wanted the First (political) Committee to decide on the Russian proposal, the Committee divided, at the end of its discussion, into two groups. Those who saw the question of defining aggression as a primarily political problem wanted to refer the proposal to the Interim Committee of the Assembly. Those who considered it as mainly juridical wanted reference to the International Law Commission. The latter desire was embodied in a joint Syrian-Bolivian resolution which was finally adopted with a large majority [1]).

The boundary between international law and international politics – for long a favourite subject of international lawyers – has, since the existence of a political world organisation, become a much debated question of practical politics. So long as the organs of individual States, with their own juridical advisers in the inner-rooms, were exclusively competent to pronounce officially on international matters, open discussion on this distinction as a practical question was excluded. But since international political organs exist and next to them juridical bodies qualified to advise these organs, on their demand, on legal matters, the question whether a certain problem has a political or rather a legal character is often a very pointed question of procedure. It is important to observe that this is a question of *aspects* rather than of *intrinsic qualities* of the matter: the question can never be answered in an abstract way. A political question becomes juridical, or takes on a juridical aspect, from the moment there exists a binding rule concerning its subject-matter. Whatever higher principles or sociological laws politics may obey, its essence remains the free decision, while the essence of law is the binding rule.

---

1) Resolution 378 (V) adopted by 39 to 12 votes with 7 abstentions.

Few will be inclined to go as far as Kelsen who in the Preface 'On Interpretation' to his *The Law of the United Nations* stamps not only law but also its interpretation as "a specific social technique for the archievement of ends determined by politics" [1]).

This doctrine denies not only the existence of any independent value of law, that is any direct relation to the aim of justice and the common good, but also the autonomy of the juridical norms which govern the legal rule after its creation. But even those who consider the creation of positive law to be subjected to higher norms and those who, in conformity with Article 36 (2a) of the Statute of the International Court of Justice, deem the interpretation of existing law a legal question, cannot deny that the creation of law itself – with few exceptions – is in the hands of political organs.

The juridical character of the definition of aggression might be defended by reference to the use of the term in treaty provisions, notably Article 39 of the Charter, in virtue of which definition of this term, as a question of the interpretation of treaties, would have become a legal question. But in the first place this argument is checked by the express decision of the United Nations Conference on International Organisation to leave 'the entire decision' as to what, in fact, constitutes aggression to the Security Council [2]). This means that, in principle, no state action is excluded from, nor *per se* included in this concept and that 'aggression' has been inserted in the Charter as a non-specific political concept to be neither positively nor negatively defined. The decision to define 'aggression' in any obligatory way must of necessity therefore be a political one.

---

1) O.c., p. xiii. Compare, on interpretation, p. xv: "The choice of interpretations as a law-making act is determined by political motives. It is not the logically true, it is the politically preferable meaning of the interpreted norm which becomes binding". However often this may be the case, the existence of an automatic process in this respect will only be assumed by those who start from the *a priori* that there exists no 'true meaning', no substantial norm for law and legal science and who, therefore, exclude the possibility that in international law, the interpretation of which is not controlled by a binding legal organ, the political powers will ever follow such norms in the interpretation of the self-created rules. Moreover, Kelsen's theory puts the whole jurisprudence of the International Court on the unsteady basis of political opportunism.

2) See above, p. 82, note 5.

The decision as to *how* 'aggression' is going to be defined is not, for that reason, a question which, contrary to the first, could be left to a body of legal experts [1]). As has been said before, the extent of the concept of aggression depends directly on the obligations which the States have assumed and are prepared to assume. And these are not only the obligations, embodied in the Charter, to abstain from the threat or use of force in their mutual relations but also the even more important obligations to participate in 'collective measures' in situations which would be more or less precisely determined if a definition of aggression were to govern the decisions of the Security Council or the recommendations of the General Assembly.

The latter circumstance was precisely the main argument of the supporters of the insertion of a definition of aggression in the Charter at the Conference of San Francisco. As was said very clearly by the New-Zealand Delegate in the First Committee discussion of 1950: "Their object then had been to reach a definition which would provide a point at which a pledge to resist aggression could be brought into effect [2]). In Chapter VII of the Chapter, as it has now been formulated, there is neither a provision obliging the Security Council to determine the aggressor – a 'breach of the peace' can be anonymous! – nor an obligation to direct the 'measures for the maintenance of international peace and security' against the State which is wrong; there is no compulsion to protect the existing legal order. The obligation for the organs of the United Nations to act 'in accordance with justice and international law' was expressly omitted from the Chapter relating to the maintenance of peace and security [3]).

The purpose of having 'aggression' "established as a condition leading up to a legal obligation" [4]) can, in fact, only be achieved by an enumerative definition in which concrete actions are listed.

---

1) As the Brazilian Delegate in the First Committee of 1950 asserted: "the decision to define aggression was political, while its actual definition was juridical", l.c., p. 283, par. 60.

2) Ibidem p. 276, par. 34. The Delegate, Sir Carl Berendsen, rejected the Soviet proposal precisely on the ground of the fact "that no such object was at present contemplated by the Soviet Union. Under its proposals, each State would be left free to decide not only what constitutes aggression, but also whether it would take the action called for under the Charter", ibidem.

3) See below, p. 105, note 2.

4) L.c., note 2 above.

Here, in the framework of a central determination of the aggressor, lies the great attraction of the Litvinof definition which is, therefore, again and again taken up notwithstanding its repeated rejection by the majority of States.

This repressive function of a definition of aggression was but secondary in the report of Politis, under whose presidence the Litvinof proposal was elaborated at the Disarmament Conference of 1933 [1]). First came the preventive function of deterring future aggressors who would no longer be able to withdraw from an accusation of aggression by an appeal to a vague concept of self-defence. And all States, even those without aggressive intentions, would, by virtue of a precise definition of what constituted the aggression against which they had the right to defend themselves, and of what, though illegal or improper, did not constitute aggression, become strictly bound with regard to their resort to force in self defence.

It is clear why these advantages weighed most heavily at a time when the right of the international authority to determine the existence of aggression had not yet been accepted. The conventions in which this definition found a place stood outside the system of the League of Nations, as did, strictly speaking, the Disarmament Conference at which it was elaborated [2]). It is now the guarantee of assistance on the part of the community of States in the cases provided for by the definition which receives the main emphasis as *"fondement de tout système de sécurité"* [3]). This guarantee cannot, however, be separated from the preventive effect indicated above.

The definition realises this guarantee in a three-fold way. It simplifies the investigation of the responsibility for the conflict to the question of fact as to which State has first committed one of the acts defined. Secondly — the guarantee in a narrower sense — it compels the collective organ to brand the aggressor

---

[1]) Politis Report, l.c..

[2]) Soviet-Russia became Member of the League only in 1934. As the Turkish Delegate in the First Committee of 1950 stated, the Convention of 1933 is still open to the adherence of other States. At the Disarmament Conference, however, no agreement was reached between supporters and opponents of the definition, which in any event could not have been adopted as the general convention on disarmament in which the definition would have been inserted was not realised.

[3]) Politis Report, l.c.

determined by this method, leaving no possibility of escape behind a *non-liquet* for opportunistic reasons. And finally it alleviates the responsibility of the individual members of the collective organ to whom the strict definition and the evidence of the facts leaves no room for considerations derived from their special relations with the aggressor State [1]).

The great objection which since the discussion on the Geneva Protocol has been voiced in all possible variations by the opponents of the formulation of strict criteria is, in fact, directed against their legal character as such. The definition was rejected by Chamberlain, in 1928, on account of the danger it created that an aggressor in circumstances not foreseen when the definition was drafted would escape his responsibility by adapting his actions to the criteria defined [2]). And in the First Committee, in 1950, the French delegate argued that "in the organic world subject to change, any automatic system for the determination of aggression might involve uncertainty and possible errors" [3]).

From such a point of view there is no room at all for the establishment of legal rules for international relations. The fact that such objections are not made against the development of rules in other fields of international relations shows that the freedom, though vaguely resticted, to resort to force for the defence of the national interests and the freedom to render armed assistance only when that would fit these interests, still constitute the firmest, though already heavily damaged, pillars of sovereignty.

More than in any other field States fear to become bound, negatively or positively, with regard to the use of armed force otherwise than in vague terms allowing full play to circumstances and opportunistic considerations. They find themselves to a certain extent in a vicious circle: because they have not established an international police force, as prescribed in Articles 43 and 47 of the Charter, application of Article 42 providing for military enforcement action remains dependent on accidental circumstances such as existed when the Korean conflict broke out. And because

---

1) Ibidem.

2) Doc. of the Dis. Conf., series VI, p. 185, quoted by Serra, l.c., p. 46. Compare above, p. 82, note 2.

3) L.c., p. 253, par. 5. This argument did not concern the Soviet definition but the Yugoslav proposal which constitutes a parallel to the automatic criteria of the Geneva Protocol, above pp. 42 and 43.

effective enforcement-action cannot be counted upon, the States are not inclined to desist from the possibility of taking the law into their own hands.

On the other hand considerable gaps exist in the system of the Charter – the lack of a guarantee for the protection of the State of international law against forceful changes, the lack of a satisfactory procedure for the creation of new law, for peaceful change, and the insufficient formulation of Article 2 (4) which prohibits the use of force. These inconveniences seem, indeed, to make a strict definition of aggression, to make the concept of aggression itself "a legal concept borrowed from a future phase of international law" [1]). These objections will be further dealt with when the elements constituting aggression are considered (below pp. 104 ff.).

The forementioned circumstances which in general prevent the development of international law constitute, on account of its most specific feature, a considerable obstacle to the adoption of an enumerative definition of aggression. To fulfil its purpose such a definition must be complete and limitative. For here 'aggression' is taken in the general sence of aggressive war, indicating the responsibility for a bilateral military conflict, and not as a separate action *in se* (see above p. 54). The Protocol of Geneva precedes the enumeration of automatic criteria with the phrase: "dans le cas d'hostilités engagées, est présumé agresseur: . . ." and the London Definition of 1933, like all recent texts and proposals based upon it, says: "Accordingly, the aggressor in an international conflict shall, subject to the agreements between the parties to the dispute, be considered to be that State which is the first to commit any of the following actions: . . . .".

Whatever the criteria to which an enumerative definition binds the qualification of aggressor, a military conflict must materially begin with the opening of hostilities and one of the parties must open them with the first bombing, with the first shooting or with the first crossing of the border. This is what is covered by the second and third paragraphs of the definition of 1933:

"2) Invasion by its armed forces, with or without a declaration of war, of the territory of another State;

---

1) The Dutch Delegate in the Sixth Committee of 1950, Doc. A/C. 6/SR. 232, p. 138.

3) Attack by its land, naval or air forces, with or without a declaration of war, of the territory, vessels or aircraft of another State;"

If such actions do not take place there can be no question of a military conflict; they form the material initiation of war. The party committing them will not, however, be considered as the aggressor if the other one commits earlier one of the three other types of actions enumerated. These are:

"1) Declaration of war upon another State;

. . . . . .

4) Naval blockade of the coasts or ports of another State;

5) Provision or support to armed bands formed in its territory which have invaded the territories of another State, or refusal, notwithstanding the request of the invaded State, to take, in its own territory, all the measures in its power to deprive those bands of all assistance or protection.".

This list can be enlarged as it was in the Bolivian proposal at the San Francisco Conference. And a reasonable application of analogy on the part of the determining organ could still bring under the scope of the definition a number of unforeseen acts which only accidentally differ from those listed, though at this point doubt and uncertainty can creep in as the argument *a contrario* could be used as well. But what is quite impossible without making the whole definition useless and a contradiction in itself is to add, as was done in the Philippine proposal of 1945 [1]), that aggression is constituted by the enumerated acts "among others", or to provide that the qualified organ may also characterize as aggression acts other than those listed, which provision is inserted in Article 9 of the Treaty of Petropolis [2]). For the fixed criteria automatically lose their binding force if an aggressor State can succesfully appeal on the grounds of an action, not mentioned in the definition, of its opponent which would then be branded as the aggressor.

1) Submitted to the U.N.C.I.O., Doc. 502/III/3/22, May 23rd, 1945.

2) Inter-American Treaty of Mutual Assistance, concluded at Petropolis, 2 September 1947, Article 9: "In addition to other acts which the Organ of Consultation may characterize as aggression, the following shall be considered as such:

a) Unprovoked attack by a State against the territory, the people, or the land, sea or air forces of another State;

b) Invasion,..." See United Nations Textbook, Leiden 1950, p. 289.

The example may be taken of a war between a State which had permitted the slaughtering of its neighbour's subjects on its territory by a raging mob, and that neighbour State whose troops had thereupon marched upon the capital of the defaulting State to take revenge and protect its citizens. If in such a case between two States bound by the Inter-American Treaty of Mutual Assistance, the Organ of Consultation would, in virtue of the powers conferred upon it by Article 9, declare that the toleration of the lynching of foreigners constituted an act of aggression against their home-country, the 'invasion' defined in Article 9(b) would have lost all value as a binding criterion of aggression.

For in the dilemma between substantial rule and rule of competence as created by the contradictory wording of Article 9, the latter will necessarily get the upperhand, in international law. And, thus, the definition intended to be binding is in fact reduced to a non-obligatory indication as which it is superfluous, both cases formulated being the classic cases of aggression covered by the term itself. The Treaty of Petropolis which, in the Assembly discussion of 1951, several Delegates of American States proposed again and again as an example to be followed by the world organisation, only apparently contains a strict definition of aggression, the Organ of Consultation being as free in its decision as the Security Council or the General Assembly.

Reference in the U.N. Charter to the definition of 1933 "in order that the suppression of aggression may be automatic in certain cases" as was proposed by the Czechoslovak delegation in San Francisco [1]) is, therefore, impossible, because strict automatism in 'certain cases' leaves no room for other cases and because any recognition of 'other cases' as constituting aggression would nullify the automatism in 'certain cases'. And as a limitative enumeration of the cases of aggression, and therewith of the cases in which a State may resort to force in self-defence, is not, in the present circumstances, acceptable to the majority of States, attempts to arrive at such a definition have for the present to be abandoned.

In support of this political rejection of strict criteria for aggres-

---

[1]) L.c., p. 82, note 3, above.

sion there is often advanced an objective argument which in fact dominated the discussions on the subject in the First Committee of the General Assembly of 1950 and in the Sixth Committee of the Assembly of the following year. It is contended that the development of modern technique and the evolution of international relations make it impossible to foresee all forms in which aggression can be committed. A cunning aggressor would always be able to find a method to accomplish his plan without committing aggression according to the letter of the definition [1]).

Before the last war it was the rather theoretical example of the small weak State which, under the threat of impending aggression from a superior neighbour, was compelled to invade the latter's territory in order to acquire a better strategical position – which was often quoted as an illustration of the forementioned proposition [2]). But during the last fifteen years the world has had the experience of more real instances of small States losing their independence and disappearing off the map as a result of what has been called 'internal' or 'indirect' aggression, that is a combination of carefully directed *coups d'état* and outside intimidation. The arguments against a strict definition of aggression are to-day no longer of a primarily strategical or technical nature but concern, as the discussions in the United Nations organs amply demonstrate, the protection of a State's independence as such. When statesmen to-day speak of aggression they include in that concept every method, every action that can lead to the destruction of the liberty or the loss of territory of a State.

It is certainly this use of the term-aggression in modern international practice which led the special rapporteur of the International Law Commission, M. Spiropoulos, to assume the existence of a "natural notion of aggression" as "a concept *per se,* which is inherent to any human mind and which, as a primary notion, is not susceptible of definition... (but) rooted in the 'feeling' of the Governments..." [3]). Instead of introducing the subjective element of 'feeling' in such a philosophical proposition it can simply be said that governments have begun to term as

1) Discussion in the First Committee of 1950, l.c., passim.

2) See for example Clyde Eagleton, The Attempt to Define Aggression, International Conciliation, No. 264, 1930, p. 609.

3) Doc. A/CN. 4/44, l.c., p. 65.

aggression every foreign action which endangers 'the territorial integrity or political independence of any State'. The latter has become the central element of the concept of aggression superseding the limitative element of use of force which alone would allow the adoption of strict criteria and of an enumerative definition.

Before discussing the elements of aggression and the different criteria proposed it must be remarked that neither in the practice of the League and the United Nations nor in the Judgments of Nuremberg and – to a certain extent – of Tokyo, have acts other than those enumerated in the first three paragraphs of the definition of 1933 – *id est* declaration of war, invasion and armed attack – ever been branded as aggression in the sense of the initiation of aggressive war [1]). Yet, in harmony with the opinion of those who deemed that or any definition too restrictive, none of these international organs was bound by a rule for the determination of aggression. Paraguay, Japan, Italy, Soviet-Russia (in 1939), Germany, North Korea and its ally the People's Republic of China, were, between 1931 and 1951, declared aggressors exclusively on the ground of committing one of these classic forms of aggression. The Nuremberg Tribunal did entitle the 'Anschlusz' of Austria and the establishment of a protectorate over Bohemia and Moravia 'aggressive acts' [2]). But though a similar term was inserted in the United Nations Charter in the sense of aggression *tout court,* the quoted qualification cannot be seen as an exception to the formulated conclusion in view of the clear distinction which the Tribunal draws between these cases and those of criminal aggressive war.

States have certainly complained before both the League and the United Nations organs of other acts which they claimed to constitute aggression. But the important fact is that these organs which are not bound by any rule on the subject have never recognized the existence of a case of aggression in any of those

---

1) See the observation of the Israel Delegate in the Sixth Committee of 1951 to the effect that the decisions of the United Nations with regard to Korea and the Chinese People's Republic would not have been different if the Litvinof definition had been binding on its organs, Doc. A/C. 6/SR. 282, p. 11.

2) See above, p. 22. These acts had been charged not as 'aggressive wars' but as evidence in support of the charge of 'conspiracy'.

unforeseeable situations on account of which a definition of aggression has systematically been rejected. And another incontestable fact is that the absence of a binding definition enabled these organs to ignore, or, anyway, not to brand as aggression, evident 'classic' cases of aggression like the Japanese 'incidents' in China [1]) and the continuous support of the Greek rebels on the part of Greece's Northern neighbours, which latter case was included in the definition of 1933.

The Elements of Aggression.

As the chances of an adoption of an enumerative definition of aggression are in the present world situation even more remote than in the past, it seems more realistic to try another more abstract method for the juridical definition of aggression. The concept of aggression can be specified and the determination of aggression in a concrete case might be facilitated by the adoption of an essential definition indicating the elements required in every case of aggression. In its session of 1951 the International Law Commission tried to elaborate such a definition and in the subsequent session of the General Assembly its report gave rise to an extensive discussion [2]).

This method comes under the heading of 'flexible criteria' of aggression as opposed to the 'rigid criteria' given in the definition of 1933. Apart from both these methods which concern the act of aggression itself, there exists the possibility of determining a case of aggression by secondary criteria, *id est* by the establishment of a procedure, of rules of conduct which the States have to follow in case of the outbreak of hostilities on penalty of being considered the aggressor (see sections 1 and 5 of this chapter). Though the procedure has by no means become rigid and automatic as was proposed in the Geneva Protocol and by Yugoslavia in the General Assembly of 1950, secondary criteria are in practice applied in the system of the United Nations, as they were already to a certain extent in use under the League. In case of use of force, provisional measures or a cease fire are *imposed* upon the parties by the Security Council while they were the subject of a

1) See Lauterpacht, l.c., p. 13 above.
2) See above, p. 80.

recommendation at the time of the League Council, and only after the reactions of the parties to the dispute have become clear does the question of determining the aggressor arise.

However, the endless negotiations, discussions, compromising proposals, efforts of mediation, and the repetition of recommendations and orders which usually follow and which constitute ninety five percent of all international interference with aggression and with the aggressors, make it difficult to speak of disobedience to Security Council orders as a test of aggression in the system of the United Nations, as was proposed already for the League of Nations system [1]). As this is a formal criteria, a legal presumption which does not regard the merits of the facts, it cannot be applied by individual States when the competent organ fails to perform its function.

Already in the Report Politis which otherwise proposed the enumerative definition, it was recognized that the reaction on provisional measures constituted an important indication for the solution of the question of culpability, especially when that question seemed to be insoluble. In this regard, however, a distinction must be made between cases of planned sudden aggression and those in which hostilities break out as the result of a gradually aggravating dispute or of the pressure of circumstances. In the latter cases an automatic method of determining the aggressor by secondary criteria is preferable and can justly determine the culpability because primary characteristics of aggression are lacking [2]). But even when this procedure does not give an unfair cover to the real aggressor, it has the disadvantage that the measures imposed on the parties, a cease fire, or a line of demarcation, can easily present a strategic advantage for one of them. And in the absence of international armed forces and of a guarantee of effective assistance by the other States, a State engaged in an armed conflict has no certainty that after the armistice its opponent will not succesfully and with impunity surprise him. In these circumstances the sacrifice of provisional measures cannot

---

1) See the definition of Quincy Wright, quoted above p. 62. See also p. 78, note 2.

2) See the statement made in the First Committee of 1950 by the Colombian Delegate, above p. 43, note 2. The importance of these criteria were also recognized in the Politis Report, l.c., par. 9.

always be asked of the conflicting parties on the penalty of being declared the aggressor [1]).

Use of force.

Notwithstanding the 'inflation' of the term aggression mentioned before, international practice and the opinions of statesmen and authors still give ample support to the contention that the use of force is the central element of every aggression [2]). Fundamental on this point is Article 2 (4) of the United Nations Charter which finally decided a vexed question, much discussed since the time of the League, by banning all use of force for purposes other than individual or collective self-defence or in pursuance of a decision by a competent organ of the United Nations. Not only war but all use of force by the States is forbidden and it is obvious that this interdiction must be the basis of and the point of departure for every attempt to define aggression.

It is indeed by this method that these definitions of aggression proposed by Members of the I.L.C. during the third session of this Commission, were drafted. For example, the definition of M. Alfaro which "as it was the broadest general definition" was taken by the Commission as a basis of discussion, ran as follows: "Aggression is the use of force by one State or group of States, or by any government or group of governments, against the territory and people of other States or governments, in any manner, by any methods, for any reasons and for any purposes, except individual or collective self-defence against armed attack or coercive action by the United Nations" [3]).

The great importance of the introduction of the notion 'use of force' in international law is the solution it brings for the depreciation of the concept of war described in Chapter I. An objective criterion is, thus, put in the place of a qualification dependent mainly on the will of the parties.

In the second place, 'use of force' comprises all cases of hostilities short of war, including reprisals and other limited coercive actions

1) These objections were extensively elaborated in the First Committee of 1950, particularly by the British Delegate, l.c., pp. 250 ff..

2) Only the initial proposal of M. Yepes contained an enumerative definition, later replaced by an abstract one.

3) Report on the work of the Third Session, l.c., p. 9, par. 46.

not directed against the independence or territorial integrity of a State but having for object the protection of nationals or acquired rights, or obtaining redress for wrongs.

The distinction which the League maintained between coercive measures which were, and those which were not in violation of the Covenant [1]) has thus disappeared. And so has the distinction between forbidden wars, wars of execution and 'neutral' wars which were still possible under the League on account of the 'gaps' in the Covenant [2]). All resort to force in international relations is henceforward banned, and though the term 'use of armed force' is used also, the history, the context and the prevailing interpretation of Article 2 (4) of the Charter make it clear that its authors have thought only of the use of military force [3]).

So far the question seems simple. The concept 'use of force' is the key to the solution of the problem of aggression. The Charter clearly seems to choose the narrow view, of military aggression, and a strict, though unspecified, criterion for the determination of the aggressor seems to have been introduced in international law. The first State to have recourse to armed force is responsible for the ensuing conflict, is the aggressor, except in the case of collective measures. For individual and so-called collective self-defence are only permitted against an armed attack (Article 51) and, as in the forequoted definition of Alfaro, in harmony with the Charter, only collective measures and self-defence are mentioned as instances of use of force apart from aggression; aggression and armed attack seem to be identical. Apart from the case of collective measures, and leaving aside the possibility of simultaneous mutual aggression, the parties must in every conflict either be in self-defence or have committed aggression, and in the system of Article 51 aggression and armed attack are therefore one and the same thing.

But at this point the difficulties arise. The formulation of Alfaro and the one tentatively elaborated by the I.L.C. do not

---

1) See above, p. 10.

2) See B. M. Telders, De juridieke waardering van de oorlog, Leiden 1931, who recognized, moreover, a fourth category of wars, *id est* obligatory wars.

3) See Goodrich and Hambro, o.c., p. 104. The draft definitions of the members of the I.L.C., Hsu and Cordova, and Spiropoulos' Draft Code of Offences against the Peace and Security of Mankind, A/CN. 4/44, p. 40. employ the term 'of armed force'.

lead to such identification. They do not formulate aggression from the point of view of an ensuing conflict as did the definition of 1933 nor do they consider aggression as the action putting the State victim of it in a state of self-defence. They envisage aggression as an isolated illicit act to be determined by an international organ in view of its repression and they tend to leave to that organ the fullest possible liberty to determine the existence of aggression in all conceivable cases and whenever it would seem opportune. Kelsen too, in his commentary on Article 51, states expressly that aggression can be committed otherwise than by armed attack [1]).

If the forementioned identification would indeed have been accepted there would have been no reason for the committees of the General Assembly to reject repeatedly the enumerative definition of aggression as being too strict and limited. For the enumerative definitions proposed comprise more actions than armed attack alone [2]).

The general opinion of States and authors does not, therefore, consider aggression in the Charter to be complementary to self-defence [3]). It is generally considered possible that aggression is committed without the victim acquiring the right of self-defence. The question of aggression is less and less discussed as the question of culpability for wars and conflicts, and every act of military force, however insignificant and limited in design and scope, including the transgression of a border by an individual patrol and the firing on a frontier sentry, including the assistance rendered to threatened nationals and the military protection of acquired rights, is considered an act of aggression.

In the concept of aggression the International Law Commission included, moreover, the 'fomenting of civil strife' and, in the final phase of its aforementioned discussions, the threat of force [4]). The resolutions and discussions of the General Assembly have proved that such inclusion is in accordance with the opinion of the majority of States [5]). In the political terminology of the pre-

---

1) L.c., p. 797.
2) Notably, in the definition of 1933, the armed blockade and the support of 'armed bands'.
3) See above, pp. 55 ff..
4) See Report on the work of the Third Session, l.c., p. 9, par. 48.
5) See below, pp. 110 ff..

sent day 'aggression' seems, therefore, to be divided into 'armed attack' against which the States may, on the ground of Article 51, have recourse to self-defence, and other forms of aggression, including indirect aggression, incidents and threats of force, upon which only the Security Council and, according to the Resolution 'Uniting for Peace', the General Assembly may react with collective measures. Neither the victim of these other types of aggression nor other States can, in the absence of collective measures, resort to force in self-defence without running the risk of being considered aggressors themselves.

Even a superficial glance over post-war disputes, like the Kashmir conflict and the Palestine question, makes it already clear that in these and in most conflicts which do not originate from the greed of conquest of a powerful State but from a complicated, unsolved situation, both parties can be considered aggressors in the wide sense of the concept indicated above. And, in the absence of a definition of aggression, it is again left completely to the Security Council to determine not only whether, but also on which side, aggression has been committed. An identification of aggression with any use of force is therefore, as a guide for the international organ and as a guarantee for the States that this organ will take action, quite useless, politically irrational and also contrary to the *practice* of the Security Council and of the States which, in theory, adopt that identification.

It is evident why the discussions in the International Law Commission took this course. The Commission had the question of aggression under consideration in connection with the drafting of a Code of Offences against the Peace and Security of Mankind [1]), that is, in view of the development of international criminal law. Resolution 378 B (V) of the General Assembly instructed the Commission to study the question of defining aggression, raised by the Soviet proposal, in that same connection [2]).

A criminal sanction presupposes an interdiction, either given separately or implied in the penal provision, and it was only logical that the first crime against peace of the draft Code was formulated in the terms of Article 2 (4) of the Charter: "The employment or threat of employment, by the authorities of a

---

1) See below, Chapter V, section 3.

2) Resolution 378 B (V) of 17 November 1950.

State, of armed force against another State, for any purpose other than national or collective self-defence or execution of a decision by a competent organ of the United Nations" [1]). The definition which the Commission, on instruction of the General Assembly, finally formulated but did not adopt, ran: "Aggression is the threat or use of force by a State or Government against another State, in any manner, whatever the weapons employed and whether openly or otherwise, for any reason or for any purpose other than individual or collective self-defence or in pursuance of a decision or recommendation by a competent organ of the United Nations" [2]).

The two definitions, though of striking resemblance, had to serve different purposes. For the Yugoslav proposal was concerned with "the rights and duties of States in the case of the outbreak of hostilities" and the Russian proposal, which occasioned the instruction to the I.L.C., was intended to facilitate and to ensure the determination of aggression by the States and their international organs [3]). The difference between both functions of the definition of aggression was indicated before [4]). Even when all use of force is forbidden it is not necessary that for every violation of that rule the machinery of Chapter VII of the Charter may be put into operation and that the right of self-defence is extended accordingly [5]). Article 51 puts a positive restriction on the right of self-defence and it is necessary that also the concept of aggression preserves its specific meaning in connection with self-defence.

---

1) L.c., p. 98, note 3, above. Already in the session of 1950 the question of the definition of aggression had been discussed as many members could not agree with the statement of the special rapporteur that an attempt to define aggression 'would prove a pure waste of time' (First Report on the Draft Code of Offences against the Peace and Security of Mankind, Doc. A/CN. 4/25, p. 24). See records of the 55th and 56th meeting of the Commission (A/CN. 4/SR. 55 and 56) and the Memorandum of Amado, l.c., p. 11.

2) Report on the work of the Third Session, l.c., p. 9, par. 49. This tentative definition was finally rejected by the Commission with only 3 votes in favour. The motives of the opponents were curiously conflicting: the proposed definition was for some members 'dangerously restrictive' while others missed in it 'one or another element which they deemed essential'.

3) See above, pp. 42 ff. and Gen. Ass. Res. 378 A (V).

4) See above, section 4 of this chapter.

5) See the Dutch Delegate in the Sixth Committee of 1951, Prof. Röling, Doc. A/C. 6/SR. 289, pp. 10 and 11.

The necessity of self-defence.

The element of use of force has not therefore to be rejected, but only to be specified by a second, proportional element of the definition of aggression. This consists in the characteristic, which in the beginning of this chapter was deduced from the historical concept of aggression but which can also clearly be traced in the practice and doctrine after 1919, that aggression brings the attacked *en état de légitime défense*. The victim of aggression finds himself in the necessity, and acquires therefore the right, of self-defence; he is compelled to react with military, warlike measures if he wants to preserve his territorial integrity and political independence, that is his existence as a State protected by international law.

Recalling the distinction made earlier in this chapter [1]) between four successive phases in the use of the concept of aggression, one can say that the element 'use of force' keeps aggression within the military framework while the element indicated above maintains the link between the concept of aggression and that of war. The remaining characteristics of the latter, its bilateral nature and its general extent, were determined in the first chapter.

In his report on the possibility and desirability of a definition of aggression, the Rapporteur of the I.L.C., M. Spiropoulos, argues that aggression cannot be defined in the following way: "Whenever governments are called upon to decide on the existence or non-existence of 'aggression under international law', they base their judgment on criteria derived from the 'natural', so to speak, notion of aggression ... and not on legal constructions" [2]). One will not so readily accept that a notion which is not only in theory but also in its practical application the subject of so many controversies – of which the discussion on the Korean aggression in the First Committee of 1950 is only an example – is a self-evident, primary notion, 'a formula in itself', the meaning of which is simply known to everybody, as the Russian delegate contended at the London Conference of August 1945 [3]).

---

1) See above, section 2.

2) L.c., p. 63.

3) Ibidem, p. 65. The statement of the General Nikitchenko is reported in the Jackson Report, o.c., p. 328. For the discussion on aggression at the London Conference, see below, Chapter IV, p. 197.

But what can, anyway, be accepted of this opinion enunciated by many statesmen and jurists after 1919, is that 'aggression' has an individual characteristic which is not proper to 'use of force' as such. The most plausible inference is that this characteristic corresponds to that of self-defence which, though redundantly as Kelsen has remarked [1]), is in Article 51 characterized as an 'inherent right', a *droit naturel.* And self-defence under international law is defence of the concrete existence of the State, defence of what since 1919 has received the now classical formulation: territorial integrity and political independence.

Such an argument may make the impression of a circular reasoning: self-defence being the reaction on aggression, the elements of the reaction should rather be linked to the primary notion which could never be clarified by the secondary one. But by adopting the proposed formulation instead of a definition derived from Article 10 of the League Covenant by which the States undertook "to respect and preserve as against external aggression the territorial integrity and existing political independence of all Members of the League" one avoids the continually recurring misunderstanding that only use of force with the *intention* to violate the territory or independence of another State constitutes aggression [2]).

Difficult as it is already to determine the intention of a body corporate like the State, it is quite inacceptable that a State author of an armed attack against another State would be able to escape the charge of aggression and the consequences of an enforcement action by appealing to the absence of a required subjective criterion.

The fact that several members of the International Law Commission proposed such criteria as necessary elements of aggression, together with objective criteria [3]), is another consequence of the confusion in its discussions between definition of aggression as a political concept, guiding the decisions of international organs and States in view of the maintenance of peace and security, and

---

1) O.c., pp. 791–2: "a theoretical opinion of the legislator which has no legal importance".
2) This requirement is made by Serra, o.c., passim.
3) Spiropoulos, l.c., p. 65, who speaks of the 'animus aggressionis' and Scelle, Memorandum, o.c., pp. 3 and 4.

definition of aggression as a criminal act for application by a tribunal. Motives and intentions, if ascertainable, are of great importance for the judge who has to determine the degree of culpabiliety. But those entrusted with the maintenance of order can, in the first instance, only count with the objective facts and their effects. The purport of the act, not the purpose of the actor is the point of attack of the law.

It is, thus, the necessity of defence on which the right of defence is dependent which determines the existence of aggression. It is not an element of fact, but one of law. Not whether an action in self-defence, and, thus, a war or military conflict, actually follows, but whether it may follow and, therefore, should follow if the attacked State is to continue its integral and independent existence, is the criterion. The necessity of defence contains a qualitative element – having for object the territorial integrity and political independence of the State – and a quantitative proportional one: the danger must be serious and imminent. Both these elements leave sufficient room for what, according to general opinion and practice, is the overriding requirement for any definition of aggression: freedom for the competent organs to take all concrete circumstances into consideration.

Territorial integrity.

Territorial integrity is far from being an uncomplicated notion. The discussions in and around the League of Nations have often concentrated on this concept. On the one hand there were the defenders of the *status quo* established by the Peace Treaties of 1919, on the other hand the States defeated in the First World War and others which wanted to undo 'injustice', territorial changes in the past, or to satisfy long-cherished aspirations and urgent needs of expansion [1]).

The Italian delegate to the League Council, Scialoja, has attempted to find a middle way by presenting Article 10 of the Covenant as a basis for a possessory action while an *action pétitoire*

---

1) See Verzijl, l.c., M. W. Komarnicki, La définition de l'agresseur, R.d.C. 1949, Vol. 75, pp. 21–28 and 58, and Réné Vignol, Définition de l'agresseur dans la guerre, Paris 1933. The latter considers the violation of the territorial integrity as the element of aggression par excellence.

would have to be based on Articles 12 ff. [1]). As long, however, as only those States which have voluntarily submitted themselves to it, are subject to an international jurisdiction for the protection of established rights and positive international law, not to speak of equity tribunals for the revision of former settlements and for 'peaceful change', it is, under the system of the League as well as under that of the United Nations, misleading to speak of *actions pétitoires*. And this is even more cogent now as the Charter, contrary to the Covenant, contains no provision for the protection of established rights, provides for no procedure for the execution of judicial or arbitral awards, and makes only in its purposes and principles, by an amendment adopted through the pressure of the small States in San Francisco [2]), a connection between the maintenance of peace and the vague concept "principles of justice and international law".

By this it is not proposed that individual States should be allowed to use force for the purpose of maintaining their established rights or obtaining redress, or that other than formal, exterior criteria should be used in the determination of aggression so that the 'principles of justice' should supersede the requirements of the maintenance of peace. Article 2 (4) of the Charter admits no other than a military concept of aggression, Article 51 permits self-defence only against military action, and no underlying questions and causes may therefore enter into the decision determining the aggressor, at least in the first instance.

But, as was observed above at the discussion of the relevance of the intention of the aggressor, an international tribunal called upon to determine the culpability of persons accused of crimes against peace will certainly have to take into account these underlying causes. Such causes do not constitute elements of aggression but as long as the ban on the use of force does not go together with the existence of effective means to acquire peacefully what before could only be obtained through military power, these underlying causes ought to be recognized as factors diminishing, or in certain circumstances even excluding, the culpability of the formal aggressor.

---

1) Quoted by Vignol, o.c.. pp. 91 ff..

2) See U.N.C.I.O., Report from committee I to Commission I, Doc. 944, I/1/34 (1), June 13th, 1945.

Verzijl[1]) has stated that the more stringent the obligations to conciliation, arbitration or jurisdiction in case of dispute, the less need there is for an investigation into the deeper causes of the conflict once this has broken out into an armed engagement. Whoever agrees with this conclusion will also agree with the proposed discretion for an international tribunal. No satisfaction of legal claims can be expected from conciliation whereby the *fait accompli* and the 'right' of the strongest and most demanding party remain of considerable influence. And binding methods for the settlement of disputes are neither mentioned in the chapters of the Charter dealing with the maintenance of peace, nor ever applied in any conflict of great and threatening extent.

Political independence.

Territorial integrity must be defended against attempts of high-handed appropriation. Political independence opposes the other classic aim of war: the imposition of one's will upon the attacked State. Both elements together comprise the concrete existence of a State which must be seriously endangered by the use of force if this is to deserve the qualification 'aggression'.

It is therefore that territorial integrity and political independence are often referred to as the 'objects of aggression' [2]). This terminology is, however, erroneous as it introduces again a subjective element into the definition of aggression, *id est* an intention on the part of the aggressor to destroy or to reduce the territorial integrity and the independence of the attacked State, which intention can hardly be ascertained by the international security organ. For the maintenance of peace and security it is the effect of the act that counts, the purport of the use of force which, to constitute aggression, must be to endanger seriously the continued integral existence of the State in question.

International status quo.

The fore-mentioned elements of aggression were introduced in Article 2 (4) through an amendment of the small States in San Francisco which was intended to guarantee, analogous to Article

1) Verzijl, l.c., No. 12644, p. 1.

2) Steinlein, l.c., above p. 47, note 4; Serra, o.c..

10 of the Covenant, their territory and independence, though negatively only. In the meantime, however, the formulation dating from Dumbarton Oaks was retained in the final phrase of the present Article 2 (4): (use of force) "...in any other manner inconsistent with the Purposes of the United Nations".

Though this addition to the paragraph seems, at first sight, to confuse the issue and to make the clear interdiction of the use of force against a State dependent on the interpretation of political purposes, it must be remembered that territorial delimitations and, in the case of newly proclaimed States, even independence, are frequently a matter of sharp disputes between States. In view of the uncertainty of frontiers and of relationships between States in different parts of the world, the ban on the use of force against the territory and the independence of States cannot be said to cover all cases of use of force apart from self-defence and collective measures. Such a ban could not be invoked against a State using force against a colony or protectorate the self-proclaimed independence of which it does not recognize. Nor could States occupying by force part of a territory they claim but the status of which has not yet been determined, be said to use force against "the territorial integrity or political independence of any State".

The post-war colonial conflicts, the action of the Chinese People's Republic against Tibet, legally under its suzerainty, and different aspects of the Korean conflict (above p. 16) on the one hand, and the question of Palestine and that of Kashmir on the other demonstrate that, apart from the case of aggressive imperialism on the part of a Big Power, the most frequent and the most dangerous conflicts are not covered by the ban on the use of force against the territory and independence of a State. The final phrase of Article 2 (4) appears, thus, to be far from superfluous though this kind of use of force could be more clearly specified than is done by the reference to the purposes of the United Nations.

It is the second part of Article 1 (1) particularly which seems to be envisaged by this reference: "... to bring about by peaceful means, and in conformity with the principles of justice and international law, adjustment or settlement of international disputes or situations which might lead to a breach of the peace". Insofar as under these disputes and situations are comprised those concerning the territorial delimitations of States or the status of territories, the final phrase of Article 2 (4) adds to it the interdiction of the use of force against the international *status quo* as protected by the United Nations.

Article 9 of the Treaty of Petropolis, already referred to [1]), tries partly to cover *sub b.* the same situations "Invasion, by the armed forces of a State, of the territory of an American State, through the trespassing of boundaries demarcated in accordance with a treaty, judicial decision, or arbitral award, or, in the absence of frontiers thus demarcated, invasion affecting a region which is under the effective jurisdiction of another State". This formulation is clearer than that of Article 2 (4) though it is restricted to the case of territorial disputes. In a universal definition of aggression the case of attack on territories the status of which is a matter of dispute, should also be provided for, and room should, moreover, be left for the decisions of the Security Council and the General Assembly as with regard to the status of territories, the observance of cease fire orders etc..

In the definition of aggression he submitted to the International Law Commission, Scelle distinguishes between resort to force "for the purpose of modifying the state of positive international law in force" and that "resulting in the disturbance of public order" [2]). The disturbance of public order is, however, too general a notion as it would also result from a forceful modification of the state of international law in force, that is the territorial and political status of the States established by treaties and judicial decisions or otherwise generally recognized.

In its observations on the Draft Code of Offences against the Peace and Security of Mankind, submitted in June 1952 following the request in General Assembly Resolution 599 (VI), the Netherlands Government includes in the definition of aggression also the threat or use of force "against a territory under international regime" [3]). This formulation, however, covers the international *status quo* only insofar as it has been established by decisions or recommendations of United Nations organs. It leaves out the

---

1) See above, p. 91, note 2.
2) Scelle, Memorandum, l.c..
3) See Observations of Governments on the Draft Code of Offences against the Peace and Security of Mankind, Doc. A/2162, p. 27.

status of territories which, though not, or not yet, the object of an international decision or recommendation, are under the effective jurisdiction of a State or non-recognized State.

Which use of force?

The proportional requirement, *id est* the requirement that the use of force must have a certain gravity before it can be called aggression has *in practice* received too much rather than too little attention on the part of the organs called upon to determine the existence of aggression. The neglect of this requirement in the formulation of a definition of aggression, however, opens the door for an irrational and very dangerous extension of the concept of self-defence, if anyway it does not render completely inextricable the problem of aggression in a conflict.

An important part of pre-war doctrine has accordingly insisted on this characteristic of aggression. The Report of de Brouckère states for example: *"tout acte de violence n'ouvre pas nécessairement à celui qui l'a subi le droit de recourir lui-même à la guerre";* he must therefore be *"victime d'une aggression évidente et d'une gravité telle qu'il y aurait pour lui danger manifeste à n'y point répondre immédiatement"* [1]). The Permanent Consultative Commission required for the existence of aggression "l'attaque d'une grande portée" [2]). And Politis drew from the discussions in the League Council in connection with the Greco-Bulgarian dispute, the conclusion "that defensive war itself will not be tolerated unless in case of absolute necessity" [3]).

De Brouckère's formulation recalls that of Secretary of State Webster who defined the necessity of self-defence as "instant, overwhelming, and leaving no choice of means and no moment for deliberation" [4]). The quantitative requirement of the concept of aggression is, in fact, already contained in the specification, given before, of the objects of legitimate self-defence. Use of force

---

1) L.c., p. 101.

2) Quoted by Rutgers, l.c., par. 116.

3) N. Politis, The new aspects of International law, New York 1928, p. 36. The same opinion is held by Giraud, l.c., p. 754, and Diamandesco, o.c., p. 113.

4) Quoted in Oppenheim-Lauterpacht, Vol. I, p. 266, note 1. Grotius, following Thomas, considers killing in self-defence only allowed "si alia salutis non suppetat ratio", De Iure Belli ac Pacis, II, i, 4. (ed. Molhuysen, p. 129).

which does not endanger the territorial integrity of a State and cannot result in a reduction of the 'attacked' State's freedom of self-determination as provided by present international law, must necessarily be of very slight proportion. It will have arisen accidentally or be due to a misapprehension, or have such a limited object — for example the protection of nationals — that, also on account of the small size of the force used, the necessity of self-defence cannot be said to exist.

It is clear that the limits of the so-called 'inherent' right of self-defence have been considerably reduced since, at the beginning of this century, a prejudice to the honour or to what were called the 'vital interests' of a State was considered as a sufficient reason for recourse to war in self-defence. The extent of the right of self-defence is dependent on the state of international law in force and for this reason also no good purpose is served by attempts to define aggression by exclusion, that is, as the use of force which is not in self-defence. This kind of definition which received considerable attention in the I.L.C. and in the sixth session of the General Assembly [1]) brings the problem of aggression in a vicious circle and it is therefore that the necessity of self-defence as an element in the definition of aggression has to be specified.

Indirect aggression.

Two questions remain with regard to the extent of the concept of aggression which have been the subject of prolonged discussion in the International Law Commission and in the General Assembly Committees. First of all the question of the so-called internal or indirect aggression, according to many delegates the most important and dangerous form of aggression at the present day [2]). It has been recalled in a previous section that the Litvinof definition included a form of indirect aggression consisting in the support or toleration of 'armed bands' invading foreign territory. The indirect aggression which is now the focus of attention is, however, of a less romantic character, and is directed against the political independence rather than against the territorial integrity of a State.

1) See statement of Dutch Delegate, in the Sixth Committee of 1951, l.c., p. 11.

2) See above, p. 52, note 3, and British and Dutch Delegates in the Sixth Committee of 1951, l.c., passim.

While it is evident that certain forms of indirect aggression ought to be included in the general concept, a sharp distinction must be made at this point. The States cannot be allowed to answer with military measures every kind of foreign support or influence on internal attacks against the established political order and the legitimate government. Foreign propaganda against a government, economic or financial boycott, political support of revolutionary parties and still less that of certain groups within a government could hardly justify a military reaction, be it on the part of the victim or on the part of the international community. The structure of a State can be so feeble, its population so heterogenous, its government so oppressive or weak that it collapses with the slightest propagandistic blow from outside. No higher justice can demand that the States or governments receive an international military guarantee against such external interference.

Here also the use of force must be the criterion to the effect that indirect aggression can be committed either by *military support* to internal groups or by direct and necessary support, of a military or non-military character, of *fighting* rebels. The use of force is, thus, either on the part of the foreign State which sends arms or manpower over the frontier or on that of the internal group which, while in armed engagement with the established government, receives the indispensable direct support from the foreign (indirect-) aggressor State. Acts which do not fall under this formulation may be illegal, may even constitute a threat to the peace, but cannot be called aggression. A State which loses all or part of its territory or independence without force having been used against it cannot complain of aggression.

The formulation given here, requiring the use of armed force in one or another stage of the process of indirect aggression, is more complete than paragraph 5 of the Litvinof definition with its purely territorial criterion. It is, moreover, in line with the criterion of the Assembly Resolution 498 (V) of February 1, 1951, which, though not strictly concerning a case of internal aggression, constitutes the first international determination of an indirect aggressor. For with regard to facts which, on the part of China, have always been qualified as a spontaneous action of volunteers, the Resolution declares that "the Central People's Government of the People's Republic of China, by giving direct aid and assistance to those who were already committing aggression in Korea... has itself engaged in aggression in Korea" [1]).

Threat of force.

The second question of current interest concerns the threat of force which in some cases, like that of Czecho-Slovakia in 1939, and recently in combination with indirect pressure through political groups and fifth columns, has had the same effect as a war or use of force on war level. Insofar as the threat of force is, therefore, part of the process of indirect or internal aggression, it falls under the scope of the definition of aggression here proposed.

According to current opinion, as, notably, expressed in the definition elaborated by the I.L.C. and in the discussions of the Sixth Committee in 1951, the threat of force is also as an isolated act included in the concept of aggression [2]). This was different before World War II when the distinction between the threat, the danger to the State's existence, and the realised danger, the aggression [3]), was maintained in doctrine and in practice.

Even now, it may be asked whether the inclusion of the threat of force in the concept of aggression is consistent with international law in force. Whatever the relation between acts of aggression and breaches of the peace [4]), acts of aggression and

---

1) In Resolution 'Peace through Deeds', adopted by the General Assembly on 17 November 1950 (Res. 380 (V)), the Assembly "solemnly reaffirms that, whatever the weapons used, any aggression, whether committed openly, or by fomenting civil strife in the interest of a foreign Power, or otherwise, is the gravest of all crimes against peace and security throughout the world". While drawing indirect aggression within the range of the concept of aggression, this resolution nevertheless adheres to the use of force as the central element of aggression, as it presupposes that in all cases of aggression 'weapons' are used.

2) See the tentative definition of the I.L.C. and most of the definitions submitted to it. Further the discussions in the Sixth Committee, l.c., passim.

3) See for example O. Hoyer, La sécurité internationale, tome II, p. 34 (with respect to Article 10 of the Covenant): "L'aggression c'est le danger réalisé, la menace c'est le danger imminent, tandis que le danger d'aggression implique un danger qui n'a pas un caractère d'imminence", quoted by Diamandesco, o.c., p. 61.

4) The 'act of aggression' is in Article 1 (1) of the Charter conceived as a species of the 'breach of the peace' while in Article 39 they are listed as separate acts. Cf. Kelsen, o.c., p. 14, note 1, who, however, does not give an explanation of this contradiction, which has apparently to be traced to a negligence on the part of the drafting committee.

threats to the peace are consistently distinguished in Articles 1 (1) and 39 of the Charter. The resolution *Uniting for Peace* of 1950, sub A, providing that the use of armed force as a collective measure shall be recommended "in case of breach of the peace or act of aggression" only, confirms the sharp distinction in legal consequences which Article 1 (1) attaches to both latter acts on the one hand and to threats on the other.

In the light of experience there is, however, reason to consider an *imminent* threat of force, like that employed by the Nazi leaders to impose their will upon Czecho-Slovakia, an act of aggression, and a breach rather than a threat to the peace. Only such an imminent threat can fulfil the requirement of aggression, developed before, to the effect that aggression leaves the victim State no other than military means to preserve its territory and independence.

* * *

As a conclusion from the forgoing arguments aggression could be defined as *the use or imminent threat of force on the part of a State, whether acting openly or indirectly, which leaves the State against which it is directed no other than military means to preserve its territorial integrity or political independence, or which disturbs the international status quo in such a way that only a military reaction can maintain the status of territories under an international regime or under the effective jurisdiction of a State.*

All other use of force and all non-violent actions against the territory or independence of a State are, therefore, not approved. The positive law of the Charter includes them in its ban. But it is good to realise that aggression is a specific concept, distinguished from the illegality attached to it and qualified by the necessity of self-defence resulting from its existence, and that the limits of aggression are not automatically enlarged in proportion to the extension of the regulation of the use of force in international relations.

If this were true there would hardly remain a limit to the right of self-defence and, while the question as to who is the aggressor would become insoluble on the international level, the rules concerning aggression would become an obstacle rather than a help in the attempts to overcome international chaos. This applies especially so long as the U.N. organs have no means of power at their disposal with which to interfere in conflicts.

Attention was drawn before to the functional difference between a definition of aggression in view of measures to be taken by the international organs and a definition in view of international criminal justice. It is logical that in an International Code of Offences a crime is included the definition of which coincides with the formulation of Article 2 (4) of the Charter and includes all use and threat of force. But so long as, in the line of the Nuremberg Tribunal, aggression is considered the 'supreme international crime' [1]), it is necessary not only to mention it expressly but also to include it in the Code as a separate crime, before and apart from the others [2]). In municipal codes murder and maltreatment are not put on the same level either.

The concept of aggression as a crime under international law should, however, have its starting-point in the concept of aggression which the international political organs have to apply. For in view of the gravity of the act an international criminal tribunal will only be able to take cognizance of acts which have already been qualified as aggression by the Security Council or the General Assembly.

But though the criminal concept of aggression has its basis and starting-point in the political concept, it is certainly not identical with it. Criminal justice will by its nature take two factors into consideration which have hardly any importance for the direct maintenance of order through self-defence and collective measures. These are the elements — already noted — of the intention of the aggressor — which is the more important as criminal justice is concerned with individuals and not with the bodies corporate in whose name they commit the aggression — and of justification on grounds of the underlying causes of the conflict. The related questions of the state of emergency and of provocation will be considered in the last part of this study devoted to aggression in international criminal law.

It is regrettable that Assembly Resolution 599 (VI) of 31 January 1952, which for the present moment has assured the con-

1) See below, p. 214.
2) See below, p. 346.

tinuation of the international efforts to define aggression "by reference to its elements", does not take into account the functional difference noted before. Considering that such a definition of aggression is 'possible and desirable' it identifies however the point of view of "ensuring international peace and security", it being "of definite advantage if directives were formulated for the future guidance of such international bodies as may be called upon to determine the aggressor", with the point of view of "developing international criminal law" [1]). So long as this confusion lasts, neither the maintenance of world order nor the development of international criminal law can benefit from any eventual definition of aggression.

1) Gen. Ass. Res. 599 (VI), of 31 January 1951.

CHAPTER III

EVOLUTION TOWARDS NUREMBERG

SECTION 1. INTRODUCTORY

The concept of aggressive war, the two constituent parts of which have, as far as possible, been delimited in the preceding chapters, has in fact entered the reign of a new science, 'international penal law', or – as some of its prominent defenders prefer it – *droit pénal interétatique,* 'interstate penal law' [1]). Aggressive war is now, after the trials and verdicts of Nuremberg and Tokyo, not only the object of the prohibition contained in international treaties, in the Charter of the world organisation, and therefore, one can say, in international law itself. Not only have sanctions, police-measures, been threatened and applied against a State committing aggressive war, and not only is an international military force, on instructions of the political organ of the world community, combatting an aggressor. These rules and actions – and even the solemn condemnation and qualification of aggressive war, in treaties and resolutions, as a 'crime' – could still be comprised within international public law. But in Nuremberg and Tokyo, *punishment* – the characteristic element of *penal* law

1) H. Donnedieu de Vabres. V. V. Pella, Fonctions Pacificatrices du droit pénal international et fin du système traditionnel des traités de paix, R.G.D.I.P. 1947, Tome II, p. 15, defends the term "droit pénal supranational". Cf. the remark of H. Donnedieu de Vabres, in his preface to M. Merle, Le procès de Nuremberg et le chatiment des criminels de guerre, Paris, 1949, to the effect that the first realization in this new field, the Nuremberg trial, already imposes a correction of its title, as the notion 'interétatique' does not correspond with individual penal responsibility, which was the basis of Nuremberg. One could, however, contend that it is more the nature of the crime than that of the responsibility, which characterizes the new field, and it cannot be denied that the criminality that forms the object of the new law essentially affects inter-state relations or takes place under the cover of the State's interior sovereignty. See section 6 of this chapter.

—has been applied to individual German and Japanese 'major war criminals' for the 'planning, preparation, initiation and waging of aggressive war'.

This was done by an International Military Tribunal, set up in accordance with and basing itself on penal Charters, agreed upon or adhered to by the majority of nations. And in two resolutions the United Nations — again the overwhelming majority of States — have 'affirmed' this 'principle' — of the penalization of aggressive war — and have charged the International Law Commission with the task of 'formulating' this and other principles in the context of an international, criminal 'Code of Offences against the Peace and Security of Mankind' [1]).

These proceedings overstep the limits of international public law, which was always essentially a law of co-ordination between independent States which were, to a certain extent, willing to restrict the exercise of their rights and limit their freedom on a contractual basis, in the reciprocal and common interest, recognizing no legislative assembly, no binding executive and no judicial power — proceeding independently — above them. The Nuremberg and Tokyo proceedings, where the leaders of two States were tried for acts committed essentially in that capacity, have laid open a perspective, that was till then considered to exist only in the dreams of ardent Utopians: the perspective that is, of the submission of States and statesmen to a common international judiciary that has the competence to take cognizance of and to investigate and judge their acts, and to sentence the authors in accordance with an international criminal code. Both post-war trials are, however, but isolated posts in this new domain, and still await their reinforcement and definite establishment by a generalization of the scope of the 'Nuremberg principles'.

But before passing to the analysis of both Charters and Verdicts regarding aggressive war, and to a survey of the efforts towards formulation and universal application of the concept of punishable aggressive war, it is interesting to throw a brief glance over the history before Nuremberg, which proceeding was neither unprepared in doctrine and planning, nor even completely un-

---

1) General Assembly resolutions 95 (I), 16 Dec. 1946, and 177 (II), 21 Nov. 1947.

precedented [1]). There was, on the one side, a constant undercurrent – driving upwards in some periods – in legal, political, and particularly moral and theological thinking, tending towards a discrimination in the concept of war. And at the same time there were, in the distant and in the recent past, some concrete efforts to arraign rulers for having waged a war or a series of wars considered as violations of treaties, and as unjust, unlawful or criminal.

SECTION 2. ANTIQUITY AND THE ORIENT

It is doubtful whether the Roman pursuit of warmongering Hannibal – exiled from Carthage, living at Antiochus' court, flying from there to king Prusias of Bithunia and finally committing suicide [2]) – whether the persecution of this private individual could be called a precedent for the new international criminal law.

It is an open question whether there would have been a trial, and not just summary execution, if Hannibal had come alive in the hands of the Romans who after Antiochus' defeat demanded his extradition from King Prusias. Though in their declaration before the Carthaginian Senate the Roman delegation said that Hannibal's conduct – incitement of foreign kings and peoples to make a coalition war against Rome and planning a rupture of Carthage's pact with Rome [3]) – could not remain unpunished, the statements in the Roman Senate, opposed by Scipio, only stressed the idea of revenge, mixed with a sense of fear that Hannibal's activity might present a danger for the peace of

1) The term precedent is, of course, used here in a historical sense, not in the technical meaning of the common law countries. Same further in this chapter.

2) See Livius, Historiae Ab Urbe Condita (Teubner ed., T. IV, 1898) L., XXX, c. 37. L. XXXIII, c. 45–47. L. XXXIV, c. 60. L. XXXIX, c. 51. Also Nepos, Vitae (Teubner, 1874), Hannibal.

3) Livius, L. XXXIII, c. 49: after recalling Hannibal's factions against the Roman nation, the fact that he had sent letters and messengers to Antiochus and the Aetolians, that he agitated to bring about a rupture of Carthage's alliance, that he had then gone to King Antiochus and that he would never rest before he had brought on a world war, the Roman envoys said to the Carthaginian Senate, that 'id ei non debere impune esset, si satisfacere Carthaginienses populo Romano vellent nihil eorum sua voluntate nec publico consilio factum esse; Carthaginienses responderunt, quidquid aequm censuissent Romani, facturos esse'. Rome asked no extradition but appealed to the State's responsibility to punish wrongdoers. Nepos, however, implies a demand of extradition, l.c. c. 7.

Rome[1]). In some peace treaties also, the Romans stipulated the extradition of their most dangerous enemies, to safeguard themselves by their elimination[2]).

But apart from the fact that in this case the idea of safety-measure prevailed over that of punishment – though such a measure could have been embodied in the form of a punishment after trial – as it always constitutes an *element* of repressive justice[3]), – the trial in Hannibal's case, which would have been concerned not with the waging of aggressive war but with an act of incitement to aggression, with warpropaganda, would not have been of international character. It could never have been an international tribunal – the Roman concept of law and their attitude towards the outside world make that unimaginable. And the 'crime' could only have been one against Rome's safety, as there was no breach of a treaty, only the State of Carthage, which had conformed to its dispositions, and not a private individual being bound by the non-aggression pact[4]).

In any event, recourse to war was, in the States of antiquity, and especially in Rome, a matter subject to law, even were it – apart from temporary treaty-stipulations – not international but national law. The Greeks, according to general opinion[5]), lived

---

1) Livius, l.c., c. 47: Scipio "parum ex dignitate populi Romani esse ducebat... factionibus Carthaginiensium inserere publicam autoritatem, nec satis bello vicisse Hannibalem, nisi velut accusatores calumniam in eum jurarent ac nomen deferrent". Scipio wanted a formal process of the State against Hannibal, if there were sufficient grounds for it, or abstention from Carthage's interior affairs (it was the Carthaginian aristocracy which, dissatisfied with Hannibal's political measures (high taxes etc.), had denounced him to the protector state). Cf. the Roman anxiety for their safety, Nepos c. 12.

2) Bauer (p. 17) affirms that there were several cases, quoting only, from Livius, the case of Brutulus Papius of Samnium, who, like Hannibal, committed suicide when his extradition was asked for breach of treaty.

3) Cf. Chapter IV, section 4, and especially the opinion of Röling, quoted there, who denying the penal element of the Nuremberg and Tokyo Verdicts, so far as aggressive war is concerned, considers – and justifies – the penalties applied as safety measures.

4) Considering the legal side of Hannibal's end the stories of the writers differ: according to Livius and Plutarch (Vitae Parallelae, T. II (Teubner, 1874), p. 279–280) Prusias, out of fear of or flattery towards Rome, acquiesced to Flaminius' demand and sent soldiers to Hannibal's castle, while Nepos states – which is an interesting point concerning the law of asylum – that Prusias did not dare to refuse, and answered that such a violation of the law of hospitality could not be asked from him, but that the Romans could go and find Hannibal themselves as his house was easy to find'. (l.c., c. 12).

5) Prof. Dr. J. H. Thiel, Het probleem van de natuurlijke vijandschap in het Romeinse oorlogsrecht, Amsterdam 1946, pp. 3, 13 en 14.

in a state of natural enmity with all States and tribes with whom no treaty of friendship had been concluded. But by virtue of their domestic rules the right to wage war was restrained by the requirements of a just cause and a formal declaration of the latter before the opening of hostilities [1]).

A formal declaration, mainly of a religious nature, was also customary in other ancient civilisations, notably those of the Hebrews and Chinese [2]). But it was especially in the strict Roman legal system that the concept of a *bellum justum* developed. War was a legal procedure, the ultimate means to realise a claim. Those claims — as in Greece — could rise out of the violation of a treaty-obligation by an opponent, from an insult to diplomatic envoys or the refusal to receive them, from the detention by the enemy of territory or possessions of the Roman State. And of course the Romans would go to war after an invasion of their country or an attack on their forces. But in all these cases a formal declaration was necessary, and, in the case of a war *rebus repetendis,* even a formal presentation of the claim to the foreign power, *clarigatio,* had to preceed the declaration of war [3]).

In the course of the Republican period, when the aggressive and imperialistic spirit grew rapidly, *bellum justum* became more and more a formal concept, *id est* that of *bellum solemne* [4]). Moreover the Romans used to provoke to war the rulers whose territories they desired or whose might they feared. But even so, the typical Roman hypocrisy which became connected with the concept of *bellum justum* and with the discussions, declarations and rites that preceeded the outbreak of war, was in the true sense of the French saying *un hommage rendu par le vice à la vertu,* here a tribute paid by aggressive imperialism to the deeply engrained idea that the use of force is subject and subser-

1) Coleman Phillipson, The International Law and Custom of Ancient Greece and Rome, Vol. II, London 1911, pp. 178 ff. and 197 ff., The Greek custom to declare war is referred to in Herod. VII, 9, 2.

2) Ibidem, p. 197.

3) The *clarigatio* and the Fecial ceremony at a declaration of war with the priest throwing a lance inside the enemy's territory, are described by Livius, o.c., L.I., c. 32, (Phillipson, pp. 329—348).

4) Redslob, o.c., p. 90. Thiel, o.c., p. 14. Grotius uses the term 'bellum justum' often to indicate the 'bellum solemne', while the substantial 'bellum justum' is mostly referred to as 'bellum ex justa causa', cf. L. III, c. 3, par. 1 (ed. Molhuysen, p. 501).

vient to law. In the case of the war against Antiochus in 192 B.C., the Roman Senate waited several months after Antiochus' landing in Greece, till he attacked and annihilated a group of Roman mariners, before declaring war upon him and starting a well prepared campaign [1]).

But, as has already been said, this law was Roman law, and did not apply to non-Romans, and it is doubtful whether, as is sometimes contended, a penal character should be attributed to the peace treaty clauses, providing for reparation and for the extradition of those responsible for the war. It seems more likely that these were just regarded as protective measures, a political exercise of the victor's right, and, like the disarmament clauses, guarantees for Rome's peace.

It was Christianity that took over the Roman legal inheritance. Stripped of its formalism, the substantial concept of *bellum justum* was developed, in an unbroken tradition, to a Christian doctrine of the law of nations from St. Augustine to Hugo de Groot, through St. Thomas, the Mediaeval theologians, philosophers and canonists, and the 'founders of international law' in the 16th century, Vitoria and Suarez.

The transformation that the traditional concept underwent in Occidental Christianity can be summarized as follows: (1) the formalised *bellum justum* acquired a true, legally substantial significance and was put – outside the scope of the unilateral, national, Roman legal institutions – above the individual parties in the multilateral commonwealth of States, ruled by the same law, having its source in the rational human nature created by God; (2) the international phenomenon of war to which the Ancients were morally indifferent, if they did not see a glorious act in it, was regarded – in principle – as an evil, a work of Satan; (3) the cases in which the waging of war is permitted to Christians and

---

1) Thiel, o.c. p. 10. Phillipson, o.c., pp. 191 ff., already reacts against those authors who deny the existence of any substantial element in the Roman just war concept, though he admits the later decline (p. 195). See also pp. 166 ff. where he puts Greek and Roman practice rather on the same line. Many present-day legal writers still adhere to that opinion already voiced by Suarez (quoted in Butler-Maccoby, The Development of International Law, London 1928, p. 107). Also de Taube (p. 365, work quoted in following note). In this question one should not judge by state-practice alone, which shows rather constant features through all ages, but also by the contemporary doctrine, the origin of the legal formulas and the public opinion of the time.

is considered just, remain cases of conscience for them and have their place in the moral precepts of the Church [1]).

To appreciate the value of this new doctrine, it is worth while considering this Occidental development in juxtaposition to the war-doctrines in the Oriental church and in Islam. Though Byzantium contributed to international law and morality by the development of the institution of diplomatic representation and that of humanitarian intervention [2]), its record concerning the position of war is entirely negative. The 'Emperor and Autocrat' was regarded as almighty, his position was even nearer to Oriental despotism than to the tradition of the Roman emperors, his wars were just by reason of his sacrosanct decision only, and it was considered a benefit to be defeated and subjected by him.

Although in the 4th century St. Basil the Great still prescribed that soldiers who had killed an enemy in the war should not approach the Holy Table for three years 'because their hands were impure with blood', the opinion of his contemporary, St. Athanasius, that it is quite legitimate and even praiseworthy to kill enemies in the war – 'because for the most courageous statutes are erected' – seems, whatever the theological disputes [2]), to have been more in conformance with Oriental and East-European thinking. The idea of the holiness of the war for the Empire, the officially decreed beatification of those killed in the wars against the infidels, dominated the thinking on this matter in the Byzantine Empire, and to a certain extent in the succeeding Czarist Russia.

For the same reason there was hardly any humanizing influence of the Oriental church on the barbarian war practices. There was nothing in the Orient analogous to the Christian doctrine of the temporary order that in its synthesis of Faith and reason was the basis of Western civilization to which the concept of just war belongs. In the East the individual religious attitude and that imposed by a cesaropapist 'divine' State were never reconciled.

The contact with the political power of Islam and its rapidly rising culture certainly drew Byzantium still further from Oc-

1) Cf. M. de Taube, Etudes sur le développement historique du droit international dans l'Europe Orientale, R.d.C. 1926, I, Vol. II, p. 365.

2) Ibidem, p. 361.

3) Ibidem, p. 366. See also, John Eppstein, The Catholic tradition of the Law of Nations, London 1935, p. 52 and p. 56.

cidental Christendom in its conception of war. After initial hesitations about the lawfulness of war Mahomet came to the idea of the 'djihâd', the holy war against the infidels, not only in defence of the faith, but – as his power grew – more and more as an aggressive action for the propagation of Islam. In such a concept there could never enter a distinction between just and unjust, lawful and unlawful motives and causes – all wars were equally just, war was of divine origin and the obligation to carry it on was a holy charge on the faithful – rulers and soldiers – whose greatest glory would be death on the battlefield. And though Islam in other respects – such as the humanization of warfare – stood originally on a higher level than either Occidental or Oriental Europe, regarding the conception of war its influence was definitely for the worse [1]).

SECTION 3. BELLUM JUSTUM IN WESTERN CHRISTIANITY

St. Augustine in the 5th century, after the more radical pacificism of earlier teachers like Origenes and Tertullianus, decided the theological question of the lawfulness of war in the sense that war is an evil and that it could only be resorted to by Christians as an instrument to attain justice, and – by that – peace. It could only be waged in extreme necessity, when no other means were left, and then only for a just cause, that is in answer to a wrong inflicted by the enemy: "Justa bella definiri solent quae ulciscunter injurias" [2]).

Most authors following in his footsteps, jurists with more casuistry than the theologians, distinguish by their causes between various types of lawful wars and give separate consideration to the war of defence. War to drive back the enemy who invades the country without a good cause is even considered obligatory but, according to a constant doctrine lasting till after Grotius, in a just offensive war the attacked are not allowed to defend themselves [3]). Suarez, the first to draw a line between natural law – directly and invariably dictated by man 's rational nature – and

1) De Taube, pp. 386 ff..

2) Quoted In R. Regout S. J., La doctrine de la Guerre Juste de Saint Augustin à nos jours d'après les théologiens et les canonistes Catholiques, Paris, 1934, p. 42, nt. 2.

3) Vitoria, De Iuri Belli, IV, prop. 1., c. 19. Grotius, o.c. II, i, 18. Gentilis quoted by him breaks with the tradition in this respect.

positive international law – formed by the usages of all the nations [1]) – regarded resort to war in self-defence as permitted by natural law itself, while the other *bella justa* found their justification in positive law [2]). The right to resort to the latter was thus conditioned by the impossibility of pacific means of redress.

Defensive war was, however, taken in a wider sense than the military one prevailing to-day [3]). Suarez divides *bella defensiva et aggressiva* according to whether the wrong is being done *in fieri* or is already accomplished [4]). The notion of war *ratione defensionis* comprises also the war of assistance to a State victim of an actual injustice as well as what the 19th century called 'humanitarian intervention'. Vitoria states this idea very clearly in his *Relectio de Indis*: "a grave offence against innocent subjects, e.g. the religious sacrifice of adults and children – and not only the actual killing, but already the existence of tyrannic, barbarous laws providing for such atrocities – is a good enough motive for a just, 'defensive' war" [5]).

The justification of *offensive* war was really the core of the scholastic doctrine of *bellum ex justa causa*. It is of this war that St. Augustin said: *Bellum geritur ut pax acquiratur* – peace not taken here in the sense of absence of war – the phrase would be a truism – but the wider, fundamental notion of *omnium rerum tranquillitas ordinis,* of peace as an *opus justitiae* and the *ordo* is a creation of justice [6]). In the necessity of creating a order is disturbed by an injustice, the victim may have recourse to war to get redress and punish the wrongdoer.

---

1) Franciscus Suarez, De Legibus, The Classics of International Law, Carnegie Endowment for International Peace, No. 20, Oxford 1944, Vol. I, the Latin Text, pp. 797–824, Vol. II, English Translation, pp. 800–865 (Selection from three works, Oxford 1944). L. II, c. 19, nos. 1, 2, 6.

2) Suarez, l.c., De Bello, sectio I, n. 4 ('ius propriae defensionis est naturale et necessarium').

3) See chapter II of this study, passim.

4) Suarez, l.c., De Bello, sect. I, n. 6.

5) Vitoria, Relectio V, De Indis Recenter Inventis, The Classics of International Law, Carnegie Endowment for International Peace, No. 7, Washington 1917, Latin text, pp. 269–297, English text, pp. 163–187, Sect. III, 15. Assistance to friends and allies as a title for just war is treated in the same section, n. 17, and that of freeing the propagation of the Christian Faith from suppression and hindrance, in sect. III, n. 9, 10, 12.

6) Augustin, ad Bonifacium, 6, and De Civitate Dei, XIX, 13, quoted by Regout, p. 40, nts 4 and 5.

This wrong done to him gives the wager of a war his just cause, be it the defence of his goods, his country, his allies or his subjects, be it the recuperation of goods taken away from him or be it the maintenance or the restoration of the law of the international community – which corresponds to the classical division of just war-aims: *propulsare hostias – repetere res – ulcisci injurias* 1). As Thomas says: "A just cause is required, which means that those who are fought deserve the fighting because of a fault" 2).

The second requirement for a just offensive war is, according to the great scholastic the *auctoritas principis* – an important question in the feudal Middle-ages when the existence of many *de facto* independent baronets and the dubious over-all authority of the Emperor of the Holy Roman Empire made the frontier between private and public wars very vague. And the third condition required by the theologian is the *recta intentio* of those who start the just war 3).

Certain supplementary conditions and finer distinctions are elaborated by other authors. Already in the 7th century St. Isidor of Sevilla required – in Cicero's footsteps – as an expression of the necessity that conditioned the just war, a notification of the impending hostilities to the wrongdoer, who had therewith his last opportunity for peaceful redress 4). This point was later elaborated by other authors. Already in the 7th century St. Isidore of settlement, e.g. arbitration by the Pope or neutral princes 5). Some writers replace, in their enumeration of the three conditions of a just war, the *recta intentio* by the *rectus modus* of warfare, observance of the customs of war. The first is certainly a non-juridical element, but the latter – as only afterwards ascertainable – can hardly be stated as a condition precedent to the initiation of a just war unless one tried to reconcile this divergence between

1) The third formulated by St. Augustine in the phrase quoted p. 122, nt. 2, the two others by St. Isidore of Sevilla, Etymologiae, XVIII, 1, quoted by Regout, p. 45, nt. 2.

2) St. Thomas Aquinas, Summa Theologica, II, II, qu. 40, 1.

3) Ibidem.

4) Regout, l.c.: "Justum bellum est quod *ex praedicto* geritur de rebus repetitis aut propulsandorum hostium causa". Also Thomas, o.c. II, I, qu. 105, prop. 13.

5) Suarez, l.c. De Bello, sect. II, n. 5 (the idea of the indirect authority of the Pope, by intervening as a judge in cases between Christian Princes), De legibus, sect. III, c. 7. n. 13 (possibility of arbitration by Emperor), De bello, sect. VII, n. 3 (justice of war conditioned by effort for peaceful solution).

the authors by regarding the belligerent's conduct during and after the war as an expression of the intention he had when initiating it [1]).

Another requirement – made by nearly all authors of the *bellum justum* school and often forgotten by its present-day students – was that the expected result of the just war – restoration of justice by redress or punishment – should exceed the expected evils [2]). The authors were well aware of the atrocities, misery, devastation and demoralisation accompanying war or necessarily resulting from it. War for them was a consequence of sin, a scourge of God on sinning mankind, to be restricted as far as possible.

In relation to the subject of the present study, some further attention may be paid to certain points of the doctrine of *bellum justum*.

The notion of 'war for a just cause' was principally formulated by theologians, as a moral code, first of all for the Christian princes and their advisers and further for all Christians likely to participate in wars. It was part of an effort to integrate Christian teaching in the world situation in which the Christians found themselves. The questions to be answered were: when can a Christian before God and his conscience justify the waging of a war? What is a Christian allowed to do during a war and what may he do after it to the defeated enemy? Its authors were seldom jurists, and never politicians: they did not consider it their task to conceive a new world-order, an international organisation. The Pope and the Emperor – the latter only nominally – were each in their field the supreme authorities. And the idea of international organisation could not yet be conceived in an epoch that saw only the beginning of internal organisation and peace.

1) According to Regout both requirements do not really form a part of the *Jus ad bellum*, and the *recta intentio* was gradually omitted, after Sylvestre de Priero and Cardinal Cajetanus had, in the beginning of the 16th century, drawn attention to the distinction between requirements for the objective justice of a war, and those to avoid individual culpability. Lucas de Penna, however, who was not a moralist but a jurist, wrote still at that time: "Intentio quoque mala justum bellum fecit injustum", in W. Ullmann, The Mediaeval Idea of Law, A study of Lucas de Penna, London 1946, p. 193. Of course the theory of bellum justum could with this addition never be applied, as wrongs and offences, robberies and attacks would remain unpunished, and unrepelled, no rulers being there with unmixed juridical aspirations.

2) E.g. Vitoria. 'Iuxta mensuram delicti debet esse plagarum modus'.

What is often regarded as a theoretical oversimplification by the authors on *bellum justum* – their contemplation of cases where the one party was completely right and the other totally wrong [1]) – can easily be explained in the theological and moral context of works which were written for the conscience of men, not for the building up of new institutions. In later episodes, Vitoria, Suarez and de Groot in particular put the doctrine of St. Augustine and St. Thomas in the living reality of contemporary political life – by elaborating it for the cases of dubious claims, and by devising means for peaceful redress at a time when the co-existence of completely independent States had become a clear fact.

The underlying idea of all thinkers from Augustine to de Groot was inherited from classic Rome: war – just war – was the realization of a legal claim in a case where the claimant – in the absence of a higher authority – had of necessity to be his own judge. This is very clearly formulated by de Groot in a passage in the first chapter of his second book, which, with regard to this question, may well be called the nucleus of *De Iure Belli ac Pacis.* After recalling the definitions of Augustine and Thomas quoted above and the phrase of the Roman Fecial ceremony of a declaration of war – calling the gods as witnesses that the enemy people is unjust and does not abide by the law – de Groot states: "It is evident that there are as many sources for wars as there are for legal actions; then where no judgments are given war begins" [2]).

The possibility and occurence of wars is the natural outcome in an unorganised international society in which the subjects are not ready to abandon their rights. But for the Christian thinkers there is not only this egoistic national point of view: the maintenance and restoration of one's rights is but a part of the just order that should reign in the world and that creates peace. This order asks also for maintenance or restoration of just relations between all nations – and the use of armed force is a lesser evil than the destruction or tolerated violation of this multilateral, universal order.

---

1) Butler-Maccoby, Development of International Law, l.c., p. 110.
2) Grotius, o.c., II, i, 3 (Molhuysen, p. 137).

It has rightly been observed [1]) that in the centuries in which this doctrine was elaborated many people's chief interest was in war as a means of change and progress, while the 20th century's chief interest lies in peace as a way to a new epoch and a new unity. The 15th and 16th centuries especially were periods of disruption of a unity which was felt to be retrogressive and oppressing, while the wars of that time were, also, less of a general evil than those of the present world, which seeks order out of chaos.

While the accent now lies on the injustice of aggressive war, as a forbidden recourse to force, and on the means of preventing it, it was at that time the justification of war, as an instrument of law, and the correct way to do justice by it that demanded attention. Correspondingly, the notion of crime was then as strongly concentrated on the violator of the law to whose punishment the just war would lead, as it is now applied to the act of the aggressive belligerent.

This difference of situation that does not necessarily imply a difference of doctrine explains why in the scholastic teaching hardly any attention was paid to the act of waging unjust war and to the fate of those who waged it. Some twentieth century writers, pre-occupied by the problems of their time, have tried to deduce from the scholastic authors the idea of the criminality of unjust war, referring to a punishment of unjust war [2]).

One is inclined to draw the opposite conclusion. The action dealing with the unjust aggressor is defensive war, and it has already been observed that the authors regard this war as a self-evident matter. As Suarez states: "Quaestio est de bello agressivo; nam potestas se defendendi penes omnes datur")[3]. St. Augustine referring to a war motivated by greediness or by the spirit of domination says: "What else is it but a great brigandage", but by making the distinction – as do all the authors after him – between wars of defence and wars waged with the aim of 'avenging injuries', he excludes the idea of punishment from the former. This difference is still confirmed and strengthened by the distinction Suarez and others elaborate as to the rights of

[1]) Butler-Maccoby, o.c., p. 3.

[2]) E.g. Bauer, o.c., p. 20, referring to St. Thomas' teaching regarding personal culpability. Also Butler Maccoby, o.c., p. 120, referring to Vitoria's opinion.

[3]) Suarez l.c., De Bello, Sect. II, no. 1.

the victor in a just war and the rights of those who have successfully repelled an unjust invader.

Self-defence, as stated, is seen as a natural, invariable right; it belongs even to the individual to protect by force his own life and goods, as well as that of others against unlawful attack, as it is still to-day expressly permitted in the criminal codes of many nations. What is allowed to individuals, groups and cities, without the *auctoritate principis,* must be regarded as obligatory for the States, for the princes, who have the duty to protect their subjects [1]). But as with regard to individuals, the scholastics consider self-defence among States to be limited to averting the danger, the attack, which must be immediate and certain and which must necessitate defence by force. The defensive action must be carried out *cum moderamine inculpatae tutelae,* within the limits of careful protection [2]). The State which acts in self-defence is not given the right to punish his opponent for the latter has only made an *attempt* to commit an *injuria* – a conquest for example – which he is prevented from accomplishing by the defensive action.

The conclusion sounds anomalous in the present-day world which considers precisely the illegal use of force as the 'supreme crime' and does not even allow the individual State to go to war to obtain satisfaction in a just cause [3]). But it is quite explainable in the scholastic doctrine which did not know the sharp distinction between public and private law and tried to create order by identifying, for all purposes, the moral and legal position of the prince, his rights and duties, with those of the individual.

As the just, offensive war was regarded as a legal procedure in which the offended State was, in the absence of a higher authority, judge in his own cause, so the position of the attacked State was identified with that of the individual in self-defence. The fact that the latter lives under the protection of the law and that his right of self-defence was restricted to the mere averting

1) Ibidem. sect. I, n. 4.

2) Suarez l.c., De Bello, sect. I, n. 6. For Grotius, see below and p. 130, nt. 1. Cf. Lucas de Penna's explicit statement that self-help in retaliatory form is forbidden, and that only permissible reaction against breaches of the peace is defence within the limits of the law (Cf. Ullmann, o.c., p. 197).

3) See above, p. 105.

of the danger only because he could have recourse to the maintainers of the law, was here overlooked.

The transition to a more realistic appraisal of the State's position in this regard becomes perceptible in the works of Grotius, on this point as on many others the link between the old doctrine and modern international law. Continuing the phrase quoted above (p. 127), he formulates the traditional opinion on the distinction between defensive and offensive war for a just cause: "Actions are taken on grounds of either an unaccomplished or an accomplished wrong. On grounds of an unaccomplished wrong a *cautio de non offendendo,* damages and *interdicta* against new violence can be asked. On grounds of an accomplished wrong one may demand either reparations or punishment which are rightly distinguished" [1]).

But further in the same Chapter '*De belli causis, at primum de defensione sui et rerum*' Grotius draws attention to the forementioned difference between self-defence of an individual in a legal order and that of a State which cannot have recourse to a judge, and he draws the conclusion: "the public authorities have with the right of self-defence also that of revenge". And he adds that, while a direct preventive war is illicit [2]), a means of indirect prevention may rightly be seen in this punishment "for a crime which has started but has not yet been accomplished" [3]).

---

1) "Dantur autem actiones aut ob iniuriam non factam, aut ob factam. Ob non factam, ut qua petitur cautio de non offendendo, item damni infecti, et interdicta alia, ne vis fiat. Factam, aut ut reparetur, aut ut puniatur: quos duos obligationum fontes recte distinguit Plato..." o.c., II, i. 2 (Molhuysen p. 127).

2) Contrary to the opinion held by Gentilis.

3) Ibidem, 16, (p. 137): "Quae vero dicta a nobis huc usque sunt de iure tuendi se ac sua, maxime quidem ad bellum privatum pertinent, sed ita ut ad publicum quoque aptari debeant, habita diversitatis ratione. Nam in privato bello ius quasi momentaneum est, et cessat simulatque iudicem adiri res patitur. At publicum quia non oritur nisi ubi non sunt aut cessant iudicia, tractum habet, et perpetuo fovetur accedentibus novis damnis et iniuriis. Praeterea, in bello privato ferme defensio mera consideratur at publicae potestates cum defensione ac ulciscendi habent ius: Unde illis licet praevenire vim non praesentem, sed quae de longo imminere videatur, non directe (id enim iniustum esse supra docuimus) sed indirecte ulciscendo delictum coeptum iam, sed non consummatum; de quo agendi erit alibi locus". A certain contradiction between this text and that quoted in the previous note cannot be denied. The latter referring to public as well as to private wars indicates the use of force as a legal remedy and restricts the *actio ut puniatur* by the judge as well as by self-help exclusively to the accomplished offence.

The conception of punishment of unlawful war, of war waged without a just cause, can thus be found in the works of de Groot, who, none the less, still considers it a lesser crime than others like conquest, robbery, insult or the illegal detention of an other State's territory. Aggressive war is considered under the aspect of its criminal object as an unaccomplished crime.

Contrary to the view of some present writers the conclusion must be drawn that, in the works of the authors on *bellum justum,* reference to the treatment and punishment of *injustum bellum gerentes* concerns what are today called the aggressors in the material sense. It concerns those who provide the victim with a just cause for a *bellum justum* [1]), the violaters of the law, the usurpers of territories that do not belong to them, and not the unjust invadors. As stated, war itself was regarded as a lesser evil, compared to an accomplished grave violation of the law of nations or of an other nations' rights.

The penal element in the just, offensive war has been a much disputed question among modern students of the scholastic war doctrine. Authors like Van der Pol [2]) and Stratmann [3]), inspired by the pacifistic doctrines of this century, have contended that the Mediaeval writers stipulated that for the waging of a just war the violator be guilty of his act in the criminal sense. They relied on the phrases of St. Augustine – *ulcisci injurias,* – and Thomas – *propter aliquam culpam impugnationem mereantur* – and on the terms *vindicandi causa,* and *ad puniendum* used by nearly all writers. They understood these terms to imply that all just wars had the character of penal measures, and that for a mere objective, not a culpable wrong no war was allowed, at least not before the 'rupture' in the tradition, the destruction of the pure scholastic wartheories, which began at the end of the 16th century with Spanish authors like Suarez and Molina.

Recent research, especially that of Regout [4]) and also those

---

1) 'Iniquitas partis adversae justa bella ingerit gerenda sapienti', Augustinus, De Civ. Dei, XIX, 7 (Regout, p. 41, nt. 4).

2) A. Vanderpol, La doctrine scolastique du droit de guerre, Paris 1919.

3) F. Stratmann O.P., Weltkirche und Weltfriede, Augsburg 1924.

4) Regout, o.c., specially devoted to the demonstration of the essential continuity of the teaching of the Catholic theologians on 'bellum justum', from St. Augustine till to-day, as against Vanderpol and others.

of Beaufort [1]) and Kipp [2]), have demonstrated the essential continuity of the doctrine of *bellum justum*. The distinction constantly made since the *Decretum Gratiani*, between wars for recuperation and those for punishment – both offensive – is the first argument against an exclusively penal interpretation. It may be added that the distinction between the fields of civil and criminal law was not yet clearly established in the Middle Ages and that the concepts *vindicta* and *injuria* were rather imprecise. As theologians, most authors were not so much concerned with the psychological degrees of guilt and responsibility, and treated the normal case of punishable, responsible act, with more emphasis on the rights of the victim than on the position of the law violator.

While the Scholastics admitted the justice of war for reparation of a simply objective wrong, caused by the *ignorantia invincibilis*, the fully sincere mistake of the opponent, the main form of just war for them was the war of punishment. It is important to stress here that war itself was not regarded as the execution of the punishment, as is sometimes proposed in modern literature on international criminal law. The misery and damages accompanying war and causing harm to innocent and guilty alike, were rightly never thought of as punishment but rather as the necessary appendage of an action, which, if succesful, made the way free for the execution of justice by the punishment of the guilty.

The authors of the *bellum justum* school divided the rights of the victor of a just war into four categories [3]):

1) Concerning the *objectum litis;* restitution if a material

---

1) Beaufort, o.c., who by an exposition of the doctrine of Early Christianity, Middle Ages, and sixteenth century on the just war of assistance and that of punishment, refutes the thesis of Prof. van Vollenhoven, according to whom Grotius had conceived a new theory based on altruism and universalism, contrary to the nationalist-egoistic doctrine of his predecessors (See C. van Vollenhoven, Grotius and Geneva, the Chapter 'Grotius Theorem'), Bibliotheca Visscheriana, vol. VI, pp. 1–81 (Lugdunum Bat. 1926).

2) Dr. Heinz Kipp, Moderne Probleme des Kriegsrecht in der Spätscholastik, Paderborn 1935, an exposition of the teaching on war of Vitoria and Suarez, pp. 55 ff.. Kipp elaborates five conditions for the just war, first the 'objective' conditions: legitimate authority, just cause, moral certainly of success (good results must exceed bad consequences); then two 'subjective' conditions: failure of all peaceful efforts, and correct conduct in and after the war.

3) Cf. Vitoria, l.c., De Iure Belli, dubium VII ex qu. 4, prop. 5, n. 54, and prop. 5, n. 19. Suarez l.c., De bello, sect. VII, n. 7.

object, otherwise the restoration of violated rule or honor is implied in the victory itself.

2) Reparation for all damages and for the costs of the war to the victor. All the property of the enemy, according to some writers even that of its subjects, could be taken for this purpose.

3) Security against future violations, as already practiced by the Romans: hostages, disarmament and possible occupations of certain territories.

4) Punishment of those responsible for the injury and therefore for the war.

One of the main objects of the scholastic treatises was to eliminate the frequently practiced collective punishment, wholesale slaughter and destruction, by a recourse to justice, which would be limited to the responsible wrongdoers. The barbaric conduct of victors, occurring regularly in Western Europe till the peace of Westphalia, had its origin in the Germanic as well as in the Ancient and Oriental tradition of warfare. As with the proclamation of the Truce of God, the notion of *bellum justum,* with its emphasis on the responbility for the execution of *justice* lying on the victor, was not in the least intended for the humanization of warfare.

The restriction of war to the 'guilty', among whom originally were numbered all soldiers who fought the unjust war, was later clearly specified by Vitoria to regard only the 'morally guilty': those who consciously participate in an unjust war and may be punished with the death penalty [1]). By the time of de Groot the idea of collective punishment was wholly abandoned, while in practice the idea of individual punishment of those responsible for the war began to recede before the modern idea of the State's competence to wage war indiscriminately, as did the whole concept of just war as a legal procedure.

As a last point it is important to stress the grounds of jurisdiction on which the doctrine of this period based a State's right to punish another State. The more it is realized that princes and nations are equal independent entities, not bound by any legal organisation, the more their position is compared to that of individuals living without any, or within an ineffective, legal

1) Vitoria, l.c. dubium V ex qu. 4, prop. 1—4, n. 45—48 et dubium VI, ex qu. 4, n. 49.

organisation: they may do justice to themselves and maintain the natural order against a violation of which they are the victim. Maintenance or resoration of order implies, in the case of a grave offence, not only material redress, but also retribution and punishment.

In other words, as Suarez says very clearly, a State may punish its equal *quae ratione delicti ei subditur* [1]), because they have, by their crime, become subject to its revenge. Thomas says that as the princes rightly protect the State against interior disturbers by punishing them, they are competent to protect it with 'the sword of war' against exterior enemies [2]). This text clearly brings out the close connection between protective measure and punishment, (referred to above, p. 118) as well as the objective basis which the scholastics give to the *jus belli,* not self-interest, but the maintenance or restoration of order.

There is in this teaching, therefore, no difference in the character and cause of a war for self-protection and that for protection and assistance to others, be it States or innocent victims of State cruelty, except that the latter comes second in the order of necessity. The idea of protection is specially emphasized by Vitoria who argues that the world cannot exist without a power to deter the malefactors and compel them to keep away from the innocents, and their goods, which in the internal order are protected by the public authorities. In the natural world-community – *orbis* – this power could only have been exercised through the princes, who therefore, after waging a just war, may as judges punish the law-violating enemies – *et hoc jure gentium et orbis totius auctoritate* [3]). In *De Jure Belli ac Pacis* Grotius widens still further this 'natural' jurisdiction by affirming that every man and every State, even outside the range of a judicial organisation, has penal competence towards malefactors, from which it appears that Grotius attributes to the States the right to wage punitive war for every wrong committed, even outside their own particular sphere of interest [4]).

---

1) Suarez, l.c. De bello, sect. IV, n. 4 et 5.
2) Thomas o.c. II, II, q. 40, I.
3) Vitoria, l.c., De Indis, I, 19.
4) Grotius, o.c. II, 14, 6 : 2. "sed aeqalibus in aequales id jus (i.e. coactionis) est a natura, superioribus in subditos etaim ex lege". And specially, chapter II, 20, 40 : 1, 4, the text on which v. Vollenhoven relies specially in

The great importance of the *bellum justum* doctrine with respect to the subject of the present study lies in the fact that over a period of thirteen centuries it affirmed on the basis of a universalist conception of mankind – of a 'United World' – the existence of law and order conform to man's reasonable nature, in the service of which law and order alone, war could find its justification. The rights of a State waging such a just war were in consequence of this service and not of its self-interest; they were based on law and not on force. The sanctions and the punishment which a State and its leaders deserved on account of their offences had, in the absence of a superior tribunal, to be applied by the victorious State. But the punishment had to be based on personal culpability, on a conscious and free committance of, or participation in, the violation of law. Collective punishment was more and more clearly excluded, though the subjects might undergo the consequences of other sanctions.

The notion of war as an executive act with no higher instance to control it, and the circumstances of the time prevented much attention being given to war itself as a punishable act, though its reprehensibility was voiced in strong terms, and was, in fact, the basis of the whole doctrine. But by the clear view of the criminality, the punishable character of grave offences against the law of nations and other peoples' rights, and by the provision of the world community's jurisdiction over them, to be exercised through the States, the doctrine laid the basis for what now, on a proper international organisational basis, is going to be realised as international criminal law. The demands of the conscience of mankind, so strongly expressed after the last World War but flowing forth from a constant aspiration to justice, reinforced by Christianity, find their reflection in the works of the authors, who from Augustine to Grotius, helped mankind to realise its aspirations, aspirations which would outlive

---

support of his 'theorem' (see nt. 1, p. 132): "Sciendum quoque est reges et qui par regibus jus obtinent, jus habere poenas poscendi, non tantum ob injurias in se aut subditos commissas, sed et ob eas quae ipsos peculianter non tangunt, sed in quibusvis personis, jus naturae aut gentium immaniter violant". Grotius adds that he differs in this respect with Vitoria, Vasquez and others. It is, however, only Suarez who expressly denies this universal right of punishment and demands a title of special jurisdiction, in the passage referred to in nt. 1, p. 134).

the period of positivist indifference and which proved stronger than an obstinate state-practice.

This state-practice, though rejected in the Middle ages – as shown by the criticism of it by the aforementioned authors themselves – for much the same reason as it was later, reflects nevertheless the moral and legal teaching of these writers. Redslob quotes the example of the alliance which the three original Swiss cantons, and the city of Zurich, concluded in 1352 with Glarus; military assistance to the new ally was conditioned by the existence of a good cause, which the cantons reserved for themselves to determine [1]).

But the Middle Ages also present an example of a trial of a prince for the waging of an unlawful war. As stated before, the mediaeval authors did not refer to this act as a crime, though such a conception could easily fit into their general doctrine on war. In conformity with that doctrine, it occurred from time to time that an officer of the defeated enemy was tried for crimes committed in that function. Such was the case of Charles the Bold's lieutenant, Peter van Hagenbach, who was tried and sentenced by a kind of international tribunal for his inhuman rule over the city of Breisach, in 1474 [2]).

Different however was the execution of the last descendant of the Hohenstaufen, Konradin, in Naples in 1269, by the new King of Naples and Sicily, Charles of Anjou, brother of Saint Louis, King of France. Although everyone examining the relevant documents and the historicial background of the case, will refrain from calling this judicial murder of 17-years old Conradin, which roused the indignation of his contemporaries, a precedent for the Nuremberg proceedings, the motivation of the sentence is worth recalling, as the expression of a legal opinion [3]).

---

1) Redslob, o.c. p. 151, nt. 103.

2) See for a description of this case, G. Schwarzenberger, Manchester Guardian, 28 Sept. 1946, p. 4 ('A forerunner of Nuremberg, The Breisach War Crime Trial of 1474').

3) See Monethault d'Egly, Histoire des Rois des Deux Siciles, Tome Premier, 1741, Paris, p. 147–156, especially.

Bartholomeo de Castro, Historia sui Temporis a morte Friderici II, Imperatoris Siciliaeque regis ab anno 1250 ad usque annum 1294 (Re-edited in: De Principe Templo Panormitano, libri XIII, of P. J. M. Amato Panormitano e Societate Jesu, Panormi (Palermo) 1728, on pp. 490 sq.). Chs. IX et X, pp. 503–506.

The facts may be summarized as follows. The kingdom of Naples and Sicily had been ruled for sixty years by the Emperors of the Holy Roman Empire, but were bound by a certain allegiance to the Holy See. At the height of the struggle between Pope and Emperor, between Guelfi and Ghibellini, Pope Clement IV gave the entire Kingdom to Charles of Anjou, who, after receiving his investiture in Rome, defeated the actual ruler, Manfred, successor of Frederic Barbarossa, in 1268. The Sicilian Guelfi, always faithful to the defeated dynasty, and others discontented with Charles' hard, revengeful and impopular policy, sollicited young Conradin, cousin and legal successor of Manfred, to come from Germany to take possession of his Kingdom.

After initial success, being inexperienced and without counsel, he was defeated by Charles through a stratagem in the battle of Tragliacozzo, captured on his flight to Sicily and delivered to Charles, who considered it "bonne politique de faire périr Conradin pour assûrer pendant son absence le repos dans ses Etats". But "afin d'observer quelque ombre de justice dans une affaire de cette importance" – as a later French historian remarks [1]) – Charles called to Naples a great council, of high French noblemen, delegates of Italian cities, and French baronets of his new court. The latters' advice to have Charles executed got the upperhand over that of the French nobility who counselled Charles to make an alliance of friendship with Conradin, or to keep him imprisoned with his associates, until his own rule in Sicily was firmly established.

Nothing is told about any further proceedings against Conradin himself, so – apart from the following 'sentence' – one can hardly speak of a trial. Bartholomeo de Castro, contemporary historian, quotes the entire sentence pronounced before the public execution on the market place in Naples on 26th of Octobre 1269, by Robert de Bari, great protonotarius of the king: "Conradinus iste filius Conradi regis, Imperatoris Friderici progenies, de Alemania surgens *arma non licita induit,* in Regem nostrum [2]) proterviit, seductor erat populi regni sui . . . . & ideo permissione Pontificum, & sapientium, ac

1) D'Egly, o.c. p. 152.
2) It was clearly regarded as a domestic trial.

scribarum consiliis, in eos [1]) sententiam, *quasi in praedones* [2]), providit praesentis judicii arbiter promulgandam: nos .... nomine et pro parte Serenissimi Regis Caroli, dictos Conradinum & socios ejus praesentes, *tamquam invasores et alterius juris praedones,* capitali sententia duximus feriendos, ita quod ab ipsa sententia resilire non possint, sed statim totaliter in conspectu omnium moriantur" (italics supplied) [2]).

Before dying Conradin declared that he had had no intention to insult the Holy See, nor to usurp the crown of Sicily, but that he was called 'ad jura . . . domestica haereditatis patriae' [3]).

It is interesting however to recall that when some years later the Sicilians had seceded from Charles' reign and had reinstalled the former dynasty, in the persons of Peter of Aragon and his wife Constance, daughter of Manfred, the deputies of Sicily, after the capture of king Charles' son, the prince of Salerno in a sea-battle, demanded his head as a reprisal for the death of Conradin. But Constance spared him; it was Good Friday, d'Egly relates, and also, the young Charles had, unlike Conradin, a father and brothers to take revenge [4])!

SECTION 4. THE PERIOD OF INDIFFERENCE

As this chapter is mainly concerned with those doctrinal developments and historical events that have certain elements in common with the principles of the new international criminal law or with the post-war trials concerning the criminality of aggression, the periods of absolutism and the succeeding democratic nationalism – with, first, the watering down of the natural law doctrine and then legal positivism with its exclusion of non-conventional elements and considerations from the field of law – are of little interest and can be dealt with briefly. With the birth of the modern State and modern political thinking a sceptical school sprang up which opposed the 'natural law' teachers.

---

1) Konradin was accompanied by Frederic, Duke of Austria, of the same age.

2) Like Hannibal, even like Napoleon (see below), Konradin was not regarded as a head or functionary of State, but as an individual bandit. This is a striking difference from the Nuremberg-trial, to which these proceedings are often compared, see on Konradin, Bauer, o.c. p. 21.

3) De Castro, caput IX, p. 504–5, and answer from Konradin c. X.

4) D'Egly, o.c., p. 234.

As in the sixteenth century Macchiavelli [1]), who wrote that Princes should give reasons for their wars as the people would otherwise complain of a war without cause, stood in opposition to Vitoria, so Hobbes' writings in the following century forms a sharp contrast with those of Grotius, the last great exponent of the Christian doctrine on war [2]). Both Macchiavelli and Hobbes were realists and pessimists. Their works were not so much based on other principles as directed towards another object, namely the description of the political practice of their time, which they saw as autonomous, guided by its own prinriples, political and psychological principles [3]), and by the rule of force, but not by law and morality.

The three causes of war Hobbes gives in *Leviathan* are: *competitio, defensio, gloria*. Nature dictates for the pessimist no natural law, but a "condition of war of everybody against everybody, so long as there is no superior coercive force". "For", he explains, "the nature of war does not consist in fighting, but in a space of time during which the will to decide matters by armed force is manifest... the other time is peace... besides, in a war of all against all it is logical that nothing can be called injust. The categories of just and unjust have no place in this condition. Force and artifice are the cardinal virtues in war" [4]).

As a concept of law, the notion of punishment can have no place in an unorganised society: only he who has normal sovereignty over a delinquent may punish him; no government, no penal jurisdiction. An attacked or assaulted State may try to strike down its opponent, but that has nothing to do with law [5]).

This is the main trend in the period of indifference; one straight line runs from the seventeenth to the twentieth century, from the last quotation from Hobbes to Strupp's affirmation

---

1) N. Macchiavelli, Il Principe (1517), Libri XVIII and XXI.

2) T. Hobbes, De Cive, (1642); idem, Leviathan (1650).

3) See e.g. M's judicious remark in Leviathan (quoted by van Vollenhoven, o.c. Appendix R.) that the cause of Kings' and individuals' restless desire for power is not the hope for more intensive delight, but the fact that they can only maintain their present power and means by acquiring more, the reason why kings at the height of their power exercise it ever more, at home by laws, abroad by the force of arms.

4) Ibidem.

5) Quoted by v. Vollenhoven in an article 'Grotius and Geneva', in 'Tijdschrift voor Strafrecht', 1926, p. 22, vol. XXXVI, Verspreide Geschriften, vol. I. p. 461—469.

that it is absolutely impossible legally to appreciate war itself which is considered a pure fact [1]), or Salvioli's statement that war is outside justice and outside law [2]). The only change during these centuries was that what was regarded as a shocking statement in the 16th and 17th, became a matter of course for most lawyers in the positivist 19th century. The fact is that the notion of law changed; its basis was no longer seen in objective rules for human relationships, but in the will of the sovereign State and in state-practice itself. The guiding principle was no more the *recta ratio* ascertained by Suarez and Grotius, but the *raison d'état*. While Hobbes and before him Macchiavelli proclaimed the divorce between state-practice and law, positivist doctrine made a clear-cut separation between law and objective rule, took law out of the moral stratum wherein it had lain for centuries and established it as the formulation of state-practice.

This state-practice, while renouncing, even formally, the control of a *jus ad bellum,* started on the other hand, in the 19th century, to regulate the procedure of resort to war and its legal consequences. The obligation of declaring war, formulated in the third Hague Convention of 1907 [3]), and the development of the *jus in bello* by means of general conventions on the laws of warfare, in part formulations of established customs, were the only remaining chapters of international law devoted to war. In his exast language Anzilotti sums up the legal position: "International law cannot determine the cases in which the States are permitted to resort to war, but it can discipline the way they must wage it". Law cannot say *when,* but only *how* war is to be waged [4]).

One cannot say that opposite this dominant trend of the last centuries, starting from Hobbes, there was another international law school continuing the tradition of Augustine and Grotius. If there were, during all this time, other currents in legal thinking, they were mostly by-currents to the main stream, coming

---

1) Karl Strupp, Elements du Droit International Public, Paris 1927, p. 332.

2) G. Salvioli, Le concept de la guerre juste chez les écrivains antérieurs à Grotius, trad. Fr. 1918.

3) See above, Chapter I, p. 3.

4) Anzilotti, Corso di Dirito Internazionale, vol. III, Rome 1915, p. 185.

for all practical purposes to the same result, be it formulations of the same state-practice in the language of the old doctrine, or moral reflections and juridical aspirations murmured *sotto voce* with an acknowledgment of their impracticality in applied international law.

After Grotius the doctrine of natural law and just war gradually fell into decay. First of all it must be admitted that the doctrine itself, even during its height, had a great deficiency which in part accounts for its neglect or abuse by statesmen as well as for its later decline. The determination of the justice of the cause was left entirely to the rulers themselves who were expressly recognized as judges in their own cause; hardly any efforts were spent on the devising of means – procedural criteria or institutions like arbitration – by which a more impartial, certain and objective judgment could be obtained than that of princes whose interest and egoïsm were only too obvious [1]).

Secondly, during the 17th and 18th century, the authors – in order to come in line with state practice – began to elaborate the doctrine in the direction of concessions to contemporary absolutism and this finally corrupted and hollowed out the whole notion of a just war. This corruption, the germs of which can already be traced in some of the minor writers of the 16th century Spanish school [2]), consisted in the doctrine of probabilism, which admitted the possibility of a war which was just on both sides, and in the related notion of war as the legal process itself in which the issue was decided by the force of arms.

---

1) Suarez and Grotius however mention already the idea of arbitration, while other writers insist on it quite strongly, especially L. Molina (obligatory recourse to arbitration in case the opponent may be completely bona fide, quoted by Regout, o.c. pp. 295–260) and the Belgian L. Lessius (who indicates a method for obligatory arbitration, Regout, pp. 244–245), both 16th century theologians.

2) See Regout, o.c., p. 248 on Grégoire de Valentia (who admits war for a prince 'qui sequitur opinionem probabilem', and admits therefore a war just on both sides, be it on one side only 'per accidens') and p. 263, ibidem, on Martin Bécan, a Dutch theologian (who states that in the same way as a private person may sue his opponent a prince may undertake an action with armed force. The difference with Grotius' and other 'orthodox' authors' analogy between war and a process is of course that they admit war *after* the sentence is given, id est, after the certainty of the prince's right is acquired, while here the impression is given that an uncertain right may be ascertained by a succesful war).

Vitoria elaborated the idea that the opponent in a just war could be *bona fide,* led by 'invincible ignorance', with the consequence that he *subjectively* waged a just war and could not be punished; the only war aim in that case could be the realization of the right of the – objectively – just party. On the other hand different proposals were offered for the conduct of a State which entertained doubts as to the justice of its cause. While the great authors all required a thorough investigation in that case and admit war only if there is no doubt as to the greater strength of its claim, others defended a right to go to war on the ground of a probable right, in which case wars might be just on both sides.

But in the 18th century Vattel, though repeating the 'orthodox' teaching of the theologians, admits that a State may wage war for the maintenance of the balance of power, which cause can of course be rightly invoked by both parties [1]), and he contends moreover that a State, for the rightness of its cause, has only to answer before its own conscience. He denies – consistently – penal or any coercive competence among sovereign nations, though he states elsewhere that the combined force of all States may suppress the overt violator of the law of nations [2]). Vattel's work, as that of Wolf who recognizes a right to punish but only in the form of a demand of reparation and guarantees against repetition [3]), offers little consistency. The fact is that both writers, like most of Grotius' successors, base their work on the reality of absolute sovereignty, repeating at the same time the arguments for warfare developed in former ages, probably in order to offer as many justifications as possible for the state-practice of their days, which still paid, especially in the formal declarations of war, tributes to a doctrine that was, in fact, no longer alive.

Then the third, the most important factor in its decay is one which touches not only the chapter of war but the whole concept of natural law. The distinction between natural law, as a basis and a principle, and the customs developed in international

1) See Butler-Maccoby, o.c., p. 232, where the inconsistent and inconclusive mixture of old doctrine and contemporary practice in Vattel's work is clearly demonstrated on the point of neutrality.

2) Van Vollenhoven, l.c. on page 138, nt. 5, above.

3) Quoted by Bauer, o.c., p. 23.

relations, positive law, which had been strictly, perhaps too strictly, drawn by Suarez [1]) and largely maintained by Grotius [2]), was abandoned, and the whole international legal field became regarded as natural law – an indiscriminate mixture of philosophical considerations, legal principles and valid customary rules of the time, all based on Roman law and regarded as of fixed universal and perpetual validity. The real principle of natural law, the objective, moral foundation of all law, could only suffer from this misrepresentation; in fact, the foundation of natural law received a more and more utilitarian accent, (Pufendorf, Thomasius) [3]), while for Hobbes, natural law meant in the first place the law of self-conservation [4]).

With the progressive disruption of the spiritual unity of Europe and the extension of the boundaries of the world by the discoveries, natural law could not but lose its authority as a standard for public life common to the whole of mankind and be reduced to utilitarian platitudes. When in the mineteenth century legal purism, on a positivist and voluntarist basis, began to do away with natural law as unscientific, natural law in the legal field had, for all intents and purposes, identified itself with state-practice; it had been hollowed out and what remained was indeed a bad scientific method. On the other side, the old doctrine was continued outside the legal field, in theological and moralist writings which no longer had any influence on the growth of international law.

Both developments are reflected in the positions the international lawyers take towards the problem of war. For apart from the main line discussed above, following in the footsteps of those who denied the existence of natural law, two lines of thought have sprang out of the 'natural law' doctrine. The first affirmed that war is waged in the exercise of a legal competence,

---

1) Who excludes natural law rules from the domain of the law of nations contrary to Thomas who does not distinguish a separate 'lex humana' in the 'ius gentium'. See above, p. 123–4, and note 1, and Kipp's exposition of this difference o.c. Kapitel 2, pp. 26 ff., 'Die Lehre vom Völkerrecht in der Spätscholastik'.

2) O.c. Prolegomena 1 (Molh. p. 3).

3) Pufendorf ('omnia quae ad istam socialitatem (sc. humanam) necessario faciunt, iure naturale praecepta'), De Iure naturae et gentium, L. I., c. 1, par. 10, n. 1, and Thomasius, Institutionum iurisprudentiae, L. I., c. 1, par. 28/31, both quoted by Kipp, o.c., p. 102.

4) Hobbes, De Cive, 'Libertas', c. 1, n. 7.

be it an entirely discretionary competence, *omnivalente et inconditionnée,* (Scelle [1])), that war is a legal remedy, a procedure provided by international law for the solution of conflicts and the development of international law (Phillimore [2]), Bluntschli [3])). Because this theory does not discriminate between just and unjust causes, but binds the legitimacy of war only to the requirement of its initiation by the competent, national authorities [4]), it regulates only, as Scelle formulates, *la competence de guerre* [5]); this opinion falls in with the main line of the extra-legality of war, the only difference remaining being one of historical approach and of legal theory. This development of the *bellum justum* terminology may well be compared to that in Roman antiquity in the time of imperialism, when *justum* was taken to mean 'declared in the formally required way'. (See above).

The other theory that qualified the legality of war, as a procedure, by a listing of causes moved rather uneasily between positive law and law as an aspiration, *jus constituendum,* or international morality as it is often called. Augustine, Thomas, Vitoria and Grotius, stated quite concretely what they regarded as just causes and what as unjust and forbidden, like the desire of conquest, the propagation of religion, the prevention of possible attack, the nation's glory or a mere interest. The authors after them who still upheld, more or less, the distinction between just and unjust causes, extended the scope of the first considerably or left it unspecified. Wheaton — inspired by Grotius — says that war is the only means to get reparation for injuries the State has received, just as between individuals if there were no civil society [6]). Montesquieu compares the right to wage war with that of individual self-defence, and admits it for the self-conservation of the State [7]). Fauchille says that the use of force is

---

1) G. Scelle, Cours de Droit International Public. 1946—7, Paris, pp. 816—818.
2) Phillimore, l.c., above p. 2, note 2.
3) Blundschli, l.c., above, p. 2, note 3.
4) So it could be said that the regulation of the *jus ad bellum* was not within the province of international, but in that of domestic, constitutional law.
5) Scelle, ibidem.
6) About Wheaton's 'discovery' of Grotius, see v. Vollenhoven, o.c., p. 35—6. 'discovery' of Grotius see v. Vollenhoven, o.c., p. 35—6.
7) Montesquieu, De l'esprit des lois, L. X, c. ii.

legitimate if used for the defence of the independence, autonomy or security of the State: a nearly unlimited field! Schücking says that before 1914 war was considered as a legitimate means for the realization of a right, but that in practice the difference between right and interest was not always observed [1]).

This remark touches one of the reasons why discrimination between just and unjust causes of war was given up, or remained in the air as with the forementioned writers, and why as Eagleton says, "responsibility for war" in the passed century was a "historical and political notion, not a juridical" [2]). It was hardly ascertainable which of the belligerents was *au fond* in the right.

But the greatest obstacle to an integration of a substantial notion of just war in international law before the first World War was the absence of sanctions on a war waged without a just cause, because war itself was no more regarded as such a sanction and because the prevailing positivist theory did not admit as law any rule that was not sanctioned or sanctionable. It was not merely the circumstance that the legal consequences war entailed, the coming into force of the separate body of laws of war, were exactly the same whatever the cause or motivation of the war, provided it had been started by an act of the competent state-authorities (see Chapter I). For this fact had in principle already been admitted by Grotius [3]), as it was by Fauchille [4]) and all writers of the last centuries. Even the fact that international practice and law [5]) – in order to prevent an extension of the conflict – did not permit of any differentiation in the attitude of neutrals as a consequence of their opinion about the right

---

1) Fauchille-Bonfils, o.c., Vol. II, p. 7.
Manuel de Droit International Public, vol. II, Guerre et neutralité, Paris 1921, p. 7.

2) C. Eagleton, The Attempt to Define Aggression, International Conciliation, 1930, No. 264, p. 584.

3) Grotius, o.c., III, 17 (Molh. p. 636).

4) Fauchille-Bonfils, o.c., Vol. II, p. 9.

5) Qualification of neutrality entered into international practice – for a long time having been an exception – with the American attitude during the First World War, before its declaration of war upon the Central Powers, and is a necessary consequence of the reappearance of the conception of just war in the form of an interdiction of aggression, cf. Harvard Draft on Rights and Duties of States in the Case of Aggression, quoted in Chapter II, p. 40. Cf. Chapter I, p. 36.

or wrong of the parties, as Grotius defended [1]), would not necessarily have eliminated the legitimacy of the cause as a notion of law, if the absence of a legal authority, and of a legal criterion to which the legitimacy of a cause could be referred, had not delivered the whole terminology about 'just war' to the ephemeral needs and caprices of the *raison d'état*. In this connection the 'pure law' theory of Kelsen, pretending to permit war only as a sanction, carried the formalization of the notion of *bellum justum* to its extreme consequence with the thesis that the illicit act which 'just war' presupposed was contained in the juridical act itself of the State going to war, the ascertainment of the illicit act being made by a supreme and therefore infallible state-organ [2]).

Certainly, as many writers admit, the fact that, on no matter what grounds, a State could bring about a state of war, did not imply a justification of the grounds invoked [3]). However the notion of just war could not, during the period of indifference, in the absence of a superior or at least impartial authority and in the absence of a legal criterion, be more closely associated with legal science than in the words of Fauchille who, after stating that only the States may appreciate the causes of the war and evaluate their urgency, expediency and opportunity, says: "This is not the point of view of the jurist who must censure and condemn the wars of ambition and of conquest, under whatever veil they hide, whatever pretext their authors invoke,

---

1) Grotius, o.c., III, 17, 'de his qui in bello medii sunt', (the term neutral is only of later date), par. 3 (Molh. p. 636). "Vicissim eorum qui a bello abstinent officium est nihil facere quo validor fiat is, qui improbam fovet causam, aut quo iustum bellem gerentis motus impediantur". But at the end of the paragraph Grotius says that it is good to make friendship with both belligerents so as to be able to stay out of the conflict with the goodwill of both and to offer both the services of the human community. See for the later doctrinal confusion at the birth of the legal notion of neutrality, Butler — Maccoby, o.c., p. 232. The necessity of rules of neutrality was certainly one of the main factors in the development of the legal indifference about war and the silence about the justice of wars from the side of the statesmen.

2) See Etienne Bibó, Le dogme du 'bellum justum' et la théorie de l'infaillibilité juridique, Revue Internationale de la Théorie du Droit, 1936, pp. 14—27; H. Kelsen, quoted by Clyde Egelton. International Conciliation 1932, l.c., p. 238, nt. 2.

3) Cf. Moore, Digest, vol. I, p. 171.

be it the development of civilisation, the defense of the oppressed, etc." [1]).

It is interesting to quote several instances of the state-practice during these centuries, testifying at the same time to the gradual decline and disappearance of the notion of just war with its penal sanction, as to its constant virtual presence, actualized on moments of great crisis or revolutionary overthrow.

The treaties of Westphalia, aiming at an assured European equilibrium for the next epoch, showed little influence of the doctrine of just and punitive war, though it was only concluded a few decades after the publication of Suarez' and Grotius' works and though Spaniards and Dutch were the principal actors in Münster [2]). Penal sanctions were provided for the protection of the treaties, but only for treaty-violators in the Holy Roman Empire, and only through the enactment of the treaty as a law of the Empire [3]).

On the international plane all parties guaranteed the pact against any violation and were bound to assist a victim of such a violation, who could not obtain peaceful redress, *ad repellendam iniuriam* [4]). The most interesting clause, however, is that prescribing a general amnesty, not only for the reciprocal hostile acts *ab initio horum motuum,* but also for all injuries, violences, hostilities, damages and costs *tam ante bellum quam in bello* so that "quicquid eo nomine alter adversus alterum prendere posset, perpetua sit oblivione sepulta" [5]). Amnesty presupposes the possibility of a penal sanction, and where the amnesty did not only concern what was done during the war — war damages and war crimes — but also what had happened before, one may conclude that the cause of the war itself, the injustice or injury that gave rise to it, was, in 1648, still regarded as being of a criminal nature.

The treaties of Utrecht (1713) [6]) and Aix la Chapelle (1748) [7])

---

1) Fauchille—Bonfils, o.c., p. 10.
2) Cf. v. Vollenhoven, o.c.. See however François, vol. II, p. 301.
3) K. Strupp, Documents pour servir à l'Histoire du Droit des Gens, 2nd edition of German edition, Berlin 1933, Tome I, p. 15.
Treaty of Osnabrück, Articulus XVII, par. 2 and 5.
4) Treaty of Münster, par. 116—117, quoted by Redslob, o.c., p. 213.
5) Treaty of Osnabrück, Art. II, in Strupp, o.c., p. 15.
6) Treaty of Utrecht, 1713, Bauer, o.c., p. 25.
7) Treaty of Aix la Chapelle, 1748, quoted ibidem.

do not use the term 'amnesty' but speak only of *oubli général* – *absolument oubliés*. They list apart from *torts, dommages,* also *injures, offenses* – but only those committed during wartime. Only the treaty of 1763 stipulates again "un Oubli général de tout ce qui a pu être fait ou commis, avant ou depuis, le Commencement de la guerre qui vient de finir" [1]). The peace treaties from the time of the French Revolution and Napoleon do not contain any more of these clauses, though perhaps the express stipulation of the exchange of prisoners of war and hostages *without a ransom* [2]), may be regarded as a reminiscence of the time that the prisoners of war were at the disposal of the victor)[3].

The French Revolution saw the idea of a just war suddenly blazing up and then dying away quickly only to revive, like many other ideas of the French Revolution, after more than a century. The ideas and forces that overthrew the absolutist order not only aimed at an internal revolution, but envisaged also a reform of international relations through an international organisation of free nations. William Penn, the 'Abbé de Saint Pierre, Leibnitz and Rousseau preconized this idea and in Kant's *Zum Ewigen Frieden* the thesis is already developed – under the influence of the French events – that the first condition of peace and the establishment of the Law of Nations is internal freedom, because an international organisation is impossible between autocracies.

Therefore the first thing to be done was the subjection of the competence to wage war to the consent of the Constituante, as decreed in 1790; this according to many Revolutionnaries amounted to the establishment of a permanent peace. For how could the representatives of the people ever decide to make a war? But the Assemblée Constituante, conscious of its mission, wanted to go further and – as Mirkine-Guetzévitch says – *constitutionnaliser la paix* [4]). In stormy enthusiasm more and more radical proposals were made, silence was imposed on conservative and nationalist objectors and the idea was advanced

1) Treaty of Paris, 1763, Art. I.

2) Treaty of Paris (France—Great-Britain) 1802, Art. 2, de Martens, Suppl. vol. II, p. 563.

3) See Butler-Maccoby, o.c., p. 122—123.

4) I. Kant. Perpetual Peace, re-edited after first English translation, N.Y. 1939, p. 12.

that all unjust aggression is contrary to natural law, as among individuals, and that a nation cannot, therefore, give to its King a right that it does not possess itself. War should only be used to repress a grave injustice and conquest should be forbidden. Finally Mirabeau introduced his project, which provided in its Article 4: If the legislative judges that the hostilities started are a culpable aggression on the part of the ministers or any other agent of the executive, the author of this aggression shall be punished *comme criminel de lèse-nation* [1]). The project was adopted, though only one clause entered the constitution of 1791 viz: "The French Nation renounces the undertaking of any war with a view to making conquets and will never use its forces against the liberty of any people" [2]).

When in 1792, before the imminent threat of an invasion, war was declared upon Austria, this article of the Constitution was repeated and it was stated that this war had to be waged for the liberty and independance of the nation, not against another nation but against the unjust aggression of a king [3]). Together with the ideas mentioned above, the French Revolution developed the concept of intervention on behalf of an oppressed nation. Though incorporation of territories was made dependent on a plebiscite the following years showed more and more clearly the realization of what the 18th century progressives and the delegates of 1790 could not have imagined: a bellicose imperialistic people's representation. The constitutions of 5 Fructidor An III and 22 frimaire An VIII only prescribed that a war be decided upon by decree of the Legislative on the formal proposal of the Directorium [4]).

While in 1814 the Senate of the Restoration only noted Napoleon's non-observance of this article, the statesmen of the Alliance – certainly after Napoleon's landing in France in 1815 – had more substantial grievances against him. In the treaty of April 1814 concerning his future status as prince of Elba, Napoleon was still treated as emperor, magnanimously abdicating because

---

1) Mirkine-Guetzévitch, La 'guerre juste' dans le droit constitutionel français, R.G.D.I.P., 1950, pp. 233, 240.
2) Constitution de 1791, titre VI.
3) Ibidem, p. 234.
4) Constitution de l'An VIII (22 frimaire), Art. 50. Constitution de 5 fructidor An III, Art. 326.

"the Allied Powers had proclaimed that Napoleon Buonaparte was the only obstacle to the peace of Europe" [1]). But after the news of his landing was received in Vienna, the Allied Powers gave a declaration on the 25th of March, stating that "en rompant ainsi la convention (that he had solemnly promised to observe) qui l'avoit établi à l'isle d'Elbe, Buonaparte détruit le seul titre légal auquel son existence se trouvoit attachée. En réparaissant en France avec des projets de troubles et de bouleversements, il s'est privé lui-même de la protection des lois et a manifesté, à la face de l'univers, qu'il ne sauroit y avoir ni paix ni trêve avec lui". And after a promise of help to France if it was requested, the Powers "déclarent en conséquence que Napoléon Buonaparte s'est placé hors des relations civiles et sociales, et que, comme ennemi et perturbateur du repos du monde, il s'est livré à la vindicte publique" [2]).

By this action of what was later going to be the Concert of Europe, Napoleon was, as an individual, internationally outlawed. Meticulous care seems to have been exercised to avoid any reference to legal rules or terminology in dealing with the case of Napoleon. When Napoleon was captured by the English, a convention was signed stating that Napoleon was "au pouvoir des Puissances Alliées" and "en vertu des stipulations du traité de 25 Mars 1815" whereby the Powers guaranteed to each other military collaboration until they had made it impossible for Napoleon to stir up trouble or disrupt again the peace in Europe), it is stated "Napoléon Buonaparte est regardé par les Puissances qui ont signé le traité de 25 Mars dernier comme leur prisonnier".

His custody was especially entrusted to the English Government, while commissars of Prussia, Austria and Russia 's'assureront de sa présence' [3]). In the Parliamentary Acts of 11 April 1816 [4]) – adopted after sharp criticism by the opposition of the arbitrary and unconstitutional treatment of Napoleon by the British Government – it was simply stated that it was necessary "for the Preservation of the Tranquillity of Europe, and for

1) Acte de renonciation, 11 Avril 1814, de Martens, N.R. I., p. 696, nt. 1. Traité de 11 Avril 1814, ibidem.

2) Déclaration des Puissances Alliées, à Vienne, de 13 Mars 1814, de Martens, N.R. II, pp. 108–109.

3) Convention sur la garde de Napoléon Buonaparte, de 2 Août 1815, de Martens, N.R. II, p. 579.

4) De Martens, N.R. III, pp. 1 ff., 5 ff..

the general Safety, that Napoleon Buonaparte should be detained and kept in Custody" and further that he "shall be deemed and taken to be, and shall be treated and dealt with as a Prisoner of War".

Though it may appear from the documents quoted that Napoleon was, after his landing, at first regarded as an individual, an international adventurer, it is obvious that after Napoleon's reappearance in France had taken serious forms, the hostilities were regarded as war: the word is omitted in the Alliance-Treaty of 25th March 1815, but occurs in an Austrian counter declaration about another matter of May 9th: "la présente guerre contre l'usurpation de Napoléon Buonaparte" [1]).

Moreover a new peace-treaty was signed with France on 20 November 1815, after the battle of Waterloo, providing for more concessions on the part of France than that of 1814. But on the other hand, the war was waged against Napoleon and not against the French people, and the King of France's adherence was sought for the treaty of 25 March 1815 while at the same time a treaty was concluded with France, and Napoleon, exempted from its benefits, was kept as a prisoner of war.

The contradictions are easily understandable in view of the differences between the Allies: Prussia (Blücher) wanted to shoot Napoleon, England wanted France to sentence and execute him, while the French government, after the restoration of the Bourbons, found itself too weak to oppose popular sentiments by such an execution. The treatment of Napoleon as an international bandit, as the British ambassador Lord Castlereagh saw it, was, according to Bauer [2]) intentional because no reference to the idea of punishment for aggressive war was wanted, freedom of going to war being already generally accepted.

This notion of war as a political action open to every nation found striking support in Bismarck's refutation of the proposal of some Germans to have Napoleon III arraigned as guilty of the war of 1870. This war was declared by France for "la défense de son honneur et de ses interêts compromis", though German intrigues (notably Bismarck's publication of the Kaiser's telegram from Ems) had played a considerable part in bringing

1) De Martens, N.R. I. p. 109 ff..
2) Bauer, o.c., p. 37

about a war that was welcomed enthusiastically in both countries [1]). As if directly attacking Suarez or *De Iure Belli ac Pacis* Bismarck stated: "Public opinion is only too ready to consider political relations and events in the light of those of civil law and private persons generally, and to demand, among other things, that in conflicts between States, the victor, with the moral code in his hand, goes to sit in judgment upon the defeated and sentences him for what he did to him and possibly also for what he did to others. Such a demand, however, is quite unjustified. Putting forward such a demand shows a complete lack of understanding of the nature of political matters, to which the notions of punishment, recompense and revenge do not belong; compliance with such a demand would mean a falsification of the essence of politics. Politics have to leave the punishment of princes and peoples for offences against the moral law to Him Who directs the battles" [2]).

If this quotation demonstrates Bismarck's political wisdom and moderation, it certainly also shows that the idea of war and the launching of it were for the ordinary man, for public opinion, always loaded with moral significance – demanding full approval if waged with right, and condemnation and punishment if without – and that this was so even during the centuries in which jurists and statesmen had accepted war as a fact, a political means among others, without legal significance.

SECTION 5. THE PERIOD OF DISCRIMINATION

Because public opinion demanded a just cause for a war, justification of war lingered on in political terminology. The aim of every war was formulated in terms of defence, if not the actual defence of territory and population, then that of honour or security, and above all the protection of interests, which justified a whole series of colonial wars of conquest throughout the 19th century. But by the end of the century a public movement was rapidly developing that turned against the notion of

---

1) See for the French declaration of war of 19 July 1870 and the German contra circulaire to the diplomatic representatives, de Martens, N.R.G., XIX, pp. 585, 586.

2) Quoted by Bauer, o.c., p. 38.

just war from another than the political realistic viewpoint mentioned above. Tolstoyism and the less radical pacifistic movements denied the possibility of any just war, even that of immediate defence; thus had the pre-Augustinian Christian rejected the use of violence.

While the efforts for humanization of warfare continued – by codification and development of the *jus in bello* – especially since at the Paris Congress of 1856 after the Crimean war – the new currents at the end of the century – haunted by the frequency of war, and by the increasing armament and the threat of a worldwide clash between the big powers – aimed at the legal restriction of the *jus ad bellum* itself. The indirect approach to the restriction of war, by the provision of peaceful methods for the settlement of international conflicts, was more or less successful and resulted in the Convention for the Pacific Settlement of International Conflicts at the First Hague Conference of 1899 [1]). But the proposals for the direct banning of war, by making obligatory recourse to conciliation or arbitration, were no match for the *raison d'état,* the national requirements of unrestrained sovereignty [2]). The Porter-convention – concerning the limitation of the use of force for the collection of contractual debts [3]), – and the Convention concerning the opening of hostilities [4]), were the poor results of the lengthy discussions of the Second Peace Conference.

The worldwide extension and the length, intensity and unprecedented suffering of the First World War brought about a more radical revision of international law. From the Peace Conference of Versailles sprung the two main lines of direct legal attack on the resort to war in international politics: the attempts at *legislative elimination* of war by the procedural regulations of the Covenant and other legal instruments, and later by most direct 'outlawry', and the *judicial repression* of war by the efforts to arraign the authors of the First World War and, in later years to penalize, in a general and permanent way, the resort to ag-

---

1) Les deux Conférences de la Paix, Recueil des textes arrêtés, Paris 1909 2me éd., pp. 77–95.

2) See for an illustration of this opposition the cynical commentary of a German delegate, quoted by Steinlein, o.c., p. 1.

3) Les deux Conférences de la paix, pp. 95–99.

4) O.c., pp. 99–103, cf. chapter I, p. 3, above.

gressive war and other offences against international law, through proper instruments and institutions of an international penal law.

Some observations concerning the first method of preventing war will be made here while judicial repression will be dealt with in the last section of this chapter. After the examination, in Chapter II, of the specific rules concerning the resort to war, and specially aggressive war, in such instruments as the Covenant of the League of Nations, the League projects and resolutions, the Locarno Pact and other regional non-aggression-treaties, and finally the Kellogg Pact, it is necessary to consider here the legal character of these instruments and the position of war in international law that resulted from them.

The legislative development towards a restriction and suppression of war in international relations took two converging directions: from indirect to direct, and from procedural to substantial regulation of the *competence de guerre* [1]). The provisions of the Covenant, contained in Articles 12 to 15, were, like the Porter-convention of 1907 and like the bilateral Bryan Treaties, which created standing conciliation commissions, mainly procedural. The competence to wage war was not itself affected but its exercise was restricted by the obligation to seek first a solution of the conflict by a peaceful method that involved the interference of an impartial body – be it the Council, be it, by a juridically binding method, an arbitral tribunal or the Permanent Court. In no case was either party to resort to war until three months after the arbitral award, the decision of the Court or the report of the Council; and never was it to go to war against the party which complied with award, decision, or the unanimous recommendations of the Council [2]).

While in this last provision the notion of a material *bellum injustum* may already be noticed, the competence to wage war was certainly restricted in itself by Art. 10 which laid down that aggression or aggressive war was never to be waged in order to

1) This expression of Scelle (Cours de Droit International Public, 3me éd., 1946–1947, p. 816 and passim) is used here because it expresses more the extralegality of resort to war that was not the exercise of a subjective right but of a power (cf. Quincy Wright, A.J.I.L. 1924, p. 755 ff.). Still better would be 'freedom to go to war'.

2) Articles 13, pararagraph 4, and 15, paragraph 6, of the Covenant.

change the territorial integrity or existing political independence of any League Member. Wars, by this Article, were discriminated between by those which were and those which were not henceforward, permanently and regardless of circumstances, forbidden to the majority of nations, Members of the League.

From this Article – itself a generalised descendant of the bilateral treaties of non-aggression and guarantee – originated the series of resolutions, projects and treaties, which in the course of the twenties gradually extended the field of illicit war beyond the limits set by the Covenant. 'Offensive war', 'aggressive war', is forbidden in the project of a treaty of mutual assistance (1923), and in the unratified Protocol of Geneva (1924), 'recourse to war', 'attack', 'invasion', – with the exception of self-defence and executive actions in virtue of the Covenant – in the Locarno-Pact, 'aggressive war' again in the resolution of the Assembly in 1927, and that of 4th Pan-American Conference in 1928, and finally war as such, 'war as an instrument of national policy', in the Kellogg Pact of 27 August 1928 [1]).

Apart from the tendency to extend the scope of the obligation not to resort to war, so that this would not be allowed even in the cases in which the Covenant had put no restrictions on the freedom to go to war [2]), the legislative and would-be legislative development indicated above showed another remarkable feature. Not only were they formulated in the language of interdictions and of obligations of States, but the forbidden war was being associated with crime. 'Aggressive war' was declared to constitute an 'international crime' in Art. 1 of Lord Cecil's project of a treaty of mutual assistance, as 'an infraction of the solidarity and an international crime' in the Protocol of Geneva, again as an 'international crime' in the League of Nations resolution of 1927 and in the Pan-American Resolution of 1928, in the

1) See documents quoted above, pp. 10–11.

2) The famous 'gaps' in the Covenant, on the 'closing' of which legal efforts in the latter half of the twenties were concentrated. The possibility of not-illegal resort to war was mainly left open by Artt. 12, 1 (after the three months, in case of failure of arbitral or judicial settlement), 13, 4 (against a Member who would not comply with the judgment, war of execution), 15, 5 (against the Member not complying with a unanimous Council report, also, in a broad sense, a war of execution), 15, 6 (failure of Council to reach a unanimous report) and 15, 7 (if Council declares dispute-matter to be under domestic jurisdiction of one of the parties).

preambles of the South-American Saavedra Lamas Treaty for the Prevention of War, of 10 Oct. 1933, and in many bilateral non-aggression treaties. In the Paris Pact resort to war 'for the solution of international conflicts' is solemnly condemned and it is denounced 'as an instrument of national politics'.

An examination into the legal import of these clauses shows that their primary significance was that they incorporated into international law a moral conviction of mankind, strongly voiced by different movements for peace and outlawry of war and by various other non-governmental international organisations like the Interparliamentary Union [1]). This public insistence accounts for the adding of the terms 'condemnation' and 'international crime' to the pacts and resolutions limiting the freedom to go to war, and the history of the Kellogg Pact shows clearly that not only were the initiative and stimulation to a universal 'peace-pact' given by non-governmental agencies [2]) but also that its actual wording was governed by the primary desire to satisfy public opinion, which was no longer willing to accept war as a political means at the disposal of statesmen [3]). It is particularly to the American Movement for Outlawry of War, of which Professor Shotwell was the most prominent spokesman [4]), that the idea and character of the Kellogg Pact can be traced.

The salient features of the Pact, the idea of 'outlawry' itself, — technically incorrect as it presupposed an existing legality of war [5]) — the radical unqualified formulation of an 'objective' abolition of war without an accompanying system for its prevention and for peaceful settlement of conflicts, and, in connection with that, the absence of executive control or judicial sanctions for the enforcement of the proclaimed norms, these three

1) See for the work of private international organisations, Wehberg, o.c., pp. 17 ff. and 93—122, and also section 6 below.

2) See Wehberg, o.c., pp. 72—93, and Mandelstam, o.c.. Professor Shotwell seems to have suggested Briand's original proposal for a peace pact with the United States, which general plan retained in the final multilateral treaty, (See introduction to Eppstein, o.c.).

3) This is quite clear in Kellog's successive notes to the French government, especially where he argues against the second French counter-proposal that added the qualification 'aggressive' to war, and made several other reservations. See this correspondence in Strupp, Das Kellog Pakt im Rahmen des Kriegsvorbeugungsrecht, o.c..

4) See his 'War as an Instrument of National Policy, and its Renunciation in the Pact of Paris', New York, 1929.

5) See below, p. 301.

characteristics by which the Pact distinguishes itself from previous and later anti-war treaties can be deduced from its unpolitical origin.

For these same reasons the Paris Pact is open to much controversy, as shown in Chapter II, on the issue of the scope of war and self-defence, the significance of the straightforward 'outlawry' being much weakened by the implicit reservations of several States. But as an almost universal pact adhered to by 63 nations [1]), it owes to its lapidary form none the less its tremendous importance in international law. At the same time it summed up the whole previous development, the main formulations of which have been mentioned, and gave a new impetus to the efforts for the effective legal suppression of war. It was confirmed in the Preamble of the Pact of Four of June 7th 1933 [2]), in the South-American Non-aggression Pact mentioned above, and in a declaration of the Pan-American Conference in Lima, in 1938; it was elaborated in the Convention concerning the definition of aggression of 1933, and in the East-European non-aggression treaties [3]). Further, it gave rise to a whole series of efforts within the League of Nations to bring the Covenant in harmony with the universal renunciation of war.

It was however only after the Second World War that the rule of the Paris Pact was incorporated in the law of the international organisation. And at the same time it was mainly on the basis of the Paris Pact that the drafters of the London Charter and the International Military Tribunals in Nuremberg and Tokyo justified the criminal and punishable character of aggressive war (see next Chapter). Though the other instruments mentioned above are also quoted beside the Paris Pact, as supporting this new notion, in positive law it could only have been the Kellogg Pact that brought this change about. The project of 1923 was never adopted; the Protocol of Geneva was signed by 19 States but never ratified so that it could only have the same force as the resolution-Sokal of 1927, which, whatever the legal significance of a resolution, could never change the positive

1) See Harvard Research, l.c., p. 865.
2) This treaty was however never ratified.
3) Quoted above, Chapter II, par. 6.

law of the Covenant that still allowed war in several cases [1]). On the other hand the Locarno Pact and the South-American treaty of 1933 are purely regional, while the first is, moreover, more restricted regarding the scope of its prohibition of war.

Though the declarations in resolutions and preambles of treaties could therefore only amount to *promises* of a predominantly moral character, the renunciation of war as an instrument of national policy, which was as stated not devoid of moral features [2]), became legally binding on the parties. Contrary to the suggestion Wehberg made [3]), this renunciation covered war as such; war as an instrument of 'religious or ideological policy', being war, could only be started by a State or a group of States, as only States had the right to wage war and as no religious or ideological entities were or are recognized in international law. And war as an instrument of international policy is a *contradictio in terminis*. The international action against a lawbreaker, to enforce exactly those rules the Kellogg Pact preconised, has (as argued in Chapter I) nothing but the laws of warfare in common with 'normal' interstate war, 'war as an instrument of national policy'. At the same time the opinion of Kelsen, that war waged in the national interest but based on a claim recognized by international law, that is by an international arbitral or judicial decision, remained licit, must be refuted [4]). If one accepts that the Kellogg Pact forms part of international law, it is impossible to maintain that international law can still give, or leave with a State, the competence to go to war for the purpose of execution of a judicial decision. In a certain sense the effect of this general 'abolition' of war

---

1) See above, p. 155, nt. 2.

2) This moral, and propagandistic aspect of the Pact is expressed in its Art. 1: 'The High Contracting Parties solemnly declare in name of their respective peoples'. The U.N. Charter has carried this still further: 'We the peoples of the United Nations. ... accordingly our respective governments through representatives assembled in the city of San Francisco ...'. The moral character was stressed by Stimson: 'The Briand-Kellog Pact provides for no sanction of force ... Indeed, it rests upon the sanction of public opinion which can be made one of the most potent sanctions of the world', (quoted in S. Glueck, The Nuremberg Trial and Aggressive War, New York, 1946, p. 17—18).

3) Wehberg, o.c., p. 72 ff..

4) Kelsen, The Law of The United Nations, o.c..

was undone by the broad scope of 'the right of self-defence' which the United States and the Commonwealth reserved and which was tacitly accepted by the signatories.

The position both countries took was a consequence of the historical guardianship they pretended in certain parts of the world, the United States in the American Continent on the basis of the Monroe-doctrine, England regarding the Commonwealth and the communication-lines between the metropole and the different dominions and overseas territories. But if both countries had referred in their reservations to aggressive wars in those parts of the world, these reservations could have been brought in line with the sanction mentioned below, according to which they would become free from their obligations under the Pact in relation to the State that resorted to war 'as an instrument of national policy'. It was not the territorial but the substantial extension of 'self-defence' – contained in the reservations – that invalidated the absoluteness of the prohibition of war.

Self-defence was taken as a political and therefore indefinable concept. Moreover, not only was the formulation of a legal criterion omitted and declared impossible but also the mere possibility of an impartial authority determining when – or if – *in concreto* self-defence was permitted, was expressly denied in Kellogg's statement that it was the States, and they alone, that would be competent to determine when self-defence was necessary.

It was exactly these deficiencies – of a legal criterion and/or an impartial authority – that – as stated in conclusion on the doctrine of *bellum justum* – caused the death of this concept in international relations. The world, after three centuries once again occupied with the suppression of the, now generalized, *bellum injustum,* was not yet ready to draw the consequences of a legal discrimination of war. And this situation was even more serious because of the fact that the discretion the States claimed in the matter of self-defence was not linked up with the mainterance or restoration of rights but with those of interests [1]).

---

1) See Chamberlain's note of May 19, 1928, quoted in Strupp, o.c., annex.

The causes for these reservations, shared or at least accepted by all signatories of the pact, were obvious. As the second feature of the Pact, the radical, direct 'abolishment' of the competence of war was mentioned. It was not an engagement they took towards the other signatories as such, but a universal, 'law-making' renunciation of their power, applicable to all their relations with all States, also non-signatories, formulated as a change in international law, not primarily as one of subjective rights; the condemnation of the recourse to war preceded the renunciation of it.

It is certainly on this ground that the Kellogg-Pact was regarded, before the war, as one of the two most important treaties in international law, the other being the League-Covenant [1]). It was this because of its radical dealing with the chief, all-important problem in international relations – war. But war would never have become the chief problem of history and it would never have remained that till today if it had been an isolated factor, an unnecessary, exclusively pernicious element. War also fulfilled necessary functions in international society – the maintenance or restoration of justice and the adjustment of international relations to changed conditions, two contradictory functions as Lauterpacht rightly remarks [2]), but both essential in a living society. If war was to be eliminated, society would need a complete structural reversal, affecting every part of its organisation, with another institution or other institutions to fulfil the functions of the eliminated war. If these institutions were not effectively set up, war would come back or would remain.

The provision of these other instruments, peaceful methods for the solution of conflicts, was called (above) the 'indirect' approach to the elimination of war. The Kellogg Pact has been severely criticized on the ground of its pre-dominantly negative character; formulating the renunciation of war before the norm making the recourse to the peaceful method obligatory (Article

---

1) Oppenheim-Lauterpacht, Vol. II, p. 165.

2) Ibidem pp. 147–8. Cf. Scelle's more elaborate distinction between wars: "guerre punitive", "guerre exécutive" (both under Lauterpacht's war as a means of self help) "guerre-révision", and "guerre révolution" (L.'s war as a legally admissible instrument of change).

2) has been characterized as placing the cart before the horse [1]). There has been a tendency to deny any legal significance to the Pact in the absence of an effective, obligatory machinery for settlement of conflicts.

The absence of detailed provisions for such machinery was, however, quite justified. Within one month of the signing of the Paris Pact the General Act of Arbitration was signed in Geneva [2]), containing a highly perfected regulation of the three chief methods of settlement of conflicts: conciliation, arbitration, and judicial settlement, based on the experience with the Hague Convention, the League Covenant and the Statute of the Permanent Court. Moreover, all regional non-aggression pacts contained provisions in this sense, so that there was in fact no need for anything else in the Paris Pact than a legal norm for the exclusive use of this machinery in the settlement of all conflicts.

Quite another question, which touches the core of the matter, is whether war could be eliminated in a society that has not yet undergone or accepted that radical structural change, that has no superior authority invested with power to enforce the law, and no legislature for the necessary renewal and adjustment of the law, whether, in a sociological sense, war *could* there be eliminated. The opinion of Kelsen (quoted before) touches a vital question: how to exclude self-help if there is no appeal to an executive for the enforcement of a States' rights, Article 13 paragraph 4 of the Covenant, like the new Article 94 of the U.N. Charter, having only a facultative character for the appropriate organ? But also how to exclude war under the regime of a Covenant that was built around a guarantee of the *statu quo* (Art. 10) and provides for 'peaceful change' only with the proviso that 'the Assembly may from time to time advise the reconsideration by Members, etc.' (Art. 19)? [3]). The dead letter of the last article was indeed one of the factors that caused Article 10 to be trampled underfoot by a whole series of aggressive armies.

Could war then, in this absence of effective executive and

---

1) David Hunter Miller. The Pact of Paris, p. 127 quoted in E. Janeczek, Nuremberg Judgment in the Light of International Law, Genève 1949, p. 113.

2) Acte Général en matière de Conciliation, d'Arbitrage, et de Règlement Judiciaire, of 26 September 1928.

3) The Charter of the United Nations, however, contains no provision at all in this respect. See above, p. 105.

legislature, be legally renounced and 'abolished' by the Kellogg Pact? For a jurist and for those who attribute any significance to law in international relations there can only be one answer: war was legally renounced and 'abolished' by the Kellogg Pact, and resort to war as an instrument of national policy, that means every formally aggressive war, every initiation of war, was henceforward an illegal act in international law. Force of circumstance might serve as an excuse for, never as a justification of, a resort to war, that is a general use of force not in self-defence.

The sanctions of the norms proclaimed in the Pact remain to be considered. Some authors have denied legal significance, at least the same legal significance which the Covenant possessed, to the Pact, on the ground that it contained no sanctions [1]). In the first place one sanction was expressly formulated in the Preamble, which was recognized by the signatories as forming part of the Pact [2]). The formulation of this sanction was certainly a concession to those who wanted the binding part of the Pact as restricted as possible. It was hardly in conformance with the universal 'law-making' character of the treaty to state that a party resorting to war should be denied the benefits of the treaty: there could be no special benefits from the treaty as resort to war was condemned before it was renounced in the mutual relations of the parties.

Secondy a whole series of legal consequences could be deduced from that sanction. At the Budapest Conference of the International Law Association in 1934 authorative conclusions were drawn regarding the deviation from the rules of neutrality that was permitted to the other parties as soon as a State had violated it by resorting to war [3]). The Harvard Draft of 1939,

1) E.g. B. M. Telders, De juridieke Waardering van de Oorlog, o.c..

2) See Australian Note of 18 July 1928, in Strupp, o.c., Annex.

3) See the Budapest Articles of Interpretation of the Kellogg Pact, (adopted at the Conference of the International Law Association, held in Budapest, Sept. 1934), reproduced in Transactions of the Grotius Society on 1935, London 1940, Annex, Part. II, p. 189 ff., art. 4, a) — d), amounting to the complete setting aside of neutrality obligations towards the Pact-breaker, who could be hindered by all sorts of measures short of war and could be attacked by all other signatories. In Art. 6, the liability of the Pact-breaker was stated for all damages caused to any signatory or its nationals by the violation of the Pact. Art. 5 contained the Stimson-doctrine (See below). Cf. F. N. Keen, The Preamble of the Pact of Paris, ibidem pp. 177—8.

referred to previously, elaborated these consequences still further, without however taking the universal interdiction of war as the point of departure [1]).

Aggressive war was 'condemned' in the Kellogg Pact, not declared a crime, as in previous and later resolutions, plans and preambles of treaties among which, however, only the regional treaty of Rio de Janeiro (1933) belongs to positive law. 'Condemn' is certainly weaker than 'international crime'; neither term, occurring in declarations without any special elaboration, can be regarded as invested with any penal significance: the meaning of both is moral, political, propagandistic rather than legal, as they are only used to strengthen the wording of a renunciation, an interdiction; not the slightest idea or suggestion came up during the preparatory work or afterwards that might be connected with the notion of international penal law, either concerning States or individuals (see following section).

The paucity of sanctions in the Kellogg Pact has been severely criticized but was in line with the whole conception of the Pact as a universal instrument, originating moreover from a non-Member of the League, the United States whose government and public opinion alike strongly opposed the idea of wars of sanction, an idea already much diluted in the League-system [2]). It was only later, in 1932, that Stimson, Secretary of State, formulated the rule named after him, amounting to the non-recognition of territorials changes brought about by the use of force. This sanction, while accepted in the League of Nations, proved unpracticable in the prevailing circumstances of international interdependence and was consequently not observed, either on the American Continent for whicht it was formulated, or outside, as the outcome of the Abyssinian Campaign manifestly proved.

It is interesting to compare the tendencies and realisations of the period of discrimination with those of the *bellum justum* doctrine. While the aim of both movements was the same – the creation of world-order – and while both saw law as the chief means to obtain it, the actual tendencies were more or less opposed as a result of a different point of view, a different accentuation imposed by the circumstances of the era. As stated, in the

---

1) Above, p. 40, nt. 2.
2) Cf. Wehberg, o.c., pp. 17 ff. and above, Chapter II, section 1.

Middle Ages and more so in the tumultuous 16th and beginning of 17th century, war – restricted in scope and intensity – was seen as the chief means for the maintenance and progress of justice. Now that war has grown, during the period of indifference, to its present monstrous dimensions, it is peace, understood as the absence of war, not in the Augustinian sense of just order, which receives the main emphasis. Now it is the suppression of war, then it was the suppression of injustice that occupied the minds and hearts of men.

While the theologians admitted war as a sacrifice of (exterior) peace to justice, the Kellogg Pact and the legal instruments drafted in its spirit manifest the willingness to sacrifice justice to peace, as the prohibition of war intervenes at a time when the machinery for peaceful settlement and adjustment is still gravely deficient [1]). Before the period of indifference it was the usurpation of rights that was the principle object of the world's condemnation and after it, now, it is aggression. But both movements were equally threatened, in the absence of a superior authority, by a formalization of these objects as a consequence of their arbitrary use in state-practice, which is unable or unwilling to accept clear, fixed legal criteria by which their freedom to decide and to act would be restricted.

The doctrine of *bellum justum* became diluted and was ignored in the practice of power politics; the movement for restriction and 'outlawry' of war had in any case developed an authority, which, though not invested with force, was able to pronounce on right and wrong in a given case and to influence morally its adherents. The discrimination between just and unjust wars had become a reality in the world between the Great Wars, but the States were unwilling to take the practical consequences of this. By thus withholding force from the superior authority injustices had to be tolerated while peace was lost as well. Only by a real world-organisation, by an authority invested with power, can both the components of world order – justice and peace – be safeguarded and integrated to a real *pax*.

---

[1]) Compare, with respect to the United Nations, Lauterpacht's observation that the Charter "in many respects preferred order to law". H. Lauterpacht, the Grotian tradition of International Law, B.Y.I.L., 1946, pp. 1–53, note 1.

SECTION 6. THE DOCTRINE OF INTERNATIONAL PENAL LAW

At the Peace Conference of Versailles where the first steps were taken towards an 'outlawry' of war, also the first efforts were made to introduce penal sanctions in international law by a system of repressive justice applicable to its violators. Contrary to the 'outlawry' of war, international penal law in this sense did not go beyond the stage of doctrine and planning.

The field covered by the term 'international penal law' consists of three parts: first the classic counterpart of private international law, that may be of international concern but is solely the domestic law of the States, regulating the limits of their penal jurisdiction. The co-existence of the national competences gives rise to national law of conflicts which is the object of international co-ordination but only in a secondary sense international law.

Secondly there are individual crimes, the nature and scope of which have led the States to combine efforts for their suppression and to assume jurisdiction over the perpetrators of those crimes, wherever committed, in line with the so-called 'universal principle of jurisdiction'. Piracy is the classic example originating from Grotius' concept of universal penal jurisdiction [1]); further examples are: slave trade [2]), traffic in women and children and in narcotic drugs, and dealings in obscene publications [3]).

The third field was an innovation of this century. The 'interstate penal law' (see beginning of this section) was suggested to comprise within its scope crimes committed in the relations between States, in violation of international rules and therefore committed by representatives of the States. As Donnedieu de Vabres defines: *le droit pénal interétatique* "régit les infractions qui sont commises dans les rapports entre les états par des personnes exercant une activité publique agissant au nom de l'Etat". It is this attribution of penal responsibility to the State or to its organs that was the essence of the doctrine

---

1) Van Vollenhoven, o.c., passim.

2) Oppenheim-Lauterpacht, Vol. I, (seventh ed. 1948) p. 665. The Slavery Convention of 1926 contains provisions for combined action for suppression of slavery and punishment of its perpetrators.

3) See the list of these 'humanitarian conventions', ibidem, p. 890–893.

of international penal law which began to play an important role after the first World War.

The period of indifference only knew state-responsibility as a civil-law concept, as a notion of the *iustitia commutativa,* wherein all obligations could be reduced to 'reparation of the moral and material wrong done'. Oppenheim-Lauterpacht quotes several instances of reparation "indistinguishable from punishment, in the form of pecuniary redress unrelated to the damage actually inflicted" [1]), but it has to be remembered that also in civil law fines can be imposed in excess of damages. Real punishment was incompatible with the notion and practice of sovereignty. The competence to resort to war and to take reprisals, to take the law – or the interests – into the State's own hands was the necessary complement to this system.

So, the revised Hague Convention relative to the laws and customs of war on land, of 1907, provided in its Article 3: "La Partie belligérante qui violerait les dispositions dudit règlement" (concerning the laws and customs of war on land) "sera tenu à l'indemnité s'il y a lieu. Elle sera responsable de tous actes commis par les personnes faisant partie de sa force armée". In the meantime it was an established customary rule that individual violators of the laws of war might be punished by the belligerent into whose power they came as prisoners of war [2]). The concept of 'war crime' was born; and that included both acts committed by soldiers on their own initiative and those committed by order and on behalf of the State.

The Commission nominated by the Peace Conference in Versailles to report on the responsibilities of the authors of the war and on sanctions [3]), not only drew the consequences of this previous development by proposing the arraignment, before a national or an international tribunal, of all those persons belonging to enemy States – upto the head of State – who had committed, or were responsible for the committing of, war crimes,

---

1) Ibidem, pp. 320 ff..

2) G. A. Finch, The Nuremberg Trial and International Law, A.J.I.L., 1947. pp. 20 ff.. M. W. Mouton, Oorlogsmisdrijven en het Internationale Recht. 's Gravenhage 1947, pp. 330 ff..

3) See Commission des Responsabilités des Auteurs de la Guerre et de Sanctions, (in La Documentation Internationale, La Paix de Versailles, No. 3), Paris, 1930, Rapport de la commission, pp. 459, sv.

– which proposal was embodied in Articles 228 to 230 of the Versailles Pact – but also proposed the establishment of the notion of responsibility for the war itself. In Article 227 the Powers concequently accused the German ex-Emperor of "a supreme offence against international morality and the sanctity of treaties". Though the substance of the accusation was predominately moral and political – as was that of Napoleon – Article 227 provided for a formally complete legal process and punishment [1]).

The 'supreme offence' for which Wilhelm II was accused in Article 227 was an amalgamation of two responsibilities alleged in the Commission's report, of which the one, of individuals 'si haut placés qu'ils soient' for the violation of the laws and customs of warfare, be it *per ommissionem,* may here be left aside. The conclusions of the Commission concerning the other responsibility "pour les actes qui ont amené la guerre mondiale et qui en ont accompagné le début" manifests clearly the duality noted in Article 227. The first and second paragraph of the Commission's conclusions reflect its consciousness of the actual state of international law: the acts that had brought about the World War could not constitute the object of an arraignment of their authors before the Tribunal, whose institution was recommended for dealing with the ordinary war criminals. The accompanying acts, the violation of Belgium's and Luxembourg's guaranteed neutrality, were regarded as such an offence against the principles of the law of nations and of the good faith in international relations that, in the Commission's opinion, they had to form the object of a formal condemnation by the Peace Conference.

The reasons were clear. As stated elsewhere in the report, the

---

1) Art. 227 Versailles: 'The Allied and Associated Powers publicly arraign William II of Hohenzollern, former German Emperor, for a supreme offence against international morality and the sanctity of treaties.

'A special tribunal will be constituted to try the accused, thereby assuring him the guarantees essential to the right of defence. It will be composed of five judges, one appointed by each of the following Powers, namely, the United States of America, Great Britain, France, Italy and Japan.

'In its decision the tribunal will be guided by the highest motives of international policy with a view to vindicating the solemn obligations of international undertakings and the validity of international morality. It will be its duty to fix the punishment which it considers should be imposed.

'The Allied and Associated Powers will address a request to the Government of the Netherlands for the surrender to them of the Ex-Emperor in order that he may be put on trial'.

premeditation of a dissimulated aggressive war was an act "que la conscience publique réprouve et que l'histoire flétrit sans qu'a raison du caractère purement facultatif des institutions créées à la Haye" (for pacific settlement of disputes) "... une guerre d'aggression puisse être considérée comme un acte rigoureusement contraire au droit positif et qui pourrait être porté, avec quelque chance de succès, devant un tribunal ..." like that proposed for war criminals; apart from this legal obstacle, an argument *de facto* was advanced which ran counter to the Commission's earlier constatation of the enemies' full and exclusive war guilt [1]): "Toute enquête approfondie sur les auteurs responsables de la guerre ... devrait s'étendre à des événements qui se sont passés pendant un grand nombre d'années dans plusieurs pays de l'Europe et qui soulèveraient forcément beaucoup de problèmes ardus et complexes, qui releveraient plutôt des recherches d'historiens et d'hommes d'état que d'un Tribunal qualifié pour juger les violations des lois et coutumes de la guerre".

It sounded more like the period of indifference and like Bismarck's conception of the problem of responsibility for a war as that of the 'square circle', than like anything else. It was these arguments that were put forward by the majority of the Members of the Commission, and particularly by the American members, in refutation of the French thesis voiced by Larnaude and De Lapradelle, according to which the ex-Emperor could be brought to trial for violations of international law before a special tribunal which by its composition and authority would at the same time, in a most solemn verdict, advance the moral and political importance of proceedings that would nevertheless be legal. And though the starting point of the French mémoire was the ex-Emperor's responsibility for the committing of war crimes, it clearly resulted from their report that they wanted the proposed trial to bear not only on the violation of guaranteed

---

1) L.c. 'La guerre est prémédité par les Alliances Centrales ... ainsi que par la Turquie et la Bulgarie ... et elle est le résultat d'actes d'libérément commis dans l'intention de la rendre inévitable' 'Une sourde conspiration contre la paix d'Europe'. Cf. with this pronouncement of a 'legal' committee 'after an examination of the relevant documents', the well-balanced, objective judgment of the French historian Pierre Renouvin in his 'La crise Européenne et la grande guerre, 1904—1918'. Paris.

neutrality but also on the launching of an aggressive war [1]). In support of this proposal they contended that: "Le droit pénal international est encore à ce premier stade de l'évolution où le droit se forme par réaction contre le fait, où la peine ne s'appuie que sur la conscience du juge, et où le juge lui-même n'apparaît que pour sauver le criminel de la vengeance" [2]).

But while this opinion was in substance rejected in the first paragraph of the Commission's conclusions, because of its complete groundlessness in positive law, the idea of a formal tribunal was retained on a non-legal basis in the third: "Sur l'ensemble des faits qui ont amené la guerre mondiale et qui en ont accompagné le début, notamment la violation de la neutralité du Luxembourg et de la Belgique, il appartient à la Conférence de la Paix d'examiner s'il ne conviendrait pas, devant une situation absolument sans précédent, d'adopter des mésures spéciales et même d'établir un organe spécial pour traiter comme ils le méritent les auteurs de ces faits". This suggestion the cautious formulation of which manifests its compromising and controversial character, was retained by the Peace Conference and found, with the Commission's allegation of Wilhelm's moral responsibility for war-crimes, its way into Article 227, where both responsibilities are comprised under the formula 'supreme offence against international morality and the sanctity of treaties'.

One is inclined here to draw a conclusion similar to that from the Allied Powers proceeding against Napoleon more than a century before: while unwilling to recognize a change in general international law, which would be generally applicable and binding on its authors, the peacemakers of Versailles nevertheless wanted to proceed in an exceptional way against the enemy deemed guilty. But while in the case of Napoleon legal proceedings were for that reason renounced and only a safety measure was applied against a person dangerous for the international order, Wilhelm II, who no longer presented a danger for the peace – at least this was not taken into consideration or

---

1) F. Larnaude et A. De Lapradelle, Examen de la responsabilité pénale de l'Empereur Guillaume II d'Allemagne, Journal de Droit International, 1919, pp. 131–159.

2) Ibidem, p. 156.

referred to –, was to be charged on moral and political grounds in a legal proceeding.

The fourth conclusion of the Commission on this point: "Il serait désirable que désormais des sanctions pénales fussent prévus pour des violations aussi graves des principes les plus élémentaires du droit international" [1]) – remained without any consequence and was not even mentioned in the Peace Treaty, or later in the League of Nations. This fact aggravates the arbitrary character of the Commission's and the Conference's compromise, that was severely criticised by the U.S. delegation which stressed the contradiction between the first two and the third paragraphs and stated in its reservation on the Commission's report [2]) that moral crimes were susceptible of moral sanctions only. Acts like the breach of neutrality should be condemned and their authors *voués à l'exécration de l'humanité.*

The other arguments of the American delegation: the non-retroactivity of penal law, conceived as a dogma valid for international law, and, what was advanced also in the Japanese reservation, "that the heads of States are . . . responsible to the people . . . and that they are not and that they should not be made responsible to any sovereignty" are open to criticism at a moment of revolutionary change of an underdeveloped international law. But the Commission's conclusions and Article 227 – half-way house between law and morality, between judicial procedure and political action, between general rule and exceptional law – could not be regarded as an advance in international law.

The Dutch government, not a signatory to the Versailles Treaty, invited to associate itself with this "acte de haute politique internationale, imposé par la conscience universelle, dans lequel les formes du droit ont été prévues, uniquement pour assurer à l'accusé un ensemble de garanties tel que le droit public n'en a jamais connu", took with respect to this ambiguous act the side of positive law. It refused extradition of Wilhelm who had taken refuge in a country with a tradition of hospitality for political delinquents because the 'supreme offence etc.' of Article 227 did not occur in the Dutch Penal Code or in any extradition treaty

1) O.c., above, p. 66, nt. 3, p. 479.
2) Ibidem, Annexe II.

to which the Netherlands were party. Though the conditions the Dutch government laid down for its collaboration in international criminal trials were rather strict, the conclusion of its note pointed in the right direction: "Si dans l'avenir, il était institué par la Société des Nations une juridiction internationale compétente pour juger, dans le cas d'une guerre, des faits qualifiés de crime et soumis à des sanctions par un statut antérieur aux actes commis, il appartiendrait aux Pays Bas de s'associer à ce nouveau régime" [1]).

It was however neither the League nor individual governments that went further in this direction, but only private institutions and individuals. The President of the Drafting Committee for the Statute of the Permanent Court of International Justice, Baron Descamps, submitted a Project for an international criminal jurisdiction to be exercised by a special chamber of the Permanent Court on cases brought before it by the Assembly or the Council of the League of Nations and which would comprise among others crimes of aggression and crimes against security [2]). But the First Assembly deemed the Committee's recommendation premature because of the absence of a positive international penal law which, however, the States were unwilling to create.

The only other direct effort to etablish permanent international criminal jurisdiction was undertaken on the initiative of the French government after the assassination of King Alexander of Yugoslavia and the French Prime Minister Barthou in 1934, but the resulting convention of 1937, never ratified, was restricted to the individual crime of terrorism, did not envisage the cases of state-responsibility and made even the extradition of the criminals dependent on the existing law and jurisprudence of the different countries [3]).

The development of the doctrine of international penal law was, in the twenties, principally marked by the resolutions concerning the creation of an international criminal court

---

1) Quoted by Mouton, o.c., p. 110–111. See also A.J.I.L., vol. 14, 1920, pp. 95–154.

2) Mouton, o.c., p. 273–4. See also V. V. Pella, La guerre-crime et les criminels de guerre, Paris, 1946.

3) Convention of 16 November 1937, Geneva, for the prevention and punishment of terrorism.

adopted at the Conferences of the Interparliamentary Union, of 1925 (draft of Pella) and following years, at the Brussels Conference on the International Penal Law Association in 1926, (report of Pella and Donnedieu de Vabres), and at the Conferences of the International Law Association of 1924, in Buenos Aires, (draft statute of Bellot) and 1926, in Vienna, and by the publications of its pioneers like Pella, Donnedieu de Vabres, Saldaña, Caloyanni, Travers, Bellot and Politis [1]).

Apart from the necessity to assure impartiality, unity and a proper international, judicial technique in the adjudication of individual criminals, who were till now entirely left to the jurisdiction of the national courts of the victors or the defeated, the principal argument invoked for the creation of an international criminal jurisdiction was that only an international criminal court, based on proper international instruments, could punish the grave violations of international law committed by States or state-organs. And among these violations the crime of war and correlated crimes were regarded as the "real domain of international criminality" [2]).

The great question in this respect, one on which the different trends of criminal theory came into collision with each other, was that of the attribution of responsibility for this crime. The exclusive responsibility of the state collectivity was defended by Donnedieu de Vabres. Exclusive responsibility of the individual agents was defended by Phillimore, while Pella in his later publications on this question proposed a double — collective and individual — criminal responsibility. The Conference on International Penal Law in Brussels adopted in its resolutions the combined opinions of its two rapporteurs:

" (3) The Permanent Court (scil. invested with criminal juris-

---

1) V. V. Pella, La criminalité collective des Etats et le droit pénal de l'avenir, 2me éd. 1926, Bucarest.
H. Donnedieu de Vabres, Les principes modernes du droit pénal international, Paris 1928.
Q. Saldana, La justice pénale internationale, Recueil des Cours de l'Académie de Droit International, 1925, V. 10, pp. 223—429. N. Politis, The New Aspects of International Law, (Chapter III) Carnegie Pamphlet Series No. 19, Washington 1928. For full details of the different conferences and for detailed bibliography see Pella l.c., Mouton, o.c., pp. 271—290. For the early development cf. Premier Congrès de Droit Pénal, Bruxelles 1926, Actes du congrés, Paris, 1927.

2) Politis, o.c., p. 43.

diction) shall hear all cases for penal responsibilities against States consequent upon an unjust aggression and for violations of International Law. It will impose penal sanctions and measures of security upon the offending State.

"(4) The Permanent Court shall hear cases of individual responsibilities which may arise from the crimes of aggression as well as crimes and accessory crimes and all violations of International Law committed in time of peace or in time of war" [1]).

In theory both categories of responsibilities, individual and collective, are quite tenable, this particularly in the age of democracy, in which, within limits and with necessary differentiation, it can be said that practically every nation has the government it demands or at least brings to power, even if it is, or turns out to be, a totalitarian one.

While individual responsibility should be the basis, the state-collectivity could very well be thought to become the subject of repressive justice. But in view of real international relations, this collective penal responsibility seems theoretical. Pella elaborated in his Draft International Penal Code a whole series of possible punishments to be inflicted on the guilty national collectivity. And in a post-war publication he argues that the security measures taken by the victors against the defeated nations should be taken as the consequence of a condemnation of those nations, whose situation would not be different for that but who would in that case know that they had bent for justice and not for the sword [2]). But apart from the question whether these proceedings would have the psychological effect Pella expects from them, the main objection must be that measures which have in any case to be taken, and will always be taken, by the victor for reasons of political and strategic security and order, could never in substance be characterized as punishment.

Criminal law concerns human beings and even if one admits that they could be held criminally responsible for their conduct as a group, one may never lose sight of the fact that the collectivity and most of all the collectivity in the international society, the

---

1) English text quoted by Mouton, o.c., p. 281, from the International Law Association Report, on the 34th Conference, Vienna, August 5th—11th, 1926, London, 1927.

2) V. V. Pella, Fonctions pacificatrices du droit pénal et fin du système traditionel des traités de paix, R.G.D.I.P. 1947, tome II, pp. 1—27.

State, being a group of human beings, has at the same time an existence of its own, only indirectly human, insofar as its aim is to care for the common good. Also in its treatment in international relations the State's exercise of this function must be given primary consideration and the duties it has to fulfill as such must prevail over considerations of retribution. Man may be held criminally responsible because he has his aim in himself, according to his own conscience. The State exists and acts not for an aim in itself but for a specific purpose, that is in its care for men, which must guide its actions as well as the measures which are applied to it. And at the same time, the conception of state criminality could lead to the dangerous idea of war itself as a punishment, which it is not one of the least merits of the leaders of the *bellum justum* school to have fought successfully [1]).

The international sanctions as against aggressive war, provided for in Article 16 of the Covenant, having not a punitive but a security character, could from the point of view of international penal law be envisaged only as an executive action to break the resistance of the State, to stop and deliver the criminals acting through it, as a police action for the seizing of delinquents [2]).

The discussions and projects mentioned remained entirely theoretical however, until the outbreak of the Second World War. The States were not willing to accept effective international sanctions, let alone a criminal jurisdiction, which would still further radically destroy the notion and reality of state sovereignty that was so jealously maintained. On the level of municipal law, where as a complementary object the doctrine of international penal law tried to introduce the penalization of the acts for which it proposed, as a more perfect solution, an international criminal jurisdiction, no direct legislation with regard to the criminality of resort to aggressive war was undertaken, while the 'conventional' war crimes entered most penal codes. Though the principle of the interdiction of resort to war was incorporated in the constitutions of Spain and several South American States [3]), no country in the 20th century went so far as

[1]) Cf. above p. 132, and also Wehberg, o.c. 107.

[2]) See below, Ch. V, section 3.

[3]) See enumeration in Wehberg, o.c. pp. 108 ff.. and Mirkíne-Guetzévitch, l.c. pp. 243 ff..

Mirabeau's decree, penalizing resort to unjust war, adopted by the Constituante on 22 May 1791 [1]).

Before 1939 the only concrete effects of the movement for an international penal law, at this point parallel to the movement for 'outlawry' of war — to which however the idea of penalization was strange —, was the 'condemnation' of war as an instrument of national policy, and the growth of the 'custom' to qualify aggressive war, in resolutions and preambles of treaties, with the term 'crime', without proper legal significance and therefore without proper legal effects.

---

1) The pioneers of international penal laws, in various countries, were, however, very active in putting forward proposals for the introduction of offences against the peace in municipal criminal codes. See, for a survey of these efforts, the Memorandum concerning a Draft code of Offences against the Peace and Security of Mankind, (written by Professor Pella). I.L.C. 2nd session, U. N. Doc. A/CN. 4/39, 24 November 1950.

CHAPTER IV

THE PUNISHMENT FOR AGGRESSIVE WAR

SECTION 1. THE SECOND WORLD WAR

The rules instituting and governing the trial of the German 'Major War Criminals' were, so far as the crime of 'planning, preparation, initiation or waging of war of aggression' [1]) is concerned, in the fullest sense *in causa posita*. Before 1939, as is evident from the previous chapter, no penal rule existed in international law concerning such a 'crime', as existed concerning war crimes, violations of the laws and customs of warfare.

Those laws and customs were, before 1939, part of international law, largely codified by the Hague Conventions of 1899 and 1907, and by the Geneva Conventions of 1929; a violation of these laws and customs was generally regarded as a criminal act over which the belligerent States, having secured custody of the offender, had jurisdiction [2]). The innovation brought about by the Charter of the Nuremberg Tribunal in this respect was chiefly a jurisdictional one. The restriction of the plea of superior

---

1) Charter of the International Military Tribunal, Art. 6 (a) in Report of Robert H. Jackson, United States Representative to the International Conference of Military Trials, London 1945, Department of State Publication 3080, released February 1949, Washington D.C.. (Further quoted as Jackson report).

2) See Report of the Commission on the Responsibilities etc. of 1919, o.c.. Also Oppenheim Lauterpacht, Vol. II. Seventh Edition, London 1950, pp. 566—7 and 587—8, and History of the U.N.W.C.C., pp. 29 ff. Theory and practice demonstrate however divergent views on the principle of jurisdiction involved. While in the U.S.A. jurisdiction over war criminals is preferably based on the universal principle, whereby the war crime is considered as a *delictum juris gentium* like piracy, British courts and authors show a preference for the protective principle. The territorial principle gives a smaller scope for jurisdiction over enemy war criminals. Cf. E. J. Janeczek, o.c., pp. 53—67; Mouton, o.c. pp. 358—362, William B. Cowles, Universality of Jurisdiction over War Crimes, California Law Review 1945, pp. 177—218.

orders and the elimination of the pleas of official position and of impunity for the same act under domestic law [1]) being not entirely without precedent [2]), the trial *by an international tribunal* of those violators of the laws of war 'whose offences had no particular geographical localization' [3]) was, on the issue of ordinary war crimes, the only new feature of Nuremberg.

The remarkable fact about the *ex post facto* penalization of aggressive war in the London Charter is that the idea did not arise when, between September 1st 1939 and December 8th 1941, the Axis countries launched their aggressive wars that brought about the Second World War, but only much later. The idea of punishing resort to war itself only appeared after the United Nations, shocked by the reports of the abominable wholesale war crimes and mass murders committed by the enemy, had decided to punish the authors, and only after these wars started by the Axis countries had reached their peak of misery and atrocity.

This fact becomes evident, not only from the growth of the plan to punish the resort to war but still more from an analysis of the Nuremberg Verdict in which the punishment of aggressive war is most often justified by reason of the criminality it entails. In other words: the *causa* in which the rule concerning the punishment of aggressive war is established appears to be the starting of such a war not in itself but taken in connection with its criminal consequences, taken as the beginning of a whole criminal proceeding which is the proper and fundamental foundation of its penalization. The Declaration of St. James's

---

1) Respectively Articles 8, 7 and 6 (c) of the Charter, and principles IV, III and II of the Nuremberg principles as defined by the International Law Commission, see report covering its second session, U.N. Doc. A/CN. 4/34 (2 Aug. 1950), pp. 32–34.

2) For precedents of the restriction of the plea of superior orders, see Janeczek, o.c., pp. 68–78; regarding the pleas of head of State and official position (the latter sometimes referred to as the plea of act-of-State) see Glueck, War Criminals, Chapters VII and VIII, and so far as the crime against peace is concerned, below Section IV of this Chapter; the plea of impunity under domestic law becomes irrelevant with the adoption of the concept of 'international crime' – first with respect to war crimes *stricto sensu*.

3) Moscow Declaration on German atrocities made by President Roosevelt, Prime Minister Churchill and Marshall Stalin, on October 30, 1943: "The above declaration is without prejudice to the case of the major criminals whose offences have no particular geographical location and who will be punished by a joint decision of the Governments of the Allies".

Palace of January 13th 1942, made by the representatives of the Governments of nine occupied European countries and referring to previous similar statements by the President of the United States and the British Prime Minister, stated: "Whereas Germany, since the beginning of the present conflict which arose out of her policy of aggression, has instituted in the Occupied countries a régime of terror characterised amongst other things by imprisonments, mass expulsions, the execution of hostages and massacres, ...

(the undersigned)

3) place among their principal war aims the punishment, through the channels of organised justice, of those guilty or responsible for those crimes, whether they have ordered them, perpetrated them, or participated in them, ...".

Thus, although reference was made to Germany's responsibility for the war, the plan for punishment was explicitly restricted to war crimes *stricto sensu*. It remained so in the succeeding notes and declarations of Allied governments [1]), including the fundamental Moscow Declaration of November 1st 1943 which only refers to 'atrocities, massacres and executions' and warns "those who have not yet imbrued their hands with the blood of innocent lives" not to join the ranks of the guilty. The announcement of punishment of the 'major criminals' 'by joint decision of the Governments of the Allies', can only be understood within the limits of the aforementioned crimes.

A few days afterwards, on the sixth of November 1943, Marshal Stalin announced "measures to ensure that all the fascist criminals who are responsible for this war and for the suffering the peoples have endured shall meet with stern punishment and retribution for all the crimes they have committed, no matter in what country they may hide" [2]). Though this

---

1) The instruments quoted and the other principal declarations, notes and proposals concerning the punishment of the war criminals are inserted in: History of the United Nations War Crimes Commission and the Development of the Laws of War, London 1948, Chapter V. See also Glueck, The Nuremberg Trial and Aggressive War, New York, 1946, Appendix B, and Mouton, o.c. pp. 141—162.

2) J. Staline, Sur la grande guerre de l'Union Soviétique pour le salut de la patrie, 5me éd.. Editions à langue étrangère, Moscou 1946, p. 120. This was stated to be the third Allied war aim. Earlier in the same speech the announcement "we will force the German criminals to answer for all their misdeeds" is only preceded by 'ordinary' war crimes and atrocities by 'the army of barbarians and bandits', ibidem p. 116.

statement was adopted immediately afterwards by the Commission on the Punishment of War Criminals of the London International Assembly [1]), as a reference to the punishment for crimes against peace, this idea is far from being clearly expressed in the quoted sentence. The addition 'for all the crimes... etc', could as well be taken to refer only to the 'ordinary war crimes' that were mentioned in the Declaration of January 1942, which also was accompanied by an indication of the responsibility for the war as such. In the light of the subsequent hesitant attitude towards a punishment for aggressive war on the part of the Russian delegates at the London Conference in 1945, a less revolutionary interpretation of Stalin's statement appears to be more consistent (see below, second section of this chapter).

Some weeks later in a statement of the leaders of the United States, England and the United Kingdom, released on December 1st 1943, at the Cairo Conference, it was said: "The Three Great Allies are fighting this war to restrain and punish the aggression of Japan" [2]). However, it is also doubtful if this statement was intended to convey any idea of individual punishment for the crime against peace. In the first place the Cairo statement makes no other reference to the punishment of war criminals: the quoted sentence is followed by an enumeration of the territories conquered by Japan that must be restituted. The term 'punish' in such a context appears to have been used in a non-criminal sense, indicating solely the international sanction of the Stimson-doctrine (see above, Chapter III).

Secondly, even the Potsdam Declaration appearing nearly two years later speaks only of the intention that "stern justice shall be meted out to all war criminals, including those who have visited cruelties upon our prisoners" [3]). And, one year later, in

---

1) See History U.N.W.C.C., o.c. pp. 100—101, and Mr. B. V. A. Röling, Strafbaarheid van de agressive oorlog, Groningen 1950, quotation on p. 20. The proposal was made by the Czechoslovak member of the Commission, Dr. Ecer, the same who later proposed the punishment for the launching of the war in the U.N.W.C.C.. See below, pp. 180 ff.

2) Official Transcript of Tokyo Trial, Prosecutions Exhibit No. 1. Keenan and Brown, o.c. below p. 201, note 1, consider this statement as an "umistakable declaration — that Japanese war leaders would be punished for the international crime of aggressive war" (p. 25).

3) Published 26 July 1945, while the London Conference for the Drafting of the Nuremberg Charter was already in session.

his commemoration address at the 27th anniversary of the October Revolution, speaking of the means of making aggression impossible, Stalin refers only to international organisation and not to the punishment of the aggressors [1]).

Consequently it may be said that in the entire course of the Second World War, until 1945, no Allied statesman definitely indicated a plan to punish the German and Japanese war leaders as authors of the aggressions by which that war was initiated and extended. The issue in a concrete form was brought up for the first time in the United Nations War Crimes Commission, established on October 20th 1943 and consisting of the representatives of 17 Allied governments, Soviet Russia not participating. Though its terms of reference included only investigation and recording of evidence of war crimes and the making of reports to the Governments concerned [2]), the Commission dealt also with important questions of substantive law. In March 1944, some months after the meeting of the War Crimes Commission of the London International Assembly mentioned above, the Czechoslovak member of the U.N.W.C.C., Dr B. Ecer, proposed to the legal Committee that the Axis leaders be charged with the 'launching and waging of the second World War' which should be considered as the 'paramount crime' [3]).

It is worth while recalling his reasoning as an illustration of what was said before about the real foundation of the plan to punish the authors of the war, which war not the conception of aggressive war as a criminal act in itself, but the conviction that the initiation of this particular war, as a chain of criminality, was a criminal act. "The criminal nature of the last war was found (according to the Czechoslovak delegate) to derive from its aims and methods. The aims were to enslave foreign nations, to destroy their civilisations and physically to annihilate a considerable section of the population on racial, political and religious grounds. The methods arose from the fact that this was a 'total' war which disregarded all humanitarian considerations lying at the root of the laws and customs of war, and introduced indiscriminate means of warfare and barbaric methods of

1) Staline, o.c., p. 157.
2) History U.N.W.C.C., o.c., p. 113.
3) L.c., p. 180.

occupation" [1]). In a minority report of a special subcommittee established to study this issue the Czechoslovak delegate expressed himself even more clearly: the Commission should decide only "whether the Second World War was a crime, and not whether this was the case with any aggressive war in general" [2]). He added another argument: as soon as international law deprived aggressive war of its legality, the latter automatically resolved into "a chain of crimes" punishable by the heaviest penalties.

The outcome of his proposal to the U.N.W.C.C. is most interesting. It met with the initial approval of the legal committee but was referred back to that body for closer study by the plenary commission which felt that governments might be 'reluctant to go so far'. It was re-examined in a special subcommittee consisting of four members the majority of whom supported the British expert, Sir Arnold McNair, who maintained that "only if it could be shown that a State had committed a criminal act the human agents responsible for it could properly be indicted for having procured that act". The *lex lata* on which the concept of punishable war should be based, recognized, in the case of a State's breach of a rule of international law, a situation analogous to a breach of contract or delict, not a crime. He referred to the 1919 qualification 'act of high international policy' and contended that the Kellogg-Briand Pact had effected no change on this point: it made war illegal, but did not convert the aggressor State into a *caput lupinum,* it did not enlarge the category of acts which international law permits States to punish as criminal. And in any event, the launching of a war could never be called a 'war crime' (with which alone the Commission was concerned).

The majority report resembles to a remarkable degree the conclusions which the Commission on Responsibilities had reached in 1919 [3]). *Lege lata,* aggression was not considered a war crime; such grave outrages of international law should, however, be the subject of 'a formal condemnation in the peace treaties', and, after 25 years, the aspiration of 1919 was repeated textually: "It is desirable that, for the future, penal sanctions

---

1) Ibidem.
2) L.c., p. 182.
3) Ibidem. For the report of 1919 see above, p. 168.

should be provided for such grave outrages against the elementary principles of international law".

While the legal committee agreed this time with the majority report of its subcommittee, it was in the plenary commission that the Czechoslovak arguments found support, among others from the future president of the Commission, the Australian delegate, Lord Wright. His arguments, like those of other delegates, turned principally around the distinction between *lex lata* and *lex ferenda* introduced by McNair whose conception of the former was strongly attacked as being inapplicable to international law. As in English Common Law, Lord Wright argued, where there was no specific statutory agreement making murder a crime – which it incontestably was – so the rules of international law were to be extracted from many sources. Absence of a *lex lata* prevented arraignment and conviction of an accused in a case of doubt, not in that of aggressive war the criminal nature of which, besides being declared as such in the Kellogg-Briand Pact, was "recognised by a general consensus of authoritative opinion" [1]).

Very interesting are the arguments of the Yugoslav member of the Commission who drew a clear distinction between the illegality of aggressive war, on which everybody agreed, and its criminality "in the sense of penal law" regarding which the difference of opinion existed. For him also, the *lex lata* in international law evolved "from such sources as the dictates of public conscience and the laws of humanity" (terms borrowed from the Preamble of the Convention concerning the laws and customs of War on Land of 1907). The Hague and Geneva Conventions embody the laws and customs of war without defining their violation as 'war crimes' and without attaching to the prohibited acts penal sanctions – which, however, were generally recognized and applied in practice. The same development should be recognized with respect to aggressive war which was clearly prohibited by the Kellogg Pact. Later, on instructions of his Government, he also added that, as peace was indivisible and as total war exposed entire populations to destruction, aggressive war was 'a crime against the international community as a whole and against all the nations'.

1) L.c., p. 183.

In this discussion, which took place in October 1944, the Commission was equally divided. The delegates of Greece, the United States and especially France (which consistently opposed the criminality of aggressive war at the London Conference [1]) ten months later) actively supported the majority report mentioned previously. For this reason, and because of the importance of the question, it was decided to postpone a decision till the delegates had had the opportunity to get instructions from their governments. As the question of the punishment of the authors of the war was for many delegates linked up with the question whether aggressive war was a 'war crime' coming within the scope of the Commission, the President asked the members to leave the latter question out of the decision to be taken. He stated that otherwise some delegates who were opposed only to the competence of the Commission, in the matter of aggressive war, would seem to be against the punishment of the Axis leaders, which was favoured by the Allied leaders. In Lord Wright's opinion the question of the punishment for aggression and that of the punishment of the Axis leaders seemed thus to be identical [2]).

Though several members transmitted the opinion of their respective governments to the effect that those responsible for launching a war should be regarded as war criminals within the scope of action of the Commission, no decision was taken. A lack of instructions to other delegates seems to have been one of the reasons for this. The Commission, and many Governments behind it, seem to have been hesitant to take a decision which would not only constitute an innovation in the plans for post-war punishment, but could also be expected to have radical consequences for all Members of the international community.

At the approach of the United Nations Conference on Inter-

---

1) See second section of this Chapter.

2) O.c., Ibidem. While definite plans were known regarding the punishment of the normal war criminals, the quoted sentence of the Moscow declaration was for one and a half years the only announcement with respect to the punishment of the major war criminals, the 'joint decision' being taken only at the London Conference. The field of their responsibility for the unprecedented amount of misery and atrocity was all this time open to all possible kinds of legal constructions, while between the governments the fundamental question — trial or summary execution — remained undecided till the end of the war.

national Organisation the Czechoslovak member of the U.N.W. C.C. suggested that agreement between the governments on the question of the punishment for aggression should be sought in San Francisco. This suggestion was rejected but a report of the Commission was submitted and examined by the Enforcement Committee in San Francisco. Two recommendations resulted from this examination: one concerning the future, the other as to the interpretation of existing law. On the basis of paragraph 4 of Chapter II of the Dumbarton Oaks proposals (later amended to Article 2, paragraph 4, of the Charter) the following rule was recommended: "Any person, in the service of any State, who has violated any rule of international law concerning the threat or use of force, or any rule concerning warfare, especially the obligation to respect the generally recognized principles of humanity, shall be held individually responsible for these acts, and may be brought to trial and punishment before the civil or military tribunals of any State which may secure custody of his person" [1]).

While this recommendation, foreshadowing some of the 'Nuremberg principles', met with general agreement, the discussion on the other question – whether the Second World War was a crime from the point of view of existing law – showed again considerable difference of opinion. France and several other States once again answered the question in the negative. The meaning and effect of the main foundation of the criminality of war, the Kellogg Pact, was found to be 'ambiguous'. Yet the following formula was drafted: "It being the original intent and meaning of the Kellogg-Briand Pact . . . that any person in the service of any Party-State who violated its provisions . . . should be held individually responsible for these acts, it is declared that the aggressions of the Axis States since the signing of the Pact violated its provisions and that *the persons in the service of such Axis States* are individually responsible for such acts and may be brought to trial and punishment before any United Nations Court or other tribunal of competent jurisdiction which

---

1) U.N.C.I.O. 103 (April 4, 1945). Recommendation to Governments concerning penal sanctions for the threat and use of force (adopted by the Third Commission on May 3, 1945).

may secure custody of such persons or any of them" [1]).

This curious recommendation of a political committee, giving a rather indefinite extent to the criminal responsibility for the war, was nevertheless adopted by the Enforcement Committee and afterwards by the Third Commission, so that it constitutes the first definite recognition by an intergovernmental body that the launching of the war constitutes a punishable offence. The Conference as a whole, however, did not deal with this subject, and the recommendation of the Third Commission to the various governments remained, therefore, an incidental pronouncement of a subordinate body on a matter not specifically entrusted to it.

As it was felt by different States that the Conference was only concerned with the future and that no statement on past events or instruments could enter the Charter, the two recommendations quoted before were submitted in separate documents. Yet no reference to the criminality of aggressive war or the punishment of war-criminals, dealt with in the former recommendation, was inserted in the Charter. The "collective measures for the prevention and removal of threats to the peace and for the suppression of acts of aggression or other breaches of the peace" in Article 1, paragraph 1, refer exclusively to the international sanctions to be applied by the Security Council and enumerated in Chapter VII. Criminal law and criminal jurisdiction as means to prevent and repress violations against peace, and as possible reinforcements of the collective security system, did not gain the attention of the drafters of the final version of the Charter in San Francisco.

The discussions on the criminality of the war which were held at this period have been dealt with rather extensively because they contain the essence of the entire discussion on the criminality of aggressive war which took place at the drafting of the Nuremberg Charter, at the Nuremberg and subsequent trials, and which continues till the present day in the International Law Commission, in the Sixth Committee of the General Assembly, in international legal associations and in legal and political

---

1) Italics supplied. U.N.C.I.O., 104 (April 4, 1945), recommendation to Governments concerning the interpretation of the Kellogg-Briand Pact (adopted by the Third Commission on May 3, 1945).

literature. The different aspects of this problem: the scope of the Kellogg Pact, the scope in international law of the rule *nullum crimen, nulla poena sine praevia lege poenali,* the nature of the development of international law and its sources, the question of state criminality and that of individual penal responsibility, the difference between illegality and criminality in a penal sense and the political question of the desirability of punishment for aggression – all these aspects of one of the most vital problems of present day international law arose the first moment the issue was brought up in a concrete form.

The terminological confusions regarding 'international crime' and 'the criminality of the war', the changing attitude of the War Crimes Commission which only gradually, as it were, became aware of the real issues involved in the proposal, and its final hesitation are striking features of the birth of a new concept in international law: criminal war. It was only in the course of the discussions that a more precise concept of the criminality of the initiation of the war emerged from the broad notion of over-all, paramount responsibility on the part of the Axis leaders for the individual crimes and criminal practices as a whole. And all the time the notion of criminality remained more attached to the 'total war', to 'this war', than to aggressive war in the abstract; only a few opinions were expressed in favour of a general penal rule concerning the latter. This was evident from the London Conference where the French, and to a certain extent the Russian, delegates wanted to restrict criminality to the "policy of aggression ... and domination ... carried out by the European Axis Powers".

It is also a remarkable fact that, while the criminality of aggressive war was heralded in several pre-war resolutions (see previous Chapter, section 6), legal literature on the punishment of war criminals during the war hardly discussed this idea [1]). Prof. Sheldon Glueck, who was later to defend

[1]) The question is dealt with, and answered in the negative, by G. Manner, The Legal Nature and Punishment of Criminal Acts of Violence Contrary to the Laws of War, A.J.I.L. 1943 (vol. 37) pp. 407–435; the idea is proposed, as a consequence of the violation of the Pact of Paris, by A. G. D. Levy, The Law and Procedure of War Crime Trials, American Political Science Review, 1943 (vol. 37), pp. 1051–1081; Röling, o.c., p. 20, mentions Hermann Mannheim, War and Crime, who suggests punishment for aggressive war on p. 171. One of the reasons for this silence on the subject in legal literature before

the Nuremberg concept of criminal war, is one of the exceptions as he combats the idea in his book on *War Criminals* of 1944 [1]). Schwarzenberger defended the outlawry of the totalitarian aggressors but only with regard to international sanctions not to individual punishment [2]). The Russian Prof. A. N. Trainin, on the contrary, devised in his book *Hitlerite Responsibility under Criminal Law* a whole system of 'crimes against peace' as 'international crimes' for which the Axis leaders could be punished [3]). But the subject only began to occupy a central place in legal literature after the penalisation of aggressive war in the Nurem-

---

the end of the war is certainly the absence of Continental European literature during this time, as it was in Europe, and particularly in French language publications, that the doctrine of international penal law and the notion of the criminality, of aggressive war found their principal upholders.

1) O.c.. In War Criminals, Glueck argues that a prosecution for an unjust war violating the sanctity of treaties 'would draw a red herring across the trial and confuse the much clearer principle of liability for atrocities committed during the conduct of a war, be it a just or an unjust one'. He considered — like Manner, o.c. — that the Kellogg Pact did not make its violation a punishable offence, that in any case the major war criminals could be punished for their other crimes, and that — under the concept of criminal war — all German military acts, whether or not in violation of the laws of war, could be branded as illegal (o.c. pp. 37—39). The last argument is directed against the opinion — voiced for example by the Czech member of the U.N. W.C.C., quoted before p. 181, — that as soon as war was deprived of its legality under international law, it automatically resolved into 'a chain of crimes'. This same reasoning is found in the opening statement of the French Delegate at the Counsel of the Prosecution in Nuremberg, Francois de Menthon, Trial of the Major War Criminals, o.c., below p. 208, note 2, Vol. V, p. 387.

2) G. Schwarzenberger, International Law and Totalitarian Lawlessness, 1943. He specially relies on the sanctions of the Paris Pact, as stated in the Budapest Articles of Interpretation (see Chapter III, above, p. 162).

3) A. N. Trainin, Hitlerite Responsibility under Criminal Law, edited by A. Y. Vishinsky, London, 1945, p. 36 ff.. His propositions, which are in line with the pre-war doctrine of international penal law, look rather abstract as he says on p. 93 that the crimes of the Hitler clique are "so vast and indisputable that substantially there is no necessity for a special investigation and judicial procedure for the determination and judgment of the monstrous misdeeds they have committed. The fate of Hitler and his clique can be settled by the political verdict of the victorious powers". This interpretation of what the 'joint decision' was going to be (substantially the same as the English attitude) seems to be more in line with the official Soviet attitude till the end of the London Conference. Also in the light of the foregoing analysis of Stalin's 1943 speech, one feels inclined to disagree with Röling (o.c., pp. 20—21) who traces the origin of the idea of punishment for aggression to Stalin and sees Trainin's book as a further elaboration of that idea. Also G. A. Finch, The Nuremberg Trial and International Law, A.J.I.L. 1947, pp. 20—37, pp. 28—29, erroneously traces this idea to Russian influence.

berg Charter [1]). Both the opponents and the champions of the criminality of aggressive war revealed themselves only after the notion had been officially adopted.

Though, as related, the legal committee of the London International Assembly, referring to Marshal Stalin's October speech, put "the waging of aggressive war and all other acts of aggression" as a specific item on its list of war crimes [2]), the impression is made that the juridical world was rather hesitant to voice an opinion. While on the one hand, as appears notably from the discussions in the U.N.W.C.C., it was generally felt that there was a criminality broader and more fundamental than the concrete war crimes and atrocities for which the Nazi leaders should be punished – a *culpa in causa* that did not exclude the *culpa in actu* – there was on the other hand a general hesitation among the jurists about the definition of this criminality which arose from a reflection on the state of positive international law.

As will appear from the following account of the London Conference and of the succeeding drafts that resulted in the Nuremberg Charter, it was finally non-juridical factors that carried the adoption of the notion of criminal war and the punishment for this crime in the judgements of Nuremberg and subsequent trials.

SECTION 2. THE CHARTER OF LONDON

In a memorandum from the Secretaries of State and War and the Attorney General, prepared to guide President Roosevelt in discussions on this subject at the Yalta Conference, it was stated as the United States attitude that "the criminality of the German leaders and their associates does not consist solely of individual outrages, but represents the result of a systematic and planned reign of terror ... (that) goes back at least as far as 1933 when Hitler was first appointed Chancellor of the Reich". Consequently it was recommended that "the German leaders and the organisations employed by them ... should be charged both with the commission of their atrocious crimes, and also with joint participation in a broad criminal enterprise which

1) See below, Section 4.
2) L.c., above, p. 179, nt. 1.

included and intended these crimes, or was reasonably calculated to bring them about". And the allegation of the criminal enterprise should "permit full proof of the entire Nazi plan from its inception and the means used in its furtherance and execution, including the pre-war atrocities ... as well as the waging of an illegal war of aggression with ruthless disregard for international law and the rules of war" [1]).

It appears from a close examination of these texts that 'the waging of an illegal war of aggression' was not yet quite clearly formulated as constituting an independent crime, but – contrary to the 'atrocious crimes' – only entered the proposed accusation as a means 'in execution and furtherance' of a 'broad criminal enterprise'. It was proposed as a component of a charge of criminal planning, by which specific concept of Anglo-Saxon law the criminal responsibility of the Nazi leaders *as a group* was to be covered. And even so, the waging of an *illegal war* was not separated from the violation of the rules of warfare.

The initial British attitude, formulated in an aide-mémoire of April 23, 1945, was against the ambitious American plan for an elaborate public trial of the major war criminals. Instead the British Government proposed the summary execution of 'the arch criminals' "for their conduct leading up to the war and for the wickedness ... in the conduct of the war". The British arguments were that a trial for "the totality of offences against the international standard which civilised countries try to observe" would take too long and could be turned against the Allies, and notably that it was not clear that "unprovoked attacks ... can properly be described as crimes under international law"; and further, that such a charge "would at any rate give the accused the opportunity of basing their arguments on what has happened in the past and what has been done by various countries in declaring wars which resulted in acquiring new territory, which certainly were not regarded at the time as crimes against international law" [2]).

After the American memorandum to the Foreign Ministers

---

[1]) Published in Jackson report, o.c., pp. 3 ff.: Memorandum to President Roosevelt from the Secretaries of State and War and the Attorney General, January 22, 1945.

[2]) Jackson Report, o.c., pp. 18–20.

in San Francisco, of April 30, 1945, in which the preparation and launching of the war were again indicated as the result of an all embracing criminal plan and in which punishment after trial was primarily motivated by its deterrent effect, by its impetus to improved standards of international conduct and by its preservation of the moral force behind the Allied cause [1]), the British government accepted in principle the United States proposals [2]). The Provisional Government of the French Republic did the same, and finally, on June 14, also the Soviet Government agreed to the establishment of an international tribunal for trial of the principal war criminals [3]).

In the 'draft of definite proposal' accompanying the forementioned American memorandum, the item of war and aggression appeared for the first time not as part of a criminal enterprise, but in the form of not less than four separate criminal acts which were to be put to the charge of "the major war criminals, their principal agents and accessories, and all other offenders who are not sent back for trial to the countries in which their atrocities and crimes were committed". After war crimes *stricto sensu* there follow in this declaration:

"b. Invasion by force or threat of force of other countries in violation of international law or treaties.

c. Initiation of war in violation of international law or treaties.

d. Launching a war of aggression.

e. Recourse to war as an instrument of national policy or for the solution of international controversies" [4]).

The structure of these four 'criminal acts' was rather confused, and in the revised draft submitted to the London Conference in June [5]) the first and the second paragraph were combined while the last one — obviously referring to the Kellogg Pact — was omitted. Until the end of the conference the American delegation

---

1) American memorandum presented to the Foreign Ministers at San Francisco, 30 April, 1945, l.c., pp. 28—38.

2) British memorandum of May 28, 1945, with preceding note, l.c., p. 39.

3) Ibidem. See also Report to the President by Mr. Justice Jackson, June 6, 1945, l.c., p. 46.

4) L.c., p. 24.

5) Revision of American draft of proposed agreement, June 14, 1945, l.c., pp. 55—60, art. 12.

adhered to the separate listing of invasion and initiation of war in violation of international law and treaties on the one hand, and the launching of a war of aggression, as a criminal act in itself, on the other. The controversial juxtaposition of 'war of aggression' and 'war in violation of international treaties, agreements and assurances' in article 6 (a) of the Charter is the result of this American insistence that, irrespective of special treaties and particular assurances, aggressive war has been outlawed and is considered a crime by the community of States.

The formulation of resort to war, and particularly aggressive war, as a separate international crime, – apart from the method of warfare, apart from the concrete Nazi-policy, apart from the whole criminal plan – appears in this way to have developed, step by step, in successive American memoranda of the beginning of 1945, upto the emphatic four-fold definition quoted above. The motive behind this development towards an abstract definition and universal establishment of the 'crime of war' went beyond the actual trial of the enemy leaders. This was formulated in a report to the President of June 6, 1945 by Justice Jackson, the designated American Chief Prosecutor who was charged with the preparation of the trial and who at the London Conference carried the American idea through against the strong objections of the other delegates: "In arranging these trials we must also bear in mind the aspirations with which our people have faced the sacrifices of war ... it was the universal feeling of our people that out of this war should come unmistakable rules and workable machinery from which any who might contemplate another era of brigandage would know that they would be held personally responsible and would be personally punished. Our people have been waiting for this trial in the spirit of Woodrow Wilson, who hoped to 'give international law the kind of vitality which it can only have if it is a real expression of our moral judgment' " [1]).

Though the British Government agreed with the idea of a legal trial, they held a more conservative idea regarding the state of international law which in their view did not admit such an abstract definition of a crime of war, but only a punishment for

---

1) Quoted above, nt. 3, p. 190, l.c., p. 50. See also l.c., p. 53.

a concrete criminal policy. It was, however, principally the French delegation in London that was to defend the notion expressed in the British drafting amendments: to substitute for the four criminal acts formulated in the U.S. proposal the following: "Pursuing a systematic policy for the purpose of dominating Europe by a war of aggression and in the carrying out of that policy.

(1) Initiating and making attacks on other countries in violation of International Law, treaties or assurances.

(2) Resorting to war as an instrument of national policy" [1]).

The American solicitude for the invigoration of international law was, however, not shared by the Soviet Government which wanted solely an *ad hoc* tribunal and *ad hoc* provisions applicable to the 'major war criminals', but not binding for the future so in international law. The Russian delegation did not object much to the proposed definition of crimes, but wanted to have 'provision' of criminal acts instead of 'declaration' which implied universal validity [2]). And it was with their obstinate desire to have the phrase 'carried out by the European Axis Powers' included in the definition of the Crime of War that, consequently, at the Conference, the American attitude came in sharpest conflict [3]).

It is fascinating to read the verbatim records of the London Conference made available in the Jackson Report published by the State Department in 1949. More than six weeks of intensive debate were necessary to reconcile not only the political views of the four Governments but also the strongly held ideas on legal and especially procedural matters of the four conferees, representatives of widely divergent legal systems. If proof is needed of the intimate link between the fundamentals of a civilization and its penal law and procedure, one can find it in this account of the drafting of the first international penal charter, that seemed sometimes, due to unexpected obstacles, in danger of not being realized. Proceedings normal for the one were regarded by other delegates as a gross denial of justice, or,

1) L.c., p. 40.

2) Aide-mémoire from the Soviet Government, June 14, 1945, l.c., pp. 61—63, sub. 4.

3) See below, pp. 196—197.

on the contrary, as a menace to the successful course of the trial.

While on procedural questions the representatives of the Common Law countries found themselves confronted with the traditions of systems derived from Roman law, and with the purely inquisitorial Russian procedural rules, there was a remarkable *chassée croisée* on the issue of the nature and definition of the crimes to be charged. The codification countries, and especially France, where the doctrine of international penal law was nevertheless the furthest developed before the war, opposed, till the end of the conference, the previous formulation of punishable offences in the matter of aggressive war, and wanted instead to leave it to the tribunal to find the law in the concrete case. This was the more striking in the light of the French proposal of 1919 for the arraignment of the German ex-Emperor, which had then been opposed by the American delegates [1]). The same applies to Jackson's insistence on the insertion of the Litvinof definition of aggression which had always been rejected by the U.S. Government, but on this occasion was rejected by the Russian delegate.

The London Charter has been severely criticised on the ground that it was drawn up by representatives of the four Powers who were going to undertake the prosecution of the case for which they laid down the law [2]). The American and British delegates themselves were designated as Chief Prosecutors [3]). It cannot be denied that these delegates especially were, in their proposals, continuously alive to their coming task as prosecutors, and that the U.S. delegate, who had already taken cognizance in large part of the evidence collected, even drew many of his arguments con-

---

1) See above, p. 170.

2) See for example, Viscount Maugham, U.N.O. and War Crimes, London 1951, (with a postscript by Lord Hankey), p. 27.

3) The combination of functions — negotiator of the Agreement and Charter, and Prosecutor — was intended by the respective governments. See Executive order of President Truman, May 2, 1945, in Jackson Report, p. 21, and announcement of Prime Minister Churchill in the House of Commons on May 29, 1945, mentioned l.c., p. 45. Attorney-General Sir David Maxwell Fyfe was as British designated Chief Prosecutor after the British elections replaced by his successor, Attorney-General Sir Hartley Shawcross, but continued as first deputy. The Russian delegate to the London Conference, General Nikitchenko, was later nominated as Russian judge on the Tribunal, the French delegate, Judge Falco, became alternate French member of the Tribunal. Their respective assistants, Prof. Trainin and Prof. Gros, became deputies in the Prosecuting staffs of their countries.

cerning the proposed provisions from the possibilities that evidence offered for a successful building of the case.

While this objection holds in principle, one must not lose sight of the difference between the state of international law and relations in which this first international trial occurred and the fully developed municipal law systems, where penal proceedings can be governed by strict rules of law and a standing judicial organisation. If one admits the principle of individual liability for grave violations of international law, the right of the victorious Powers to improvise the organisation of a trial must also be admitted. The participation therein of other States, and of neutrals if they had consented to it, would not have made any difference in principle. Nor would it have made any difference, in principle, if the contracting parties in London had been represented in London by delegates other than the designated prosecutors. For in either case they would have been representatives of the same level, not acting upon their own views but on the instructions of their governments.

Moreover it must be recognized that the advantage of availability of evidence and the identity between drafters and future prosecutors were *in casu* hardly relevant. The evidence was abundant and unambiguous, and the provisions which were proposed to limit the defence and to avoid recriminations – like Jackson's proposal for a limited definition of aggression – did not enter the Charter.

Little as such a procedure is to be recommended for the future, its actual adoption cannot have diminished the right of the Allies to hold enemy persons criminally responsible for their acts – notably the preparation and waging of aggressive war – once that right and that individual responsibility are admitted, which are the points in question.

As stated, the opposition to the introduction in the Charter of individual liability for the 'crime of war' came from the French side on the ground of its non-conformity to existing international law, and from the Russian side on the ground that the conference could not make a general pronouncement on what constituted law but could only occupy itself with the present case against the Axis criminals. The English, after their initial opposition, confined themselves in the main to a mediatory role at the conference, in order to achieve a compromise between the conflicting views.

Apart from the procedural questions the question of the criminality of aggressive war and of the extent of that criminality turned out to be the most controversial of the conference. It was only settled at the last session after an interval in which the United States delegate consulted with his Government at the Potsdam Conference.

The divergent opinions of the delegates regarding this issue may be analysed in an examination of three questions involved: what was the nature of a declaration of criminal acts in the Charter?; what was the criminal act related to aggressive war and how should it, accordingly, be defined?; and on what basis could individual criminal liability for such a violation of international law be founded?

For the future of international law the most significant aspect of the Charter is that it contains in Article 6 a *declaration,* abstractly formulated and therefore universal in character, of 'crimes under international law'. Guided by this decision the tribunal gave a judgement on the basis of which the General Assembly could afterwards affirm the validity of the Nuremberg principles which were later formulated by the International Law Commission as the point of departure of a universal "Code of offences against the peace and security of mankind".

It was the American point of view, stubbornly defended by Justice Jackson, that the conference was called upon to *declare,* in the Charter, that the defendants were personally answerable for definite international crimes: "*International law is indefinite and weak in our support on that, as it has stood over the recent years.* This definition" (the French one, see below) "seems to me to leave the Tribunal in the position where it could be argued . . ., that no personal responsibility resulted if we failed to say it when we are making an agreement between the four powers *which fulfills in a sense the function of legislation.* I think there is greater liberty in us to declare principles as we see them now than there would be in a court to use *new principles* that we had failed to declare in an organic act setting up the court" [1]).

1) Italics supplied. Jackson Report, l. c., p. 331.

The French proposal to which Jackson objected attributed to the Tribunal "jurisdiction to try any person who has . . . directed the preparation and conduct of:

a) the policy of aggression against, and of domination over, other nations, carried out by the European Axis Powers in breach of treaties and in violation of international law;

b) . . .

c) . . .

and who is responsible for the violations of international law, the laws of humanity and the dictates of the public conscience..." [1]. The French delegation definitely wanted to leave it to the Tribunal to declare the criminal responsibility for the acts enumerated, because, contrary to those mentioned under b) and c) (atrocities against the civilian population and ordinary war crimes), the series of acts, the policy, defined under a) had not been 'declared or deemed' to be a criminal violation of international law. The American approach would amount to *ex post facto* legislation, by 'just four individuals', to 'settling a question as if we were a codification commission' [2].

Though supporting the French attitude, the Russian delegate, Prof. Trainin, took, in fact, a quite different view: "the question of declaration of law remains. That is, the four countries may, for the purposes of this trial, declare certain acts to be criminal; and for the purposes of this trial the laws declared by the Four Powers should be sufficient" [3]. Throughout the conference the Soviet delegation relied on the *ad hoc* political declaration of Axis criminality in the Moscow statement of 1943. As General Nikitchenko said *à propos* of a definition of aggression – "The policy which has been carried out by the Axis Powers has been defined as an aggressive policy in the various documents of the Allied Nations . . ., and the Tribunal would really not need to go into that . . . The fact that the Nazi leaders are criminals has already been established. The task of the Tribunal is only to determine the measure of guilt of each particular person

1) English translation of the draft article on the definition of crimes, submitted by the French delegation, July 19, 1945, l.c., p. 293. A similar, amended, draft was later submitted by the Soviet delegation, l.c., p. 327.

2) L.c., p. 335.

3) Ibidem.

and to mete out the necessary punishment – . . . ." [1]).

With respect to the second question, the determination and definition of the 'crime of war', it is not amazing that the Russian delegation at the one time proposed a definition of specific criminal acts, following the American line, and the next backed the French formulation of 'a policy of aggression and domination'. The question was rather irrelevant to them so long as the *ad hoc* character of the definition was clearly emphasized. They therefore insisted strongly on the introduction in the definition of the phrase 'carried out by the European Axis Powers'.

The suggested insertion was, of course, rejected outright by the U.S. delegation. As Jackson stated: "If it is a good rule of law, it should bind us all, and if not, we should not invoke it at this trial" [2]). It was, however, inconsistent with this attitude that, for reasons of expediency and limitation of the defence at the trial, the American delegation insisted on the insertion of an enumerative definition of aggression, which was at the time rejected by the American Government, strongly averse to all specifications of this concept proposed before or after the London conference [3]). Especially the final paragraph of that definition: "No political, military, economic or other considerations shall serve as an excuse or justification for such (aggressive) actions" would have amounted to an entirely 'partial' rule. As the French delegate, Prof. Gros, stated: "in this last paragraph (the draft) wants to dispose of the whole question of reprisals – the question of reprisals in international law is one existing for the last 500 years and you cannot wipe it out in just one word" [4]).

The motives for the American delegations proposal to charge not only "invasion and initiation of war in violation of international law, treaties" etc., but also the "launching of aggressive

1) L.c., p. 303.

2) L.c., p. 336.

3) See above Chapter II, p. 58. The U.S. squarely opposed every attempt to formulate aggression in the framework of the United Nations; see for example the U.S. delegate in the First Commission of the General Assembly, U.N. Doc. A/C. 1/SR. 386. p. 261 ff..

4) Jackson report, p. 381. See for the American-proposed definitions of aggression, pp. 294 and 375. Here as in the previous chapters there is of course only question of reprisals in interstate relations during peace time and not of reprisals taken against a belligerent or his subjects in order to retaliate for acts of illegitimate warfare.

war", as a separate crime, were closely connected with the policy of the United States in the beginning of the Second World War and its subsequent participation in it. And the arguments for this policy as well as for the new charge were drawn mainly from the Kellogg-Briand Pact. As it was argued at the conference: "Our attitude as a nation, in a number of transactions, was based on the proposition that this was an illegal war from the moment that it was started, and that therefore, without losing our rights as neutrals or non-belligerents, it was our right to extend aid to the nations under illegal attack, and the lend-lease program, the exchange of bases for destroyers, and much of American policy was based squarely on the proposition that a war of aggression is outlawed... Therefore, our view is that this is not merely a case of showing that these Nazi Hitlerite people failed to be gentlemen in war; it is a matter of their having designed an illegal attack on the international peace, which to our mind is a criminal offence by common-law tests, at least, and the other atrocities were all preparatory to it or done in execution of it" [1]). "The launching of war of aggression, regardless of agreements, treaties, or assurances is in itself, as it is in our judgment, a crime. We are supported by a course of dealings in which the countries have given up war as a means of promoting policy" [2]). "We want this group of nations to stand up and say, as we have said to our people... that launching a war of aggression is a crime... and that no political or economic situation can justify it... that the great crime of crimes of our century was the launching of a needless war in Europe... we want the Germans and anybody else to know that, as far as the United States is concerned, it regards any attack on the peace of the world as an international crime" [3]).

Prof. Gros stated the difference succinctly: "The Americans want to win the trial on the ground that the Nazi war was illegal, and the French people and other people of the occupied countries just want to show that the Nazis were bandits" [4]). While admitting the illegality of the war on the German side and while

---

1) L.c., p. 299.
2) L.c., p. 380.
3) L.c., p. 384.
4) L.c., p. 382.

determined to draw this illegality into the case, the French delegation did not want to "start from the top and say what will be a criminal violation of international law (but)... start from the bottom, say that there have been indisputable crimes and go up the line of responsibility to the instigator of the war" [1]). If Germany had only started a war of aggression, the French argument ran, without committing war crimes and atrocities, a court could never have been set up for the judgment of the members of the German Government [2]). Now it was a question of indirect accusation, with the court to decide whether on the basis of the facts put before it these defendants were war criminals: "There has been organized banditry in Europe. The result was crimes, and we want to show that those crimes have been executed by a common plan. The result of that will be to show that the Nazis have launched and conducted an illegal war" [3]).

The French put the emphasis on the construction of individual responsibility, the third point mentioned above and in the drafting of a penal charter the most important question. The statement that an act was a violation, a criminal violation, or even a crime under international law, did not, in their view, necessarily imply that the individual perpetrators of the act where criminally responsible for it. First of all, as observed before at the beginning of the third Chapter, the term 'crime' was, and is, used in several international documents to express a strong moral or political condemnation, without implying any idea of criminal responsibility. Secondly, at least in the pre-war theory of international penal law there existed the concept of state criminality, excluding or not necessarily implying individual criminality. Apart from the removal of the 'act of state' plea, a positive rule was necessary for individual statesmen to be held criminally responsible for acts recognized as criminal violations of international law. This rule was not inserted in the original drafts, in which it was merely stated that the Tribunal was bound to consider the enumerated acts as criminal violations of

1) L.c., p. 296.
2) L.c., p. 386.
3) L.c., p. 382.

International Law. The French admitted state responsibility for the criminal violation of the Kellogg Pact and of specific treaties and assurances, but wanted to leave it to the Tribunal to pronounce upon the responsibility of those 'who had directed or participated in the preparation or conduct of' the policy that resulted in and comprised these criminal violations.

The notion of a 'common plan or enterprise aimed at domination over other nations' had a different significance in the American drafts. It was seen as an additional charge, a crime separate from the more specific crime of aggressive war, the war crimes and the atrocities, but embracing them all so as to make all members of the criminal group responsible for all the crimes committed in execution of the plan and included in the enterprise [1]).

The real *novum* of the Charter, the new rule of individual responsibility for the crime of war and for the common plan of aggression and domination, was, after the French objections, made explicit in the introductory part of the American 'definition of crimes' which ran: "the following acts, or any of them, are crimes coming within its (the Tribunal's) jurisdiction for which there shall be individual responsibility ...". While for the Russian delegation the individual responsibility resulted only from the previous declarations of the Allied Powers, the American considered the attribution of that responsibility *in casu* as the consequence of a new rule, the first formulation of which was in the Charter a necessary and logical completion of international law, a normal and admissible process of development. As Justice Jackson said: "Now the difficulty ... is that there is no prescribed sanction, no criminal penalty provided for that kind of what we may call 'common law' crime of violation of international law. Neither is there a criminal sanction or penalty prescribed for the other violations of international law (war crimes and atrocities) which the French draft considers to be punishable. In other words, we have no statute which states any penalties or individual responsibilities for any offences under whatever formula we attempt to arraign them" [2]).

1) See U.S. draft, l.c., p. 169. See discussions, e.g. pp. 363 and 388.
2) L.c., p. 300.

After this lengthy analysis of the discussions in London, which seems, however, justified in view of the fundamental significance of the Nuremberg Charter as starting-point of the notion of 'criminal' war, it may be useful to quote the final text of Article 6 of the Charter on this point: "The Tribunal established by the Agreement referred to in Article 1 hereof for the trial and punishment of the major war criminals of the European Axis countries shall have the power to try and punish persons who, acting in the interests of the European Axis countries, whether as individuals or as members of organisations, committed any of the following crimes.

The following acts, or any of them, are crimes coming within the jurisdiction of the Tribunal for which there shall be individual responsibility:

(a) CRIMES AGAINST PEACE: namely, planning preparation, initiation or waging of a war of aggression, or a war in violation of international treaties, agreements or assurances, or participation in a common plan or conspiracy for the accomplishment of any of the foregoing;

(b) WAR CRIMES: . . .

(c) CRIMES AGAINST HUMANITY: . . .

Leaders, organizers, instigators and accomplices participating in the formulation or execution of a common plan or conspiracy to commit any of the foregoing crimes are responsible for all acts performed by any persons in execution of such plan" [1]).

The American idea of an abstract formulation thus prevailed, while the restriction to the Axis criminals which the Russians wanted to express received a twofold emphasis in the introductory paragraph only, limiting the Tribunal's jurisdiction. The 'common plan' charge formulated in the final paragraph was also especially incorporated in the formulation of the 'crime against peace', as the less concrete character of the acts involved in this crime would otherwise make it difficult to prove the personal responsibility of the German cabinet ministers. The final definition with its three categories of crimes further owed its clarity to the influence of the French drafts, while the

---

1) Agreement and Charter of the International Military Tribunal, London, August 8, 1945, l.c., pp. 420—428. Protocol for Amendment, Berlin, October 6, 1945, p. 429.

term 'crimes against peace', now definitely accepted in international law, was proposed by the Russian delegation, instead of the American 'crime of war'.

The Charter of the International Military Tribunal for the Far East, that was enacted by special proclamation of the Supreme Commander for the Allied Powers, by virtue of the authority conferred upon him by the three Powers of the Moscow Conference of December 26, 1945 [1]), contains but few alterations of the London Charter [2]).

A marked difference from the London text is however shown in the formulation of crimes against peace in Law No. 10 issued by the Allied Control Council for the punishment of war criminals in Germany – that is the 'minor war criminals'. Article II provided: "Each of the following acts is recognized as a crime: a) Crimes against peace: Initiation of invasions of other countries and wars of aggression in violation of international laws and treaties, including but not limited to planning..." (here follows Article 6 (a) of the London Charter) [3]). This rather unclear formulation extended the criminality to 'invasions' not followed by a war, but limited the responsibility in that case, as in the case of 'aggressive wars' that had to be in violation of international *laws and* treaties, to acts of 'initiation'. The subsequent inclusion of the definition of London, which also embraced acts of planning, preparation or waging, and also the war of aggression as such, *within* the former concept, makes this whole definition of Law No. 10 inconsistent.

SECTION 3. THE JUDGMENTS

Without the subsequent judgment of the Nuremberg Tribunal the rules formulated in the Charter would never have come

1) Special Proclamation of the Supreme Commander for the Far East, 19 January 1946, General Headquarters APO 500. This is a rare example of international legislation by a single, individual organ. The Charter, with opening statement and indictment of the Tokyo Trial, is also to be found in: Trial of Japanese War Criminals, Dept. of State Publ., 2613, Far Eastern Series 12, U.S. Govt. Printing Office, 1946.

2) See above, p. 25.

3) Allied Control Council for Germany, Law No. 10: Punishment of persons guilty of war crimes, crimes against peace and against humanity, in Law Reports of Trials of War Criminals, selected and prepared by the U.N. W.C.C., Vol. XV. The law and the cases.

within the domain of international law. The definition of the crimes finally reached may have had the form of general law, the Charter as such remained none the less an *ad hoc* legal instrument, and without acceptance and implementation by the Tribunal it would no doubt have been added to that pile of documents, draft conventions, proposals and resolutions on international criminal law and jurisdiction which before the war expressed and entertained the aspirations of many international lawyers and others, without having any direct legal significance.

From this therefore it can be concluded that the law of the Charter must be seen in the light of the interpretation and application given it in the judgment of the Tribunal by means of which it came to reality in the international legal community. Only in so far as it has been applied by the Tribunal has it become 'part of international law' whatever is the significance of this phrase. Even the fact that 19 Allied governments adhered to the Agreement and Charter does not alter this fact, because by that they adhered, strictly speaking [1]), only to the establishment of an International Military Tribunal whose 'constitution, jurisdiction and functions' were "those set out in the Charter... which shall form an integral part of this Agreement" [2]).

Although this applies also to the judgments of the Tokyo Tribunal and of the tribunals set up in accordance with Law No. 10, which judgments therefore will also have to be examined in the course of the present section, the Nuremberg judgment is of far greater importance. It was the first to be pronounced, it received the widest publicity and it met with legal and political comments in nearly all countries. More important, its Charter was the model for the other instruments mentioned and its judgment was followed in the main by the subsequent tribunals

---

1) The adhering States certainly assumed a grave moral obligation to make the rules of the Charter applicable to themselves, see below, pp. 284–8.

2) Agreement by the Governments of the United States of America, the French Republic, the United Kingdom and the Union of Soviet Socialist Republics for the Prosecution and Punishment of the Major War Criminals of the European Axis, London August 8, 1945, Artt. 1 and 2, in Jackson Report, p. 420. See further on the legal nature of the Charter, below, Section 4 of this Chapter.

which recognized it as the authoritative statement on the law concerned.

The analysis of the 'law of the Nuremberg Tribunal' is preceded here by a survey of the main views and arguments brought to the fore by Prosecution and Defence concerning the crime against peace, which was the most ardently discussed question throughout the Trial. In accordance with the definition of paragraph a) of Article 6 of the Charter, the Indictment contained two categories of crimes against peace. Count One charged, along with an over-all 'common plan or conspiracy', also the common plan defined in the second part of the paragraph, Count Two the crimes formulated in the first part.

Count One: "... The common plan or conspiracy embraced the commission of crimes against peace, in that the defendants planned, prepared, initiated and waged wars of aggression, which were also wars in violation of international treaties, agreements or assurances".

Count Two: "All the defendants with divers other persons, during a period of years preceding 8th May, 1945, participated in the planning, preparation, initiation and waging of wars of aggression, which were also wars in violation of international treaties, agreements or assurances" [1]).

The principal argument on which the Prosecution relied was, naturally, the binding character of the Charter.

The basis of the right of the victors to draft a Charter and prosecute and judge the vanquished according to it was, in the opinion of the American Prosecutor, the necessity to punish the morally and legally guilty. Hardly any neutrals were left, and "either the victors must judge the vanquished or we must leave the defeated to judge themselves", which later course had proved abortive after the First World War [2]).

In the name of the French government, M. François de Menthon submitted another basis of jurisdiction: since the

---

1) See text of Indictment in Trial of War Criminals, Department of State Publication, No. 2420, Washington 1945.

2) Trial of the Major War Criminals before the International Military Tribunal, Nuremberg, 14 November 1945 — 1 October 1946, Published at Nuremberg, Germany. Opening Statement for the United States, Volume II, p. 101.

German declaration of unconditional surrender of May 5, 1945, the German Reich had ceased to exist, and the four Powers who had undertaken the prosecution exercised the supreme authority over what before was the German State [1]).

Though Sir Hartley Shawcross, the British Chief Prosecutor, went even so far as to say that the arguments of the Defence against the conformity of the Charter with general international law were beside the point [2]), he undertook to show in his opening and closing statements that the Charter, like the old English Statutes, "merely declares and creates a jurisdiction in respect of what was already the law of Nations" [3]). The Briand-Kellogg Pact was the cornerstone of the proposition that war was already a crime before 1939. With other treaties and declarations it made aggression "illegal and a crime beyond all uncertainty and doubt"; "it is fundamentally on that universal treaty that Count Two of this Indictment is principally built" [4]).

Both he and Justice Jackson saw this 'profound change' in international law – that had completely overthrown the position of neutrals and belligerents, as was proved by English and American state-practice – as a re-introduction of the distinction between just and unjust wars which had long been upheld by the early Christian international law scholars and by Grotius. For Jackson, the 18th and 19th 'imperialist' centuries were a mere interval with their 'foul doctrine' that on the one hand all war is legitimate and that on the other one could never be regarded as a criminal for committing the usual violent actions in the course of legitimate warfare [5]).

Though admitting the absence of a definition of aggressive war in the Charter and the difficulties such a definition presented in international law, the U.S. Prosecutor asserted that all Nazi-

---

1) Opening Statement of the French Prosecution, l.c., Vol. V, p. 389.

2) Final Statement for the United Kingdom, l.c., Vol. XIX, p. 459. By agreement between the four Chief Prosecutors they divided their task, so that the British Prosecution would deal with the charge of Count Two, the U.S. with the conspiracy charge, Count One, while France would deal with the war crimes and crimes against humanity committed in the West, Soviet Russia with those committed in the East of Europe. See M. Teitgen, Le jugement de Nuremberg, R.D.I., 1946, p. 171.

3) Opening Statement for the United Kingdom, l.c., Vol. III, pp. 93, ff..

4) L.c., p. 103.

5) L.c., Vol. II, p. 145. See also his report to the President of June 6, 1945, Jackson Report, p. 51.

wars were "unambiguously aggressive" and that notably the application of the definition of 1933 presented no difficulties in the light of the evidence; the remote causes invoked were "too insincere and inconsistent, too complicated and doctrinaire to be the subject of profitable inquiry in this trial". It was asserted moreover that it was a general view in international law that no political, military or economic situations could excuse aggressive actions: all methods, other than aggression, for the solution of international controversies were, in the 1920's and '30's, open to the State [1]).

The competence of the State to determine when resort to self-defence was necessary, expressly reserved by the U.S.A. and other States at the conclusion of the Pact of Paris, did not mean, according to Shawcross, that the State was the ultimate judge on the propriety and legality of its conduct; this latter thesis was already rejected by the Council of the League of Nations when it condemned Japan's military actions in Manchuria notwithstanding the alleged defensive character of these actions, and this view was now definitely disproved by Article 51 of the Charter of the United Nations. A contrary opinion would nullify the Kellogg Pact and any other pact in which the right of self defence was admitted [2]).

Neither Shawcross nor Jackson admitted a distinction between illegality and criminality on this point. Like Jackson, Shawcross said, referring to the magnitude of the consequences of this war: "No law worthy of the name can allow itself to be reduced to an absurdity in that way...", *id est,* by the proposition "that such a war is only an offence, only an illegality, only a matter of condemnation perhaps sounding in damages, but not a crime punishable by any Tribunal" [3]).

But the assertion, on the ground of treaties and resolutions, that aggressive war was a crime, remained in the air so long as the criminal responsibility for its commission was not determined. Who was responsible and should therefore be punished: the collectivity, the State on whose behalf these acts were committed,

---

1) L.c., Vol. II, p. 149.
2) L.c., Vol. XIX, pp. 461–2.
3) L.c., Vol. XIX, p. 460; Vol. III, p. 107.

or the human agents who represented it? The Charter envisaged only individual responsibility, but the English Prosecutor added that "conscience shrinks from the rigors of collective punishment". It was individual responsibility that mattered: "The State is not an abstract entity. Its rights and duties are the rights and duties of men. Its actions are the actions of men. Those who counsel and procure a crime are themselves criminal . . .", a commonplace in English law, and also in international law not altogether new, as was evidenced by the criminality of piracy, of breach of blockade and of ordinary war crimes [1]).

The plea of acts of State was rejected on the ground that it would lead *ad absurdum,* as its acceptance would imply that the individual agents could not be held responsible as they acted on behalf of the State while the State itself would be immune because it was sovereign. The British Prosecutor held that the national and international tribunals that had asserted that no State had authority over another State or its sovereign, had done so less on the basis of law than of comity the very foundations of which Germany had destroyed [2]). The criminal responsibility of the individual agent was the direct consequence of the committing of a crime by the State. There was nothing startingly new in the adoption of the principle that the State is responsible for its criminal acts: international arbitral tribunals had imposed penal damages on States for affronts of the sovereignty of another State and the League's sanctions were 'if necessary' of a penal character [3]).

The French prosecutor put forward a different construction for the individual responsibility fixed in the Charter. For him collective responsibility of the State was indeed the rule, but the dissolution of the German State had the consequence that only its former agents could be held responsible for the criminal acts they committed on its behalf [4]).

The other Prosecutors, on the contrary, affirmed the principle

---

1) L.c., Vol. III, pp. 105–6; Vol XIX, p. 464.
2) L.c., Vol. III, pp. 104; Vol. XIX, p. 465.
3) L.c., Vol. III, p. 104. Compare Oppenheim-Lauterpacht o.c., Vol. I, pp. 320–322, also for the "I'm alone" Arbitration between the U.S. and Canada on which Shawcross relies in support of his contention regarding penal damages in international law.
4) L.c., Vol. V, p. 389.

that individuals were direct subjects of international law, and found reinforcement of this principle in Article 4 of the constitution of the Weimar Republic: "The generally accepted rules of international law are to be considered as binding, integral parts of the law of the German Reich" [1]).

With regard to the nature of the responsibility for the crimes against peace the French Prosecutor presented a view that is also, though only as additional support for their main arguments, found in the American and English statements. According to this view the acts committed during a war against persons and goods in themselves prohibited and sanctioned by all legislations, were only legal if that war itself were legal. Since the Paris Pact stripped aggressive war of that legality these acts became purely and simply common crimes; such a 'war' is no longer a war in the legal sense but an enterprise of systematic banditry. The fact that the laws of war are nevertheless applied in such an enterprise is no proof to the contrary, because these laws are applied even in civil wars which have nothing international in character [2]). Jackson and Shawcross used this conception only to show that as a 'very minimum consequence' the defendants were, as war-makers, "subject to judgment by the usually accepted principles of the law of crimes" [3]). But such a construction that denies war as an international phenomenon and that is based on the notion of previous legality of war, could nevertheless be the basis of an, in principle unlimited, accusation of all those who in any capacity participated in acts of illegal warfare [4]).

While defending thus, in different ways, the two fundamental principles of the accusation, the criminality of aggressive war and the individual responsibility for it, the Prosecution dealt also with the alleged retroactivity of the law concerning the crimes against peace.

According to Shawcross there was no "substantial retroactivity in the Charter. It merely fixes the responsibility for a crime already clearly established as such by positive law upon its actual perpetration. It fills a gap in international criminal

---

1) Shawcross, Vol. III, pp. 105—7; Jackson, Vol. II, p. 146.
2) L.c., Vol. V, p. 187—8.
3) Shawcross, Vol. XIX, p. 458; Jackson, Vol. II, p. 146.
4) See under Section 4, below.

procedure" [1]). And referring to unpunished acts of aggressive war committed by Italy and Japan in the thirties, he stated that the temporary impunity of the criminal neither deprived law of its force nor legalized the crime: it was a failure of the policeman, not of the law [2]). The American Prosecutor admitted that there was no judicial precedent for the accusation of crimes against peace but pointed to the fact that international law which lacked a central legislator was of a mainly customary character. "Unless we are prepared to abandon every principle of growth for international law, we cannot deny that our own day has the right to institute customs and to conclude agreements that will themselves become sources of a newer and strengthened international law". International law "grows as did the common law through decisions reached from time to time in adapting settled difficulties to new situations". The law, advancing by the case method, advanced at the expense of those who wrongly guessed the law and learned too late their error, but "the law, so far as international law can be decreed, had been clearly pronounced when these acts took place" [3]).

It is most interesting to confront these opinions with that expressed on behalf of the whole defence counsel by the German Prof. Jahrreisz. Though not published outside the records of the Trial, his critical examination of the law with respect to the crimes against peace is an interesting contribution to the abundant literature on the subject.

At the conclusion of his examination Jahrreisz rejects not only the principle of individual criminal responsibility for 'crimes against peace' and for any other act of state, as non-existent in general international law, but he denies also the illegality, *a fortiori* the criminality, of aggressive war, or any war, in international relations in, or prior to, 1939.

His arguments, which concern only the state of law and not the concrete facts, which he does not question, may be summarized as follows. The prohibitions and condemnations of war in the Covenant of the League of Nations, in treaties, resolutions and

---

1) L.c., Vol. III, p. 106.
2) Vol. XIX, p. 460.
3) Vol. II, p. 147.

finally in the Kellogg Pact, were part of a system of collective security that the States, on the instigation of some far seeing statesmen, tried to set up after the First World War. "Before the commencement of the Second World War the whole system of collective security, even in the scanty beginnings it had made, had collapsed, and this collapse was acknowledged and declared expressly, or shown by unambiguous actions, by three world powers" [1]).

England declared so in a note to the League of Nations after the outbreak of the war in 1939. Russia treated the German-Polish conflict in accordance with 'the old rules of power politics' and took its stand upon classic international law when it attacked Finland in the winter of 1939/1940. The President of the United States stated, on 5 September 1939, that there existed a state of war between several States with whom the U.S. lived in peace, and demanded strict observance of the neutrality regulations [2]). The later 'non-belligerent' conduct of the U.S. to which Justice Jackson had referred had a political basis; the legal arguments invoked for its justification could not create international law.

Quoting many contemporary English and American authors, Jahrreisz contended that the classical rules regarding war and peace were not set aside by the Kellogg Pact, which did not contain a definition of what was forbidden, left the right to resort to self defence as an arbitrary power to the individual States and did not provide for the necessary 'peaceful change'. The irrelevancy of the Kellogg Pact for international law is shown by the maintenance of the laws of war that presuppose the equality before the law of the belligerents; it was most clearly shown in the Italo-Abyssinian conflict by the neutrality declarations of many Members of the League and by the recogni-

---

1) L.c., Vol. XVII, pp. 458—494, pp. 464 ff.. The Breach of Peace between States and its Culpability, Plea before the International Military Tribunal in Nuremberg by Dr Hermann Jahrreisz, Transcript pp. 2—76 (hereunder quoted as Transcript) pp. 13 ff.. A summary of Jahrreisz opinion is also given by Prof. H. Donnedieu de Vabres, Le Procès de Nuremberg devant les principes modernes du droit pénal international, in R.d.C., 1947 (I), Vol. 70, pp. 481—577; p. 496 ff..

2) On this and on the previous U.S. Neutrality Act of 1935, once described as the 'deathblow' to the collective security system, see G. A. Finch, The Nuremberg Trial and International Law, A.J.I.L., 1947, pp. 20—37.

tion of Abbyssinia's conquest by Italy, which facts amounted to a complete discrediting of the League of Nations and of the system of the Kellogg-Briand Pact. Classic international law was put back in its old position.

While thus asserting that "in the general international law at present valid there is no distinction between forbidden and not forbidden wars" [1]), Jahrreisz contended that the rules of conventional international law – treaties, etc. – must be examined as to their validity and interpretation in the light of the disappearance of the collective security system [2]). And if, as a result of such an examination, it were found that Germany had violated such a treaty, that violation would not differ in consequences from any other violation of international law, from which there arises normal State liability according to the ordinary rules of international law, having nothing to do with criminal responsibility. Jahrreisz hardly found it necessary to prove that in existing international law no individual, even if he were the head of a State, could in any way be held responsible for such acts. There was not a single precedent; those who waged war in the thirties were never punished, nor was such a punishment seriously proposed. "Punishment of individuals by the legal family of nations for breach of the peace between States would signify the abandoning of the fundamental principles of international law and the European 'scale of values' according to which the State, one's own sovereign State, forms the indispensable foundation for free personality" [3]).

The regulations of the Charter anticipate the law of a world State. Even if the French construction, based on the supreme territorial authority of the Four Powers over Germany, were followed, punishment for the crime against peace would violate the rule *nullum crimen, nulla poena sine lege:* the defendants could never have realised the criminality of what they did, and moreover, their individual acts were deeply rooted in the past of the German State which was a living reality, while at the time the existence of a conspiracy between them was impossible because they were all subjected to Hitler's superior orders and

1) Transcript, p. 22.
2) Ibidem, p. 43.
3) Ibidem, pp. 47–8.

authority [1]). Sentences against individuals for crimes against peace would be something completely new, legally, fully retroactive, and moreover not corresponding to the laws in force [2]).

* * *

The international Military Tribunal, faced with these conflicting statements regarding the state of international law, did not deal with all the arguments quoted heretofore. Its judgment of October 1, 1946, however, derives its importance particularly from the fact that it contains, apart from an application and interpretation of the provisions of the Charter in view of the facts submitted, an extensive argument to justify these provisions in the perspective of general international law as existing in 1939 [3]).

The Tribunal regarded the law of the Charter as decisive and binding. It borrowed its main argument for the competence of the Powers to determine the law and to institute the trial from the French Prosecutor: the enactment of the Charter was the exercise of sovereign legislative power by the countries to which the German Reich had unconditionally surrendered. It overstepped, all the same, the limits of strict legal argument by asserting that this undoubted right of the occupying countries had been recognized by the 'civilised world'. The signatory Powers of the Charter had done together what any one of them might have done singly, as any nation has the right to set up courts to administer law.

As this Charter made "the planning or waging of aggressive war" a crime, it was "not strictly necessary to consider whether and to what extent aggressive war was a crime before the execution of the London Agreement". But in view of the great importance of the questions of law involved, the Tribunal had heard full argument from the Prosecution and the Defence, and undertook to show that: "The Charter is not an arbitrary

1) Ibidem, pp. 52—75.

2) Ibidem, p. 76.

3) Judicial Decision of the International Military Tribunal, Judgment and Sentences, October 1, 1946, in A.J.I.L., 1947, pp. 172—333. Trial of the Major War Criminals, l.c., Vol. XXII, pp. 411—589. Regarding crimes against peace: findings of fact, pp. 427—458, findings of law, pp. 458—469, declarations regarding criminality of organisations, pp. 505—520, convictions of individual defendants pp. 526—585.

exercise of power on the part of the victorious Nations, but... is the expression of international law existing at the time of its creation; and to that extent is itself a contribution to international law" [1]). The following arguments for the criminality of war had, thus, the character of *obiter dicta,* in the interest of the development of international law.

The tribunal began its justification of the Charter with a determination of the scope of the maxim: *nullum crimen sine lege, nulla poena sine lege.* Against the argument of the Defence that *ex post facto* punishment for aggressive war was abhorrent as no statute had defined this crime, no penalty was fixed and no court was created at the time the facts *in casu* were committed, the Tribunal observed first that the maxim was "not a limitation of sovereignty, but in general a principle of justice".

From the Tribunal's reasoning it can be deduced that it regarded only the *nullum crimen* part of the maxim as essential. The fact that no punishment had been determined could not be invoked "as the defendants must have known that they acted in defiance of treaties and of all international law. It would therefore, on the contrary, be unjust to let them go unpunished" [2]). In other words: if it could be shown that aggressive war was already a crime when the acts of the defendants were committed, the Tribunal would consider the demands of justice to be satisfied: individual responsibility for it would be a logical and justifiable consequence of the criminality of such acts.

The main issue was, therefore, the state of international law in 1939. In this the Tribunal adopted the reasoning of the American and English Prosecutors, which was built on the legal effect of the Kellogg-Briand Pact to which by 1939 63 Nations had adhered, the German Reich being one of them. "The solemn renunciation of war as an instrument of national policy *necessarily involves* the proposition that such a war is illegal; and that those who plan and wage such a war, *with its inevitable and terrible consequences,* are committing a crime in so doing" [3]).

The first conclusion to be drawn from this central finding of the Tribunal is that it equalized on this point, the illegality and

---

1) Ibidem, p. 461.
2) Ibidem, p. 462.
3) Ibidem, p. 463. Italics supplied.

the criminality of aggressive war, as did the Prosecution. The Tribunal supported this view with a reference to the criminality of the ordinary war crimes which were nowhere in the Hague Convention of 1907 designated as criminal, or penalized, while military courts had for many years punished individuals guilty of violations of the rules of land warfare laid done by this convention [1]).

The second salient conclusion drawn from the finding quoted above regards *the nature* of the criminality of war as seen by the Tribunal. Planning and waging an aggressive war is seen as producing evil consequences, not particularly war crimes but all the acts of warfare. And therefore the crimes against peace are the central and most important crimes. Earlier in the Judgment the Tribunal had already referred to "charges of the utmost gravity (the) consequences (of which) are not confined to the belligerent States, but affect the whole world". "War is essentially an evil thing"; "to initiate a war of aggression, therefore, is not only an international crime; it is the supreme international crime, differing only from other war crimes in that it contains within itself the accumulated evil of the whole" [2]).

The Tribunal does not go so far as to subscribe to the construction of the Prosecution that illegal warfare resolves automatically into a chain of common murder and criminality. But neither does it reject this thesis, which since the beginning of the discussions on the subject during the war has hovered over the concept of criminal war [3]).

The judgment reinforces the basis of this concept by referring to a number of legal instruments which, for lack of ratification or for other reasons, have in international law a less direct significance than the Kellogg Pact. The Draft Treaty of Mutual Assistance of 1923, the Preamble of the Geneva Protocol of 1924, the Sokal Declaration of the Assembly of the League of Nations of September 1927, the Havana Resolution of the Pan-American Conference of 1928, and finally Article 227 of the Treaty of Versailles, "important to remember", all declare or suppose the "criminality of aggressive war" and the non-implementation of

1) Ibidem.
2) Ibidem, p. 427.
3) See above, pp. 181 and 208 and below, section 5 of this chapter.

most of them was not, in the Tribunal's opinion, the consequence of doubt about this criminality.

Reference to these documents invites the question whether the Tribunal considers the international rule about the criminality of aggressive war as a customary rule resulting from a general opinion of law expressed in the quoted documents, or as a conventional one, embodied in the Pact of Paris. The quoted sentence (note 3, p. 213 above) seems to indicate the latter opinion. Elsewhere in the Judgment, however, the Tribunal speaks about the fact that, in the absence of an international legislature, international agreements like the Pact of Paris have to deal only with general principles of law and not with administrative matters of procedure. And the Tribunal adds: "The law of war is to be found not only in treaties, but in the customs and practices of States, which gradually obtained universal recognition, and from the general principles of justice applied by jurists and practised by military courts. This law is not static, but by continual adaptation follows the needs of a changing world. Indeed in many cases, treaties do no more than express and define, for more accurate reference, the principles of law already existent" [1]).

If this means that the rule of the criminality of war does not, in the opinion of the Tribunal, arise solely from the Paris Pact, it is all the more surprising that the Judgment does not deal in any way with the contemporary 'customs and practices of States', whereupon the Defence had built its main argument against the criminality of war in international law.

After thus affirming the principal thesis of the Prosecution with respect to the criminality of aggressive war, the Judgment deals with three objections against the attribution of individual responsibility for it.

It is the opinion of the Tribunal that international law is not only concerned with the actions of sovereign States, but "imposes duties and liabilities upon individuals as well as upon States". "Crimes against international law are committed by men, not by abstract entities, and only by punishing individuals who commit such crimes can the provisions of international law be enforced" [2]).

1) Judicial decision, ibidem, p. 464.
2) Ibidem, p. 465.

Consequently the Tribunal rejects also the acts of state defence, in conformance with Article 7 of the Charter and adding the important statement: "It is the very essence of the Charter that individuals have international duties which transcend the national obligations of obedience imposed by the individual State. He who violates the laws of war cannot obtain immunity while acting in pursuance of the authority of the State, if the State in authorizing action moves outside its competence under international law" [1]).

Article 8 of the Charter, restricting the validity of the plea of 'superior orders', was held by the Tribunal to be "in conformity with the law of all nations". And the Judgment gave as the "true test" of responsibility "not the existence of the order, but whether moral choice was in fact possible".

If the Tribunal followed the Prosecution in its justification of the Law of the Charter, it restricted its application to the accused to a considerable degree.

First of all it considered, in Count One, only the common plan to prepare, initiate and wage aggressive war. The last paragraph of Article 6 did not, in the opinion of the Tribunal, add "a new and separate crime to those already listed", and therefore it could only refer to the responsibility of persons participating in the common plan mentioned under paragraph sub a) in the definition of the crimes against peace [2]).

The Tribunal took, moreover, a much narrower view of the concept of conspiracy than the Prosecution for whom any significant participation in the affairs of the Nazi party of Government was evidence of a participation in a conspiracy that was in itself criminal. The Tribunal declared that a conspiracy "must be clearly outlined in its criminal purposes" and "not be too far removed from the time of decision and of action". Adherence to the Party program therefore did not suffice: "The Tribunal must examine whether a concrete plan to wage war existed, and determine the participants in that concrete plan" [3]).

Consequently, none of the organisations accused of being criminal was declared so with respect to crimes against peace.

---

1) Ibidem.
2) Ibidem, p. 469.
3) Ibidem, pp. 467–8.

The pre-1934 atrocities of the S.A. were not considered as "part of a specific plan to wage war". Only as individuals were the Reich Cabinet members involved in the conspiracy to make aggressive wars. And though the Tribunal found the S.S. Units were "active participants in the steps leading up to aggressive war", and that without the military guidance of the General Staff and High Command "the aggressive ambitions of Hitler and his fellow Nazis would have been academic and sterile", neither of these organisations was held guilty under Count One [1]).

It is especially in the Verdicts on the individual defendants that the Tribunal's opinion on the nature and the limits of the responsibility for crimes against peace becomes manifest. Once the principle of this responsibility is admitted, the most troublesome question raised by the criminality of aggressive war arises – how to assess the accused individual's relation to unlawful enterprise? What degree of knowledge must he have had? What type of action must he have performed? How important a position must he have held? What influence must he have exerted in determining national policy? At what stage of the criminal enterprise must he have become involved: is mere 'waging' sufficient if he had no share in planning and preparation before the inception of the war? [2]).

While all defendants were accused under Count One of the Indictment, the Tribunal held that the evidence established the common plan to prepare and wage war by *certain of the defendants* only, and proved "the existence of many separate plans rather than of one single conspiracy embracing them all" [3]). But it held, against the Defence, that the relation of leader and followers did not preclude responsibility or make a common plan based on co-operation impossible.

The eight defendants convicted under Count One – Göring, von Ribbentrop, Rosenberg, Keitel, Hess, Jodl, Räder and von Neurath – were all the highest officials in the Party, the Army

---

[1]) Ibidem, p. 517 and p. 522. Regarding the other organisations accused, pp. 505, 511, 519 and 520.

[2]) Telford Taylor (Brigadier General, successor to Justice Jackson as Chief of Counsel for the later Nuremberg Trials), The Nuremberg War Crimes Trials, in International Conciliation, Carnegie Endowment for International Peace, N.Y., April 1949, No. 450, pp. 243–371, p. 340.

[3]) L.c., Vol. XXII, p. 468.

or Foreign Affairs. The Tribunal considered as sufficient evidence of their knowledge, their connection with the four secret conferences between 1937 and 1939, at which Hitler disclosed his aggressive plans. All of them had either attended one or several conferences or had had the decisions immediately communicated to them. This becomes still clearer from the fourteen acquittals from the conspiracy charge, several of which were expressly founded on the fact that the defendant concerned was never present at one of the conferences (Fritzsche, Streicher, Doenitz, Bormann), or that he was never informed of the decisions taken there (Doenitz, Fritzsche), or on the fact that he was not one of the inner circle around Hitler (Schacht, Streicher, Fritzsche).

Also the fact that the defendant did not hold a sufficiently high position was used as a ground for acquittal (Funk, Speer, Fritzsche, Doenitz). In other instances it was merely said that the defendant was "not sufficiently connected with the common plan to wage aggressive war" (Frank, Sauckel), or "not involved in the development of Hitler's plan for territorial expansion" (von Schirach).

But even if the defendant were a central figure, and if his actions were responsible for Germany's readiness to wage aggressive war, unambiguous evidence for his criminal intention had, in the Tribunal's opinion, to be offered. This becomes particularly clear from the case of Schacht who had been responsible for Germany's rearmament program. "Rearmament in itself is not criminal under the Charter. To be a crime against peace under Article 6 of the Charter, it must be shown that Schacht carried out this rearmament as part of the Nazi plans to wage aggressive war". Also with respect to von Papen, it was "not established beyond a reasonable doubt" that the occupation of Austria by aggressive war if necessary, as a step in the direction of further aggressive action, "was the purpose of his activity" [1]).

The Tribunal was, however, satisfied with much less evidence of criminal intent for a defendant to be held responsible under

---

1) Ibidem, p. 573. See for Schacht, pp. 554—5, for von Schirach, p. 565, for Sauckel, p. 568, for Frank, p. 542, for Doenitz, p. 556, for Fritzsche, p. 582, for Speer, p. 577, for Funk, p. 550, for Streicher, p. 547, for Bormann, p. 584 and for Frick, p. 545.

Count Two, 'the planning or waging' of specific aggressive wars. It is remarkable that the Judgment does not pay so much attention to 'preparation and initiation' of these wars, also included in the definition of crimes against peace [1]), and that the individual verdicts mostly establish either 'planning' or 'waging', or both. On the other hand, the Tribunal held 'planning' under Count Two to constitute a crime separate from the 'participation in a common plan' under Count One. The difference between the charges of Counts One and Two, in the general part of the Indictment supported by the same evidence, becomes manifest only in the part devoted to the accusation of the individual defendants. Göring, Hess, von Ribbentrop, Keitel and Jodl were convicted on Count Two for their participation in planning and waging of the whole series of aggressive wars. The three others, convicted on Count One, were also convicted on Count Two, but only on the ground of their responsibility for specific actions. Four others were found guilty under Count Two only: Funk, Frick, Doenitz and Seiss Inquart.

The case of Räder is clear: the ex-admiral devised and waged the aggression against Norway and urged action against Greece. Rosenberg's responsibility as head of the Party's Foreign Planning Bureau, though further 'removed from the time of decision and action', was also rather obvious so far as his participation in the planning and preparation of the action against Norway was concerned [2]). With Funk's conviction a new field was drawn within the scope of the crimes against peace: his guilt rests on his participation in the economic preparation for the wars against Poland and the Soviet Union.

So far, the actions of the defendants convicted under Count Two have a clear connection with the bringing about of aggressive wars. This is not the case with the four others found guilty on this point. They were only involved in the waging of wars already initiated. Doenitz, recognized as a line officer not privy to the conspiracy, is said to have been 'active in waging aggressive

---

1) For example ibidem, pp. 461 and 468. See further below, pp. 304 ff..

2) Ibidem, p. 539–540. See for Räder, p. 562, for Jodl, p. 569, for Keitel, pp. 533–4, for von Ribbentrop, pp. 530–3, for Hess, p. 529 and for Goering, p. 526.

war'; he directed the U-boat arm and did therefore 'wage aggressive war within the meaning of that word in the Charter'. Though after Räder's retreat in 1943 he became Chief of the German Navy and in April 1945 succeeded Hitler, and though it is said that at the end of the war, knowing it hopeless, he urged the Navy to continue its fight, his conviction seems to rest mainly upon the key position submarine warfare held in the German war efforts.

Merely administrative was Frick's part in the waging of the war. He devised an administrative organisation for wartime standards, but as he was not involved in the common plan this seems hardly a material basis for conviction. His guilt lay in more concrete activities: as Minister of the Interior he signed the laws uniting Austria with the Reich and incorporating certain territories, and as head of the liaison office for Bohemia, Moravia, Poland and Norway, he directed occupation policies. As the actions against Austria and Czechoslovakia were not charged as wars of aggression, Seiss Inquart's conviction on Count Two must also rest upon his administrative activities in occupied countries during the war [1]). The Judgment says indeed that he "assumed responsibility for governing territories which had been occupied by aggressive wars and the administration of which was of vital importance in the aggressive war being waged by Germany".

It is possible that a similar finding also accounts for the conviction of von Neurath, one time Reich Protector in Bohemia and Moravia. He resigned as Foreign Minister before Munich, but as he was convicted under Count One, it may be that the results of his activities in that period were deemed part of the plans in which the seizure of Austria was a step to further aggression [2]). In Rosenberg's case which was mentioned before, the defendant's "major responsibility for the formulation and

---

1) Seyss Inquart was in occupied Poland, however, the subordinate to Frank, who was not convicted of Crimes against Peace, because he was charged only under Count One, not under Count Two like Seyss Inquart. Cf. Taylor, o.c., p. 269. In drawing conclusions from the individual verdicts this dependence on the Indictment must be kept in mind.

2) Cf. the grounds for the acquittal of Schacht, above p. 218. L.c. Vol. XXII, pp. 580—1. Von Neurath was with the seven defendants listed on p. 217, convicted under Counts One and Two.

execution of occupational policies in the occupied Eastern Territories" was only part of the grounds on which he was convicted on Count Two.

In conclusion it may be said that, while the Tribunal restricted the conspiracy charge to the few top officials, it considered various foreign political, military, administrative and economic activities under the specific crimes against peace, as well as some which were carried out by subordinate officials after the inception of wars in the planning, preparation and initiation of which they had no part. The limits of this criminality were not defined; a vague line appears in the reasons for Speer's acquittal: "his activities in charge of German armament production were in aid of the war effort in the same way that other productive enterprises aid in the waging of war", but these activities were judged to involve neither engaging in the common plan to wage, nor the actual waging of, aggressive war.

On the other hand it is clear that the Tribunal did not find that the 'supreme crime' against peace deserved the heaviest punishment. Hess, the only one convicted on Counts One and Two alone, was sentenced to life imprisonment [1]). His fellow conspirators who were condemned to death were found heavily guilty of war crimes and crimes against humanity. Räder, Doenitz and von Neurath, who had committed other crimes in addition the those against peace, got respectively condemnations for life, twenty years and fifteen years.

* * *

The Tokyo Tribunal, which in Chapter I was found to have been less scrupulous in determining hostilities as aggressive wars, also extended, in certain ways, the limits of culpability beyond those fixed or indicated by the Nuremberg Tribunal. What was done in practice by the Nuremberg Prosecution was made a rule in the Tokyo Charter: Article 5 "The Tribunal shall have the power to try and punish Far Eastern war criminals who

---

1) The Soviet Judge, General Nikitchenko, was of the opinion that Hess should have been sentenced to death by hanging, and disagreed with the acquittal of Schacht, von Papen and Fritzsche, and with the failure of the majority judgment to hold the S.A., the General Staff and the Reichscabinet to be criminal organisations.

as individuals or as members of organisations are charged with offences which include Crimes against Peace" [1]). All twenty eight government ministers, high officials, diplomats and military men brought before the Tribunal were in a series of seventeen Counts accused of participation in a common plan or conspiracy to wage aggressive wars, and of actual planning and preparation of twelve aggressive wars. And after the two and a half years trial all 25 defendants still alive were convicted and sentenced for these crimes against peace.

In this text it is impossible and unnecessary to give a survey of the arguments of Prosecution, Defence and Judgment, which on many points of law closely followed the Nuremberg pattern [2]). But the main features by which the Tokyo Trial distinguished itself from its predecessor may be briefly mentioned.

Group One of the Indictment, charging crimes against peace on 36 counts, was followed by Group Two, comprising 16 counts, charging crimes of murder being at the same time Crimes against Peace, Conventional War Crimes and Crimes against Humanity. These charges resulted, in a certain way, from the construing of criminal war as a 'chain of common crimes' as suggested by the Nuremberg Prosecution [3]). The charges were based on the argument that, by initiating unlawful hostilities, viz. sudden attacks without a previous declaration of war, as in the case of Pearl Harbour, the Japanese armed forces had 'killed and murdered' such soldiers and civilians 'as might happen to be in the places at the times of such attacks'.

Without rejecting the basic concept behind them, the Tribunal pointed out the lack of consequence in these charges: if the war was not unlawful, these charges would fall; if it was, then this involved unlawful killings not only at the places and upon the dates stated in these counts, but at all places in the theatre of war and at all times. The Judgment avoided a decision on this point by stating that 'no good purpose' was

---

1) Charter of the International Military Tribunal for the Far East, Article 5 (see above, p. 202, note 1).

2) See for an extensive account of Trial and Judgment Solis Horwitz, The Tokyo Trial, International Conciliation, Carnegie Endowment for International Peace, N.Y., 1950, No. 465. Also D. N. Sutton, The Trial of Tojo, American Bar Association Journal, February 1950, pp. 93—96 and 160—165.

3) See above, pp. 208, 214, and, below, section 5 of this chapter.

served "in dealing with these parts of the offences by way of counts for murder when the whole offence of waging those wars unlawfully is put in issue upon the counts charging the waging of such wars" [1]).

To a greater extent than in Nuremberg, the crimes against peace formed the central and dominating element of the Tokyo Trial and Judgment, and greater emphasis than in Nuremberg was placed on the interpretation of the *facts* alleged to constitute these crimes.

The first argument of the Defence Counsel for its denial of the conspiracy charge was that all acts committed were acts of self-defence against provocative acts of other nations which threatened and interfered with Japan's recognized and legal rights in Asia and its right of national existence [2]). This was alleged not only regarding the 'incidents' in China, which were said to have been caused by the conditions prevailing there prior to 1931, the hostilities and threats against Japanese persons and goods, and in 1937 by the conspiracy of Chinese communists to draw Japan into war with China, but also and particularly with regard to the Western Powers. Their deliberate and coordinate economic and military pressure against Japan would finally have created a situation so oppressive and acute that Japan would have been forced to fight for its very existence and – in accordance with the secret desires of the Western Powers – strike the first blow [3]).

Rejected by the Tribunal as a whole, these arguments found a certain amount of support in the dissenting opinion of its Indian member, Justice Pal, who denied the guilt of all defendants on the ground of the legal non-existence of a crime against peace as well as on the ground of the whole policy of the Western Powers in Asia, notably that of the U.S. whose embargoes on Japan were a method of war not dissimilar to armed conflict [4]).

In the alternative, the plea of self-defence was repeated as the personal, subjective defence of all the accused, who pretended to

1) Transcript Judgment, p. 36, Official Transcript, pp. 48, 452–3 (l.l.c.c., above, p. 24, note 1).

2) Horwitz, o.c., p. 526.

3) Ibidem, pp. 529–531.

4) Dissenting Opinion of Mr. Justice Pal, Separate Transcript, pp. 227–8, quoted by Horwitz, o.c., p. 550.

have believed in the defensive character of the Japanese wars. It was found, however, that in point of fact no defendant ever believed that the actions concerned were necessary for the defence of Japan [1]).

With regard to the law, the Defence reinforced its objection to the retroactivity of the Charter by denying the jurisdiction of the Tribunal to take cognizance of accusations of crimes against peace. Japan had surrendered on the conditions of the Potsdam Declaration, in which the term 'punishment of war criminals' could at the time (July 1945) only have referred to the punishment for conventional war crimes [2]). The Tribunal overruled this contention on the ground that factual evidence showed that the Japanese Government had actually foreseen, at that time, the punishment of those responsible for the war [3]).

Like Jahrreisz in Nuremberg, on the question of law the Tokyo Defence Counsel tried to "establish the present state of international law through the pronouncements and actions of other nations". The evidence offered to prove that other nations, including certain of the Prosecuting Powers, had from 1928 to 1945 committed acts similar to those for which the defendants were being tried, and had made pronouncements contrary to the view that aggressive warfare was a crime under international law, was, however, rejected by the Tribunal. The relations between the Soviet Union and the Baltic States, Poland and Rumania, between England and Iran and between the United States and Denmark were deemed collateral and irrelevant to the issues of fact before the Tribunal. To the extent that they were proper sources of international law, these facts might, according to the Tribunal, be used in arguments on questions of law [4]).

But no more than the Nuremberg Judgment did that of Tokyo deal with these 'sources of international law', and even more exclusively than the first did it rely on the Kellogg Pact: whether

---

1) Ibidem, pp. 533—5.

2) Justice Pal, o.c., pp. 18—21, and the French Judge, Bernard, in his dissenting opinion, p. 4, disagreed with the majority judgment on this point, see Horwitz, o.c., p. 545. See also the Separate Opinion of Mr. Justice Röling, Member for the Netherlands, transcript, pp. 8—10.

3) Horwitz, o.c., p. 544.

4) Ibidem, p. 527.

aggressive war is a crime depends on the legal effect of the Pact of Paris. The Tokyo Tribunal further quoted the opinions of the Nuremberg Tribunal on the criminality of aggressive war and expressed its unqualified adherence to it. It abstained from reasoning the matter anew in a somewhat different language "so as not to open the door to controversy by way of conflicting interpretation of the two statements" [1]).

The concurring and dissenting opinions that form one of the chief elements of interest of the Tokyo Trial reflect quite different legal opinions on this point. For the French Justice Bernard, who urged the dismissal of all charges on procedural grounds, accepted, however, the criminality of aggressive war on non-positivist grounds: "such a war is and always has been a crime in the eyes of reason and universal conscience, – expressions of natural law upon which an international tribunal can and must base itself to judge the conduct of the accused tendered to it [2]). Also the President, the Australian Judge Sir William Webb, saw the emergence of a customary international law, supplemented by rules of justice and general principles of law [3]).

Justice Pal rejected the rule concerning criminal war as *ex post facto* legislation, as he considered that any distinction between just and unjust war belonged only to the theory of legal philosophers [4]). The Dutch member of the Tribunal, Justice Röling, submitted in a dissenting opinion the theory which he elaborated in later publications and which will be examined in the next section, to the effect that the sentences imposed for crimes against peace were not proper punishments for *legal crimes,* but were acceptable as political safety measures aimed at the elimination of persons who were dangerous for the peace of the world [5]).

The Judgment of the Tribunal for the Far East contains some novel conceptions concerning the scope of conspiracy and individual responsibility for aggressive war. As stated before, the conspiracy charge, more particularly Count One, was the "heart of the case". The charge held that the defendants "conspired

---

1) Transcript Judgment, pp. 25–26, Official Transcript, pp. 48, 439.
2) Dissenting Opinion, p. 10, quoted by Horwitz, p. 546.
3) Concurring Opinion, pp. 3–5, 10–11, quoted by Horwitz.
4) Dissenting Opinion, pp. 151–152, Horwitz, pp. 546 and 548.
5) See below, pp. 272–7.

that Japan should ... *wage* declared or undeclared war or wars of aggression ..." while later counts (6—17) contained the charges that all the defendants "planned and prepared" specific aggressive wars. Without questioning the validity of the latter charges, the Tribunal found all defendants guilty under Count One, stating: "A conspiracy to wage aggressive or unlawful war arises when two or more persons enter into an agreement to commit that crime. Thereafter in furtherance of the conspiracy follows planning or preparation for such war. Those who participate at this stage may be either original conspirators or later adherents. If the latter adopt the purpose of the conspiracy and plan and prepare for its fulfillment they become conspirators. For this reason as all the accused are charged with the conspiracies, we do not consider it necessary in respect of those we may find guilty of conspiracy to enter convictions also for planning and preparing" [1]).

All defendants were found guilty of conspiracy, in this sense wider than the Nuremberg conception in that many of the defendants were subordinate officials and that the activities of some of them were rather far removed from the time of decision and action. A number of defendants were moreover found guilty of 'waging' specific wars; 'initiating aggressive war' was held to mean commencing the hostilities and therefore to involve the actual waging of war. "After ... such a war has been commenced by some offenders others may participate in such circumstances as to become guilty of waging the war" [2]). It is curious that the Tribunal seems to go further, in law, than the Prosecution which had contended: "No man has been charged in this proceeding because of any act committed by him in the course of his official duties pursuant to an already established policy if those matters were his only connection with the aggressive policy" [3]).

In his dissenting opinion Justice Röling found that the norm contained in the quoted statement of the Prosecution, one which in his opinion should be generally recognized, was not followed by the Tribunal in a number of cases, notably that of Hata [4]).

1) Transcript Judgment, pp. 32—3, Official Transcript, p. 48,447—8.
2) Ibidem, pp. 33 and 48,448, respectively.
3) Transcript of Proceedings, p. 40,539, quoted by Sutton, o.c., p. 93.
4) Röling, o.c., p. 179, and on Hata, pp. 179—190.

While this difference of opinion seems to be a question of the interpretation of facts, the forequoted finding of the Tribunal indicates an inclination towards the view, suggested by the conviction of Doenitz in Nuremberg, that the mere waging of a war by a military officer can constitute a crime [1]).

* * *

The trials conducted in the American Occupation Zone of Germany, under the authority of Law No. 10, contain a number of interesting cases involving charges of crimes against peace. These trials were in more than one sense based on the Nuremberg precedent.

Law No. 10 was enacted by the representatives of the four Powers in the Allied Control Council "in order to give effect to the terms of the Moscow Declaration ... and the London Agreement ..., and the Charter issued pursuant thereto, ...", which instruments were at the same time made "integral parts of the Law (Preamble). But also the substantial provisions of Law No. 10 were largely similar to those of the Charter. The rather unsatisfactory deviation from this general conformity, by the extension of the formulation of the crimes against peace to 'initiation of invasions', discussed above [2]), was made, as an authoritative commentator states, to furnish "a basis for charging the Austrian and Czechoslavakian conquests as crimes against peace". It is difficult to see in this inclusion, as well as in the incorporation of "membership of a criminal organisation" as a separate crime [3]), anything else but an arbitrary exercise of power on the part of the Control Council. The authority of the moderate Nuremberg judgment, that was in the full sense

1) See below, pp. 300, 305, ff..
2) See p. 202.
3) Alarmed by this provision, the Nuremberg Tribunal, called upon to make a declaration of criminality with respect to six organisations, fortunately prevented its indiscriminate application by requiring that, for conviction of an individual, in addition to his membership of a criminal organisation, at least personal knowledge of the criminal purposes or acts of the organisation must be proved. A similar restriction was given to the concept of conspiracy. Cf. The criticism of Law No. 10 by Justice Biddle, Le Procès de Nuremberg Revue Internationale de Droit Pénal, 1948, pp. 1—19, p. 15.

accepted as a precedent by the subsequent Nuremberg Trials [1]), mitigated the application of this Law.

Law No. 10, designed "to establish a uniform legal basis in Germany for the prosecution of war criminals", was, however, only applied in the U.S. Zone. The trials in the British Occupation Zone were conducted on the basis of a Royal Warrant which had already been given on the 14th of June 1945, and which, perhaps as a consequence of the initial British opposition to the accusation of 'crimes against peace', did not contain this crime [2]). Little is known of the proceedings in the U.S.S.R. Zone and the law applied there. The French did not proceed on the basis of Law No. 10 either, though in one trial at Rastatt, in the French Zone, conducted before an international tribunal of the Western European countries, this Law was applied. The defendant Roechling, a Ruhr industrialist, was *inter alia* accused, and in the first instance convicted, of 'waging aggressive war'; but he was acquitted on this point on a reconsideration of his sentence in 1949 [3]).

The judgments in the four American trials, involving charges of crimes against peace, derive their interest from the fact that, apart from confirming the law of the Nuremberg Trial, they elaborated this law with respect to the personal responsibility for these crimes and contain explicit statements on points that the latter judgment passed in silence. The evidence brought before these tribunals related to acts of military men, industrialists, diplomats and other high officials, and therefore gave the judges an opportunity of indicating the limits of personal responsibility for crimes against peace far more precisely than could be done in the case of the major war criminals.

Only in the last trial of this series, the so-called 'Ministries' or 'Wilhelmstrasse' case, five defendants, von Ribbentrop's State Secretary, von Weiszäcker, and four other high officials, were convicted, on Count One of the Indictment, of crimes against peace, in that they '*participated* in the initiation of invasions...'

---

1) To what extent the precedent of the I.M.T. was followed is, for example, shown by the findings of law, regarding personal liability for crimes against peace, in the Judgment in the I. G. Farben Trial; see Law Reports, Vol. X, pp. 30—40. (U.S. Military Tribunal 1947—8, Nuremberg).

2) See Lord Maugham, o.c., p. 20.

3) Taylor, o.c., p. 399.

etc. (see Article II of Law No. 10 quoted before). In the German High Command Trial, in the I. G. Farben Trial and in the Krupp Trial [1]), the accused, high ranking officers and industrialists, were found 'not guilty' on the count charging crimes against peace.

It may be of interest to mention certain of the opinions pronounced by the latter three tribunals in their lengthy examinations of the law, before giving a brief analysis of the 'Ministries' case.

The acquittal in the High Command case rested upon an analysis of war as the 'implementation of a national policy', in close connection with the wording of the Pact of Paris. Like the International Military Tribunal, the U.S. Military Tribunal in this case considered the applicable law, as based on this Pact "evidence of a sufficient crystallisation of world opinion to authorize a judicial finding that there exist Crimes against Peace under International Common Law" [2]). Even more consistently than its predecessor this Tribunal rejected the allegation of *ex post facto* legislation, and applied Law No. 10 therefore within the limits it considered imposed by the Pact of Paris. The Tribunal attached the criminality, consequently, not to the war but to the policy from which it originated: "If the policy under which it (war) is initiated is criminal in its intent and purpose it is so because the individuals at the policy-making level had a criminal intent and purpose in determining the policy. If war is the means by which the criminal objective is to be attained, then the waging of the war is but an implementation of the policy, and the criminality which attaches to the waging of the war should be confined to those who participate in it at the policy level".

Abstaining from the formulation of a general rule on this point, the Tribunal considered that "somewhere between the Dictator and Supreme Commander . . . and the common soldier

---

1) Trial of Alfred Felix Alwyn Krupp von Bohlen und Halbach and eleven others U.S. Military Tribunal, Nuremberg, 1947–8; see Law Report, Vol. X, pp. 69–189, on crimes against peace pp. 102–130.

2) The German High Command Trial, U.S. Military Tribunal, Nuremberg, 1947–8; see Law Reports, Vol. XII, on crimes against peace, pp. 65–71, p. 70.

is the boundary between the criminal and the excusable participation in the waging of a war of aggression" [1]).

From the state of 'International Common Law' at the time of the making of Law No. 10, the Tribunal deduced two requirements for criminality of participation in the waging of a war: a) "actual knowledge that an aggressive war is intended and that if launched it will be an aggressive war"; b) on the part of the possessor of such knowledge "after he acquires it", that he shall be "in a position to shape or influence the policy that brings about its initiation or its continuance after initiation, either by furthering, or by hindering or preventing it" [2]). "It is not a person's rank or status, but his power to shape or influence the policy of his State, which is the relevant issue for determining his criminality under the charge of Crimes against Peace". Participation in the war on the part of a soldier or officer who was but the policy makers' 'instrument', 'below the policy level', was, however 'morally reprimandable', not regarded as a 'criminal offence in and by itself' by 'International Common Law' at the time the acts of the defendants were committed [3]).

It is clear that under this ruling Doenitz would not have been convicted on Count Two [4]). It is by the application of similar standards but more in accordance with the judgment of the I.M.T. that the industrialists of I. G. Farben and Krupp were acquitted of crimes against peace. In the trial of the latter it was rejected "that industrialists as such, could not under any circumstances be found guilty upon such charges" [5]). As in the I. G. Farben case the burden of proving that the defendants had conducted the armament-production with the knowledge that they were thereby preparing Germany for participating in an aggressive war, was laid upon the Prosecution. At the same time it was said that if military experts were tried for the same acts, and if it could be shown that they had knowledge of the extent of rearmament, the conclusion might be justified that they had known that the armament production was in excess of the require-

---

1) L.c., p. 67.
2) L.c., p. 68.
3) L.c., p. 69.
4) See above, p. 219 and on the whole question, below, pp. 305 ff..
5) Law Reports, Vol. X, p. 105.

ments of defence. Liability was held to be limited to "those who are responsible for the formulation and execution of the policies that result in the carrying out of such a (aggressive) war" [1]).

On the other hand, it seems that the Tribunal in the I. G. Farben case held that only 'major war criminals' could be convicted of crimes against peace, as the Moscow Declaration did not include a warning to that effect to the rest of the German population. The non-official function of the accused seems, moreover, to have strongly influenced the Tribunal which several times refers to them as 'average citizens' who could scarcely be charged with "knowledge that the rulers of the Reich were planning to plunge Germany in a war of aggression", and which made high demands for proof of their criminal intent [2]).

These requirements were made still stricter by the dissenting judges in the Krupp case, Judges Anderson and Wilkins. The first held that "to extend criminal liability beyond the leaders and policymakers and their privies to private citizens called upon to aid the war effort necessarily embodies the concept of mass punishment" [3]). Judge Wilkins considered that it must be shown that a person "acted in a manner which actually and substantially influenced the course of international events" [4]).

These opinions, leading in the Krupp case to a dismissal of the charges of crimes against peace, on a motion of the Defence, even during the trial, reflected the influence of the deteriorating state of international relations in the course of 1948. Both judgments seem, however, to overlook the circumstance that, just because they are private citizens, industrialists who participate in the preparation of war generally do so voluntarily and may usually withdraw from such activities without any danger to themselves, unlike soldiers and government officials. The requirements of guilt should accordingly be lowered in the case of the former.

The Tribunal that on 11 April 1949 condemned von Weiszaecker, Keppler, Woermann, Lammers and Koerner, *inter alia* for the preparation or waging of specific wars or invasions, set

---

1) L.c., pp. 36—7.
2) L.c., p. 34, cf. the Tribunal's argument on pp. 38—9.
3) L.c., p. 126.
4) L.c., p. 130.

definitely wider limits to the responsibility for aggressive war [1]). The majority judgment ruled that criminal sanctions could be applied "to the individuals by whose decisions, co-operation and implementation the unlawful war or invasion was initiated and waged". Making a distinction between "those who plan, prepare, initiate and wage aggressive wars and invasions", and those who "knowingly, consciously and responsibly participate therein", the Tribunal held that also the latter "violate international law and may be tried, convicted and punished for their acts" [2]).

The Tribunal, after a careful examination of the law and the facts, restated the findings of the I.M.T. as to the existence of individual responsibility for crimes against peace and as to the aggressive character of Germany's war. It put, however, in accordance with the wording of Law No. 10, the 'invasions' in Austria and Czechoslovakia and the later aggressive wars on one line, and notably condemned Weiszaecker and Keppler for their responsibility with respect to the invasion of Czechoslovakia alone. On this point, among others, Judge Powers dissented, on the grounds that these 'invasions' were neither comprised by the London Charter, nor included by the I.M.T. in its convictions on Count Two, and that even Law No. 10 could be interpreted as not requiring convictions of responsibility for these acts that would never be regarded as 'breaches of the peace' [3]). Telford Taylor, who was the Chief of the Prosecution in this case, was, however, of the opinion that the holding of the Tribunal on this point "lays at rest the notion that a great power can, with legal impunity, mass such large forces to threaten a weaker country that the latter succumbs without the necessity of a 'shooting war'. And, coming when it did, he found the judgment

---

1) Trial of Ernst Weiszaecker and twenty others (also called the 'Ministries' or 'Wilhelmstrasse' case), U.S. Military Tribunal, Nuremberg, 1947—1949. Transcript of Judgment, regarding crimes against peace, pp. 1—191, and Transcript of dissenting opinion of Judge Powers, regarding crimes against peace, pp. 1—44. As the Judgment in this most interesting case was delivered after the series of Law Reports had been closed, there was unfortunately no publication of its main findings. The case is discussed by Taylor, o.c., pp. 340 ff..

2) Transcript, p. 14. The statement is important as the Tribunal, like the U.S. Tribunals in the forementioned cases, dismissed, on a motion of all the defendants, the conspiracy charge which aroused, as Taylor states (o.c., p. 345), the deep suspicion of European jurists.

3) Transcript dissenting opinion, pp. 15—20.

"a powerful reminder that legal principles which have been judicially enforced cannot easily be buried and exhumed with each shift in the international winds" [1]). He fails, however, to demonstrate why this Tribunal, or the Control Council, could 'lay at rest' notions that the London Charter and the I.M.T. did not consider it in accordance with international law to provide with a criminal sanction [2]).

This judgment, at variance with the others mentioned, did not find that the 'power to shape and influence policy' is a necessary element of a crime against peace. Though "Weiszaecker did not originate this invasion (in Czechoslovakia) and his part was not a controlling one, we find that it was a necessary implementation of the program" [3]). Criminal intent, that is "full knowledge of the facts", was, however, deemed necessary and extensively demonstrated 'beyond reasonable doubt' in the case of each defendant, who was convicted on the ground of specific acts, and not on that of his mere function or of his being involved in a common plan [4]). This latter charge did not, however, form part of the indictment in this case.

Most of the defendants were, moreover, of the stature of 'major war criminals'; von Weiszaecker was the close assistant of von Ribbentrop; Lammers, chief of the Reich Chancellery, was condemned on the ground of administrative acts, as was Frick; Woermann played a specific role in the planning and preparation of the war against Poland. Keppler and Koerner were convicted on the ground of their activities in the Four-Year Plan, in a similar, though somewhat lower, function to that of Funk. In the opinion of Judge Powers, however, the evidence ought to have established that the defendants convicted had "committed some act intended to have some effect in bringing about a war, knowing it would be a war of aggression", an evidence that he considered 'conspicuous by its absence' in this case [5]). He took, thus, the

1) Taylor, o.c., p. 341.
2) See the reasons for von Papen's acquittal, above, pp. 22 and 218.
3) Transcript, p. 69.
4) See, for example, the acquittal of v. Weiszaecker with respect to the invasion of the Low Countries, ibidem, p. 102, and with respect to the invasion of Russia, ibidem, pp. 109—110.
5) Transcript dissenting opinion, pp. 37, 40 and 44.

stricter line of the 'policy-making level' characteristic of the previous Tribunals.

Though these judgments did not make the limits of individual responsibility quite clear and though they did not express an entirely consistent doctrine, they offer an interesting contribution to the law with respect to the crimes against peace. Firstly these judgments and the appendant dissenting opinions affirmed, with independently reasoned conclusions, the existence of individual criminal responsibility for these crimes, and they did so in the full light of the changed international atmosphere and of the criticisms brought against the Nuremberg Judgment. Secondly they elaborated this law by applying it to categories of officials and industrialists not belonging to the 'major war criminals', and they did so with great care, not led astray by the indiscriminate wording of Law No. 10. Though some of their findings may be open to criticism, these judgments, given by American Military Tribunals but based on the international authority of the London Charter, incorporated in Law No. 10, and on that of the I.M.T., have their place in international penal law and cannot be overlooked in the further development of this law.

Two other trials involving charges of crimes against peace took place before national tribunals, which in both cases convicted the defendant of these charges. Ex-Gauleiter Artur Greiser was judged by the Supreme National Tribunal of Poland, and Takashi Sakai by a Chinese War Crimes Military Tribunal at Nanking [1]). No legal consideration was given in either of these cases to the degree of personal connection with the war, though in Greiser's case it was said that he was an instrument of Hitler.

Volume XV of the Law Reports contains several references to judgments wherein the construction of some Prosecutors in Nuremberg is sustained, to the effect that in an illegal, criminal war all military acts are criminal. This was never carried so far that normal acts of war or occupation were held to be punishable, but served only to rule out certain defences, like that of military necessity in cases of wanton destruction [2]). Like a Polish Court,

---

1) See Law Reports, Vol. XV, Digest of Laws and Cases, on Crimes against Peace, pp. 138–150, pp. 138, 141 and 142.
2) See High Command Trial, Law Reports, Vol. XII, pp. 124–5.

one of the Dutch Special Courts held that all acts committed against the Netherlands or Netherlanders by the German Occupational Authorities were war crimes, on the ground of the illegal nature of the war launched by the German Reich. The Special Court of Cassation stated that this opinion went too far, without however explicitly rejecting the construction behind the opinion [1]).

SECTION 4. THE DOCTRINE ON NUREMBERG

Among the issues discussed in the world wide legal debate which the proclamation of the London Charter and the pronouncement of the Nuremberg Judgment have aroused, the most vividly disputed is certainly that concerning the existence of 'crimes against peace'. An impressive number of international lawyers have contested either the existence of the rule of individual criminal responsibility for aggressive war or the arguments with which the Tribunal has argued the existence of this rule.

And even among the majority of authors on the subject who agree with the proceedings at Nuremberg and with the principles embodied in Charter and Judgment, there is a remarkable tendency to rely more on this judicial decision itself as a precedent, or on arguments borrowed fom natural law, than on the finding of the Tribunal that the Charter "is the expression of international law existing at the time of its creation".

The number of authors who completely endorse the views of the Tribunal on crimes against peace is therefore relatively small [2]). On the other hand, few have gone so far as to reject

1) Zuehlke Trial, Law Reports, Vol. XV, p. 149. See on this whole question below, pp. 297 ff..

2) Under this category may be classed Sheldon Glueck, The Nuremberg Trial and Aggressive War, o.c., Lord Wright, War Crimes under International Law, in Law Quarterly Review, 1946, pp. 40—52, and in History of the U.N. W.C.C., o.c., pp. 547—556, and A. N. Trainin, o.c., who even before the Judgment expressed their opinion. The comments on the Judgment by the former Members of the Tribunal, Lord Lawrence (Lord Oaksey), The Nuremberg Trial, International Affairs, 1947, pp. 151—159, Francis Biddle, o.c., Justice Norman Birkett, International Legal Theories evolved at Nuremberg, International Affairs, 1947, pp. 317—325, and H. Donnedieu de Vabres, o.c., and Le Procès de Nuremberg, Revue de Science Criminelle et de Droit Pénal Comparé, 1947, pp. 171—183, reveal on several points curiously varying interpretations, and the latter does not hide his disapproval of certain findings.
The legality of the Judgment in its findings on crimes against peace is, on

outright the inculpation and conviction of the authors of 'crimes against peace' as unauthorized under international law

---

various grounds but further without qualification, upheld by the following authors: Dr. A. Balasz, Die Rechtliche Begründung des Nürnberger Urteils, Friedenswarte, 1946, pp. 369–375; H. R. Balmer-Basilius, ibidem, pp. 289–293; J. Descheemaecker, Le Tribunal Militaire International des grands criminels de guerre, R.G.D.I.P., 1946, pp. 210–311; Nicholas Doman, Political Consequences of the Nuremberg Trial, Annals of the American Academy of Political and Social Science, 1946, pp. 81–90; F. Eccard, La signification suprême du procès de Nuremberg, R.D.I., 1946, pp. 82–84; D. van Eck, Berechting van oorlogsmisdadigers en de gronden voor een internationaal strafrecht, Nijmegen, 1947; Stefan Glaser, Le principe de la légalité des délits et des peines et les procès de criminels de guerre, Revue de Droit Pénal et de Criminologie, 1947–1948, pp. 230–238; A. L. Goodhart, Questions and Answers concerning the Nuremberg Trial, International Law Quarterly, 1947, pp. 525–531; J. B. Herzog, La répression des criminels de guerre, Revue Pénale Suisse, 1948, pp. 13–38; Solis Horwitz, The Tokyo Trial, o.c.; L. Hugueney, Le procès de Nuremberg devant les principes modernes du droit pénal international, Revue International de Droit Pénal, 1948, pp. 277–280; W. E. Jackson, Putting the Nuremberg Law to work, Foreign Affairs, 1947, pp. 550–565; J. B. Keenan and B. F. Brown, Crimes against International Law, Washington, 1950; Manfred Lachs, Le Jugement de Nuremberg, Revue International de Droit Pénal, 1946, pp. 398–404; A. de La Pradelle, Une révolution dans le droit pénal international, Nouvelle Revue de Droit International Privé, 1946, pp. 360–368; Oppenheim-Lauterpacht, o.c., Vol. II, pp. 191–193; J. A. Maynard, Crimes et criminels de guerre, problème étudié par un groupe de juristes aux Etats-Unis, Revue International de Droit Pénal, 1946, pp. 333–342; Marcel Merle, Le procès de Nuremberg et le châtiment des criminels de guerre, Paris 1949; M. W. Mouton, Oorlogsmisdrijven, o.c.; W. P. J. Pompe, Enige aspecten van het politieke strafrecht, Utrecht 1947, and Les trois degrés du droit pénal, Revue de Droit Pénal et de Criminologie, May 1950, extrait pp. 12–15; A. Sottile, Les criminels de guerre et le nouveau droit pénal international, seul moyen pour assurer la paix du monde, R.D.I. 1945, pp. 225–248; Henry L. Stimson, The Nuremberg Trial, landmark in law, Foreign Affairs, 1947, pp. 179–189; D. N. Sutton, The Trial of Tojo, o.c.; Telford Taylor, The Nuremberg War Crimes Trials, o.c.; M. Teitgen, Le Jugement de Nuremberg, R.D.I., 1946, pp. 161–173; Herbert Wechsler, The Issues of the Nuremberg Trial, Political Science Quarterly, 1947, pp. 11–26; Quincy Wright, The Law of the Nuremberg Trial, A.J.I.L., 1947, pp. 38–72.

Though critical towards the Judgment or not expressly affirming the legality of crimes against peace, the following authors nevertheless support the new rule: M. Caloyanni, Memorandum on International Criminal Legislation and Peace, Revue International de Droit Pénal, 1946, pp. 305–332; Hans Ehard, The Nuremberg Trial against the Major War Criminals and International Law, A.J.I.L., 1949, pp. 223–245; François, o.c., Vol. II, p. 70; Jean Graven, De la justice internationale à la paix: les enseignements de Nuremberg, R.D.I., 1946, pp. 183–210, and 1947, pp. 3–17; Paul Guggenheim, Die Schweiz, das alte und das neue Völkerrecht, Schweizer Monatshefte, 1946, pp. 321–33; F. Honig, Nuremberg, Justice or Vengeance?, World Affairs, 1947, pp. 79–88; Janeczek, The Nuremberg Judgment in the Light of International Law, o.c.; Ph. C. Jessup, The Crime of Aggression and the Future of International Law, Political Science Quarterly, 1947, pp. 1–10; V. V. Pella, La Justice Pénale Internationale, R.D.I., 1945, pp. 88–139 (pp. 93–94); Georges Scelle, Manuel de droit international public, Paris 1948, pp. 964–999; Hans Wehberg, see note under Balmer-Basilius, l.c..

and as a violation of justice [1]). Those denying the legal character of this charge have, for the greater part, considered its inclusion as an exercise of political power by the victorious nations, under the cloak of legal proceedings. Some of them have even recognized the 'punishments' inflicted for the committing of this crime as legally admissible safety-measures for the protection of the international community [2]).

Also among the partisans of the rule of individual responsibility for aggressive war applied in Nuremberg, many differences and nuances of opinion can be noted. These are related not only to the foundation of the rule, but also to the range of its validity whether it is already a part of general international law or, on the contrary, needs a further implementation to become generally binding, and whether or not the Nuremberg Judgment has the legal force of precedent in international law. And finally there is the problem of the interpretation of the criminality of war with respect to its precise effects on the individual and collective plan, a problem – or a whole set of problems – unjustly overshadowed by the discussions on the legality of the Nuremberg proceedings.

In this section the legal basis and the nature of the rule of criminal war applied in Nuremberg will be examined in the light of the legal comments on the trial. The question of the extent of individual responsibility for this crime and of its effects

---

1) This opinion, that of the Defence Counsels in the Nuremberg and subsequent Trials, seems to be held by E. Borchard, International Law and International Organisation, A.J.I.L., 1947, pp. 106–108; W. Grewe and O. Küster, Nürnberg als Rechtsfrage: Eine Diskussion, Stuttgart, 1947; F. B. Schick, The Nuremberg Trial and the International Law of the Future, A.J.I.L., 1947, pp. 770–794.

2) The charge of Crimes against Peace is considered as a political, or otherwise non-legal, charge by the following authors: Montgomery Belgion, Victor's Justice, London 1948; F. H. Comtesse, Betrachtungen zum Nürnberger Prozess, Schweizer Monatshefte, 1946, pp. 457–463; G. A. Finch, The Nuremberg Trial and International Law, l.c.; L. Gross, The Criminality of Aggressive War, The American Political Science Review, 1947, pp. 205–225; Lord Hankey, Politics, Trials and Errors, Oxford 1950; Hans Kelsen, Will the Judgment in the Nuremberg Trial constitute a Precedent in International Law, International Law Quarterly, 1947, pp. 153–171; Otto Kranzbühler, Nürnberg als Rechtsproblem, in Um Recht und Frieden, Festgabe für Erich Kaufmann, Stuttgart–Köln, 1950, pp. 219–237; Viscount Maugham, U.N.O. and War Crimes, o.c.; Max Radin, Justice at Nuremberg, Foreign Affairs, 1946, pp. 369–384; B. V. A. Röling, Strafbaarheid van de agressieve oorlog, o.c.; G. Schwarzenberger, The Judgment of Nuremberg, Tulane Law Review, 1946–1947, pp. 329–361.

on interstate relations will be dealt with in the final section of this Chapter.

As shown in the analysis of the Judgment, the Nuremberg Tribunal, applying the law of the Charter, relied chiefly on the formal argument that this law was decisive and binding on the Tribunal [1]). Therefore not only its substantial argument as to the pre-existence of the rules applied, but also its arguments for the competence of the Powers to draft the Charter have the character of *obiter dicta;* in strict consequence, it would, according to the Tribunal, have been sufficient to determine the facts and to apply the rules of the Charter to these facts.

It is regrettable that the Tribunal followed the method of the Prosecution in cumulating more or less contradictory legal arguments to support its statements, a proper method in view of the functions of Prosecution and Defence, but one that is not favourable to 'the development of international law', an object that the Tribunal had also in mind.

As it often did in the substantial part of its argument, the Judgment in order to justify the Charter appealed to three different constructions of its enactment and implementation; the first as an exercise of 'sovereign legislative power' over the German territory by the four occupying Powers setting up a municipal court, administering municipal law; the second as an exercise of the municipal power of each of the four signatories doing "together what any one of them might have done singly", which amounts to the construction of an inter-allied court; and the third, the only admissible construction, indicated by the statement that "the Charter is not an arbitrary exercise of power on the part of the *victorious Nations,* but . . . the expression of *international* law . . .". The Charter belongs to international law, it was enacted on behalf of the international community of the United Nations and applied by an independent international court. Any construction of these proceedings under municipal law, either that of occupied Germany or that of the Four occupying Powers, necessarily comes in conflict with the following facts.

---

1) In the following sections no special reference will be made with regard to the findings of the Nuremberg Tribunal reproduced in the foregoing section.

If there existed on the part of the occupying countries 'sovereign legistlative power' over Germany, this was not in consequence of the unconditional surrender of the Reich, but of the assumption of 'supreme authority' by the Four Allies, embodied in the Declaration of Berlin, June 5, 1945 [1]). Whatever may be the outworn doctrine of *debellatio,* to which the Tribunal seems to adhere [2]), it is certainly a postulate of common sense that there can be no government without the consent of the *governing*. Before the Declaration mentioned, no authority of the Allies existed in Germany, only *de facto* power. The authority assumed was, however, exclusively exercised in the name of their respective governments by the Supreme Commanders of the Four Nations, and, since the Potsdam Agreement, for the whole of Germany jointly by these Commanders as Members of the Allied Control Council [3]). It was not exercised by the representatives of the Four Powers at the London Conference. This difference of functions is demonstrated beyond all doubt by the later enactment of Law No. 10 by the Allied Control Council indeed as an exercise of legislative power over Germany "in order to give effect to the terms of the . . London Agreement" . . "to establish a uniform legal basis in Germany for the prosecution of war criminals" [4]). The London Agreement was a proper international legal instrument concluded in accordance with United Nations Declarations – not restricted to the leading Powers – and "in the interest of all the United Nations".

---

1) See text in C. A. Colliard, Droit International et Histoire Diplomatique, Paris 1950, pp. 632 ff.. H. Kelsen, who held that the German State had ceased to exist (The Legal Situation of Germany according to the Declaration of Berlin, A.J.I.L. 1945, pp. 518 ff.), yet stated that the sovereign power over the German territory was only assumed by the Allies in the said Declaration (Will the Judgment in the Nuremberg Trial Constitute a Precedent in International Law?, l.c., p. 168).

2) See the criticism of G. Scelle, Manuel de Droit International Public, 1948, p. 976. According to Jennings, (Government in Commission, B.Y.I.L. 1946, p. 112), the assumption of authority by the Occupying Powers is a "new departure which uses control to provide a machinery of international conquest instead of a machinery of aggrandizement . . . a sublimation of the old law of conquest which may prove an important advance in international law" (quoted by François, II, p. 874).

3) According to Kelsen, Int. Law Quarterly, l.c., pp. 166–7, the Charter could, on the contrary, only have been justified had it been enacted, as Law No. 10 was, precisely on a national basis. The same opinion is held by F. B. Schick, l.c., p. 780 and by L. Gross, l.c., p. 224.

4) L.c., above, p. 202, note 3.

Moreover the Charter was not designed for the punishment of *German* 'major war criminals' only, but for those of "the European Axis countries", including countries over which the Allies had not assumed supreme authority and therefore had no legislative power whatsoever. And it mentioned the return of minor war criminals "to the countries where they committed their crimes", a provision that was neither intended to apply nor applied to German nationals only.

The nature of the London Agreement as a multilateral international legislative instrument is still more evident from its adherence clause, Article 5, of which nineteen governments availed themselves [1]). What was 'recognized' by this adherence was certainly not the 'sovereign legislative power' of the Allies over Germany, as the Tribunal constructs it, but the implementation of a policy in the initial formulation of which some of them had participated. By adhering to the Charter the nineteen governments confirmed it as an international legislative act of the United Nations, endorsed the principles on which the major war criminals were going to be tried and took a certain responsibility for these proceedings. The drafters of Law No. 10 showed their awareness of this situation by including a provision that the governments which adhered to the London Agreement could not interfere with the trials that were going to take place under that law [2]).

The conclusion must be that the Nuremberg Tribunal was an independent international tribunal instituted, with the concurrence of many other nations, by the principal victorious Powers, who had secured custody of enemy persons charged with criminal violations of international law. Prof. Scelle defines the role of the Powers very well when he says that they acted as a *gouvernement de fait international,* a *de facto* international government, and that the judges, contrary to the prosecutors who were national agents, were *des magistrats internationaux* with an even wider power than is suggested by this term, as they were free to fix certain procedural matters and the punishments

---

1) See Oppenheim-Lauterpacht, Vol. II, p. 581, note 3.
2) See text of Law No. 10 l.c..

applicable [1]). Even the function of the prosecution had an international element in that the Chief Prosecutors had to put forward the case of other Nations as well, and that notably the French and Russian Prosecutors had on their staffs representatives from West- and East-European Nations respectively who collaborated in the task of the Prosecution.

In connection with the Tribunal's ruling that the Charter was binding upon it as the law to be applied in the case, the question arises as to what extent the judges were free to disregard certain rules of that law, *e.g.* that of individual responsibility for aggressive war, as not in conformance with existing international law or with the principles of justice. Apart from the Charter, the general rules of international law were also certainly binding upon the Tribunal, and were in fact applied by it [2]). The municipal law of the Nations to which the judges belonged, or that of Germany or any other Nation, could only be applied in so far as the general principles of law recognized by civilised nations are a subsidiary source of international law [3]).

Article 6 of the Charter declares that "the following acts ... are crimes coming within the jurisdiction of the Tribunal for which there shall be individual responsibility". It results, moreover, from the discussions analysed in Section 2 above, that instead of the French proposal, which intended to leave the determination of legal responsibility entirely to the Tribunal, the American view — that the rule of individual responsibility should be explicitly 'declared' so that this question would no more be open for argument and decision at the trial — was

---

1) Scelle, o.c., pp. 965—7. The power of the four Nations to establish the Tribunal was, therefore, independent of the power they acquired in virtue of Germany's capitulation as well as from the authority they assured by the Declaration of Berlin. The opinion of Schwarzenberger, l.c., Kranzbühler, l.c., p. 220, and others, to the effect that the Nuremberg Tribunal was more a joint international Tribunal under the municipal law of the Four Powers as co-soverreigns over Germany, a court international in form but not in substance, must on these grounds be rejected.

2) See for example the Tribunal's findings with regard to the acts-of-States defence. The view that international law was directly binding upon the Tribunal underlies its whole argument concerning the criminality of aggressive war as existing law.

3) Statute of the International Court of Justice, Art. 38 (1 sub c). Such a principle of 'the law of all nations', 'the criminal law of most nations' was invoked by the Tribunal when dealing with the defence of 'superior orders'.

accepted. The imperative 'shall' used in the quoted paragraph and in the whole section on "Jurisdiction and general principles" and the express mandates given to the Tribunal, for example to draw up rules of procedure not inconsistent with the provisions of the Charter and to consider the fact of 'superior orders' only in mitigation of punishment, make it clear that according to the Charter its provisions were binding upon the Tribunal, and that the Tribunal could not let a defendant go unpunished if his actions were proved to correspond to the definition of 'crimes' in Article 6.

The Tribunal in fact avoided the question by finding that the provisions of the Charter were merely declaratory of existing international law, but if it had found both laws conflicting it could have applied the law of the Charter on the ground of the rule *lex specialis derogat lege generali.* But such a finding presupposed the recognition of the competence of the Powers to legislate in criminal matters for the present case. The application of the Charter presupposed likewise that the Tribunal did not deem such an application in conflict with elementary justice. Here again the Tribunal avoided open conflict with the Charter by putting an extremely restrictive interpretation on provisions the application of which might otherwise, in the view of the Tribunal, have been contrary to international law or principles of justice. This was notably the case with the provisions regarding the criminality of organisations, the common plan or conspiracy, and the crimes against humanity from which the Tribunal excluded the atrocities against German civilian populations committed before the beginning of the war [1]).

The freedom of the International Military Tribunal to apply general international law and to decide according to principles of justice was thus limited by the positive provisions of the Charter. This implied, on the part of the individual judges who agreed to become member of the Tribunal, a previous acceptance of the Charter as a valid and binding legal instrument in

---

1) Judgment, o.c., p. 498. Cf. the severe criticism of the Charter and of the Indictment on the points mentioned, by the French Judge, Donnedieu de Vabres, in his course before the Academy of International Law, o.c., where he states moreover that the Tribunal "jugeait qu'il *fallait* rattacher les règles ...improvisés ...de la Charte à des principes antérieurs" (p. 486, italics supplied).

harmony with international law. As the Tribunal's jurisdiction rested solely upon the Charter, it could never declare its substantial provisions inapplicable and could only interpret them [1]).

It is necessary to stress this point in view of the criticism levelled at the constitution of the Tribunal as a mere victor's tool [2]). The members of the Tribunal sat as individuals, and not as representatives of their countries or of their governments. The fact that two of the judges belonged to a country that had made itself, to say the least, an accomplice in German aggressions and the fact that neither neutral nor German judges served on the bench, are – however objectionable from a political point of view and however detrimental to the Tribunal's authority in the eyes of public opinion – legally irrelevant [3]). Both neutral and German judges would have had to accept the law of the Charter as the basis for the trial. It is at the unilateral enactment of this Charter or at its substantial provisions or at their application in the Judgment, that legal criticism may be levelled.

On the other hand, if it was to be accepted as an international judicial organ, the Tribunal was bound to justify, in the light of international law, the substantial provisions of the Charter it had accepted, to prove their conformity to, or to account for their departure from, the hitherto accepted general rules. The tacit application of provisions which *prima facie* appeared to be partial and incidental would not have been consistent with the international character of the Tribunal.

---

1) See Röling, dissenting opinion, o.c., pp. 45–45a. In this respect it is surprising that after having served two an a half years on the bench, two Members – the French and the Indian Judges – of the Tokyo Tribunal declared the Tribunal incompetent to apply the provisions of the Charter on the facts proved during the Trial.

2) Schick, l.c., p. 783; Kelsen, l.c., p. 171. In general all those who consider the punishment of the authors of the war as a political act regard the Tribunal – consequently, one may say – in this respect as an instrument of the victors. It is, on the part of some upholders of the Tribunal's Judgment, however, an abuse of words to refer to the Judges as 'representatives' of the Powers that nominated them. Though the Judgment can, to a certain extent, be fairly considered as an expression of the public opinion prevailing in the United Nations, it is incorrect to regard it as part of a *policy,* as Henri Stimson tends to do (The Nuremberg Trial, Landmark in Law, Foreign Affairs, January 1947, pp. 179–189, pp. 184–5). The conception of the Judgment as an authoritative case under an International Common Law eloquently defended by Stimson, (see below), stands or falls with the independence of the Tribunal as a court under international law.

3) See Judge Francis Biddle, Le Procès de Nuremberg, l.c., pp. 1–19, pp. 2–3.

There may exist no rule of international law which prohibits such an application of *ad hoc* provisions to captured enemy leaders. But no more than summary execution would such a proceeding have had any connection with international law. It would have been an exercise of power outside the range of law, without any significance for its development.

It is therefore that the Tribunal's statement that it was "not strictly necessary to consider whether and to what extent aggressive war was a crime before the execution of the London Agreement", that it had heard full argument from the Prosecution and the Defence, and that it would give its opinion on this question only "in view of the great importance of the questions of law involved", came, as has been observed, "to say the least, unexpectedly" [1]. The significance of the Judgment is, as Schwarzenberger has said, entirely dependent on its 'persuasive authority", on "whether, and to what extent, the Tribunal has done more than merely apply its Charter; whether it has convincingly declared international customary law" [2]. One can go further and say that without such an argument the punishment of the individuals responsible for the war would have been no more than a political incident under the guise of a judicial proceeding; the Tribunal had to demonstrate that it had its own judical responsibility for the application of *law*.

In order to substantiate its statement that the Charter was "an expression of international law at the time of its creation" [3], the I.M.T. had to prove two premises: first that aggressive war was illegal, outlawed and regarded as criminal, in international law; secondly, that there existed individual criminal responsibility for its preparation and waging, *id est,* that the perpetrators of these acts could be punished under international law, the term 'criminal responsibility' presupposing a penal rule attaching a penalty to the act it defines.

The Judgment, however, supplied arguments from positive

1) Scelle, o.c., p. 979.

2) Schwarzenberger, l.c..

3) The interpretation of Scelle, o.c., p. 975, to the effect that '*its* creation', '*sa* création', refers to 'sa propre création' (of the new international law, and not of the Charter), is, however ingenuous, still more in conflict with the English than with the French text, and certainly with the obvious intention of the Tribunal.

law for the first proposition only and it deduced from that the existence of individual criminal responsibility with arguments proper to a legislator; finding that aggressive war was "illegal in international law", the Tribunal argued that it was desirable, necessary, and not unjust nor contrary to any compulsory principle of public international law that its authors would be punished. Two links had to be provided to connect Article 6 a) of the Charter with the Kellogg Pact: that between illegality and criminality, and that between State and individual responsibility in the sphere of international relations. However much one may agree with the principles enunciated by the Tribunal, they must be recognized as new law, neither applied nor recognized, though not repudiated either, before 1939, when the whole notion of international criminal law was conspicuous by its non-existence in international relations.

That the Tribunal was well aware of this situation is evident from its argument concerning the maxim *nullum crimen, nulla poena sine lege*. In the Tribunals opinion adequate homage was paid to this maxim in the field of international law when only the aggressor had known that he was doing *wrong* [1]). The new penal rule formulated by the Charter could, according to this view, be applied once it was proved that aggressive war was "an illegal thing", and that the defendants were aware of that. It does not add to the authority of the Judgment that this situation was not explicitly admitted, and that the Tribunal tried to uphold a positivist basis by interchanging the words 'illegality' and 'criminality', and by drawing an analogy to the punishment of ordinary war crimes not penalized in the Hague Convention. This comparison overlooked the fact that grave violations of the rules of warfare had for a long time been held punishable by virtue of the criminal laws of all civilized nations [2]).

Most critics of the Judgment have, however, concentrated

---

[1]) This natural law concept of crime squarely contrasts with the axioma of critics like Schwarzenberger, in whose opinion the notion of international crime presupposes an international criminal law which presupposes in turn a strong central government (Schwarzenberger, l.c.). The historical implication of this view, namely that penal justice can only exist within a well organised community, is contradicted by the facts of legal history.

[2]) See Donnedieu de Vabres, Revue de Droit Pénal et de Criminologie, l.c., p. 820, and Kelsen, l.c., p. 160.

their efforts on a refutation of the Tribunal's opinion that aggressive war was in virtue of the Kellogg Pact 'an illegal thing' in international relations before 1939, and that it was in state-practice universally regarded as 'a crime' as evidenced by a series of declarations and resolutions made during the twenties.

Like the Defence [1]), the critics have invoked the reality of state practice in the inter-war period, particularly in the thirties, which, in their view, had nullified any legal effect that the Pact of Paris and other instruments may ever have had. These critics have relegated the Pact of Paris to the moral sphere on account of its lack of sanctions and the absence of an objective legal criterion for the 'outlawed' war, and they have contended that no customary rule could be deduced from resolutions and unratified treaties if the practice of States did not reflect such a rule and showed, on the contrary, acquiescence in aggressive wars and recognition of their consequences [2]).

In particular it has been pointed out that the gross violations of the alleged rule by one of the Prosecuting Powers, Russia, which shared in Germany's aggression against Poland, subsequently went to war against Finland and afterwards incorporated the three Baltic States with which it had concluded non-aggression treaties, demonstrated beyond doubt the non-existence of such a thing as illegal war in general international law, and the partial and incidental character of the rule applied. Attention has even been drawn to infringements of the territorial rights of neutrals during the Second World War by various Allied States, such as the British operations in the Norwegion territorial sea, the drastic occupation of Iran by the U.S.S.R. and Great Britain, and the occupation of Iceland by American troops, and to the British plans for an occupation of Norway [3]), all of which had been, or would have been approved of by world conscience [4]).

---

1) See above, pp. 209—212.

2) See Finch, l.c., pp. 26—28; Gross, l.c., p. 219; Ehard, l.c., p. 238; Röling, o.c., p. 15.

3) Some of these instances are discussed by Hankey, o.c., pp. 14—16, and on the Allied plans regarding Norway, pp. 70—79. During 1941 the American naval forces in the Western Atlantic Area and round Iceland received orders to attack any German forces appearing in these parts of the high sea, see John L. Zimmerman, A Note on the Occupation of Iceland by American Forces, Political Science Quarterly, Vol. LXII, pp. 103—7.

4) See Röling, o.c., p. 43, note 7.

Like the Defence Counsel in Nuremberg, George Finch, the editor in chief of the American Journal of International Law, has concluded that the thesis of the criminality of aggressive war in September 1939 was not acceptable [1]). "Under a cloak of justice" – Lord Hankey has said – "these trials were just the old, old story – one law for the victors and another for the vanquished. *Vae Victis*" [2]).

When discussing the Allied conduct during the war, one must beware of generalizations; for the occupations of Iceland and Iran did get the consent of the local governments, and while the mining of Norwegian Leads was a violation of Norwegian neutrality, no aggressive action against Norway was ever considered by the British Cabinet [3]). The Russian record is different.

It has rightly been said that "the obvious omissions from the recital" (in the Judgment) "make it difficult to accept it as an impartial historical document" [4]). The veiling, if not the distortion, of history of which the Tokyo Judgment gives some examples and which, according to Röling, are inevitable in such 'political' processes [5]), was, in the Nuremberg Trial anyway, a hardly-avoidable consequence of the composition of the Tribunal and of Russia's presence among the Prosecuting Governments.

But the question submitted here is whether or not there existed a rule of law concerning aggressive war. If such a rule existed, it was not invalidated by the fact that another violator of the law remained, because of his power, beyond the pale of justice, nor even by the fact that such a violator was among the accusers and that two of its nationals were among the judges. This circumstance was regrettable and certainly diminished the prestige of the trial in the eyes of the public. But should this have been a compelling reason to leave the law unapplied and

---

1) Finch, l.c., p. 33.
2) Hankey, o.c., p. 56.
3) If the facts and documents published by Churchill in his book The Second World War, Vol. I, ("The Gathering Storm"), pp. 421–439, had, however, been submitted to the Nuremberg Tribunal, there would certainly have been ground for a milder judgment regarding Räders part in the planning of the invasion in Norway (see above, p. 219). See Hankey, o.c., pp. 63 ff.. The fact that only Germany's archives were available in the Nuremberg Trial makes the Tribunal's recital of recent history and Germany's aggressions though not untrue, yet onesided and disproportionate.
4) Finch, l.c., p. 26.
5) Röling, o.c., pp. 3 and 37–38.

to let its flagrant violators go unpunished? It must not be overlooked that the Nuremberg Trial was the first attempt to contribute to world order by criminal justice and that the possibility to administer justice was, and is, conditioned by the relative power of the international policemen to get hold of the criminals.

The situation is different with respect to the pre-war conduct of the States which had signed the Kellogg Pact and joined in resolutions and declarations to the effect that war was a crime. It is not on the ground of violation, but of non-application of these instruments by their signatories, on the ground of the latters' indifference towards aggressions and of their neutral attitude towards aggressors, that legal effect has been denied to those instruments. The Defence in Nuremberg submitted this contention in yet another form: not only the Pact of Paris, but also many of the non-aggression treaties to which Germany was a party, were concluded on the basis of the collective security system that the nations of the world tried to construct after the First World War. This attempt failed, however, and according to the rule *rebus sic stantibus* these treaties must be considered as having lost their binding force.

The first objection to these contentions must be that, whatever the validity of this controversial rule in international law, it would certainly go too far to apply it in favour of those members of the international community whose ruthless law-breaking was the precise cause of the political insecurity that brought about the breakdown of the collective system. The fact that the other Powers did not have the courage, the sense of solidarity and the political wisdom to confront the aggressors with a united force, to apply sanctions effectively, or even to refuse recognition to their illegal conquest, can – of itself – never lead to the conclusion that the law they laid down, prohibiting and outlawing aggression, thereby lost its binding force. For the mere fact that a wrong is tolerated does not make it any the less wrong.

Much more serious is the argument that the other signatories lost the power subsequently to punish acts which they themselves sanctioned by their recognition or by an agreement at the time they were committed. The plea of condonation should indeed be admitted for such actions as the annexation of Austria, the seizure of Sudetenland after the Munich Agreement, the aggression in Manchuria and the wars, if wars they were, between Japan and Russia, each of which was followed by recognitions, treaties or agreements with the Powers concerned. Unhappily this principle was not applied by the Far Eastern Tribunal [1]) or by the U.S. Tribunals, but it was applied in Nuremberg where none of the acts mentioned was charged as an independent crime, and where they were included in accusations and convictions only in so far as their planning or execution had been perpetrated as steps "to further aggression" [2]). But this condonation is a question of fact, it does not affect the law. And it is, therefore, no sound conclusion from pre-war history "that certain acts not treated as criminal by the Prosecuting Governments at the time they took place, were subsequently transformed into crimes or conspiracies against peace..." [3]). A penal rule may have been added in Nuremberg but if the Paris Pact and the other documents mentioned before had legal effect, no 'transformation' took place. The illegality of aggressive war was not nullified by the temporary failure of the Governments to draw from that illegality practical consequences. The Powers acted too late to forestall the outbreak of the Second World War, but they acted finally.

The second objection is of a similar nature, but deals with the allegation that frequent breaches of the law finally abrogate it. Referring to Jahrreisz *tableau saisissant* of the pre-war failure of collective security, Donnedieu de Vabres, former French judge in Nuremberg, stated that it had only one fault: it applied the thesis of the nineteenth century positivists, Hegel, Laband and Jellinek, that facts only create law and that law is finally dependent on force: "La fréquence d'infractions à la loi pénale n'entraîne pas l'abrogation tacite de cette loi — ça serait exclure toute répression organisée, et, faute de répression, toute société viable" [5]). The existence of a *loi pénale* may be doubted;

---

1) See above, p. 29, and, on the Weiszaecker Trial, p. 232.
2) See above, pp. 22 and 218. The Tribunal did not, however, invoke the principle of condonation, and based its decision on the circumstance that the acts in question did not have the character of wars.
3) Finch, l.c., p. 28.
4) See Stimson, l.c., pp. 184–5.
5) O.c., p. 498–9. Cf. Ehard, l.c., p. 244, who states that the universal importance of the trial lies in the fact that in Nuremberg was recognized the priority of law over force.

the statement applies no less to the prohibition and outlawry of war.

On what legal basis did this rule rest? Of the dual construction of the Tribunal, the conventional part, based on the Paris Pact, is certainly the stronger, and it is doubtful whether the Tribunal would ever have invoked the other documents as evidence of a customary rule if the term 'crime' as starting point for the assumption of a penal rule had not been absent from the wording of the Kellogg Pact. The Pact had another disadvantage for the purpose of the trial: it did not use the term 'aggressive war'. The Tribunal did not deal with this point, but as such a war must *per se* be waged "as an instrument of national policy" the difference could well be neglected.

Critics of the Charter and the Judgment have, however, argued the inconclusiveness of the Pact on the ground of the absence of an objective criterion for such a war and of a central organ to determine its occurrence. The opinion of the Defence and of some authors that it is impossible to prohibit, with legal effect, an undefined or indefinable act must be rejected [1]); high treason has never received a satisfactory definition, yet it is punished regularly by municipal courts. Schick argues that it is difficult to give a comprehensive definition of "the somewhat popular term 'war of aggression' ", but that it is "quite possible to determine on the basis of positive international law whether or not the resort to or the provocation of war constitutes a violation of an international obligation". He adds however that "so long as the exercise of the right to render this vital decision is reserved to the victor, his verdict pronouncing that the vanquished resorted to an illegal war will constitute a legally problematical and politically hazardous act" [2]).

Both statements are erroneous. It has been argued in Chapter Two that illegality, the violation of an obligation, can never constitute an essential element of the concept of aggression; that opinion reduces the problem of aggression to a vicious circle. This is still more evident in the present case, as Article 6a) juxtaposes 'war of aggression' and 'war in viola-

1) Finch, l.c., p. 36: "An indefinable act cannot be prohibited unless we are willing to acknowledge our customary heresy with regard to *ex post facto* legislation".

2) Schick, l.c., p. 783.

tion of international treaties, agreements or assurances'. The Tribunal, having decided that Germany's wars were aggressive, did not deem it necessary to "discuss the subject in further detail and to consider to what extent they were also in violation of treaties...", etc. [1]). Obviously, the waging of a war of aggression, first mentioned in Article 6a), was considered to be a graver breach of law than that of a war in violation of treaties. It was considered thus precisely because of the Kellogg Pact, a general 'law making' treaty of the community of nations. Only by virtue of this treaty did aggressive war become an 'illegal thing' under international law and a matter of concern to all States, signatories of the universal Pact. As Stimson said in what he called "an exact, not a rhetorical description of the crime of aggressive war": " 'Peace is indivisible'. The man who makes aggressive war at all makes war against mankind" [2]). Universal interest in the preservation of peace lay at the root of, and was expressed in the Pact of Paris. It is only by overlooking this basic difference between a bilateral treaty and the universal proclamation of a new law that Finch draws this anomalous conclusion from the Nuremberg dictum: "Individuals may now be punished for violations of treaties in the absence of express agreements to that effect" [3]).

The other observation of Schick is equally incorrect in that it attributes to the victor a judicial decision given by an independent court after a lengthy trial during which abundant evidence was produced, not only of the aggressive character of Germany's wars, but also of the plainly aggressive intent with which these wars had been planned and prepared over many years. Though the difficulties of defining aggressive war remain unsolved and indeed prove at the present moment to be the main obstacles to a codification of the penal rule concerning aggressive war (see Chapters Two (Section 6) and Five), they constituted no obstacle in the 'clear case' before the Nuremberg Tribunal. The Judgment could leave aside the whole question of the definition of aggression, as that question became *une pure question de fait.* As Paul de La Pradelle said "Le déclenchement d'une guerre

1) Nuremberg Judgment, l.c., p. 458. See above p. 21.
2) Stimson, l.c., p. 184.
3) Finch, l.c., p. 35.

recevait sa qualification criminelle en fonction d'un plan d'agression". And Prof. Donnedieu de Vabres: "Au lieu et place d'une détermination automatique, tirée de la seule évidence momentanée de l'acte, l'incrimination de l'agression par le Statut supposait une récherche d'intention, d'évidence prolongée, de durée, que l'accusation de complot, plus expressément, rendait indispensable" [1]).

Though to a lesser degree than in the Tokyo case, – which was far less clear than that of Nuremberg [2]) – the analysis of the Nuremberg Judgment and particularly of the individual convictions demonstrates that the Tribunal sought less to attribute responsibility for the wars prepared and waged, than to disclose a criminal intention aimed at such preparation and waging [3]).

The disclosure of documents evidencing this criminal intent, like the records of Hitler's four secret conferences in the Nuremberg case, must in the present state of international relations be considered a condition for a judicial determination of aggression and, therefore, of any punishment for crimes against peace. So long as the international community has not established unambiguous objective criteria for aggression and self-defence, has not defined concrete acts that are in themselves forbidden, no convincing proof of personal responsibility for aggression can be given from the facts constituting that aggression alone. The plea that the accused thought they acted, and had to act in self-defence, cannot be ruled out except on the ground of evidence to the effect that the accused in fact did not think so. The maintenance of world order demands the effective suppression of every use of force endangering the community of States [4]). But in addition to the determination, by the competent international organ, of such an act as a violation of the rule against the use of force, evidence of the intention to violate the rule on the part of the authors of the act is required for the establishment of their guilt.

---

1) Donnedieu de Vabres in R.d.C., l.c., p. 495, and de La Pradelle, quoted ibidem in note.

2) See above, p. 24.

3) See further above, pp. 27 ff..

4) See above, Chapter II, pp. 69 ff., on the distinction between political aggression and aggression as a criminal act.

Apart from the contradictory state practice, and apart from the lack of a definition of aggressive war, the absence of sanctions in the system of the Kellogg Pact has also been put forward against its use as a legal basis for the Nuremberg dictum on crimes against peace. In so far as this argument has been used to demonstrate that no penal rule was established by the Pact, it is evidently correct. From the consideration of the Pact in the foregoing Chapters it is manifest that such a preoccupation was foreign to its authors. Even Henri Stimson, the authority the Tribunal quoted in support of its finding that the Pact of Paris made aggressive war illegal and its authors 'law breakers', said in the same speech from which that quotation was taken: "The Kellogg Briand Pact provides for no sanctions of force . . . Instead it rests upon the sanctions of public opinion which can be made one of the most powerful sanctions of the world. Any other course . . . would have confused the broad simple aim of the treaty and prevented the development of that public opinion which lies behind all international intercourse in time of peace. Its efficacy depends upon the will of the people of the world to make it effective. If they desire to make it effective, it will be irresistible" [1]).

But did this interpretation also mean, as some critics have alleged, that the Pact did not create a legal obligation for the signatory States? It is said that the Pact, brought about by the pressure of public opinion, notably that in the United States, and expressing the public condemnation of war, formulated only a moral rule, a desirable standard for international conduct. And Schwarzenberger has accused the Tribunal of ignoring the discrepancies between public opinion and that of governments on the standards for conduct of international relations [2]). But it is making a rather strange distinction between treaty commitments to deny, on the ground of its popular support, any legal effect to an express renunciation of "war as an instrument of national policy" and to an undertaking that the solution of international controversies shall be sought by pacific means only.

---

1) Quoted by Maugham, o.c., pp. 71–2.
2) Schwarzenberger, l.c., p. 345 ff..

Even if the consequences drawn from this general prohibition of war were for the time being restricted to a denial of its benefits to the State violating the rule by going to war, and even if the international atmosphere did not favour the acceptance of the further conclusions embodied in the Budapest Articles of Interpretation, the fundamental legal obligation was nevertheless created. It was recognized as such by the majority of the authors [1]) and could only have been abrogated by express provision to that effect in a subsequent treaty of the signatory States. Further provisions and sanctions for the strengthening of the rule could have been taken at any time, but with the growing insecurity in the world this machinery was only devised after the conclusion of the Second World War, when the rule of the Pact of Paris, extended to all use of force, was embodied in the Charter of the United Nations.

The legal situation is quite different with respect to the second argument invoked by the Nuremberg Tribunal in support of the criminality of aggressive war: the customs and practices of States. As the Tribunal, after mentioning this source of international law, referred to a number of unratified treaties and some resolutions, it must be concluded that it offered these documents as evidence of the existence of an international customary rule. This rule was understood to be more explicit than that of the Kellogg Pact; in the view of the Tribunal these documents added something to the condemnation and renunciation of war, otherwise it would not have quoted the documents concerned, none of which had any legal value of its own, in support of a binding treaty provision. The designation of aggressive war as an 'international crime' in the Draft Treaty of Mutual Assistance, in the unratified Geneva Protocol, in the Assembly Resolution of 1927 and in the Havana Resolution of 1928, was evidently relied upon as a basis for the contention that aggressive war was not only illegal and outlawed but also brought its authors within the scope of criminal justice. This becomes clear from the

---

1) See for example Oppenheim-Lauterpacht, Vol. II, p. 191. See further Chapter II, section 5, above.

addition to these documents of the 'precedent' Article 227 of the Versailles Treaty, announcing the constitution of a special tribunal for the trial of the ex-Emperor of Germany "for a supreme offence against international morality and the sanctity of treaties".

These documents must therefore be discussed as arguments for the rule of individual criminal responsibility for the war which was found to be illegal, the second rule the existence of which in pre-war international law the Tribunal had to prove in order to substantiate its contention that the Charter was an expression of international law at the time of its creation. Though the Tribunal held that the renunciation of war in the Pact of Paris 'necessarily involved' the proposition that the planners and wagers of war 'committed a crime in so doing', it expressed its awareness of the indecisiveness of the Pact in this respect by adding: "The law of war is to be found not only in treaties but in the customs and practices of States, which gradually obtained universal recognition, and from the general principles of justice applied by jurists and practised by military courts". Evidently the Tribunal had in mind Article 38 of the Statute of the International Court of Justice, listing the sources of international law.

The Tribunal's reference to the forementioned documents as evidence of a customary rule making war a crime on the part of those who plan and wage it, has been severely criticised. Those who disagree with the punishment of the authors of the war have, indeed, had no difficulty in showing the extreme weakness of this argument which the Tribunal adopted from the American Chief Prosecutor [1]). While Sir Hartley Shawcross relied more exclusively on the conventional rule of the Pact of Paris, Justice Jackson built part of his case on an alleged development of the practice of States in the interwar-period.

Neither of the two elements constituting an international custom, viz. a general practice and its acceptance as law, had

---

1) Finch, l.c., p. 26; Gross, l.c., pp. 210 ff.; Röling, o.c., pp. 12 ff.. Also Wechsler, who supports the Judgment, states that there is among its defenders too large a disposition to look for stray tags of international pronouncements to argue that the law was already fully laid down, l.c., p. 24.

been realized in the present case. In the first place, in order to deduce from the use in solemn declarations and eloquent preambles of the ambiguous term 'international crime' the intention to establish a penal rule at a time when the notion of international penal law was entirely absent from international relations, the Tribunal should have been able to offer explicit evidence of such an intention. Not only is this evidence lacking in the Judgment, but in the case of many of the documents quoted evidence can be offered to the contrary; as in the case of the Pact of Paris, the authors of the Geneva Protocol and of the Resolution of 1927 made it quite clear that their terminology did not have a penal significance

The aim of the Geneva Protocol was, as Benes said, "to make war impossible, to kill it, to annihilate it", and the Polish delegate Sokal saw the significance of his resolution in its great moral and educative value [1]).

But even if it had been otherwise, the objection of Finch must be accepted to the effect that "unratified protocols cannot be cited to show acceptance of their provisions, and resolutions of international conferences have no binding effect unless and until they are sanctioned by subsequent national or international action" [2]). Only such action, in the domain of criminal law, could have given rise to the gradual development of a customary rule within the limits of that action. But action was not undertaken, it was not thought of by the governments who rejected or ignored the proposals of international legal associations for the constitution of an international criminal jurisdiction in this and other matters. Hence there could be no question of the emergence of a customary rule whose content — to serve the purpose of the Tribunal's argument — should have been that aggressive war is a crime the individual perpetrators of which may be punished by the State which may secure custody of them.

Sheldon Glueck, who strongly defended Jackson's point of view which was later accepted by the Tribunal, may well be taken literally when he says that "during the present century

---

1) Quoted by Gross, l.c., pp. 213—3; see also Röling, o.c., pp. 48—50.
2) Finch, l.c., p. 26.

a widespread custom has developed among civilised States to enter into agreements expressive of their solemn conviction that unjustified war is so dangerous a threat to the survival of mankind and mankind's law that it must be branded and treated as criminal" [1]). If one replaces 'enter into agreements' by the more exact term 'make declarations', and if the term 'treated' is omitted as not based on the documents quoted, this is an exact description of what happened in Geneva and elsewhere in the inter-war period, but what could never amount to the development of a customary rule. The "mere habit of repeating a certain formula" has to be well distinguished, as Gross [2]) remarks, from the legally obliging practice or usages of States.

No single obligation was undertaken, no right was established by this use of the term 'crime', and the whole reference to a practice of States would be better omitted in connection with the illegality or criminality of war before 1939, as this practice, by commission or omission, was often hardly consistent with the obligations of the Kellogg-Briand Pact. It was only in virtue of the latter that aggressive war, notwithstanding an ambiguous practice of States, became illegal in international law and outlawed in the sphere of international relations prior to 1939. The Pact of Paris resumed and extended all the previous efforts to abolish war, including the provisions to that effect in the Covenant of the League of Nations, including previous non-aggression pacts, including also the forementioned drafts and resolutions. The latter, together with the resolutions of non-governmental international associations like the Interparliamentary Union, and of national pacifist movements in the interwar-period, can, however, be regarded as a moral reinforcement, as evidence of a universal public endorsement of the prohibition and outlawry of war.

In addition to its strict legal effect, the rule embodied in the Pact of Paris received, in virtue of this continuous public insistence, the quality of a fundamental law of the international community. Those who planned to violate this law knew that they were preparing more than a mere breach of international

1) Glueck, o.c., p. 26.
2) Gross, l.c., p. 219.

law; they knew that they were going to break a solemn pledge given to a world longing for peace, that their act which would bring unforeseeable suffering to mankind had received the strongest possible universal moral condemnation, and that they, as authors of a war, would, therefore, expose themselves to the accusation of world conscience and to the general desire for retribution, repeatedly expressed in legally imperfect, but morally unmistakable terms [1]).

If this is a correct statement of the legal and moral position of war prior to 1939, the step from there to the allotment of punishment to the authors of the Second World War in Nuremberg and Tokyo does not seem so revolutionary. The penal rule that the Tribunals obstinately attempted to read into positive law certainly did not exist; but indeed was a positive rule needed for the punishment of those responsible for the war?

The strict limitation of municipal criminal justice to the application of previously formulated penal rules, in obedience to the maxim *nulla poena sine lege,* is certainly an expression of the high legal development in most civilized States during the last century and a half. But this practice of legal security can never obliterate the fact that it is not because of the existence of a formulated threat of punishment but because of a grave outrage upon the order of their community that malefactors deserve punishment. The wilful violation of the basic law of the community calls for retribution, for punishment, for a redress of the violated order on the part of the offended community, and it is only later that, on a secondary plan, the requirement of formulated penal sanctions has been added to increase the legal security, to safeguard the liberty of the citizen, to exclude, as far as possible, doubt about the limits of what is punishable and to restrict the power of the judge in favor of the legislature, elected by the people.

As such a legislature is absent in the international community, as international law for its development is still mainly dependent on the casual agreement of its principal subjects, the States, and as the will of the people can thus only indirectly be expressed in

1) Cf. Justice Birkett, l.c., p. 315, stating with regard to war that, since the Kellogg Pact, "People embark upon it at their peril".

international legislation, it must be assumed that the administration of international criminal justice is reduced to its essentials and that the power of the judge to invoke in a concrete way the law of the community is correspondingly greater.

These essential conditions of punishment are: the perpetration of a grave outrage upon the international order and its fundamental law, and the awareness of this outrage as such, *id est* the criminal intent on the part of the perpetrator. The judge meting out punishment to the accused after both these facts had been established beyond reasonable doubt, no penal sanction having previously been attached, by a positive rule, to the committing of this crime, made himself the interpreter of the community whose law had been offended. He thus redressed, on his own authority, the violated law in the spirit of the original legislator: the members of the community [1]). This amounts to saying that of the oft-quoted maxim only the part *nullum crimen sine lege* is essential for justice; in the forementioned conditions the punishment may be added in virtue of the judge's authority.

This is what happened in Nuremberg. The objective factor, the perpetration of a grave outrage, was the waging of an aggressive war, indeed, in view of its consequences, the greatest possible attack on the international community and the violation of its most fundamental rule. And the criminal intent of the perpetrators was established beyond doubt. Both the necessary requirements being thus fulfilled, "it was not the question whether it was legal, but whether it was just to punish Goering c.s." [2]). As Justice Biddle said, the answer to this question was evident. The concept of *ex post facto* law, says Stimson, rests on the assumption that if the defendant had known that the proposed act was criminal he would have abstained from it. This state of mind was wholly absent [3]).

The state of international law, in view of which the punishment of the authors of the war is considered just, has often

---

1) Similar arguments are put forward by Stimson, l.c., p. 185; Lord Wright, l.c., p. 552 ff.; Quincy Wright, Legal Positivism and the Nuremberg Judgment, A.J.I.L., 1948, pp. 405–415, p. 407.

2) Biddle, l.c., p. 9.

3) Stimson, l.c., p. 183.

been called 'primitive'. This qualification is erroneous in so far as it could lead to the conclusion that, in the international community, law could be administered according to the methods and standards of the historical primitive societies. But while international law may still lack a standing legislature and a central executive, and for that reason have its own characteristics that call for a special juridical technique different from municipal law, it has none the less developed in co-existence with domestic law, it is part of the same civilization, an expression of the sense of justice of the present age, and it must therefore comply with the standards of justice deemed essential in civilized States.

Legal security and the liberty of the individual which require that no doubt regarding the law can reasonable exist on the part of the law violators, are in municipal law safeguarded by the demand of 'legality' of the crimes and punishments. The international tribunal, which in a *de facto* situation received the power to try the violators of international law, had to restrict the application of punishment to those of the accused the grave illegality of whose offenses could not have been in doubt either in the eyes of the world or according to their own consciences. This limitation was chiefly maintained by the Nuremberg Tribunal, and the Trial and Judgment must therefore be qualified as the legal proceedings not of a 'primitive' but of an imperfectly organised community.

Traces of a similar justification of the punishment of crimes against peace, on a non-positive basis, are certainly to be found in the Tribunal's argument on the *nulla poena* maxim. In the subsequent part of the Judgment, however, attempts to construe a customary *rule* as a basis of such punishments dominate. The Tribunal wanted to keep up the appearance of criminal jurisdiction under positive law, and did so at the price af an authentic interpretation of treaties and not without "stretching to the breaking point the accepted notions of custom in international law" [1]).

Ehard has drawn attention to the danger, for the reputation of the judge, of stretching "the law upon the bed of Procrustes

---

1) Gross, l.c., p. 220.

until it seems to serve the requirements of the hour" [1]). And Manley Hudson has pointed out that it is impossible to make substantial progress in the development of international law "unless a scrupulous respect obtains for the integrity of international instruments", and he has censured the tendency, of which evidence was supplied by the I.M.T., "to undermine that respect by torturing the meaning of great international instruments and by forcing them to serve purposes for which they were never designed, purposes at variance with the desires entertained by Governments when the instruments were brought into force" [2]).

To a certain extent, however, the Tribunal was forced to such methods by the nature of the Charter which by a declaration of "crimes for which there shall be individual responsibility", among which was the "planning, preparation, initiation or waging of a war of aggression", gave the impression that the relation between the Tribunal and the law was identical with that existing under municipal systems. But it follows from what has been said above that the judges had power to punish in the specific case, and not that the victors had power to legislate in penal matters for the vanquished. The impression of an arbitrary and partial exercise of the victors power would have been avoided if the drafters of the Charter had contented themselves with the French proposal, put forward by Prof. Gros, and had laid down only that the Tribunal had *jurisdiction* to try persons responsible for the 'policy of aggression', or for the aggressions themselves [3]). It would have then been up to the Prosecutors to convince the Tribunal, and it would have been up to the Tribunal to formulate the *ius in causa* to the effect that: "if a man plans aggression when aggression has been formally renounced by his nation, he is a criminal" [4]). But as things stand, the law of Nuremberg is nevertheless to be found in the Tribunal's

---

1) Ehard, l.c., p. 241.

2) Quoted by Prof. E. Wahl, Defence Counsel in the I. G. Farben Trial, Transcript of statement on The Breach of Peace and its Culpability, pp. 1—66, p. 20.

3) See above, p. 196.

4) In these terms Stimson formulates the basic proposition of the American and British Chief Prosecutors concerning the charge of aggressive war, which was adopted by the Tribunal, l.c., p. 184.

Judgment and not in the Charter, as it could only be the judge who in those circumstances had the power to invoke and apply a new penal rule to the specific case.

Many of those who have defended the punishment of the authors of the war as justified under international law, have, indeed, not defended the rule of the Charter but the Judgment of the Tribunal which they considered "a great new case in the book of international law". In his important comment on the Nuremberg Trial *Landmark in Law,* Henry Stimson has devised a concept of international law: "a gradual expression, case by case, of the moral judgment of the civilized world." [1]).

Though this seems too general a conclusion from the single instance of the Nuremberg Trial, Stimson's reasoning can be accepted where he draws the analogy with the origin of criminal justice, when a tribunal replaced the victim's family as judge of the offender as soon as murder was recognized as an offence against the whole community: "all case law grows by new decisions and where those new decisions match the conscience of the community, they are law as truly as the law of murder" [2]). This concept of an 'International Common Law' has been accepted by many authors [3]), and it was relied upon by the later Nuremberg Tribunals under Law No. 10 [4]).

The decision of the I.M.T. to inflict punishment on those responsible for the war has not, in itself, aroused much criticism. Only by a few writers have the constitution of the Tribunal and the declaration of the law in the case been considered illicit acts on the part of the victorious Powers [5]). The German Defence Counsel in Nuremberg and in later trials has done so on the

1) Ibidem, p. 185.

2) Ibidem.

3) For example Wechsler, l.c., passim; Donnedieu de Vabres, o.c., p. 502, and Le jugement de Nuremberg et le principe de légalité des délits et des peines, Revue de Droit Pénal et de Criminologie, 1947, pp. 813—833, p. 833; Stefan Glaser, l.c., p. 230—232 and La Charte du Tribunal de Nuremberg et les nouveaux principes du droit international, Revue Pénale Suisse, 1948, pp. 13—38, pp. 23—24; Merle, o.c., pp. 114—5 and 137. The latter continental writers speak, with reference to Nuremberg, of 'un droit pénal coutumier'.

4) See above, p. 229.

5) Apart from the Defence Counsels in the Nuremberg, Tokyo and later Trials, also Grewe-Küster, o.c., and Borchard, l.c., seem to hold this opinion. Cf. the latter's statement that the Nuremberg Judgment is a violation, not an authority in international law.

ground of a violation of an alleged rule against *ex post facto* law, but otherwise severe critics of the Judgment like Kelsen [1]) and Schick [2]) have rightly stated that no such rule existed in international law. While several authors have rejected the legality of the punishment for crimes against peace, they have agreed with the Tribunal's dicta concerning the desirability and the justice of such punishment.

The rejection of the act-of-State plea and the Tribunal's statement that individuals have obligations under international law, have been hailed as a progress in law. According to Kelsen, the greatest merit of the London Agreement is that it "puts into force the idea of individual criminal responsibility for violations of international law and thus improves – though not in general but for some particular cases – the primitive technique of general international law with its collective responsibility" [3]).

The necessity of taking measures against those who had plunged the world into the horrors of a modern war was, moreover, generally recognized, and some critics of the Judgment have even admitted the moral guilt of these men and approved of their punishment as a requirement of justice [4]).

It is not, however, the fate of the major war criminals but the question of the relation between the Nuremberg law and general international law and the question of what impact this dictum will have on the future, which have stirred up the legal debates. Was the Nuremberg Trial, so far as the authors of the war were concerned, a legal or a political proceeding, and if the first, is it a precedent or an incident in international law?

It is evident that the question of the value of the Nuremberg Judgment as a precedent does not arise for those who accept strictly the Tribunal's statement that the Charter of London is the expression of international law existing at the time of

---

1) Kelsen, l.c., p. 164.

2) Schick, l.c., p. 793.

3) Kelsen, l.c., p. 165. The same idea is expressed by Glaser in Revue Pénale Suisse, l.c., pp. 13–22; Scelle, o.c., pp. 969–970, who remarks, however, that the principle of individual responsibility was in Nuremberg not accepted 'par considération de technique juridique' but 'par considération d'exemplarité' which is the basis of criminal law. The principle of exclusive State responsibility is, at the present day, indeed still firmly established in the domain of public international law.

4) See Kelsen, ibidem, and Maugham, o.c., pp. 74 ff..

its creation. If a penal rule existed already before 1945, it certainly did not cease to exist; and there would be no more need of a precedent than there is in the codification countries. The Nuremberg Judgment would only be significant in so far as it gave an authoritative interpretation of the law.

Wechsler has, indeed, stated that as the Charter was binding upon the Tribunal, "the generalisations set forth in the Agreement demanded, as legislation always does, creative interpretation in its application to the challenging facts of a concrete case" [1]. But at the same time he shows his awareness of the unilateral character of this 'legislation', stating that Nuremberg, far more than San Francisco, was the assumption of an irrevocable obligation [2]. This obligation could be no other than that which the American Judge, Francis Biddle, felt when he insisted in his letter to the President "that the United Nations as a whole re-affirm the principles of the Nuremberg Charter" [3]. Afterwards he stated that there was no doubt that after the General Assembly Resolution of 11 December 1946 "the principles of Nuremberg are now part of the edifice of international law" [4]. A great confidence in the Charter was expressed by the former President of the Tribunal, Lord Justice Lawrence, who stated in an address that "no greater step has been taken in the history of the world than was taken on August 8, 1945" [5]. The French Judge, Donnedieu de Vabres, spoke more carefully, and more in line with those who see the Nuremberg Trial as a single instance of "une oeuvre qui a ses racines dans le passé, mais qui ne manifestera sa pleine raison d'être et ne sera justifiée aux yeux de l'opinion publique que si elle est continuée" [6].

All the partisans of the Judgment, whether they based the law applied therein on the Charter, as did the authors quoted, or on the authority of the Tribunal under an 'international common law', as did most of them, have with varying emphasis indicated the need of a further implementation of this law in order that the statesmen of all States, victors, vanquished and

1) Wechsler, l.c., p. 14.
2) Ibidem, p. 27.
3) See below, p. 311.
4) Biddle, l.c., p. 7.
5) Lawrence, l.c., p. 155.
6) Donnedieu de Vabres in R.d.C., o.c., p. 487.

neutrals of to-day, would be liable to punishment if they ever perpetrated crimes against peace. This amounts to an admission that, far from existing at the time of the enactment of the London Agreement, the penal rule invoked and applied in Nuremberg does not even after the trial exist as a universally applicable rule in general international law.

The consideration of the Nuremberg Trial as an "act of faith" [1]) and the frequent invocations, by the Prosecutors and by later commentators of the Trial, of history as its 'ultimate judge', reflect the view that not only the justice, but also the legality of proceedings and judgment depend on the effect that the members of the world community are going to give to the principles which were for the first time formulated in the London Charter and which received in Nuremberg an unprecedented application, not justifiable by ordinary legal arguments [2]). In this light the opposition between supporters and some adversaries of the Judgment can be reduced to a difference of degree, more properly speaking to one of mentality, where the basic convictions as to the nature of law, more than the legal opinions on the state of positive international law, are at stake.

Those critics who have not founded their objections against the Judgment on the alleged violation of the *nullum crimen* maxim, have, indeed, rejected the jurisdiction over crimes against peace on the ground of its incidental character. They would have admitted the 'revolutionary change' as a legal one if the victors had at the same time subjected themselves to the same rules they formulated for the vanquished. But they have demonstrated that the Charter of San Francisco did not contain any of the 'Nuremberg Principles', that, by the reservation of the veto power, the Prosecuting Powers of Nuremberg have made themselves safe from the application of any sanctions, that no sanctions against individuals are provided for, and that the

---

1) Wright, Legal Positivism and the Nuremberg Judgment, l.c., p. 408.

2) See Birkett, l.c., p. 318, who observes that the frequent assertion that history is the ultimate judge of the Nuremberg Proceedings indicates the uncertainty of the positive legal basis of the Trial. Later in his article the author, who was alternate member of the Nuremberg Tribunal, states with respect to the London Charter: "If it continues to apply only to the enemy, then I think the verdict of history may be against Nuremberg", ibidem, p. 325.

doctrine of acts-of-State is still valid without restriction.

Not in the absence of a pre-existing rule, but in the fact that nearly all the provisions of the London Agreement are absent from the Charter of San Francisco, Schick sees the clear proof that the London Charter was "a temporary derogation of general customary international law', and that the solemn promises that "the four Nations... have enunciated standards of conduct..." which "will become the condemnation of any Nation that is faithless to them" are not real [1]). In order to be effective, the resolutions and recommendations of the General Assembly have to be accepted by the Members and to be implemented by national and international legislation. If those referring to the Nuremberg Principles are not thus implemented, Schick concludes, they will share the fate of so many pre-war proposals and declarations "that far from being declaratory of a general practice of States evidence that the international law of the future is not accepted by the States" [2]).

The objection is serious, and it would, indeed, be the most serious argument that could be brought against the Nuremberg proceedings if it could be said that these were based on an alleged change of the law that it afterwards appeared had not taken place. The question of the acceptance of the Nuremberg Principles in the law of the United Nations will be examined in the following Chapter. But here it is important to note the difference in conclusions drawn from the same fact, the present absence of a criminal jurisdiction in the system of the United Nations; the upholders of the Nuremberg dictum insist on the duty to implement its principles, the adversaries deny for the same reason the legal value of the Judgment.

The difference is not primarily that between optimism and pessimism on the outcome of the present efforts to implement the Nuremberg Principles. It is first of all that between those who affirm and those who deny that, apart from the obligatory rules of treaties and those evidenced by a general practice accepted as binding, there can exist any law deserving the name. Those holding the latter view must necessarily conclude that

---

1) Schick, l.c., p. 770.
2) Ibidem, p. 794.

the Nuremberg Judgment had no other foundation than *ad hoc* provisions, the will of the victors or the personal opinion of *ad hoc* judges. They can only approve of the sentences as "morally justifiable political acts" (Finch)[1], motivated by "high reason of State" (Radin)[2], and they can never admit any effect whatsoever of these exceptional political proceedings on the state of international law. Speaking of Jackson's claim that "our own day has its right to institute customs and to conclude agreements that will themselves become sources of a newer and strengthened international law", Schick adds that this right has to be applied in strict conformance with the prevailing rules of the law of nations[3]. And leaving more room, but not enough to let the Nuremberg Judgment pass, Schwarzenberger has stated that even if international law may be called a 'growing and dynamic body', the law-making by the judge must be organically connected with what has happened before in order to be accepted as a declaration of existing law[4].

It may be thought that those who ban the Nuremberg Judgment from the field of general international law would nevertheless recognize it as proper *law* between the parties to the London Agreement and in its application to the concrete case. Here, however, an insuperable obstacle comes in the way, viz. the fact that the Charter was framed as an instrument, unilaterally applicable to the vanquished whose consent to these proceedings was never sought. Kelsen writes thus: "What really impairs the authority of the Judgment is that the principle of individual criminal responsibility for the violation of rules of international law has not been established as a general principle of law, but as a rule applicable only to vanquished States by the victors"[5]. And Gross states that the passage of three centuries has not materially improved the condition of the enemy that has unconditionally surrendered, of whom Grotius said that it did not make any difference whether he surrendered himself "to the wisdom, or to the moderation, or to the mercifulness of the

---

1) Finch, l.c., p. 35.
2) Radin, l.c., pp. 377 ff..
3) Schick, l.c., pp. 777—8.
4) Schwarzenberger, l.c., p. 344.
5) Kelsen, l.c., p. 170.

victor because the fact remains that the victor becomes absolute master" [1]).

How, in the absence of German state-machinery, could this consent of the defeated have been obtained? Surprisingly enough, both authors quoted would have been satisfied if the Four Powers had not acted in their own name, but on behalf of Germany, as by their supreme authority over the occupied territory, and had, thus, proceeded on a national instead of an international basis [2]). It is difficult to see how such a formal change could have done anything else but veil the arbitrariness of the exercise of power on the part of the victors, if arbitrariness there was. The unilateral and *ad hoc* character of the provisions now embodied in the London Agreement would have been still more emphasized if they had been couched as municipal rules. And validly then could the *nullum crimen* maxim governing all municipal criminal law have been brought against any charge of crimes against peace.

The fact is that the critics of the Charter have seen in the institution of an international jurisdiction over the leaders of a defeated State, a violation of the "fundamental principle of international law prohibiting the unauthorized interference by force of one legal order in the jurisdictional sphere of validity of another, national legal order", the scrupulous observation of which alone permits and guarantees the peaceful co-existence of independent States [3]). It will be remembered that also the French Prosecutor in Nuremberg admitted the validity of this rule, because he gave to the Nuremberg Trial the construction of a municipal proceeding, where exceptionally the responsibility of the individual statesmen could be considered, because the really and normally responsible German State had been dissolved and could not be arraigned. In the same line the French Judge, Donnedieu de Vabres, who before the war was always the champion of an exclusive collective responsibility in international penal law, justified the Judgment on the ground that "la

---

1) Gross, l.c., p. 224.

2) Kelsen, l.c., pp. 167–8; Gross, l.c., ibidem. The same view is held by Schick, l.c., pp. 780–1.

3) Schick, l.c., pp. 778–9; The same view is expressed by Kelsen, Collective and individual responsibility in International Law, Californa Law Review, 1942–3, pp. 530–571, p. 540.

carence de l'Etat allemand... mettait les puissances occupantes en contact nécessaire avec les individus à qui devait être imputée l'initiative de ses actes" and he considers therefore that the penal responsibility of the State — *la personnalité morale* — was not excluded by the Judgment [1]). The idea of the primary criminality of the State can also be traced in the statements of the British Chief Prosecutor who saw the responsibility of the defendants for crimes against peace as that of those who had counselled and procured a crime committed by the State [2]).

Behind this resistance and this hesitation regarding the transition from the traditional notion of sanction to "the more refined technique" of law enforcement through individual punishment, are two different ideas: the first, expressed in the alleged rule of international law, that immunity exists for acts committed on behalf of a State, and the second, formulated as a procedural rule, to the effect that only on the ground of an express rule of international law, or by express consent of his government can an individual be subjected to a jurisdiction other than that of his own State.

Regarding the first proposition, the Tribunal stated that "the principle of international law, which under certain circumstances protects the representatives of a State, cannot be applied to acts which are condemned as criminal by international law". The Tribunal saw the immunity of State-representatives, therefore, as a principle, but one subject to qualifications. It did not accept the view of the British Prosecutor that this immunity was granted by courts only as a matter of comity [3]). It must further be noted that although the Tribunal considered the principle applicable only under certain circumstances, it restricted its non-application to the case of violations of the laws of war, to which it assimilated crimes against peace.

---

1) Donnedieu de Vabres, l.c., p. 486, and in Revue de Droit Pénal et de Criminologie, l.c., p. 822.

2) See above, p. 207.

3) Trial of the Major War Criminals, o.c., Vol. XIX, p. 465. Glueck, o.c., p. 49, deems this immunity restricted "to the normal, peaceful intercourse of nations". The 'théorie de l'Acte d'Etat' is according to Scelle only supported by the "franc-maçonnerie utilitaire des détenteurs de la compétence du Droit des Gens", o.c., p. 971.

The immunity rule would certainly have no meaning if it never applied when "the State in authorizing action moves outside the sphere of its own competence", because it is only then, in cases of violation of law, which the State can never have *competence* to authorize, that immunity can play a role, by imputing the act of the agent to the State, as an international delinquency [1]). In the same way other pronouncements of the Judgment can only be within the strict limits of the Tribunal's jurisdiction, especially because the boundary between international criminality and international delinquency is far from being clearly drawn and the terms are often interchanged in literature.

Ehard qualifies as a truism the much quoted sentence of the Judgment that "crimes are committed by men, not by abstract entities", and rightly states that it proves nothing with regard to individual responsibility in the individual case [2]). The whole question of international criminal law, to be solved by an international code of offences, is: what specific acts of State may be attributed, as crimes, to the individual agents? The frequent reference, in connection with the Nuremberg Trial, to the universal jurisdiction over piracy and similar "crimes against the law of nations", misses this point. The customary rules of universal jurisdiction for these offences may prove that exceptionally individuals were responsible under international law, but this was no departure from the general rule according to which only States were responsible for the violations of international law committed on their behalf by their agents.

Regarding the punishment for aggressive war, however, the doctrine of the Tribunal is acceptable. It assimilated the jurisdiction over these crimes to that recognized long before with respect to conventional war crimes and to its jurisdiction over crimes against humanity which were mostly likewise committed as acts of State. The fact that the crimes in the two latter categories were also crimes according to the municipal law of most countries, according to that of Germany as well to a certain extent, does not on this point make any difference to the fact that the generally recognized jurisdiction over these crimes was

---

1) See however Glueck, o.c., p. 56.
2) Ehard, l.c., p. 240.

equally at variance with the traditional notions of state sovereignty and personal immunity [1]).

The requirement of an express rule or the special consent of the State to a foreign or international jurisdiction over its nationals was met in the case of the Japanese major war criminals to whose trial the Japanese government consented with its unconditional surrender, by accepting the provisions of the Potsdam declaration [2]). Would it have been necessary, in the German case, to put the trial formally on a municipal basis, or otherwise to wait on the reconstitution of the German state-machinery? Once it is admitted that the authors of an aggressive war are criminally responsible, the same consequence may be drawn in the case of ordinary war criminals and perpetrators of crimes *iuris gentium,* that is, that the State in whose power they are may put them to trial according to the universal principle of jurisdiction. *De facto* situations play a dominant role after a war [3]), and though it may be regretted that it was only the victor States who decided to put the criminals in their custody to trial, they certainly did better to proceed that way than to let law and justice be frustrated by a repetition of what happened after the First World War with the Leipzig Trials [4]).

The authors whose views have been discussed above regard the jurisdiction over crimes against peace in the Nuremberg Trial as a political act, an imposition of the will of the victor, which if not in violation of international law, was in any case outside its scope. As the very notion of law supposes the permanence of *rules,* the qualification of a provision as *ad hoc* puts it outside the field of law and implies that its application can only have the outward form of a legal proceeding. The punishment of the authors of the war was for this school of thought a political decision under a legal cloak. While some have scornfully exposed the political decision [5]), others have praised the legal cloak, the safeguards of a trial with which the victor sur-

---

1) See further on this subject below, pp. 290 ff..
2) See Keenan-Brown, o.c., p. 26.
3) See Cowles, l.c., p. 281; Biddle, l.c., pp. 1—2.
4) See Glueck, o.c., pp. 55—7; Scelle, o.c., p. 967.
5) For example Lord Hankey, o.c., passim, and in postscript to Maugham, o.c., p. 114.

rounded his measures, as a progress whose import should not be underestimated [1]).

The legal objections against the punishment for crimes against peace have been closely examined, but it is evident that the views on the legality of the punishment and on its effect as a precedent are not quite separate from the views on the appropriateness and desirability of a penal rule concerning aggressive war. Apart from the general criticism that the announcement of the policy of war crimes trials prolonged the war and that its execution embittered the relations with ex-enemy countries and may make real peace impossible [2]), it has been said that as a matter of legislative policy individual criminal responsibility for aggressive war was inappropriate. Such a rule would not deter future aggressors as wars are waged in the conviction not that they are legal but that they will be successful. Neither would there be any preventive effect on the people to the effect that they would not elect, or would dismiss, an aggressive government, because aggression will always be disguised as defence. And finally, the attribution of personal responsibility for a war could not hide the fact that remote causes and the forces of history are moulding the decision between peace and war in an international society that has not yet found an effective substitute for war in the bringing about of change [3]).

Led by these considerations and by the fact that there was no penal rule concerning aggressive war prior to 1945, Prof. Röling, the Dutch judge at the Tokyo Tribunal, has in his dissenting opinion given a non-penal interpretation of the sentences imposed, which interpretation he has developed in later publications [4]).

Röling started from the necessity to interpret the Charter of Tokyo – and that of Nuremberg – in accordance with international law. The Nuremberg Tribunal had declared it so, and

---

1) Comtesse, l.c., p. 462.

2) Hankey, o.c., pp. 125–126.

3) Röling, o.c., pp. 4–5, and Over Psychologische Aspecten van het proces tegen de Japanse "Major War Criminals", Publication No. 32 of the Psychiatrisch-Juridisch Gezelschap, Amsterdam, 1950; Maugham, o.c., p. 98; Finch, l.c., p. 35. See also C. A. Anderson, The Utility of the proposed Trial and Punishment of Enemy Leaders, American Political Science Review, 1943, pp. 1081–1100.

4) Dissenting Opinion of Mr. Justice Röling, o.c., pp. 46–54; Röling, Strafbaarheid van de agressieve oorlog, o.c..

it could be presupposed that the Allied Powers did not intend to create rules in violation of international law, which would, in Rölings opinion, be the case if a penal rule concerning crimes against peace had been formulated. The formulation of such a penal rule would have constituted a violation of international law not because such a rule did not exist before, the *nullum crimen* maxim being only a rule of policy, but because "the relations of the Nations did not change in the sense that even at this moment every illegal war could be qualified as a vile crime" [1]). But 'crime' could have different meanings in international law, and 'crimes against peace' should be understood in the sense of 'political crimes' in domestic law, where "the decisive element is the danger rather than the guilt, where the criminal is considered an enemy rather than a villain, and where the punishment emphasizes the political measure rather than the judicial retribution" [2]).

For Röling the 'only admissible conception' of the Verdicts of Nuremberg and Tokyo must be based on the fact that "powers victorious in a *bellum justum,* and as such responsible for peace and order thereafter, have, according to international law, the right to counteract elements constituting a threat to that newly established order and are entitled, as a means of preventing the recurrence of gravely offensive conduct, to seek and retain the custody of the pertinent persons" [3]). The elimination of Napoleon, and the proposal of judicial action against Wilhelm II "according to the highest motives of international policy" would be evidence of such a rule. And while this interpretation was in apparent conflict with the Judgment of Nuremberg, it could be based "upon the sentence proper rather than upon the reasons given for it", as only imprisonments were inflicted upon those convicted of what was nevertheless called 'the supreme crime' [4]).

The difference between this opinion and that of the authors quoted before, who considered the sentences imposed as a "morally justifiable political act", must be seen in Röling's af-

1) Dissenting Opinion, o.c., p. 45.
2) L.c., p. 48.
3) L.c., p. 46.
4) L.c. p. 49 and note 2.

firmation of the Charter provision concerning crimes against peace as a rule of international law, and not as a legally unqualified, incidental act. The measures which could be imposed according to such rule would, however, differ from punishments in that they would lack the elements of retribution and general prevention, and would only aim at security, at special prevention with regard to the authors of an unjust war. Enforcement of such measures by a judge would not constitute a necessary element of this rule; it should in the present case be seen as a concession to public opinion, having at the same time the advantage of judicial guarantees for the vanquished.

It is evident that this interpretation runs counter not only to the Judgments of the Tribunals, on whose authority, as has been shown, the legal significance of 'crimes against peace' nevertheless rests, but also to the intention of the drafters of the Charter. As in this opinion the Charter is the more important act, it is difficult to establish a distinction between the terms 'crime' and 'individual responsibility' as applied to 'crimes against peace' and as applied to the other acts which Röling considers as 'crimes' in the usual, penal sense of the word. On the other hand the reasons for the relative moderation of the sentences imposed on those responsible for 'the supreme crime' should properly be sought in the fact that the relationship between the individual acts and their terrible consequences is in the case of crimes against peace less direct than in the case of the other crimes [1]).

It must be admitted that this theory is more satisfactory than that of the authors who have approved of the Nuremberg Trial as an act of 'high policy' outside the field of law. Like those who would have preferred a 'drumhead court martial' to deal summarily with the enemy leaders, they completely overlook the fact that some time has elapsed since captured enemy rulers, soldiers and population were considered to be at the mercy of the victor, and that since the mediaeval authors, since Vitoria, Suarez, Grotius and others began to turn against this practice, international law has extended its protection to the life, liberty and property of the vanquished. The victor's power has been subjected to the customs of warfare and the law of the Hague and Geneva

---

1) Cf. Quincy Wright, The Law of the Nuremberg Trial, l.c., p. 44.

Conventions; summary execution of the enemy leaders would have been a grave violation of those laws and customs [1]), and if the Nuremberg proceedings had not been based on law, they would have been illegal. Regarding life and liberty of enemy persons there is no more a no-mans land – between law and violation of law – for *auszerrechtliche Masznahmen* [2]), non-legal measures.

But does there exist a rule permitting States to 'eliminate' enemy leaders who are a danger for international peace? The precedents invoked by Röling do not sound convincing. Napoleon's elimination occurred long before the rules of warfare were explicitly formulated, and the ambiguous character of England's custody, not based on a verdict of a court, aroused widespread misgivings, repeatedly voiced in the British Parliament. The Kaiser's trial did not materialize, and the treatment of the matter by the Allied Powers and the Dutch refusal to extradite him, approved by most authors [3]), indicate that there was no rule of international law on which such an 'act of high international policy' could be based.

The fact alone that the alleged right is reserved to 'the victor in a just war' arouses doubt as to the existence of such a positive rule of long standing. International law did not work on such a concept, and it is certainly no guarantee against what Röling condemns most in the penal conception of 'crimes against peace', the arbitrariness of the victor's decision about what is the law. And why should the certainty of the application of a 'special safety measure' not have the effect Röling and others attribute to the prospect of punishment, that is, driving the

---

1) Biddle, l.c., p. 3; Wechsler rightly speaks of the 'curious position' of those who attack the Nuremberg Trial as a 'judicial application of principles of liability politically defined' but defend the drumhead court-martial dealing, l.c., p. 24. Though it is admitted that the Allied occupation of Germany was not subject to the limitations imposed by the Fourth Hague Convention and that the defendants in the Nuremberg Trial did not benefit from the dispositions regarding the treatment of prisoners of war, the occupying Powers were, in the exercise of their 'unlimited power', certainly limited by the principles of law and justice to-day prevailing in 'civilized States'. It is submitted that summary execution of enemy leaders, however guilty, after the hostilities had ceased, would have constituted a violation of those principles. See however, Oppenheim-Lauterpacht, Vol. II, pp. 602–603.

2) Comtesse, l.c., p. 462.

3) Among those who support the Nuremberg Trial in general, for example, François, Vol. II, pp. 21 and 35; Merle, o.c., p. 27; Scelle, o.c., p. 979.

enemy leaders to fight till the bitter end? The theory discussed does not escape the *a priori* of those who confer upon the victor's administration the power which they refuse to the judge.

Moreover, the concept of 'political crime' in municipal law to which Röling assimilates the crime against peace is highly problematic [1]). Certainly the element of eliminating a danger to the established order constitutes an important factor in the repression of such crimes. And there is truth in the saying: if treason succeeds, who dares call it treason. But every crime presents a danger; the character of safety measure is an element of every punishment, and municipal penal legislation of civilized countries does not offer any evidence that the crimes called political, like the attempt to overthrow a government by force or the plot against the life of a statesman, are considered to lack the element of guilt. They are treated on the same line as other crimes the punishment of which requires the establishment of guilt. This view is confirmed by the statement of Roux [2]) that if the maxim *nullum crimen* is subject to exceptions, it may never be pushed aside with respect to political crimes.

There are many historical examples of another category of 'political crimes'. Murders of kings or defeated political leaders under judicial cover have not been infrequent, and it may be remembered that Robespierre said of Louis XIV: "Il n'était pas un accusé, mais un ennemi; il n'y avait pas de procès à faire mais une mésure de salut public à prendre". Would such a proceeding be approved of in the twentieth century, by civilized countries? On the other hand there has always been popular admiration for the courage of revolutionaries and natural sympathy for those who lost in a bold enterprise. Radin says that "preparing a scheme for dominating the world is a grandiose undertaking, however evil" [3]). Fortunately, the judges in Nuremberg understood from the Pact of Paris that the world had lost the sense of such grandiosity, even before it had to offer some many millions of men to the rulers of Berlin and Tokyo.

---

1) Also Donnedieu de Vabres gives this qualification to crime against peace but without excluding from it the proper characteristic of a crime, demanding punishment. R.d.C., l.c., p. 501.

2) J. A. Roux, A propos de la non-retro-activité de la loi pénale, R.D.I., 1947, pp. 179–186.

3) Radin, l.c., p. 384.

Rölings interpretation, thus, seems to merit the same objection he raised against the *punishment* of the authors of the war. Positive international law prior to 1945 knew neither penal rule with respect to crimes against peace, nor right of the victor to eliminate the enemy rulers. And he cannot claim for his interpretation what is the only justification, the only legal basis, of the Nuremberg Judgment: not the power of the victor over his enemy, not the holding of supreme authority over the German State, not a competence unilaterally to change the rules of international law to the prejudice of the enemy, but the power of the judge to punish those who were proved to have knowingly prepared and perpetrated the gravest possible violation of the law of the international community, bringing thereby untold misery to the countries and peoples who were their victims.

Some upholders of the Nuremberg Judgment have invoked the doctrine of natural law maintaining that international law, in the absence of a central legislature, should in itself have the means of its own development according to the needs of a changing world, and they have contended that the criminality of aggressive war had always been implicit in international law. Teitgen, the late French Minister of Justice, went furthest in this direction when he said: "Le droit international consiste dans la conscience humaine et dans les principes fondamentaux et les états n'ont qu'à s'y soumettre et les appliquer". In such an opinion international custom is binding because it is an expression of the human conscience and it would be sufficient to prove, before an international court, that a treaty formulates rules of that conscience to convince the court that even non-signatory States are bound to respect the rules of that treaty. In this sense the Nuremberg Tribunal would rightly have designated the Charter as an expression of international law [1]).

Without admitting such far reaching consequences Lord Wright had stated that international law, unlike municipal law, is not based on the acts of a central law-making authority, and therefore has other sources like natural law "as flowing

1) Teitgen, l.c., p. 161 ff.. In the same direction, though not so far, tend Glaser, in Revue de Droit Pénal et de criminologie, l.c.; Sottile, Graven and Balmer Basilius, l.l.c.c..

from the instinctive sense of right and wrong possessed by all decent men" or "as derived from the principles common to all civilised nations". Basing his ideas on such a concept, he regarded the acts enumerated in Article 6 of the Charter as crimes, not by virtue of the Agreement but by virtue of international law. The Governments only defined the jurisdiction of the Court which on any other assumption, "would not be a Court of law but a manifestation of power" [1]). The Nuremberg Judgment adopted nearly the exact text of the statement of Lord Wright to the effect that the criminality of war rested upon "the very nature of war as a thing evil in itself... the accumulated evil of the whole" (viz. other criminality) [2]). Similar opinions of Shawcross, Jackson, and some members of the Tokyo Tribunal have already been quoted [3]).

As to the opinion that the 'rules' of world conscience would *by themselves* amount to 'existing international law', it is doubtful whether one instance, in classic or modern international law, could be quoted of a court or a State accepting such a source. In so far as universal public opinion has been referred to above, it has been quoted as the driving force behind a legal instrument and as being expressed in resolutions and declarations, in an effort to assess the specific value of such an instrument – the Kellogg Pact – and to interpret the dominant trends of the world community. These trends were different from the mere pacifist movements before the First World War in that they expressed the conviction that war was legally abolished. They were concerned with law and not only with morality. The importance of such a difference is emphasized by Lauterpacht: "If general opinion throughout the world presumes that sovereign States are under no obligations except those they have explicitly accepted, then international relations will be little affected by a sense of legal obligation. It is for this reason that periods of jural positivism have been periods of jural pessimism, in which men see little hope of improvement through the law. Unless men believe in justice and the possibility of

---

1) Lord Wright, l.c., p. 547.
2) Ibidem, p. 552. For the statement of the Tribunal see above, p. 214.
3) See above, pp. 207 and 208, and for the Tokyo Tribunal, p. 225.

realising it through law, there is not likely to be much either of justice or law" [1]).

A similar qualification applies to the invocation of natural law the value of which depends on the conception which is, in a certain period, in a certain legal community, made of 'law in force'. While the present period, unlike the last century, is characterized by "a growing awareness of the fact that treaties and custom cannot tell the whole story of international law" [2]), it is an anachronism to invoke legal concepts held by Grotius and his predecessors as evidence of valid rules of international law. Natural law is concerned with the permanent and unchanging dictates of human reason, with men's innate sense of justice. A good case can be made for the contention that in the eyes of public opinion, for the human conscience, war was never allowed except in extreme necessity, for the defence of what was right or for the punishment of what was wrong. But how can it be said that war is criminal according to natural law, that there is anything like an 'inherently criminal character of war', if at the same time it must obviously be admitted, that, as Stimson said, until quite recently any legal judgment against a war-maker would have been absurd? [3]). If, according to such standards, the London Charter is considered as an expression of international law at the time of its creation, it cannot escape the reproach of containing unilateral, *ad hoc* rules, because the concept of 'international law' applied is one not admitted in other fields of international relations [4]).

Neither the legal security and the universal validity which international law owes to its positive incorporation in binding treaties and to the establishment of general custom, nor the contribution which world conscience and the law of nature can give to the progressive development of international law, are served by a loose invocation of the latter where that is convenient.

The drafters of the Charter, and the victorious States which enacted it, could not validly declare, on the basis of such sources,

---

1) Lauterpacht in B.Y.I.L., 1946, quoted by Quincy Wright, Legal Positivism and the Nuremberg Judgment, l.c., p. 407.

2) A. Nussbaum. A. Concise History of the Law of Nations, N.Y. 1947, p. 275, quoted by Wright, ibidem.

3) Stimson, l.c., p. 181.

4) See Graven, l.c., p. 10.

that there *existed* a rule in international law by virtue of which the planning, etc., of an aggressive war were crimes for which there was individual liability.

The fact that nineteen States adhered to the Agreement does not alter its legal character: they adhered to the establishment of a temporary tribunal on a certain basis, not to a codification treaty. The Agreement ceased to produce legal effects after the Judgment had been rendered and the Trial was over. Only the international judge could, in addition to treaty rules, and custom, invoke these exceptional sources of international law to deduce that the planners and wagers of the war in the case submitted could be punished. Quincy Wright in discussing the Nuremberg Judgment refers to the inclusion of the "general principles of law recognised by civilised States" as a source of law in the Statute of the International Court of Justice and concludes that the makers of the Statute "recognized that international law should not be limited by the positive consent of States, but should be capable of developing through juridical deduction from normative principles endorsed by prevailing world opinion" [1]).

At the London Conference Jackson rightly observed that it was not merely a case of showing that the Nazi leaders had failed to be gentlemen in war; "it is a matter of their having designed an illegal attack on the international peace, which to our mind is a criminal offence by common law tests, at least" [2]). But he forgot that such common law tests can, by the very nature of common law, be used by the judge only. Contrary to his opinion that "there is greater liberty in us to declare principles as we see them now than there would be in a court to use new principles that we had failed to declare in an organic act setting up the court" [3]), the Charter should have been restricted to the attribution of jurisdiction to the Tribunal to take cognizance of acts constituting the planning, etc. of aggressive war and to try persons accused of such acts. The decision that such acts constituted, as many Governments, legal authorities and a good

1) Quincy Wright, l.c., p. 408.
2) See above, p. 198.
3) See above, p. 195.

deal of the public held, offences against the law of the community which could and should be punished, had to be left to the Tribunal which was called upon to fulfil a major role in the development of a customary international penal law. The inescapable consequence of the opinion of all authors who, like Stimson, Quincy Wright, Donnedieu de Vabres and Scelle, have justified the Nuremberg Judgment as a case in an international common law, in a customary criminal law, is that it was not the Charter but the Judgment that made the crime against peace enter into positive law [1]). If "no greater step has been taken in the history of the world", it was not so much, as Lord Justice Lawrence says, on August 8, 1945, that this epoch-making event took place but on October 1, 1946.

There is nothing startingly new in the idea of such a development of international criminal law by the judge. As Pella wrote in 1929 there were among the champions of such a law two currents. The one, dominant at the Conferences of the International Law Association, aimed at the creation of an international criminal jurisdiction "à prononcer, avec l'objectivité nécessaire, des sanctions pénales contre les organismes ayant perpétré des faits de nature à troubler profondément l'ordre internationale". The other thesis, prevalent in the codification countries which adhered to the *nullum crimen* maxim and proposed by Pella as the guiding principle for the Interparliamentary Union, required the previous and precise determination of the infractions coming within the jurisdiction of the Court [2]). Events drove international penal law in the first direction, and even some champions of the second opinion admit that for the time being this law will remain customary [3]).

In all countries law has been developed by the judge before it was codified, and in the present state of international law, in which there is certainly no lack of juridical techniques, of legal doctrines and of ingenuous interpretations regarding what is the law, the primary need of the international community is not in the legislative field but in that of law-enforcement. It

1) As is admitted by Lord Wright, l.c., pp. 548 and 555.
2) V. V. Pella, 'La Nature Criminelle de la Guerre', discutée par l'Union Interparlementaire, et quelques aspets du Pacte Kellogg, Bulletin Interparlementaire, 1929, pp. 1—11, p. 1.
3) See authors quoted above, p. 262, note 3.

is not codification that is needed primarily in international public and criminal law but judges who can impose their decisions in the case of international controversies, who can impose sanctions upon law violators and make binding declarations as to what is law among the divergent interpretations. It is in this sense that, with respect to the present subject, de La Pradelle wrote that before Nuremberg the rule concerning the justice or injustice of the war "échappait au droit par cela seul qu'il échappait aux juges" [1]).

It might even be said that a penal rule concerning illegal war was only absent because there was no international criminal tribunal, and that the Charter, properly speaking, the Tribunal, only made explicit what was already implicit in international law, notably in the Kellogg Pact. Though the question of the sanctions of a rule of law is a question of substantive law, and the Charter did therefore more than merely fill a procedural gap as Shawcross alleged, the development from the Kellogg Pact can in this sense be called a necessary one.

This element of necessity, as a justification of the Nuremberg Proceedings and Judgment, is relied upon by many writers who recognize the novelty and the *ad hoc* character of the Charter. Scelle who states that positive international law provided neither the penalty nor the judge, that the threats of an enemy (the Moscow and other declarations) are no law, that, with respect to the argument of universal condemnation, morality in itself does not constitute law, and that precedents lose much of their force and prestige by their unilateral character, nevertheless holds that the precedent of Nuremberg was "nécessaire au développement du Droit" [2]). For Scelle the only positive basis of the Judgment is Article 38 (3) of the Statute of the I.C.J. which assimilates the general principles of law to general custom.

A remarkable recognition of the necessity of a legal development in the direction subsequently taken by the Nuremberg Tribunal is contained in the report Lauterpacht presented in 1943 to the International Commission for Penal Reconstruction and Development in Cambridge: "The law of any international

---

1) A. de La Pradelle, quoted by Graven, l.c., p. 189.
2) Scelle, o.c., p. 976.

society worthy of that name must reject with reprobation the view that between nations there can be no aggression calling for punishment, and it must consider the responsibility for the premeditated violation of the General Treaty for the Renunciation of War as lying within the sphere of Criminal Law" [1]).

The element of necessity has played a certain role in a number of international dealings, settlements of territorial questions, permanent neutralisations, and general treaties of a political, technical or humanitarian nature, which, effectively enforced by the Great Powers or enacted by the overwhelming majority of Nations, have been considered as binding also on non-signatory States [2]). The legal value of provisions like Article 17 of the Covenant of the League of Nations and Article 2 (6) of the Charter of the United Nations can be said to rest upon a consideration of the requirements of the international society, which necessitates the universality of certain minimum standards of conduct and therefore makes an infringement upon the independence of States. Equally non-positive, the principle of necessity differs from the principles of natural law in that it is based on factual situations rather than on justice, that it is determined by the changing state of international relations and that its relative value is essentially dependent on the effective enforcement, by political or moral pressure, of the rules concerned.

In matters of criminal law, where the element of justice is paramount, the invocation of necessity seems therefore less appropriate, unless a more utilitarian view is held of criminal proceedings, that is primarily as means of prevention, prevention of future violation of the law, or, as was occasionally put forward in the Nuremberg case, prevention of private vengeance by the victims of the accused [3]).

Like the appeal to natural law and world conscience, the

---

1) Quoted by Glaser in Revue Pénale Suisse, l.c., p. 35, note 1.

2) See Oppenheim-Lauterpacht, Vol. I, pp. 831—834, and the present author, Toepassing van multilaterale verdragen op derde staten, Rechtsgeleerd Magazijn 'Themis', 1951, pp. 322—344, pp. 335 ff..

3) See Wechsler, l.c., p. 14, who states that the Nuremberg Trial had two functions, a negative one in forestalling private vengeance, and a positive one in deterring others from similar crimes. He adds that the preventive efficacy will in the present case be reduced by the fact that the victor will always be immune, whether or not he is the aggressor.

consideration that punishment is necessary is in customary criminal law a criterion for the judge, not a justification for *ad hoc* legislation. The Nuremberg Judgment contains several references to this criterion: "This law" (of war) "is not static, but by continual adaption follows the needs of a changing world ... only by punishing individuals who commit such crimes can the provisions of international law be enforced" [1]).

The penetration of natural law view-points in the Nuremberg Judgment, considered by Wehberg as a new demonstration of how little international legal positivism is able to deal with the great problems of the international society, can never detract from the very notion of law that is made, developed and applied by men, by legislators, judges and subjects of the law and is not an automatic, immanent, self-generating process. It is difficult to agree with Wright when he states: "In such a situation" (the lack of a workable, legislative authority in international law) "the law must have within itself the means of its own change, and that element is what the seventeenth century jurists called 'natural law' and which in modern terminology can perhaps be better expressed by the word 'justice' as interpreted by the dominant world opinion" [2]).

It is especially important to bear this in mind when examining to what extent Nuremberg has created a precedent. If the planning and waging of an aggressive war would necessarily, or by natural law only, be punishable offences, this question would not need to be discussed. The development of the present efforts of the United Nations in the field of international criminal law, to be discussed in the following Chapter, should bring back the reality of international law to anybody who holds such a view.

Kelsen has strongly denied that the Nuremberg Judgment has any value as a precedent on account of the lack of the formal and material conditions required for a judicial decision to serve "as a model for subsequent decisions of similar cases" [3]). First

---

1) See above, p. 215.

2) Quincy Wright, l.c., p. 407; the final phrase makes it clear that the element Wright has in mind is the same as Rousseau's 'volonté du peuple' which decides in the political democracy and has nothing in common with the objective concept of natural law.

3) Kelsen, l.c., pp. 153 ff..

of all such a judicial decision must establish a new rule of law while the Nuremberg Tribunal applied the law of the Charter. It is therefore the authority of the pre-existent statutory or customary rule that is the source of law, the law-making act. Behind this argument lies the positivistic opinion that a rule of law cannot be determined by different sources in a concurring development, as the pronouncement of the Tribunal was, which indeed partly relied upon the Kellogg Pact, partly upon general principles of law and partly upon world conscience, which latter two sources are moreover not recognized by Kelsen.

But, what is more important, the Judgment was, with respect to crimes against peace, only apparently based on the Charter. The Charter could not create new international crimes; it could only establish a jurisdiction. It is the Tribunal which, accepting a view expressed in the Charter, pronounced *in casu* that the evidence before it established acts which in view the state of international law could be punished. The Tribunal pronounced its sentences under international law, and it is this law-making decision that lifted the rule of individual liability for aggressive war out of the *ad hoc* sphere of a unilaterally enacted provision and put it on the level of an international criminal case-law.

As a second argument Kelsen states that Article 59 of the Statute of the international Court of Justice denies binding force to a decision of the Court outside the particular case. New Tribunals could only administer the law of Nuremberg in application of their basic treaties. Article 59 is, however, only concerned with the International Court and with international public law. However closely related, coming from the same origin and serving the same legal community, the new international criminal law should be considered in view of its specific nature and its own requirements. It is true that the particular system under which the Nuremberg Tribunal was set up ceased to exist after the subsequent Trials in Nuremberg were over. But the Tokyo Judgment, established under a separate system, already shows the extent of the influence and authority of the International Military Tribunal.

Is then the significance of the Judgment as a precedent only dependent on "whether or not ... other tribunals will actually decide other cases in the same way" [1])? The eloquent assertions of the Prosecutors that Charter and Judgment will be considered as a precedent are said to be 'premature at least', and Kelsen sees hardly any chance for the Nuremberg Trial "to be recognized as a worthy example to be followed" [2]). "If the principles applied in the Trial", he concludes, "were to become a precedent – a legislative rather than a judicial precedent – then after the next war, the governments of the victor States would try the members of the governments of the vanquished States for having committed crimes determined unilaterally and with retroactive force by the former. Let us hope that there is no such precedent" [3]).

What a future victorious State will do with the enemy leaders in its power might well be a violation of the law but it would not need a precedent for such action. The only relevant question on this point is what future independant courts under international criminal law will do. The curious fact is that in literature and in the practice of the United Nations the emphasis is laid on the moral, perhaps even legal, obligation of the States to codify, after Nuremberg, the principles it applied in a universal treaty applicable to all States. It is evident that there is a certain moral obligation especially on the side of the victors and on the part of those who associated themselves with the Agreement and the Nuremberg Proceedings. The declared intention of the prosecuting Powers even pointed in the direction of the undertaking of a legal obligation to make the new law applicable to themselves and to all States. Such a *pactum de contrahendo* could in this sense hardly create a legal obligation because the very content of such an obligation – the terms of the treaty to be made – cannot be determined.

But is the moral obligation of the prosecuting and associated powers primarily to affirm, formulate and codify principles, to determine the law? As a consequence of what has been said before, it is submitted that the primary need is not for a perfectly formulated, all-embracing law but for a jurisdiction to apply the law that exists. And an international criminal court

1) Ibidem, p. 163.
2) Ibidem, pp. 163–4.
3) Ibidem, p. 171.

created under international criminal law by the United Nations or a group of its Members, without an accompanying code of offences, could apply existing law: the law of the Nuremberg Tribunal as pronounced in and by the Judgment. What substance 'International Common Law' or 'Inter-State Penal Law' has at this moment, it owes to the Nuremberg Tribunal which was the first Tribunal called upon to formulate and administer that law. And a court set up under international penal law would not be at liberty "to decide other cases in the same way" but would by its very nature be bound to do so.

It may be that the Nations of the world favour a change from customary to statutory international criminal law. In that case the Nuremberg Judgment would be superseded by a criminal code which would instead be binding upon courts set up under that law and its significance would be reduced to that of an authoritative interpretation of the Nuremberg Principles in so far as these would be embodied in that code. But the essential fact remains that, for the general application of the principles of Nuremberg and international criminal law, such a Code is not strictly necessary, while without the creation of an international criminal jurisdiction even the most perfect codification remains valueless and international criminal law inapplicable, a law applied unilaterally and *ad hoc* by the victors to the vanquished. Unlike international public law, criminal law can only be applied by the judge. So long as there is none, it is impossible to agree with Stimson that the Four Nations and the nineteen adherents to the Agreement "firmly bound themselves to the principle that aggressive war is a personal and punishable crime" [1]).

The validity and justice of the Judgment of the post-war international trials of war criminals may be expressed by the endorsement of world public opinion as evidenced by the political organs of the world community [2]); it may be said that if the Tribunal had been wrong in holding individuals criminally

1) Stimson, l.c., p. 188.

2) See however Radin, l.c., p. 381, stating that it is impossible to determine with certainty whether public opinion at the present time supports the doctrine of individual guilt for crimes against peace "due to the fact that the three types of crimes are inevitably fused in the public mind by being combined in a single trial".

responsible for aggressive war, it was open to the civilized States to deny the validity of any such proposition [1]); so long as no effective action is taken in international criminal law, such open or silent approval will remain suspect and will not remove from the post-war judgments the taint of victor's justice. Only after such unanimous action can the world have greater confidence that, as Jessup says, "earth's law: 'the conquered are the wrong' will become 'the wrong will be conquered' " [2]).

SECTION 5. CONSEQUENCES OF NUREMBERG

After this evaluation of the basis and the legal value of the Nuremberg Judgment, some clarification is needed as to the content of the rule concerning aggressive war. In the beginning of the fourth Chapter it was said that the law of Nuremberg was *in causa posita;* that in the discussions during the war, preceding the enactment of the London Charter, the point of departure had been the criminality of the Second World War, launched and carried on by Germany, as a whole, and that only during the London negotiations, on American insistence, was an abstract rule of individual criminal responsibility for the planning, etc. of a war of aggression formulated.

Lord Wright states very clearly the difference between the two lines of approach to the question of crimes against peace; in the concrete method the argument is centred around the Second World War announced as one of atrocities, degradation and extermination and executed as one of systematic crimes; Hitler and his government "are thus seen, in accordance with elementary principles of criminal law, to be the criminals guilty of the crimes against peace, in that they initiated this particular war in the form in which it was in fact carried out, that is, as a vast series of separate crimes, all traceable back to Hitler and his gang". Next to this establishment of the 'totalitarian crime against peace' there is a more abstract argument, resting upon the very nature of war as 'a thing evil in itself'. This argument, which is adopted by Wright, is based also upon the fact that the

---

1) Lawrence, l.c., p. 157.
2) Jessup, l.c., p. 10.

war of 1939 was "one of the greatest calamities that ever befell the human race", but he concludes that even "if it were possible to conceive of a war conducted on the most chivalrous and humane methods possible, the initiation of the war, if it were an unjust war, would still be a crime. It would be a crime against peace" [1]).

It has been seen that the Tribunal, departing from the concrete case and from the legal materials it invoked, adopted the latter opinion and ruled that in international law, as determined from its several sources, those who plan and wage a war "with its inevitable and terrible consequences" are committing a crime in so doing. Even so, the criminality of aggressive war remains *in causa posita*.

First of all, the Tribunal, being no legislative but a judicial organ under international common law, could not create an abstract rule but could only give a concrete decision, which was, and will eventually be, followed by subsequent international criminal courts. The penal decision more than the reasoning on which it is based, is the important factor, though, on the authority of the Tribunal, the latter may be regarded as evidence of rules of international criminal law.

Secondly, the Tribunal, which separated the crime of war from the war crimes committed during its conduct, did not isolate the criminality of war from its 'inevitable' consequences, having in mind therefore a specific war, modern war. In this respect, the two approaches to the criminality of war are quite close to each other: as every modern war will necessarily be of the scale and the total, ruthless character of the last one, the concrete criminality of the latter includes every modern war as such. The most important feature of the Judgment remains, in this respect, that it punished the crimes against peace as such, while it could have considered the over-all conspiracy charge only and not have convicted under the second Count of the Indictment.

The third and most important reason why no abstract rule can be deduced from the Judgment lies in the concrete approach to the question of aggression, defined in neither Charter nor Judgment, and in the case determined through a consideration

---

1) Lord Wright, l.c., p. 552.

of the intention of the accused. So long as aggression is not satisfactorily defined or definable, international criminal law will necessarily betray several features of case law. The only other course would be to adopt the alarming proposal made to the effect that a system similar to that of Nuremberg "will provide for the punishment of individuals who ignore the advice and directions of the Security Council" [1]).

The Tribunal did not consider to what extent the wars proved to be aggressive were also wars in violation of international treaties, agreements and assurances. Unlike wars of aggression, these wars of the second category could not have been declared criminal and punishable in themselves. Aggressive war is, in virtue of the Kellogg Pact, which recognized the indivisibility of peace, an attack on the order of the international community, a grave violation of its fundamental law, and as such therefore, a criminal act [2]). Were it not for the Kellogg Pact, and were such a war not in conflict with that Pact, a war in violation of treaties, agreements and assurances would not, however condemnable, amount to a crime punishable by the judge of the international community and would merely be a breach of particular international obligations.

Three different points must be specified with respect to the consequences of Nuremberg; first the consequences of the criminality of war for the collectivity, the State; secondly the consequences for the legal position of warfare; thirdly the limits of individual responsibility.

The rejection by the Tribunal of the act-of-State plea raises the question as to what is the impact on the State of the criminal act perpetrated on its behalf. The three schools of thought in the pre-war doctrine of international penal law appear again in the literature on Nuremberg with the difference that some of those who then defended exclusive State responsibility, like Donnedieu de Vabres, now, faced with the facts of Nuremberg, admit also individual responsibility, while those who, like the Defence Counsel in Nuremberg, like Finch and Schick, have opposed

1) Honig, l.c., p. 82.
2) Stimson, l.c., p. 184.

themselves to the latter and upheld the act-of-State doctrine, likewise deny the criminal liability of the law-violating State and recognize only the latter's civil liability. But even so the champions of the Nuremberg Judgment are divided between those who have deduced from it the acceptation of the doctrine *universitas delinquere non potest* [1]) and others who have with equal emphasis contended that collective criminal responsibility of the State is not excluded by the Judgment [2]).

Quincy Wright, who sees in the Judgment a rejection of the notion of collective responsibility, admits to a certain extent the principle, upon which the Defence and some adversaries of the Judgment relied, to the effect that a State cannot be subjected to foreign jurisdiction without its consent [3]). Unlike the French Prosecution who escaped the question by referring to the non-existence of the German State, Wright asserts that the principle was not violated because in Nuremberg nothing happened that does not happen in national courts which regularly determine the effects of treaties on States in order to judge the rights and liabilities of individuals under their jurisdiction. No jurisdiction over the German State was therefore, according to Wright, involved in Nuremberg, where the Tribunal did not make its findings to judge Germany's liability but only that of individuals, the findings on Germany's acts and obligations being therefore more findings of fact than of law [4]).

On the other hand Wright states, as a matter of substantive law, that, as in national, administrative law, in international law *ultra vires* acts of State are null and void, and that the resort to war in violation of the Kellogg Pact is therefore no act of State but one for which only individuals are responsible [5]). This argument approaches that of the construction of the

---

1) Quincy Wright, l.c., and International Law and Guilt by Association, A.J.I.L., 1949, pp. 746—755; Jessup, l.c., p. 6; Glaser, l.c., p. 20.

2) Donnedieu de Vabres in Revue de Droit Pénal et de Criminologie, l.c., p. 822.

3) Quincy Wright. Legal Positivism and the Nuremberg Judgment, l.c., pp. 411—2. He quotes in support of this principle the decision of the Permanent Court of International Justice in the East Carelia case of 1923 in which the Court refused to give an advisory opinion to the League Council. See World Court Reports, ed. by Manley O. Hudson, Vol. I Carnegie Endowment, Washington 1934, pp. 191—206.

4) Wright ibidem.

5) Ibidem, p. 410.

conspiracy charge as put forward by the American Prosecution: the defendants were accused of a conspiracy begun long before they took control in Germany and their seizure and use of the German State machinery were represented as acts of individuals, using the State as a mere instrument in the furtherance of their conspiracy, which consequently could not act independently [1]).

Still further consequences from the individual responsibility for acts of State are drawn by Levy, who , in an article in 1943, contends that from the formulation of the Kellogg Pact as a treaty concluded by the governments "in name of their respective peoples", it may be concluded that governments cease to represent their peoples as soon as they resort to aggressive war. The war would be a police action rather than an interstate struggle, unconditional surrender would take the place of an armistice and would be followed by trials of the guilty leaders rather than by a peace treaty that would perhaps not follow at all. The advantages of such a course would be that no 'carving up' and redistribution of territories would take place, but only a return to the *status quo ante crimen commissum,* and that after the criminals had been brought to trial a new government could be recognized with which the United Nations could deal as with equals, so that – without solutions by force and without relations as between victors and vanquished – it would become a 'moral' rather than a political victory [2]).

Such a separation between guilty leaders and a guiltless population, widely claimed as a major advantage of war crimes trials, was not in reality, however, admitted by the Allies, apart from the fact that the Four Powers, in contradiction to the principles defended by the American Prosecutor in Nuremberg, proclaimed, immediately after the unconditional surrender, the 'collective guilt' of the German people as a basis for their

---

[1]) Opening Statement for the United States, l.c., Vol. II, pp. 103 ff.. Compare also the Indictment in the Nuremberg case. See the sharp criticism on this concept of conspiracy as a 'romantic conception for striking the popular imagination' by Donnedieu de Vabres in R.d.C., o.c.. This concept of conspiracy was not, however, adopted by the Tribunal; see Stimson, l.c., p. 187, who considers this the great weakness of the Judgment, and Merle, o.c., pp. 110–1.

[2]) A. G. D. Levy, The Law and Procedure of War Crime Trials, American Political Science Review, 1943, pp. 1051–1081, pp. 1068–1071.

occupational policy [1]). And the continuity of the German State has been admitted as readily by the German authorities, notably by the Federal Republic which has recognized its international 'civil' responsibility for the acts of the former Reich, as by the victors who still consider the conclusion of a peace treaty, at the present time already made with Japan, and in part have received, in part still claim reparations.

A tendency 'to destroy the State mentally', as Jahrreisz said, was indeed inherent in the Nuremberg proceedings, and he was quite right when he observed, as against Jackson's conspiracy conception, that the German State cannot be reduced to "a mere shadow or tool", that it had long been in existence and that the "enormous weight of its history" was an important factor in Hitler's coming to power and "guided, urged on, limited or put a brake on Hitler in his choice of aims and means" [2]). Whatever may be the future development of international law with respect to individuals, at the present stage the States firmly hold the position of its primary subjects; the reality of the independent State dominates international life and, consequently, international law. State responsibility thus remains the normal basis of its enforcement.

The Nuremberg Judgment did not destroy this basis but strengthened it by the addition of individual criminal responsibility. This is recognized by Quincy Wright when he states that "the individual crime of aggressive war . . . differs from the international delinquency of aggressive war, though both are involved in determining the criminal liability of a defendant" [3]). The difference is not only one of subject and of sanction, but also one of quality. While Wright sees as the international delinquency of aggressive war "any resort to hostilities by the government or from the State's territory in violation of the State's international obligations", the individual crime has been shown to be limited to the grave violation of the fundamental law of the international community, the attempt to destroy that community itself [4]).

---

1) See Guggenheim, l.c., p. 327.
2) Jahrreisz, l.c., Vol. XVII, pp. 458—494; Transcript, pp. 46 and 53.
3) Quincy Wright, The Law of the Nuremberg Trial, l.c., p. 66.
4) Ibidem, and above, p. 259.

At the other side stand those who, far from ignoring and eliminating the State, consider aggressive war also, and even in the first place, as a crime of the State. Reference has already been made to Shawcross' conception of the crime of the individual as one accessory to that of the State; to constitute an individual crime aggressive war had first to be proved a crime of the State. This opinion is closely related to that of Lauterpacht who, dealing with international delinquencies, states that the responsibility of States is not limited to restitution and to damages of a penal character. "The State, and those acting on its behalf, bear criminal responsibility for such violations of international law as by reason of their gravity, their ruthlessness and their contempt of human life place them within the category of criminal acts as generally understood in the law of civilised countries" [1]).

Apart from the preparation and launching of an aggressive war, he gives as a possible example the wholesale massacre of alien residents. Article 16 of the Covenant of the League of Nations can only, however, be partly relied upon in support of these contentions; that is, in so far as its last paragraph provides for the measure of exclusion of a State from the League. The 'corresponding provisions of the Charter of the United Nations', which Lauterpacht quotes also in this connection, prescribe like the rest of Article 16, only international sanctions, police measures, which must be well distinguished from penal sanctions, from punishment, in that they aim only at the counteracting of the aggressor State, and in the most serious case at the removal of the danger by a military police action to restore peace and order.

Criminal responsibility is only considered when the judge intervenes after the police action has resulted in the seizure of the law-breaker, and in this respect nothing is provided by the Charter. Doubt must also prevail regarding Lauterpacht's reference to the "universal recognition as part of International Law of rules penalising war crimes", "as another instance of the criminal responsibility of States" [2]). Though these crimes are, as

---

1) Oppenheim-Lauterpacht, Vol. I, p. 321.
2) Ibidem, p. 322.

a rule, committed "not in pursuance of private gain and lust but on behalf of and as organs of the State", and though the Convention of 1907 envisaged only the ('civil') responsibility of the State for these acts, the development has, specially through the incorporation of the violations of the laws of war, been precisely in the sense of an exclusive, criminal responsibility of individuals. Lauterpacht says in conclusion that, in view of the legal and ethical difficulties "inherent in the notion of collective responsibility and punishment", the extreme drastic consequences of criminal responsibility of States are capable of modification in the sense that such responsibility is additional to and not exclusive of the international criminal liability of individual . . ." [1]).

Like other authors [2]), Donnedieu de Vabres sees, on the contrary, in the State "le seul, le vrai coupable de la guerre aggression". The accusation of individuals as accomplices of the crimes committed "c'est prendre la question par le petit côté". And he agrees in this respect with Jahrreisz: "l'inculpation du représentant au lieu du représenté, ne méconnait-elle pas le caractère public de l'acte reproché?" [3]). Pella has given strong arguments for a recognition of the criminal responsibility of the German State: the criminals of Nuremberg acted on behalf of this State with the means provided by it; the condemned régime was established by an act of will of the national collectivity; the measures taken after the capitultion were security measures against the international danger of a State collectivity and the situation of the German population would be the same if these security measures — "ou mêmes sanctions pénales" — had been applied to the State collectivity pursuant to a condemnation [4]).

The far-reaching possibilities Pella considers as a consequence of the collective criminality of the German Nation are interesting in comparison with the ideas of Levy discussed above. While the latter sees the relationship between victors and vanquished

1) Ibidem, p. 322—3.

2) Sottile, l.c., pp. 237 ff.; Pella, l.c., and La Guerre-Crime et les Criminels de Guerre, Paris 1946, passim.

3) Donnedieu de Vabres, in Revue de Droit Pénal et de Criminologie, l.c., p. 821.

4) V. V. Pella, Fonctions pacificatrices du droit pénal et fin du système traditionnel des traités de paix, R.G.D.I.P., 1947, pp. 1—27, pp. 10—11.

and the necessity of a peace treaty disappear after a condemnation of the only guilty leaders, Pella proposes "un statut de défense internationale" to be *imposed* on the vanquished criminal State as "un traité-sanction", instead of "le système traditionnel des traités de paix" *concluded* with the defeated enemy. With criminals, he argues, no contracts are concluded; peace treaties in the past rested on the conception of the 'guerre-institution'; the 'guerre crime' can only be followed by the imposition of measures to safeguard the peace of the community. He draws attention to the different treatment of Germany's former satelites, with whom peace treaties have been concluded, and Germany itself. The former, as the Allies admitted, did participate in the war *contre leur gré,* and "en se retirant de la guerre contre les Nations Unies ... en prenant un part actif à la guerre contre l'Allemagne", as the Preambles of the Peace Treaties of 1947 state, they have, in Pella's opinion, acquired the right to invoke, in the international organised community, "le désistement volontaire, le répentir actif et, dans une certaine mesure, la réparation volontaire du préjudice" which at least diminish, if not remove, their responsibility for the criminal act committed [1]).

It may be true that, as Sottile states, "l'immense majorité des criminalistes sont unanimes à l'heure actuelle pour admettre la responsibilité pénale internationale de l'Etat". But this opinion the doctrinal merits of which have been discussed in a previous Chapter [2]), cannot up to the present moment rely upon one single instance of its recognition or application in international law and practice [3]). However much one might have preferred another course, the present treatment of Japan and Germany falsifies the conclusions of Pella, just as definitely as the postwar policy of the United Nations disproved the alleged separation between criminal leaders and an innocent nation. Both theories, the one by a process of personification, the other by individualization, amount to a denial of the independence of the State as a subject of international law, which notion is still firmly rooted in the ground of international reality.

Between both extremes, neither denying nor admitting the

---

1) Ibidem, pp. 18 ff..
2) Sottile, l.c., p. 238. See further above, pp. 172 ff..
3) As Lauterpacht admits, Oppenheim-Lauterpacht, Vol. I, p. 322.

criminal responsibility of the State, the Nuremberg Judgment remains as an affirmation "that individuals have international duties which transcend the national obligations of obedience" and that "only by punishing individuals who commit such crimes can the provisions of international law be enforced". Far from negating the basis of international law and anticipating the law of a world State [1]), these pronouncements have their roots in the past and as a 'landmark in law' point to the future. The Nuremberg Judgment comes in the middle of and contributes to the transition from the traditional system of sovereignty and personal immunity to that of a real world community which will be built primarily upon the responsibility of men.

The danger inherent in legal conceptualism which loses sight of the *phenomena* of international life, becomes strikingly apparent in an interpretation of the criminality of war which has made its threatening appearance in the discussions before and after Nuremberg as well as at the Trial itself. The opinion is held that since war has been "stripped of its previous legality" which constituted the sole justification of the murders, destructions and others acts of violence of which the conduct of war consists, these acts become automatically what they would be without the justification of war: ordinary villainous crimes, according to the laws of all civilized nations punishable by the heaviest penalties. As has been shown this argument underlay the first proposal for punishment of aggressive war, in the U.N.W.C.C. [2]), and it was used by Jackson in the London negotiations and by the Chief Prosecutors at the Trial, where it even had a prominent place in the exposition of the French Chief Prosecutor [3]).

It must immediately be admitted that this conception of the criminality of war was only used, in London and Nuremberg, to justify the criminal liability of those responsible for the war. The hideous consequence of the criminal responsibility of all those millions who committed acts of warfare in an aggressive war, which consequence must follow from such a theory, was

1) Röling, Strafbaarheid, o.c., pp. 30—1.
2) See above, pp. 181 ff..
3) See above, p. 208.

in fact not envisaged or intended by the authorities quoted. But their argument opened the door to such consequences which were in fact suggested by a few writers.

Trainin, for example, speaks of the liability of all Hitler criminals "from the lance-corporal in the army to the lance-corporal on the throne" [1]). Glueck, though speaking of the punishment of the Nazi *leaders* only, does not hesitate to state "the fact that if the launching of such a (aggressive) war is found to be criminal then *all* acts in pursuance of such a master-crime are criminal – whether they be within or without the laws and customs of warfare, whether they be classifiable as ordinary soldierly deeds or atrocities" [2]). And Doman sees "nothing fantastic in the trial of a few million persons", where the same yardstick would be used for common and for international crimes [3]).

But more serious than these individual suggestions which one hesitates to consider as the result of earnest reflection on the part of their authors, is the fact that the provisions which guided the punishment of the war criminals are formulated in such a way as to allow such a "systematic holocaust" [4]). The inclusion, in the definition of the Crimes against Peace in the London and Tokyo Charters, of the ambiguous term 'waging of a war of aggression' and, in the last paragraph, of the responsibility of "accomplices participating in the . . . execution of a common plan or conspiracy to commit any of the foregoing crimes", leaves room for the conviction of all "those who were members of the forces, or even those who marched in an army or fired a shot . . ." [5]).

The Charters were, in their application, limited to the 'major war criminals', but Law No. 10, which restated these formulations even more loosely, was not. Several writers, among whom is the former Lord Chancellor, Lord Maugham, who has recently devoted a book to the subject, have severely critised these formulations "which continued to convert into a criminal

1) Trainin, o.c., p. 82.
2) Glueck, o.c., p. 101.
3) Doman, l.c., p. 87.
4) Maugham, o.c., p. 19.
5) Ibidem.

everyone who had participated in aggressive war". Regarding Lord Maugham's dramatic warnings against the dangers of these provisions, it may in the first place be observed that no such application was given to the Charter or Law No. 10. These provisions have in the meantime, moreover, ceased to be applicable. As has been pointed out, it is on the moderate decision of the Nuremberg Tribunal, followed by the later United States Tribunals, that the new criminal law concerning aggressive war must be based. It follows moreover from the Jackson Report and from the speeches of the Prosecutors that no such wide responsibility was envisaged by the drafters of the Charter. Its loose formulation, due to indistinct conceptions and a shortage of time, would, indeed, have been exposed if 'a single democratic nation had made such a law' which would then have been subjected to parliamentary discussions, clause by clause [1]). The Tokyo Trial contained, however, in its murder charge an interpretation of the Charter in this dangerous sense, and its rejection by the Tribunal has anything but cleared the issue.

But the chief danger is not to be found in the formulation of the Charter, nor has it consequently been dispelled by a limited and moderate application in the Judgments by means of what Lord Maugham considers as 'strange but almost inevitable devices'. The danger lies in the forementioned justification of the criminality of aggressive war to which that author himself adheres and which was neither accepted nor rejected by the Tribunal. So long as the charge of crimes against peace is considered to be based not on the Kellogg Pact but on the fact that this Pact removes any excuse for an utterly unjust war, that it is "not a weapon for the injured State, but ... removes a shield from the individual malefactor", the limitation of punishment to "the actual authors of a clearly aggressive war" remains a question of restricted formulas, of human moderation, of common sense perhaps, but not of legal principle; the virtual criminal liability of all participants in such a war remains inherent in the very concept of crimes against peace.

The interpretation which, together with other authors, some of the judges of Nuremberg have in later publications given

---

1) Hankey in postscript to Maugham, o.c., p. 119.

to their Judgment, is not reassuring in this respect. Lord Justice Lawrence states that the words of the Charter might have been interpreted in such a wide sense as to include everyone who fought in an aggressive war, but that the convictions of individuals and organisations "show that the Tribunal did not put any such wide interpretation on the words" [1]. Justice Biddle says that the conviction of Doenitz indicates that the *waging* of an aggressive war was established as a crime under international law, that the standards fixing this conception more precisely and applying it were not formulated in the Judgement, but that it is a question of degree of direct responsibility for the war from which, in the majority of cases, the ordinary soldier will be excluded by the defence of superior orders [2].

These authoritative interpretations seem to indicate that in principle the Tribunal accepted the view that the criminality of war entails the criminality of all the acts committed in its furtherance and that the personal liability for these acts must be assessed in accordance with the individual defences recognized in criminal law. It is submitted that this construction is erroneous and not in conformity with international law.

The root of this justification of the punishment of crimes against peace by reference to the acts constituting war as crimes under common law, is the unwillingness or hesitation to accept the notion of an international crime as an act made criminal by rules of international law. It may appear paradoxical but those who, like the French Prosecutor de Menthon, put forward this concept of criminal war, with its drastic consequences in international relations, which were only avoidable by practical devices, do not in fact accept the existence of an international penal law. And it is evident that it is the reluctance to accept the latter notion and not the desire to have such consequences realized which is behind this conception of criminal war.

For in this conception the common rules of domestic criminal law of civilised nations – penalizing murder, ill-treatment, destruction of public and private property, etc. – and not the Kellogg Pact, qualify the planning and waging of an aggressive

1) Lawrence, l.c., p. 156.
2) Biddle, l.c., pp. 8 and 12.

war as criminal acts. Not the resort to war as an instrument of national policy, but crimes under domestic law, according to this view, are punishable. Consequently, every municipal court in the countries where the war was carried on would have jurisdiction with respect to the local acts of war; no international tribunal would be needed and no international law would be involved in such criminal proceedings. If the Kellogg Pact would remove a 'legalizing' shield from the individual malefactor, it would indeed make the war-makers, and all of them, "subject to judgment by the usually accepted principles of the law of crime" [1]).

But the Kellogg Pact and similar legal instruments did, at the same time, more, and less, than "strip those who incite or wage (aggressive) wars of every defence the law ever gave". These legal instruments did more in that they made such acts, resort to war, violations of the fundamental law of the international community, of such gravity that they could henceforward be qualified as criminal acts, within the scope of jurisdiction of a future international judge. This is the basis of the Nuremberg Trial, and whoever denies this, minimizes the latter's importance to that of extraordinary proceedings under the combined municipal law systems of the victor States.

At the same time the Kellogg Pact did less than is suggested by the forementioned doctrine. The term 'outlawry of war' on which the doctrine is based and under the heading of which the movements for condemnation and renunciation of war proceeded, lends itself in this respect to inaccurate interpretations. In the first place it presupposes a previous legality of war, which in fact did not exist before the Kellogg Pact. There was in international law no rule permitting war. War was a fact, an international phenomenon, and classic international law was indifferent towards it; law began to regulate the conduct of war with a view to its humanization, later established formal requirements as to its opening, and after the World War the Covenant of the League of Nations and other documents limited the States' power to resort to war by obligatory procedures and substantial restrictions, before the Kellogg Pact finally gave a

---

1) See above, p. 208.

universal and unqualified prohibition of the initiation of war [1]). A 'legality' of war supposed distinction between just and unjust wars, which may have lingered on in public opinion and may have been defended by some authors, but was not, according to the majority of them, part of international positive law.

Only if it is accepted that war was neither legal nor illegal, that it was an international phenomenon outside the domain of law, does the effect of the Kellogg Pact become clear. It prohibited the *resort to war,* its use as an instrument of national policy, a use that can only be made by those who have, under domestic law, the competence to decide between peaceful means and war, the leaders of the State. The Kellogg Pact was not concerned with the *conduct of war* which remained subject to the laws and customs of warfare previously established by international law and not abolished by the Kellogg Pact. If some politicians and public movements had the intention to outlaw war in the sense that all its constituant acts would become illegal, legally to 'annihilate' war as an international phenomenon in which acts prohibited by municipal law can be and are committed, they could only have realized this intention by positive rules of international law to that effect. These rules were not established either in the Kellogg Pact or in any other international legal instrument. But the international phenomenon of war could never, before or after the Kellogg Pact, become subject to the rules of municipal law.

It has been rightly put by Mosler in an interesting article on the present subject: "those parts of the politico-social happenings that we call war, which produce legal effects, become evident from an examination of the legal rules which lift them — as imputable acts — out of the chain of development of these happenings and submit them to a juridical order" [2]). A number of acts of war became violations of municipal law after they had been declared violations of law against the enemy, violations of international law. This was the development of the conventional war crimes, violations of the laws of warfare, and the criminality of all acts

---

1) See above, Chapter III, section 5.

2) Dr. H. Mosler, Die Kriegshandlung im rechtswidrigen Kieg, Jahrbuch für Internationales und Ausländisches Offentliches Recht, I, Hamburg 1948, pp. 335—357, p. 344.

of war would imply that these laws were suspended or superseded as no rules can exist concerning the conduct of acts which are in themselves, inherently, criminal. That these laws are still in force results from the charges of warcrimes which were the most serious accusations in Nuremberg and all other post-war trials, and the ones calling for the heaviest punishment. That the development is not in the direction of their abolishment is apparent from the conclusion of the new Geneva Conventions of 1949 concerning the treatment of prisoners of war and of the civilian population during war or hostilities.

The validity of the *jus in bello* is only compatible with what is now called the criminality of aggressive war if the latter is understood in the sense of, and as based upon, the Kellogg Pact which abolishes the *jus ad bellum*. Even if the theory of a previous legality of war is held, the Kellogg Pact can only have made it illegal and prohibited to bring about a situation wherein, as before, from both sides, acts can be and are committed which, in this view, are protected by international law as acts of war. France and England proclaimed in 1939 the state of war with Germany. While the notion of 'state of war', as has been shown in the first Chapter, has lost much of its significance in international law as a consequence of the occurrence of hostilities short of war, the essential fact has remained that the hostile acts which are committed by the armed forces of a State are unaffected or, hypothetically, permitted by law in so far as they are not in violation of the laws or customs of warfare [1]).

Only in this restricted sense, in conformity with the Kellogg Pact as well as with the law of the United Nations, can the terms 'outlawry of war' and 'illegality' or 'criminality' of aggressive war or aggression be used. There exists no criminal liability for normal acts of war, not because of the absence of a *mens rea* on the part of the perpetrators, as the forementioned school of thought holds, but because there is no *actus reus*. Whoever holds the contrary opinion and avoids the consequences of mass trials by alleging that in the modern State only those who act directly for the State can appreciate the regularity of the

1) Ibidem, p. 348, and authors quoted. See also Oppenheim-Lauterpacht, Vol. II, p. 218.

orders received [1]), could not, logically, oppose himself to a conviction of soldiers, especially volunteers, who knew or reasonably could be expected to have known that the war in which they participated was illegal. Abstention from participation in such a war may be a testimony of farsighted ideas and high morality, yet such moral courage cannot be demanded by a law and by a world which still recognize the State as the dominant legal and social community of men.

The main forms of individual liability for aggressive war – which liability constitutes the principal consequence of Nuremberg – must be established in the light of these considerations. The Charters and Indictments contained five types of crimes against peace: planning, preparation, initiation and waging of a war of aggression and participation in a common plan or conspiracy for the accomplishment of any of the foregoing. The convictions by the Tribunals of Nuremberg and Tokyo, on which the new law is based, did not, however, involve all these separate activities. While this restriction was partly the result of the limitations of the cases, of the evidence and of the particular structures of the Indictments, an element of logical simplification certainly played a role.

From this point of view the formulation of the Charters, hurriedly arrived at, lent itself to criticism. The inclusion of initiation seems illogical; those who initiate a war necessarily wage it and must either have planned and prepared it, or have been involved in a common plan to do so. Planning, on the other hand, must be either preparing or participation in a common plan. An analysis of the Judgments (see above pp. 219, 226), shows that the Nuremberg Tribunal considered, apart from the conspiracy, only acts of planning and waging, while the Tokyo Tribunal considered only the waging, in the sense of the initiation of the specific wars, separately, while it deemed their planning and preparation included in the dominating conspiracy charge.

The charge of conspiracy, as explained by the Tribunals, requiring in addition to 'naked conspiracy' personal acts on the part of the individual conspirators in the execution of the plan,

---

1) The French Prosecutor, de Menthon, Opening Statement, l.c., pp. 388 ff..

and the charges of planning and initiation of a war of aggression, do not present any difficulties from the point of view of criminal law. They presuppose the relation of causality between the incriminated acts and the resort to war, and, at the same time, the necessary knowledge, the criminal intent, on the part of the perpetrators. If the resort to aggressive war is criminal, these acts are punishable according to the generally accepted principles of criminal liability. Therefore the opinion of Kelsen – that only the resort to war could be punished, because that was the only act condemned by the Pact of Paris – must be refuted.

More difficulties are presented by the acts of preparation which do not involve planning, and by those of waging which do not involve initiation, acts which were nevertheless punished in Nuremberg as crimes against peace [1]). Especially the incrimination of the waging of an aggressive war has, as shown before, aroused misgivings, and misunderstandings, in legal and political literature.

In the first place it must be stated that, apart even from the intention of the drafters of the Agreement, the inclusion of the term 'waging' cannot in itself be seen as evidence of the opinion that all acts of war are 'inherently criminal'. 'Waging' contains the element of venturing, and originally it had even the same significance as declaring war [2]). Its meaning has been extended to that of 'carrying on' a war, in the French translation 'la poursuite d'une guerre (d'aggression)'. But can it be said, without an abuse of language, that ordinary soldiers, or even high officers, 'carry on' a war, that they 'wage' it? In former times wars were 'waged' by kings, supreme rulers, by commanders-in-chief of the army, and in modern times, with the modern notion of the State, it can only be said that the State, the nation, the people, and, in a secondary sense, that its government, eventually the Supreme Command of its armed forces, carries on or 'wages' a war. Only if the participation in the execution of a common plan to wage war were included, according to the last paragraph of Article 6 (a) of the Charter, in the crimes against peace, might a wider circle of officers and functionaries be included

---

1) See above, pp. 218–221.
2) See the Concise Oxford Dictionnary, 3rd ed. 1946.

in such a charge. But the Tribunal, far from giving such a forced interpretation, did not consider this text.

While the foregoing, textual interpretation can be opposed to that of those who have based either their justification of the criminality of war, or their apprehensions as to its consequences, upon the term 'waging of a war of aggression', yet the conviction of a number of defendants in Nuremberg and in the 'Wilhelmstrasse' case seems a departure from the basic law, the Pact of Paris. This Pact prohibits the resort to war; it would seem that, apart from those who initiate war, only those whose acts have 'some effect in bringing about a war' which they know will be a war of aggression [1]), should be punished. A position 'on the policy making level', as demanded in the High Command and Krupp Trials [2]), does not seem required, as industrialists who voluntarily and knowingly made an essential contribution to the preparation of an aggressive war would fulfill all requirements for criminal responsibility.

But the difficulty is found in the case of those who acquired knowledge of the aggressive plans only after the wars had been initiated, or in that of those whose activities were outside the main line of actions that led up to a resort to war. On the one hand, for instance, there is the example of Doenitz, builder and war commander of the submarine forces, convicted because he had been 'active in waging war' [3]), and on the other hand that of administrators like Frick and Seyss Inquart, and those who, put in charge of occupied countries, assumed an active role only after the beginning of the war.

In each of the cases mentioned the conviction of the Tribunal is understandable and involves more than acts of waging war. All these defendants were, before the war, active and important assistants in Hitler's policy; they were on the edge of Hitler's inner circle though their actual knowledge of the aggressive plans could not be established beyond reasonable doubt. It would, indeed, be odd if a man like Doenitz, who made an essential contribution to Germans state of readiness for war and who consequently led one of the main war operations, would

---

1) See above, p. 233.
2) See above, p. 229.
3) Judgment I.M.T., l.c., p. 557.

escape punishment on the ground that before September 1939 he had not known of the plans for war and that afterwards he only followed superior orders to use the weapon he had prepared.

Doenitz, his pre-war and war activities taken as a whole, might thus deserve a place among those responsible for the war. So might the other defendants mentioned. But it would have been preferable if the Tribunal had established their guilt in terms of a general responsibility, instead of subsuming their successive acts under the loosely formulated and ambiguous provisions of the Charter which lends itself to an interpretation not in conformity with the fundamental Kellogg Pact and with the present state of international law and relations.

But in the light of the Judgment's significance as a precedent under international penal law as case law, the verdicts of the Tribunal are more important than the reasoning on which they are built. In the absence of a more clearly formulated, general rule, the criminal liability assessed by the Tribunal may thus be said to have been limited, in accordance with the Pact of Paris, to *those responsible for an aggressive war.* Such a broad but restrictive formulation of the crimes or of the crime against peace as the causing of a consequence – war –, as an act 'materially defined' [1]), and *not* the language of the Charter, is the point of departure of the criminality of aggressive war.

International penal law as inaugurated by the Nuremberg Tribunal is concerned with the resort to war, with the authors of a war, which category is henceforward associated with that of the violators of the laws of warfare which were established in an earlier period of international law. In a future phase of international law, when this law has penetrated still further in the domain of the independent States and further reduced their role in prescribing the conduct of their citizens, the sphere of criminal responsibility in a war may be further extended. At the present stage of development international law does not contain any rules concerning war other than those described above, and

---

1) See above, p. 54, note 1. Graven speaks of 'l'acte générateur de guerre'. Biddle, stating that the guilt of Doenitz and Funk was not "d'être les auteurs de la guerre, mais de l'avoir poursuivie", concludes that the 'waging of a war' is a crime though the standards "fixant plus précisement et appliquant cette conception" are not formulated, l.c., p. 13. See however Wechsler, l.c., pp. 18 ff..

neither the state of international relations nor that of world opinion affords any basis for their extension. The Nuremberg Judgment is a half-way house between classic international law and the law of a world federation, and it is in the interest of justice and legal development to realize that while a good distance has already been covered the end of the journey is not yet even in sight.

CHAPTER V

IMPLEMENTATION OF THE 'NUREMBERG PRINCIPLES'

SECTION 1. THE AFFIRMATION OF THE 'NUREMBERG PRINCIPLES'

A study of the efforts undertaken by the United Nations to make the law recognized and applied by the Nuremberg Tribunal generally applicable, has necessarily a different character from that of the judgment itself. The latter and the judgments of the other post-war tribunals discussed above can be considered as accomplished facts. The work of the United Nations relative to these Judgments is still, however, at the present moment, after the Sixth Session of the General Assembly, in full development. Apart from the affirmation by unanimous resolution of the General Assembly of "the principles of international law recognized by the Charter of the Nürnberg Tribunal and the Judgment of the Tribunal" on December 11, 1946, and apart from the formulation of these principles by the International Law Commission during its Second Session, in June and July 1950, no positive steps have been taken in this field and no definite conclusions can be drawn.

As the present study is concerned primarily with the criminality of aggressive war, the following observations will bear only on the impact the two steps mentioned have had on the law of Nuremberg, of which the criminality of aggressive war is a part, and there will further be a commentary on the proposals made for the implementation of the Nuremberg law, in the light of the conclusions reached in the previous chapter regarding its legal nature and scope. These proposals under discussion in the United Nations tend in two directions: first towards a codification, in a "Draft Code of Offences against the Peace and Security of Mankind", of that part of international criminal law with which the Nuremberg Tribunal was concerned; and, second, towards the creation of an International Criminal Jurisdiction. The efforts in the latter direction – indicated before as the most important step to be taken in view of an implementation of the Nuremberg Principles – will be discussed in the final section of this Chapter. As a preliminary remark it may be observed that while the two tendencies indicated do not exclude each other, and should, perhaps, as in municipal systems, go together, no such close connection is envisaged at the present time between the Codification of Offences against Peace and Security and the establishment of an International Criminal Court.

Resolution I (95) unanimously adopted on 11 Dec. 1946 during the First Session of the General Assembly of the United Nations reads as follows:

"THE GENERAL ASSEMBLY

"*Recognizes* the obligation laid upon it by Article 13, paragraph 1, subparagraph a, of the Charter, to initiate studies and make recommendations for the purpose of encouraging the progressive development of international law and its codification;

"*Takes note* of the Agreement for the establishment of an International Military Tribunal for the prosecution and punishment of the major war criminals of the European Axis signed in London on 8 August, and of the Charter annex thereto, and of the Charter of the International Military Tribunal for the trial of the major war criminals in the Far East, proclaimed at Tokyo on 19 January 1946;

"*Affirms* the principles of international law recognized by the Charter of the Nürnberg Tribunal and the judgment of the Tribunal;

"*Directs* the Committee on the codification of international law established by the resolution of the General Assembly of 11 Dec. 1946, to treat as a matter of primary importance plans for the formulation in the context of a general codification of offences against the peace and security of mankind, or of an International

Criminal Code, of the principles recognized in the Charter of the Nürnberg Tribunal and in the judgment of the Tribunal."

The proposal to adopt a similar resolution had been made by the American delegation to the General Assembly on November 15, 1946. Six days before that date the American Judge in the Nuremberg Tribunal, Justice Biddle, had recommended in a report to the President of the United States "that the United Nations as a whole reaffirm the principles of the Nürnberg Charter in the context of a general codification of offences against the peace and security of mankind" [1]). In his answer to that report, President Truman had supported that opinion [2]). Though the subsequent proposal of the United States delegation can obviously be traced to this correspondence, the actual wording of this proposal and that of the final resolution demonstrate different lines of thought, and it was only on account of this change that the United Nations resolution became of immediate significance.

A comparison between the texts shows three differences. Firstly while the proposal of Biddle aimed at a re-affirmation of the Nuremberg principles *by means of* a codification of offences against peace and security, the affirmation of these principles was made a separate act of the General Assembly in the final resolution. Secondly, the resolution referred to the principles "recognized by the Charter ... *and* in the Judgment of the Tribunal". And thirdly, the Assembly 'affirmed' these principles instead of 'reaffirmed', — as Biddle and the American delegation had proposed.

The purpose and effect of this resolution have since been a matter of controversy among legal authorities and the question of its interpretation has, as will be shown, played an important role in the subsequent discussions with regard to the nature of a 'formulation' of the Nuremberg principles, in both the International Law Commission and in the Sixth Committee of the General Assembly. On the one side it has been contended that since the adoption of this resolution there is no doubt that

---

1) Department of State Bulletin (1946), Vol. 15, pp. 954–957.
2) Ibidem, p. 954.

the principles of Nuremberg are part of international law [1]). Other writers, however, have pointed out that resolutions and recommendations of the General Assembly have no effect in law unless they are implemented by national or international legislation [2]). In the light of these divergences, close attention must be paid to the formulation of the resolution as compared with that of the preceeding proposals.

If the action to be taken by the United Nations after the promulgation of the Charter and the rendering of the Judgment of the Nuremberg Tribunal had been envisaged as one single act – the affirmation of the Nuremberg principles by means of their incorporation in a general codification – the resolution could not be claimed to have had any effect on international law. The resolution would not have constituted the act of affirmation. It would merely have entrusted a subsidiary organ to do some preparatory work in order that such an affirmation by the United Nations might be given at some future date. To recognize that – in the words of President Truman – the setting up of a "code of international criminal law to deal with all those who wage aggressive war . . . deserves to be studied and weighed by the best legal minds the world over", does not imply any approval of what was done in Nuremberg. In the twenties and thirties, before even Utopian thinkers imagined a similar trial, such a 'recognition' was embodied in the proposals and resolutions of international legal associations which were conspicuous by their platonic character. Every year many matters are entrusted – for study and planning – to the International Law Commission, and exactly as is shown by the fate of the Draft Code of Offences against the Peace and Security of Mankind, if that were all that had been done, the Nuremberg Judgment would still be the sole responsibility of the Prosecuting Powers and the nineteen adherents to the Charter.

But regardless of the outcome of the instructions given to the Codification Commission, and, later, to the International Law Commission, the General Assembly affirmed the principles of international law recognized by the Charter and in the Judgment.

---

1) Biddle, Revue International de Droit Pénal, l.c., p. 7.
2) Schick, l.c., p. 794; Finch, l.c., p. 26.

What was the scope of this affirmation? In the discussion, which the Sixth Committee of the General Assembly held in 1950 on the formulation of the Nuremberg principles presented by the International Law Commission, several South American delegates contended that the General Assembly had affirmed only those principles acknowledged in Nuremberg which were at the same time well established in international law [1]. However, such an interpretation would make the resolution senseless – it is only necessary to affirm principles the international legal validity of which would otherwise be open to doubt. As is confirmed by the subsequent resolution of the General Assembly on this matter (that of 21 November 1947, see below), the third and fourth paragraphs of the resolution under discussion refer to the same principles and the addition of the phrase 'of international law' in the third paragraph can only mean that exclusively those principles which come into the field of international law, and not, for example, those of criminal procedure or those relating to criminal organisations, were affirmed by the Assembly.

The Nuremberg Tribunal founded its judgment on international law, to which it gave at the same time a new development, and this development was recognized as international law by the Assembly which invoked in the introduction of the resolution the obligation laid upon it by Article 13 (1) of the Charter "to make recommendations for the purpose of encouraging the progressive development of international law..." The other part of that obligation, "to initiate studies" for the *codification* of international law, was taken into account by the last paragraph of the resolution. This consideration of the Nuremberg principles as a new development of international law was indicated – during the aforementioned discussion of the Sixth Commission – by the English delegate, FitzMaurice: "...what had happened was that, between 1939 and 1945, concepts of aggressive war and offences against peace and humanity which had hitherto existed only as concepts, had become definite rules

1) See discussion in the Sixth Committee at the Fifth Session of the General Assembly, concerning Part III of the Report of the International Law Commission, in U.N. Documents A/C. 6/SR. 233–239, A/C. 6/SR. 235, pp. 165–6 (Delegates of Venezuela and Argentina).

of international law accepted by all civilized nations. The Charter and Judgment of Nuremberg were based on those rules . . ." [1]). It is, however, more exact to say that in the civilized nations during those years, what had been but a vague notion of the 'criminality' of war and other grave violations of law had become a strong conviction, a sense of justice in the civilized nations and was subsequently, for the first time, applied in law by the Nuremberg Tribunal, so as to become a 'definite rule of international law'.

In this connection it is important to consider the significance of the addition of the phrase 'recognized . . . in the Judgment of the Tribunal' to the original proposal, which referred only to the principles recognized in the *Charter*. This 'minor deviation' from Biddle's and Truman's idea was, according to Röling, a consequence of the awareness of the fact that the Tribunal, though it declared the law of the Charter binding upon itself, departed from rules of the Charter where it deemed that necessary, and of the fact that its findings were necessary for the interpretation of vague concepts like "the waging of a war of aggression" [2]). As, however, there existed on different points a contradiction between the law of the Judgment and the provisions of the Charter, it was impossible to affirm, and formulate, the principles recognized in both instruments without making a choice between them. This choice had to be in favor of the Judgment which was of later date, embodied the effective application of the abstract provisions and restricted moreover, as has been shown [3]), the scope of these provisions. Once the principles recognized in the Judgment were also affirmed, they had to prevail over the wider formulations of the Charter. In fact, the formulation of the Nuremberg principles by the International Law Commission of 1950 embodied the concept of conspiracy and the exclusion of the defence of superior orders within the limits set by the Judgment of the Tribunal. Where it did not do so, as with regard to the 'waging' of aggressive war

---

1) A/C. 6/SR. 237, p. 181.

2) Prof. Mr. B. V. A. Röling, Stand en Ontwikkeling van het internationaal strafrecht, Tijdschrift voor Strafrecht, 1951, pp. 1 ff., p. 2.

3) See above, pp. 299 and 304 ff..

and the concept of complicity, its formulation aroused strong criticism from the delegates in the Sixth Committee [1]).

In these circumstances, however, mention of the Charter seems to be superfluous: the principles it embodied were 'affirmed' only if, and in so far as, they were applied by the Tribunal, whose Judgment, thus, appears the more important document. This is in conformity with the legal significance of the Judgment and its justification as given above [2]), and only such an interpretation gives true meaning to the resolution of the General Assembly. The Charter of London established a Tribunal and defined its jurisdiction but after the Judgment it could no longer produce legal effects [3]). An affirmation of the principles of the Charter would be a separate, independent act, the legal value of which would depend entirely on they legislative powers of the General Assembly. Such powers have not been given under the United Nations Charter. Resolutions and recommendations made in virtue of Article 13 (1) can only 'encourage the progressive development of international law', and can never give legal significance to principles which would not otherwise have such significance.

But the Judgment, as has been argued in the foregoing Chapter, does have legal significance. It was given by the first international tribunal called upon to apply international criminal

---

1) See particulary the Dutch Delegate in the Sixth Committee, A/C. 6/SR. 232, p. 138 and A/C. 6/SR. 236, p. 172; also Report of the Sixth Committee, A/L 639, p. 12.

2) See above, pp. 258–260.

3) An exception has to be made for the statute of the Office of the United Nations High Commissioner for Refugees, Annex to Gen. Ass. Resolution 428 (V) adopted on 14 December 1950, by virtue of which is excluded from the mandate of the High Commissioner a person "in respect of whom there are serious reasons for considering that he has committed a crime mentioned in Article VI of the London Charter of the International Military Tribunal". The same provision was included in Resolution 429 (V) of the same date, recommending a definition of refugees for the purpose of a draft Convention relating to the status of Refugees. The Convention as adopted by a Conference of Plenipotentaries in Geneva, on 25 July 1951, does not contain any reference to the Charter of London on account of the opposition to such express reference by the German Delegation to the conference. The relevant paragraph (Art. I, par. 1) now gives as criterion the committing of "a crime against peace, a war crime, or a crime against humanity, as defined in the international instrument drawn up to make provision in respect of such crimes". Article 6 of the London Charter thus remains decisive in this respect (Cf. Prof. Dr. B. V. A. Röling, Internationaal Strafrechterlijke Organisatie, Tijdschrift voor Strafrecht, 1952, reprint p. 5, note 9).

law. Established by the Agreement and Charter which defined its jurisdiction, the Tribunal found, as world conscience demanded, that the accused, who had gravely and with terrible consequences violated the fundamental rules of international law, deserved punishment. The I.M.T. inflicted such punishment on the guilty, and thus marked the beginning of an international criminal law developed, and to be developed, by judges. The substance of this new law, since it is case law, cannot be expressed as much in precise and fixed rules, as in the principle that the Judgment rendered serves as a model for the future, that is, that all those who violate international law in the way of the major war criminals in Nuremberg will be liable to punishment by an international tribunal.

Even had it not been declared again and again by the Prosecutors and other spokesmen of the Prosecuting Powers that the law applied would also bind their own countries and statesmen, that it was under international, and not under an *ad hoc* law that the defendants were judged, and that the aim of the trials was that successive generations of men might say 'So perish all who do the like again', – even if this had not been promised and admitted, it would have been evident that the post-war trials could only be classified as administration of justice if they were accepted as precedents in the sense indicated above, that is if the law applied in, and resulting from these cases, would be one for victors and vanquished alike.

In this light the affirmation of the Nuremberg principles by the General Assembly was the affirmation of the existence of an international criminal law as case law inaugurated by the International Military Tribunal. It was an affirmation of principles, not of a special way of dealing with the German major war criminals. The Assembly did not pronounce on the way in which the Tribunal was set up, its actual composition of judges drawn exclusively from the victor countries, the organisation of the prosecution or the specific rules of procedure which were in certain respects objectionable and defective, and these remain the responsibility of the signatories and later adherents to the London Agreement. But what was affirmed, after the event, by the organ of the international legal community – which quality the General Assembly certainly possesses when the nearly sixty

Member States all concur in a resolution – was the essential fact that the Nuremberg Tribunal was a court of law, that it was in virtue of law that the defendants were punished and that in the international community the Tribunal had, indeed, the extraordinary power to develop and create the law in the concrete case, which power is the proper characteristic of a common-law tribunal.

While the affirmation of the Nuremberg principles by the United Nations did not indicate a full and formal endorsement of the trial, as was given by the nineteen governments which adhered to the Charter, its consequences in law reached further, were less ambiguous and more permanent. When the London Agreement was signed and adhered to, the law of Nuremberg had not yet come to life; there was, properly speaking, not yet a law to recognize and affirm. Only a jurisdiction had been established and defined, for the trial of the enemy statesmen, and what was tentatively put down as 'the law' of the case, could only, at least so far as the criminality of aggressive war was concerned, be brought into real, legal existence by the judgment the Tribunal would render.

What signatories and adherents *did not do* in London – that is create new rules of international law applicable to themselves – *could not* be done by resolution of the General Assembly because it lacks legislative authority. But the Members of the international community could, and did, by resolution recognize and accept what had happened in the meantime – a judicial development of the law by the decision and punishment of Nuremberg. In any case these facts would have constituted irremovable milestones in international relations, threatening indications for all those who planned to go the way of the condemned Nazi leaders. But their existence could have been ignored or dismissed to the field of mere political action by the States not directly involved in the Nuremberg proceedings. The resolution signified a recognition that judicial not political action had been taken, that Nuremberg did not signify an ephemerical, opportunistic deviation from the established rules, but a permanent, irrevocable change, and that it was not a unilateral provision but general law, binding the whole community, which had been applied. The process of development of international common law was, as such, accepted and encouraged by the Resolution of December 1946, which constitutes powerful evidence of the universal scope of the legal development which occurred before and in Nuremberg. The resolution was not a creation, but a recognition of the existence of international criminal law and of individual criminal liability for aggressive war which, as Politis said, is "the real domain of international criminality" [1]).

The replacement of the term 'reaffirm' proposed in the Biddle-Truman correspondence, by 'affirm' in the final resolution, was in line with the other changes the original proposal underwent. The United Nations as a whole had never before pronounced itself on the Nuremberg Trial; the resolution constituted its first action in this field. But the re-affirmation proposed was not identical with the affirmation given by the Assembly; the former was – in fact – suggested as a new action, not, like the affirmation, dependent on the Nuremberg Judgment, adding to its authority, but separate from it – a general codification of new law incorporating in more or less identical rules the provisions of the London Charter. That the original proposal referred only to the Charter and not to the Judgment, was fully consistent with the different type of action envisaged. The fact that the Nuremberg Judgment was a law-making case could be ignored if international criminal law was not going to be case law but codified law.

As soon as there is codification the judgments lose their strict and decisive value as precedents; it is no more the case or series of cases but the code which contains the law applicable; no more the judge but the legislator who says what is law and develops it. Of course the judgments would remain authoritative interpretations of the law, and their authority and influence would remain very great if the code were formulated in summary rules and contained vague conceptions like 'aggression' and 'conspiracy'. But the difference in legal nature between a codification and a common law system, and the corresponding difference in the role of the judge, remain essential.

The two parts of the resolution of 1946 thus embody two completely different types of action: the first recognized the

[1]) N. Politis, The New Aspects of International Law, o.c., p. 43.

existence of international criminal law as customary law, growing from case to case; the second envisaged the transformation of judge's law into legislator's law, a complete change of legal foundation and structure. It would go too far to speak here of a contradiction in the resolution. After an affirmation of the binding character of the Nuremberg Judgment, one would have expected the decision to create a permanent international criminal jurisdiction which would be entrusted with the task of applying and developing the principles recognized in the Nuremberg Judgment in all cases of grave violations of international law by statesmen of any Member of the United Nations. But in view of the general preference for codification, among the authorities on international penal law and among the majority of Members of the United Nations – having a codification system in their domestic law – the desire to formulate the principles of Nuremberg "in the context of a general codification of offences against the peace and security of mankind or in an International Criminal Code", seems quite understandable and justified.

Two points, however, must be stressed with regard to the connection between the two different decisions embodied in the Resolution of 1946. First of all, the decision to prepare the codification and extension of the Nuremberg law did not detract from the value of the affirmation, the acceptance of that law as the existing law of the international community. So long as an International Criminal Code does not exist, or is not ratified by the United Nations, the law of Nuremberg remains valid and applicable law in virtue of the Judgment of Nuremberg affirmed by decision of the United Nations.

In his supplementary report to the General Assembly, of 24 October 1946, the Secretary General of the United Nations stated: "In the interest of peace, and in order to protect mankind against future wars, it will be of decisive significance to have the principles which were employed in the Nürnberg Trials, and according to which the German war criminals were sentenced, *made a permanent part of the body of international law* as quickly as possible" [1]). This statement, the correctness of which was

---

1) Official Records of the second part of the First Session of the General Assembly, pp. 699–700 (italics supplied).

already doubtful at that time, was textually repeated in the Memorandum of the Secretary General of 3 March 1949 [1]). After the resolution of 1946, however, there can be no doubt that the principles of Nuremberg do constitute a permanent part of the body of international law – because they were applied by an international tribunal recognized as such by the United Nations. The codification of these principles may be deemed desirable and may, in the opinion of most Member States, re-inforce and consolidate their legal nature, and such a codification may even constitute a moral obligation for the States who organized the Nuremberg proceedings, but the existence of international criminal law, based on the Nuremberg Judgment, can no more be denied.

But criminal law, to be really applicable, needs a judge, a criminal jurisdiction. Where in the foregoing argument the Nuremberg law was qualified as applicable law, it was in the meaning that a future international criminal jurisdiction could proceed on the principles employed in Nuremberg. The primary moral obligation assumed by the States which instituted the Nuremberg and subsequent war crimes trials and by those which endorsed the judgement rendered, is not, consequently, to ensure an affirmation, or even a codification of the law, but to establish such a jurisdiction. The Nuremberg principles are not rules of behaviour. Those existed already, notably by virtue of the Kellogg Pact, and could not be extended or developed by the Tribunal. They are principles of individual criminal responsibility. The Tribunal created new sanctions attached to the existing rules of conduct and the General Assembly affirmed that it was just and lawful that those sanctions were applied.

Whether, therefore, the principles – the rules of sanction affirmed as applicable to the law violators, in the name of whatever country they may act – are incorporated in a criminal code or whether they remain customary rules, the first task of the General Assembly was, and is, to create an international criminal jurisdiction, and the absence of any reference to such a step is a fundamental deficiency, the real objection against the Resolution of 1946.

1) The Charter and Judgment of the Nuremberg Trial; History and Analysis, A/CN. 4/5 (U.N. Publication 1949/V/7).

SECTION 2. THE FORMULATION OF THE NUREMBERG PRINCIPLES

Though of less importance than the resolution discussed till now, the formulation which the International Law Commission in its 1950 Session gave to the Nuremberg principles [1]), ranks nevertheless as another positive step taken within the framework of the United Nations with the purpose of continuing and developing what was begun in Nuremberg. Like the resolution and contrary to the draft codification of international criminal law and to the draft statute for an international criminal court, this formulation may be regarded as an accomplished fact, having what value it has in itself and not depending on further approval, ratification or implementation. Though the formulation is by no means universally accepted in all its details, it remains an important interpretation of the law of Nuremberg by the principal juridical body in the world, charged with the restatement and development of rules of international law on specific subjects [2]), and composed of outstanding authorities on international law, representing as a whole the chief forms of civilization and the basic legal systems of the world.

A closer examination of the nature and of the specific principles of the formulation must be preceded by a brief survey of the Assembly resolutions leading up to it.

The Assembly Committee on the Progressive Development of International Law and its Codification, entrusted with the task of devising plans for the formulation of the Nuremberg principles within the context of a general codification, did not really devise substantial plans but submitted instead a recommendation which amounted to a revision of the original instructions of the Assembly.

In its report of June 17, 1947, the Committee recommended that the International Law Commission, the establishment of which it had proposed, should be invited to prepare:

"a) a draft convention incorporating the principles of inter-

---

1) Formulation of the Nuremberg Principles, Part III of the Report of the International Law Commission covering its Second Session, A/1316, pp. 11—14.

2) Cf. Statute of the International Law Commission, Articles 1 and 15, in Gen. Ass. Resolution, 174 (II).

national law recognized by the Charter of the Nürnberg Tribunal and sanctioned by the judgment of that Tribunal; and

b) a detailed plan of general codification of offences against the peace and security of mankind in such a manner that the plan should clearly indicate the place to be accorded to the Nürnberg principles" [1]).

In addition the Committee expressed its opinion that these tasks would not preclude the I.L.C. from drafting in due course a code of international penal law.

A preliminary remark may be made on the use of the term 'sanctioned by the judgment of the Tribunal' instead of 'recognized' in the resolution of 1946. At first sight it seems as though, taken in the sense of 'attach a penalty to', this expression changed the meaning of the original resolution; the rules to the violation of which the judgment indeed attached a penalty were recognized principles of international law, like the prohibition of resort to war. But as the principles affirmed by the Assembly were obviously those of criminal responsibility, the term 'sanctioned' must be taken in the sense of 'made binding', 'made effective', and as such, distinguished from 'recognized by the Charter', which interpretation confirms the view given above to the effect that the Judgment and not the Charter was the source of the new criminal law. Unhappily, this expression was dropped again in the later resolutions.

The striking aspect of the recommendation of the Codification Committee is that it considered as three different actions, as three subsequent phases, what was presented as one in the Assembly resolution: first the incorporation of the Nuremberg principles in a draft convention, which would entail their formulation and the transformation of case law, affirmed by the Assembly, into written law, ratified by the States; secondly the drafting of a code of offences against the peace and security of mankind wherein the place of the Nuremberg principles had only to be 'clearly indicated', an obvious recession from the position the Assembly had taken in its resolution of 1946, in which the

1) Quoted by J. Spiropoulos in The Formulation of the Nürnberg Principles, report presented to the International Law Commission at its second session, A/CN. 4/22 (12 April 1950), pp. 20–1.

Nuremberg principles were envisaged as the chief element of the general codification in the context of which they would be formulated; and finally the drafting of a, still broader, international penal code.

Subcommittee 2 of the Sixth Committee of the Assembly of 1947 adhered in the main to the foregoing proposal, while on the recommendation of the Sixth Committee the Assembly finally adopted the following resolution:

"THE GENERAL ASSEMBLY

"*Decides* to entrust the formulation of the principles of international law recognized in the Charter of the Nuremberg Tribunal and in the judgment of the Tribunal to the International Law Commission . . .

"*Directs* the Commission to

a) Formulate the principles of international law recognized in the Charter of the Nuremberg Tribunal, and in the judgment of the Tribunal, and

b) Prepare a draft code of offences against the peace and security of mankind, indicating clearly the place to be accorded to the principles mentioned in sub-paragraph a) above" [1]).

The proposed separation of what was regarded as one single act in the resolution of 1946 – formulation of the Nuremberg principles and codification – was thus adopted by the Assembly. By the phrase 'clearly indicating . . .', the Assembly gave the I.L.C. liberty regarding the inclusion of the Nuremberg principles in the draft code. The discussions of the Sixth Committee show that this decision had its main origin in an uncertainty as to the conformity of the principles of the Nuremberg Tribunal with general international law, and, even more, in an uncertainty as to the consequences of a formal and specific acceptance of these principles as binding law. Apart from the criticism of the trial (see foregoing Chapter), the change in international relations, the growing tension between the great Powers, had an influence on this decision.

---

1) Gen. Ass. Resolution 177 (II) of 21 November 1947.

It must be noted however that an open challenge of the Nuremberg principles was avoided and that there were no proposals to go back on the affirmation of 1946. The fact that in Germany and Tokyo other war crimes trials based on the same principles were still going on offered a welcome motive to delay for the moment the decision on penal codification. With regard to the formulation of the Nuremberg principles in the context of such a codification, to which the General Assembly in its previous resolution had attached 'great importance', "several delegates expressed their conviction that this work should be held over until the trials of war criminals were further advanced" [1]). The expected judgments would perhaps show new developments and, on the other hand, these trials might be unduly influenced by a critical position the United Nations might adopt towards the principles applied there. Legal discrimination towards the vanquished sometimes cast its shadow over the discussions in Lake Success in 1947.

On an important point however, the new resolution of the Assembly differed from the proposal of the Codification Committee adopted by Subcommittee Two: instead of a draft convention a mere formulation of the Nuremberg principles was demanded from the I.L.C.. A draft convention would not have been of any use, as the following draft code would either incorporate or modify the Nuremberg principles. As it was, the whole idea of formulation of the Nuremberg principles was changed; from the uncertain plans for codification it was drawn into the field of unwritten law where the General Assembly, by its affirmation, had already taken a positive stand, and where an analysis of the Nuremberg law in a number of principles by a body of the highest scientific authority could emphasize the significance of, and benefit the proper development of the new criminal law. This law was already in force and the Assembly could no more talk it out of existence. The scope and definition of this law remained, as always in unwritten law, a matter open to discussion. Only courts can with full authority develop a penal case-law, but in the present situation of international

[1]) Official Records of the Second Session of the General Assembly, Sixth Committee, Summary Records of Meetings, 16 Sept.–26 November 1947, p. 212, quoted by Röling in Tijdschrift voor Strafrecht 1951, l.c., p. 7.

relations the opinion of a body like the I.L.C. may be taken into consideration as evidence of the state of law.

There was, initially, a divergence of opinion among the delegates in the Sixth Committee and among the members of the I.L.C. with regard to the nature of the task entrusted to the latter, and the foregoing interpretation of this task, as an independent restatement of the Nuremberg law by an authoritative body, will be seen to have developed but gradually in the course of the discussions in the Commission and in the Assembly.

The Commission, elected in 1948, considered the question of the formulation of the Nuremberg principles during its First Session, in 1949, and submitted in its Report to the General Assembly the conclusion that "since the Nuremberg principles had been affirmed by the General Assembly in resolution 95 (I) of 11 December 1946, the task of the Commission was not to express any appreciation of these principles as principles of international law but merely to formulate them". Though the report containing this passage was approved by the General Assembly of 1949, and the Commission, thus, proceeded on this basis in its Second Session [1]), the opinions expressed by some of its members and the strong criticism voiced in the General Assembly of 1950 against this conclusion demonstrate that it did not clear the confusion regarding the nature of the formulation produced.

Apart from the fact that the principles to be formulated had already been affirmed there was another factor which drove the Commission to such a modest attitude. In the Draft Code of Offences which the Commission had begun to elaborate at the same time, the place to be accorded to the Nuremberg principles had to be clearly indicated. As it was probable that the Code would deviate on certain points from the Nuremberg principles and as the Commission desired entire liberty with regard to such deviations, it seemed more logical that the Commission should postpone expressing its opinion on the Nuremberg principles till drafting the Code. In his First Report on the Draft Code the special rapporteur of the I.L.C., Jean Spiropoulos, had already stated that the incorporation of the

1) A/1316, p. 11, par. 96.

principles in the Code would not be a mechanical process but would entail 'appreciation' of them [1]).

It is understandable that in these circumstances several members of the Commission did not show great enthusiasm for the task assigned to it. For the Commission had to formulate principles on the subject-matter of which it had decided and already undertaken to draft more or less divergent rules for real use in the future. In the view of several members such a 'mechanical' formulation of the Nuremberg principles could as well have been entrusted to the juridical personnel of the Secretariate; an authoritative body like the I.L.C. was not needed for such work [2]). The task of the International Law Commission would have had more substance if the Commission had put a broader construction on the term 'principles'. An effort to formulate "the general principles of law on which the provisions of the Charter and the decisions of the Tribunal were based", as proposed by Professor Scelle [3]), would not, perhaps, have led to an agreement because of the wide divergencies of legal and scientific opinion regarding these matters which are hardly suitable for decision by majority-vote. But, as will be seen below, some of the 'principles' adopted by the Commission look more like precise provisions of a Code than like the basic principles of a series of trials on which a system of international penal law was to be based [4]).

Contrary to the view of those authors who regretted the distinction made by the resolution of 1947 between formulation of the Nuremberg principles and the drafting of a Code, it may be held that the development of international penal law would have benefitted from a more complete separation between the two tasks, in the sense outlined above. The elaboration of a Code should have been seen more clearly as an entirely new

---

1) J. Spiropoulos, Draft Code of Offences against the Peace and Security of Mankind, report presented to the I.L.C. at its Second Session, A/CN. 4/25 (26 April 1950), p. 18.

2) See Prof. Mr. Dr. J. P. A. François, De codificatie van het internationale recht, Economisch-Statistische Berichten, 1949, Nos. 1686 and 1687; reprint pp. 9–10.

3) See Report of the I.L.C. covering its First Session, A/925, Chapter III, p. 4, par. 27, and Report on Second Session, l.c., p. 11, note 3.

4) See the criticism of this method in the Sixth Committee of the General Assembly of 1950, Report of the Sixth Committee on the Report of the I.L.C., A/1639, (8 December 1950), p. 9.

chapter of written law, for which the essentials of the post-war judgments, restated by the International Law Commission, were the point of departure.

Such a view of the formulation of the Nuremberg principles by the International Law Commission supposes the acceptance of this formulation as a pronouncement of an authoritative legal body not subject to approval by governments or by the General Assembly. The work of the commission is not however generally regarded this way, as was shown particularly by the subsequent discussion of the Nuremberg principles in the Sixth Committee.

The question of the autonomy of the International Law Commission has arisen on various occasions since its establishment in 1947. The original proposals of the Preparatory Committee, envisaging a body constructed on more or less the same lines, regarding structure and position, as the International Court of Justice, had been modified by the General Assembly so as to make the Commission a subsidiary organ, not continuously functioning [1]). During the discussion on the Nuremberg principles the question presented itself in this way: certain delegates in the Sixth Committee argued that the I.L.C. before presenting its report on the Nuremberg principles should have consulted the governments as provided in its Statute. A thorough examination of the formulation submitted, it was asserted, was therefore impossible. Against this view it was argued that the Commission had in this matter been entrusted with a special task which did not come under the procedural rules of either Article 16 (governing the progressive development of international law) or Article 21 (governing codification) of the Statute, both requiring consultation of the Governments [2]).

While the question whether or not the formulation of the Commission should be discussed in substance was, also for practical reasons, decided in the positive, no decision was taken concerning the nature of the Commission's formulation. Strong criticism was voiced, in various directions, on the formulation chosen, and in drafting its final resolution the Sixth Committee

---

1) See Resolution 174 (II) and François, Vol. I, p. 624.

2) See the forementioned resolution, and Report of the Sixth Committee, l.c., p. 8.

took great pains to avoid any terms which might suggest an approval of the formulation. Though the resolution still invited the Governments of Member States to furnish their observations on the formulation of the Commission, it requested the I.L.C. to take into account such observations and the observations made by the delegates only "in preparing the draft code of offences against the peace and security of mankind" [1]. The Commission was not requested to reconsider its formulation.

In view of this provision, and in view, moreover, of the fact that part of the criticism of delegates was counterbalanced by the approval of others, that a great deal of the arguments advanced had already been taken into account by the Commission, and that some criticism had been made by one or two delegates only, the special rapporteur of the Commission refrained the following year from positive suggestions on this matter [2]. In its report covering its Third Session [3] the Commission has accordingly dropped the item and only mentions that while considering the draft Code it took into account the observations made on its formulation of the Nuremberg Principles by delegates during the Fifth Session of the General Assembly — as summarized subsequently by the special rapporteur [4] — and those received from various governments.

The formulation of the Nuremberg principles presented by the International Law Commission to the General Assembly in 1950 must accordingly be regarded as a closed chapter, a document of international law deriving its significance as a succinct restatement of the law of Nuremberg from the international body which formulated it.

The final text of the Commission is divided into seven principles and runs as follows:

Principle I. "Any person who commits an act which constitutes a crime under international law is responsible therefor and liable to punishment."

1) Gen. Ass. Resolution 488 (V); see Report of the Sixth Committee, l.c., pp. 12–14.

2) J. Spiropoulos, Second Report on a Draft Code of Offences against the Peace and Security of Mankind, presented to the I.L.C., A/CN. 4/44 (12 April 1951), pp. 6–7.

3) Report of the I.L.C. covering its Third Session, A/1858, Chapter IV, p. 11, par. 57.

4) Second Report on a Draft Code, l.c., pp. 7–36.

Principle II. "The fact that internal law does not impose a penalty for an act which constitutes a crime under international law does not relieve the person who committed the act from responsibility under international law."

Principle III. "The fact that a person who committed an act which constitutes a crime under international law acted as Head of State or responsible Government official does not relieve him from responsibility under international law."

Principle IV. "The fact that a person acted pursuant to order of his Government or of a superior does not relieve him from responsibility under international law, provided a moral choice was in fact possible to him."

Principle V. "Any person charged with a crime under international law has the right to a fair trial on the facts and law.

Principle VI. "The crimes hereinafter set out are punishable as crimes under international law:

"a. Crimes against peace:

(I) Planning, preparation, initiation or waging of a war of aggression or a war in violation of international treaties, agreements or assurances;

(II) Participation in a common plan or conspiracy for the accomplishment of any of the acts mentioned under (I).

"b. War crimes:

Violations of the law or customs of war which include, but are not limited to, murder, ill-treatment or deportation to slave-labour or for any other purpose of civilian population of or in occupied territory, murder or ill-treatment of prisoners of war or persons on the seas, killing of hostages, plunder of public or private property, wanton destruction of cities, towns, or villages, or devastation not justified by military necessity.

"c. Crimes against humanity:

Murder, extermination, enslavement, deportation and other inhuman acts done against any civilian population, or persecutions on political, racial or religious grounds, when such acts are done or such persecutions are carried on in execution of or in connexion with any crime against peace or any war crime."

Principle VII. "Complicity in the commission of a crime against peace, a war crime or a crime against humanity as set forth in Principle VI is a crime under international law."

As was observed before, and as was stated by numerous delegates in the Sixth Committee, this formulation contains precise rules rather than basic principles. These rules moreover – notably Principles III, IV and VI – appear more like a copy of the corresponding provisions of the Nuremberg Charter – respectively Articles 7, 8 and 6 (paragraph 2) – than like the results of an analysis of the Tribunal's Judgment. That this had been the avowed intention of the Commission appears already from a passage in the report covering its First Session, in 1944 [1]. The result, which the representative of the United Kingdom, FitzMaurice, approvingly called "a species of small code on the subject to serve as a point of departure for further efforts in the field" [2], could, however, no longer serve that purpose since the 'further effort', the draft code, was going to contain a different set of rules. For the view of the Commission that it was not bound to insert the Nuremberg Principles in their entirety in the draft code was at the same session approved by the majority of delegates [3].

The problem for the Legal Committee, to "avoid affirming now what we would deny next year", would, according to the Dutch delegate, Prof. Röling, have lost its difficulty if "only those general ideas which mark the importance of Charter and Judgment", which are not questioned, but which "stand and ... will be applied in the draft code of the future", had been formulated [4]. But the majority of the delegates approved of neither

1) Report on First Session, l.c., p. 4, par. 26 *in fine*.
2) Statement of the Delegate of the United Kingdom, A/C. 6/SR. 233, p. 143.
3) Report of the Sixth Committee, l.c., p. 10.
4) Statement of the Dutch Delegate at the 232nd meeting of the Sixth Committee, (A/C. 6/SR. 232), transcript p. 12; cf. Röling in Tijdschrift voor Strafrecht, l.c., p. 11.

the vaguer formulation of principles, introduced by Röling, nor the proposal of the French and Chinese delegates to formulate "the general principles of law underlying the Charter and Judgment" [1]).

Yet it is doubtful whether any text, however general, stressing the importance of the Nuremberg Trial could have received the approval of the General Assembly in 1950. For, precisely as the discussion on the most fundamental principle, number II, showed, four years after the Assembly's 'affirmation' of the Nuremberg Principles no principle was left the validity of which is not questioned by a substantial number of States. For Principle I, generally approved by the delegates, has no significance except in connection with a definition of 'crimes under international law' [2]) as embodied in Principle VI. The Soviet proposal to add to the text of the first Principle "whenever a relevant treaty exists" only emphasized the real situation [3]).

It was precisely on the question by which *modus operandi* the concept of individual responsibility for crimes under international law could be realized, that a great divergency of views was shown in the discussion on Principle II. It appeared that a great number of delegates was not willing to accept the idea of direct individual responsibility under international law, a concept "convenient and picturesque but... unscientific". The British delegate argued that the aim of individual punishment for crimes under international law could in fact be achieved by establishing "the position in which the States admitted that the individuals under their jurisdiction would be subject to punishment for certain acts recognized as crimes under international law" [4]). While the delegates supporting this view relied principally on "the classic concept that international law solely governs relations between States", other representatives, notably of South American States, took exception to the statement made by the Commission in its commentary on Principles I and II to the effect that these implied the supremacy of international law

---

1) Statement of the French Delegate, A/C. 6/SR 232, p. 141, and statement of the Chinese Delegate, A/C. 6/SR. 235, p. 164.

2) Cf. Statement of the Peruvian Delegate, A/C. 6/SR. 237, pp. 179—180.

3) Statement of the Soviet Delegate, A/C. 6/SR. 234, p. 156.

4) Statement of the Delegate of the United Kingdom, A/C. 6/SR. 233, p. 145.

over national law, which doctrine they rejected as not universally accepted and as contrary to the constitutions of their countries.

For all these delegates there was no question of individual obligations. The obligations involved could only be those of States to punish the guilty individuals themselves or to allow them to be punished by other States or by a legally constituted international tribunal. It may be remembered that it was exactly to these arguments, and to the absence of such a State obligation in their cases, that the Defence in Nuremberg, in Tokyo and in other post war trials vainly appealed in defence of the lives of the accused. The Nuremberg Tribunal decided that the existence of individual duties under international law, transcending national obligations, was the essence of the law it applied, and the Tribunal drew from this the consequence that the accused could be judged and sentenced by an international tribunal without the interposition of a consenting or law-enforcing State.

Several delegates contesting the views of the International Law Commission alleged that the Commission had not followed its own decision to formulate only the principles of international law and not the general principles underlying them, and then relegated the questions of the supremacy of international law and of the individual responsibility under that law to the field of legal theory [1]). But the fact that all those rejecting one or other of these principles contested at the same time what the Tribunal called 'the essence of the Charter', demonstrates that the Commission, departing from its own rule, had attacked the core of the question [2]).

As the Report of the Sixth Committee stated, opinion was generally too divided to permit conclusions as to the meaning of the Committee on the controversial issues [3]). But one conclusion may be recorded, that is that, on whatever theory they proceeded, four years after the Nuremberg Judgment at least two of the Prosecuting States, and a large number of those adhering to the Charter or affirming the "Nuremberg Principles" in an Assembly Resolution, had actually adopted the principle that no one may be subjected to trial for the international crimes they had recog-

1) Report of The Sixth Committee, l.c., p. 11.
2) As the Delegate of Israël, Mr. Robinson, remarked, A/C. 6/SR. 236, p. 175.
3) Report of the Sixth Committee, l.c., p. 10.

nized before, except by or with the consent of the State of which he is a national.

While the Commission's formulation on this point accurately reflects the basis of the Nuremberg Judgment, the same cannot be said of Principles VI and VII. That the Commission, in Principle VI, simply copied the definition of crimes of Article 6 of the Charter is all the more surprising as it took the liberty to modify the provisions of Articles 7 and 8. The former provision was softened, in Principle III, by the omission of the rule that the official position of the defendants could not be considered in mitigating punishment, because the Commission was of the opinion that the question of mitigating punishment was a matter for the competent court to decide [1]). It omitted the same provision in Principle IV and mitigated the elimination of the plea of 'superior orders' by making the condition of the possibility of 'moral choice' [2]). This ambiguous phrase borrowed from the Judgment has been much criticized and was rejected by a great number of delegates [3]).

Apart from the incorporation of the limitation of crimes against humanity to acts committed in time of war, which had not been a limitation of the criminality but only of the competence of the Nuremberg Tribunal [4]), it is the fact that the Charter's formulation of the crimes against peace was retained that deserves strongest criticism.

If anywhere, it was on this point that the Commission should not have limited itself to repeating the careless and useless definition of the Charter hastily arrived at in London, not applied as such by the Nuremberg and other Tribunals and the defects of which had been demonstrated extensively in legal literature [5]). As shown before [6]), the Nuremberg Tribunal had surrounded the concept of conspiracy by strict limitations: only a concrete plan to wage war, clearly outlined in its criminal purposes and not too far removed from the time of decision and action, was to be regarded

1) Formulation of the Nuremberg Principles in Report on Second Session, l.c., p. 12, par. 104.
2) Ibidem, pars. 105–6.
3) Report of the Sixth Committee, l.c., p. 11.
4) Ibidem, pp. 11–12.
5) See above, pp. 297 and 303 ff..
6) See above, p. 215.

as a criminal conspiracy. None of these limitations was included in the definition of the International Law Commission.

Nor did the Tribunal follow the arbitrary summing up of some of the activities by which the defendants could become guilty of the crime against peace. Neither 'planning' nor 'initiation' of an aggressive war were considered separately by the Tribunal which gave by its decision such a restrictive interpretation to the criminality of 'preparation' and especially 'waging' of a war that it can be said that the real test for the Tribunal was whether a defendant was responsible for a war of aggression [1]).

The formulation became still more defective on this point by the fact that the Commission listed the criminality of complicity in the committing of any one of the crimes defined under VI as another principle recognized in Nuremberg. The Commission had been led to this conclusion by the fact that, though the Tribunal had interpreted the last paragraph of Article 6 of the Charter as establishing only the responsibility of those participating in a common plan to wage war, it had at the same time applied the ordinary rules of complicity in assessing the guilt of the defendants with respect to war crimes and crimes against humanity which are perpetrated by individual action [2]). But in that case the Commission should have excluded the crimes against peace from the scope of the complicity rules.

By not formulating the limits drawn by the Tribunal to the concept of conspiracy, by including the dangerous word 'waging' and further by adding the rules of complicity, the Commission gave the false impression that the law of Nuremberg admitted the possibility of an, in principle unlimited, number of convictions for crimes against peace. That the members of the Commission had been aware of this danger appears from paragraph 117 of its report, which, however, oddly concludes with the statement that the Commission understands the expression 'waging' "to refer only to high-ranking military personnel and high state officials, and believes that this was also the view of the Tribunal". If this was the belief of the Commission it should have included this most important restriction in the formulation itself. With

---

1) See above, p. 306.
2) Report on Second Session, l.c., p. 14, pars. 125—7.

its general scope the formulation is now open to the criticism that it does not take into account the circumstance that, as the Nuremberg law was made in a Judgment on *major* war criminals only, its rules cannot always be applied to ordinary war criminals [1]).

It should not be forgotten that, as was argued in the previous chapter, the Nuremberg law is not the written law of abstract rules in a code, but case law, judge's law, originated and developed by the Judgment of the I.M.T. in view of a concrete case, and further elaborated by the subsequent tribunals. It is always a hazardous undertaking to deduce abstract rules from precedents, especially when these are of recent date. This applied even more in the case of the International Law Commission which could only take into account one single precedent of a very limited nature. The limits set by the precedent and the conditions under which it was established should have been carefully observed in formulating the new law.

It is regrettable that in this situation the I.L.C. adhered so closely to the wording of Articles of the Charter which were writen for the prosecution of major war criminals and which were, moreover, only partly and with carefully drawn limitations followed by the Tribunal. It may seem in contradiction to the concept of criminal law as understood in civilized States that there should be different sets of rules for different categories of persons, for major and minor criminals, as has been suggested with respect to the law of Nuremberg [2]). Just as there should not be rules of law applying only to 'European Axis Criminals', so, in a sound legal system, should there not be special rules for 'major' and 'minor' war criminals, to the effect that acts criminal when committed by the former would not be so when committed by the latter, or that the latter could appeal to pleas which are not open to the former. Of course there can be, and there are in different municipal systems, crimes which by definition can only be perpetrated by persons in a certain profession, for example civil servants. And the judge, and sometimes the law, takes into account the special responsibility and the degree of independence of the accused when measuring the punishment.

---

1) Cf. Report of Sixth Committee, l.c., p. 9.
2) See for example Röling in Tijdschrift voor Strafrecht, l.c. pp. 10–11.

The fact that this was different in the Nuremberg Charter qualifies this document as *ad hoc* law, not integrated into a system. When the General Assembly affirmed the law of Nuremberg and entrusted the International Law Commission with its formulation, it intended precisely to integrate this law into a system. The principles should therefore have been formulated in such a way that they would lose both their restriction to European Axis Criminals and their restriction to major war criminals. As is evident from its formulation of Principles VI and VII, the Commission had lost sight of the latter aspect of its task while, on the other hand, a great number of delegates, as appears from their comments on Principles I and II, may be said to have forgotten the former.

As was said before, the affirmation of the Nuremberg Principles by the Assembly amounted to the recognition, by the community of States, that the Nuremberg Judgment was given by an international tribunal applying international law. This amounted, it was said, to a recognition that every statesman, every soldier, every person of no matter what country, who violated the fundamental rules of international law in the way the Nuremberg criminals did, would be punishable before a competent tribunal, national or international, existing already or established for that purpose. It is, in principle, possible to give a more detailed formulation of the Nuremberg principles, but after a review of the achievement of the I.L.C. and of the way this was received in the General Assembly, it seems that it would have been preferable if the Assembly had immediately and unambiguously formulated this one consequence of its affirmation and left the matter there. The 'principles of Nuremberg' would have remained safe and intact in the Judgment of the Tribunal where later international tribunals could find them.

Criminal law stands or falls with the recognition of crimes, whether defined in codified rules or in the decisions of criminal courts. Only when it is admitted that there are international crimes, crimes under international law, and only when it is agreed which they are, can an international criminal law, in the modern sense of the term, be said to exist. Any competent tribunal can judge the authors, provided of course the individual is regarded as responsible for his acts. And the discussions of 1950 show indeed that the individual is universally seen as the real perpetrator of international crimes, though a few delegates advocated in addition to the concept of individual responsibility that of collective criminal responsibility of the State [1]).

All the questions discussed above, that of the supremacy of international law, that of the position of the individual under international law and of the intermediary position of the State, dissolve in the one question whether there are acts recognized as international crimes. Once this is the case, the consequence should be drawn that the States recognizing such crimes agree that their nationals committing them be brought before any tribunal having jurisdiction with respect to crimes against international law, when they are not judged in their own country.

It appears from the forementioned discussions that there is a number of States agreeable to this conclusion. A greater number of States is not so. The fact is that they do not admit the existence of crimes under international law, though some do not say this openly but hide their opinion behind arguments to the effect that the concept of a possibly existing crime is not yet definite. It is regrettable that the International Law Commission, by adopting the loose definition of crimes of the Nuremberg Charter, especially of the crime against peace, the central crime under international law, played into the hands of the delegates of countries which are not willing to accept the consequences of Nuremberg. A clear view of the positions of States in this matter was therefore obscured. And by not adopting the point of view that since the Assembly had recognized the principles of Nuremberg there was no more doubt that these principles *were* part of international law, the Commission allowed the Sixth Committee to keep its distance from the Nuremberg law it had affirmed before, to discuss the definition of crimes as if their existence was completely in the air and to talk on the concept of international criminal law as on a matter of pure speculation. But the facts of the judicial decisions of Nuremberg and Tokyo and of their execution cannot be reasoned away and the solemn decision of the General Assembly of 1945 cannot be revoked. Even if States declare that they do not regard the law

---

1) See Report of Sixth Committee, l.c., pp. 10–11.

of Nuremberg as binding on themselves and on their nationals, these facts and decisions stand as the irrevocable beginning of international criminal law.

SECTION 3. THE DRAFT CODE OF OFFENCES AGAINST THE PEACE AND SECURITY OF MANKIND

In its Third Session from May 16 till July 27 1951 the International Law Commission adopted a Draft Code of Offences against the Peace and Security of Mankind which it submitted for consideration to the Sixth General Assembly in Paris [1]). At one of its first meetings, however, on November 13th, 1951, the Assembly decided, especially for reasons of political convenience, not to discuss the Draft [2]) but to invite the Governments of Member States to furnish their observations on the text proposed. This is therefore the third time the Governments have had the opportunity to express their opinion on the subject, an opportunity of which few States availed themselves on the previous occasions [3]).

When the I.L.C. at its First Session considered the task conferred upon it by paragraph (b) of Resolution 177 (II), it decided to circulate a questionnaire to Governments "inquiring what offences, apart from those defined in the Charter and judgment of the Nürnberg Tribunal, should, in their view, be comprehended in the draft code" [4]). At its Second Session the Commission took the report of its special rapporteur, Jean Spiropoulos, as a basis of discussion, while also taking into consideration the replies received to its questionnaire [5]). As the place to be accorded to the Nuremberg principles had to be clearly indicated in the Draft Code, the formulation of these principles received priority as has been seen, and was submitted to the Fifth Assembly. The

---

1) Report on Third Session, l.c., Chapter IV, pp. 10—14.

2) C. G. Fenwick (Draft Code of Offences against the Peace and Security of Mankind, A.J.I.L., 1948, pp. 98—100, p. 100) rather bluntly states with reference to the U.S. Mutual Security Act of 1951: "The terms of the law made the consideration of the Draft Code by the General Assembly wholly impracticable, with the result that the Code was taken off the agenda of the Sixth and postponed until the Seventh Session of the General Assembly". See also Pitman B. Potter, ibidem, pp. 101—2.

3) See Observations of Governments on the Draft Code of Offences against the Peace and Security of Mankind and on the Question of the Definition of Aggression (1952), A/2162 and Add. 1.

4) Report on First Session, l.c., p. 5, par. 30.

5) Report on Second Session, l.c., p. 17, par. 148.

provisional Draft Code of a special subcommittee of the I.L.C. was referred to the special rapporteur who was requested to submit a further report at the Third Session, after the Commission had taken a number of general decisions concerning the content of the Draft Code [1]). Resolution 488 (V) of December 1950 invited the Governments, thereupon, to express their observations on the formulation of the Nuremberg principles and requested the Commission to take these observations into account while preparing a draft code at its Third Session.

At this moment, therefore, the Draft Code continues, representing only the opinion of the International Law Commission on the form international criminal law should take in the future. The Draft Code does not contain an element of positive law, like the formulation of the Nuremberg principles which represents the view of the Commission on the content of the law recognized and applied by the Nuremberg Tribunal. The Draft Code does not take the place of the formulation. Only if the Draft Code, whether or not modified, were accepted by the States and enacted, in the form of a treaty or a statute, as positive law between them, could the Nuremberg law be said to have been superseded and replaced by the new rules – and this, of course, only in so far as the Code would regulate the same subject matter as the Nuremberg law. If, for example, the bringing about of an aggressive war were not incorporated as a crime in the new code, the criminality of aggressive war pronounced by the Nuremberg Tribunal would retain its entire validity as law, case law, for the international society.

That it is the final object of the work started by the International Law Commission, on the request of the Assembly, together with the preparation of the Draft Code, to replace the law of Nuremberg by written rules of criminal law is evident from its procedure. In accordance with its terms of reference, especially Resolution 177 (II), the Commission indicated in its comment on every article of the Draft Code the corresponding principle or rule of Nuremberg. It took its own formulation of these principles as point of departure, but it also took into account the observations of delegates and governments on this

---

1) Ibidem; see for the text of the subcommittee's draft, Doc. A/CN. 4/R. 6.

formulation. The interpretation of the terms of reference as not meaning that the Nuremberg principles should be inserted 'in their entirety' in the draft code has not precluded the Commission from drafting a text which covers the field of the Nuremberg law. As will be shown, the Commission has not gone so far in "suggesting modification or development of these principles" as to bring about that a future international tribunal, administering justice on the basis of this code, would be forced to dismiss as not guilty an accused who for the same acts would have been sentenced in Nuremberg.

And this is precisely the way in which the binding force of the Nuremberg law should be interpreted [1]). Within this limit the international society is free to adopt any definition of crimes and of rules of responsibility it considers suitable and in conformity with justice. Pursuant to enacting this Code the States would have to permit that any individual violating the basic rules of international law in the way the major war criminals did, will be tried and sentenced by an international tribunal having jurisdiction with regard to crimes under international law.

The Draft Code goes, indeed, far beyond the minimum prescribed by the precedent. The text proposed by the International Law Commission reads as follows:

Article 1.

Offences against the peace and security of mankind, as defined in this Code, are crimes under international law, for which the responsible individuals shall be punishable.

Article 2.

The following acts are offences against the peace and security of mankind:

(1) Any act of aggression, including the employment by the authorities of a State of armed force against another State for any purpose other than national or collective self-defence or in pursuance of a decision or recommendation by a competent organ of the United Nations.

---

1) See above, p. 336.

(2) Any threat by the authorities of a State to resort to an act of aggression against another State.

(3) The preparation by the authorities of a State for the employment of armed force against another State for any purpose other than national or collective self-defence or in pursuance of a decision or recommendation by a competent organ of the United Nations.

(4) The incursion into the territory of a State from the territory of another State by armed bands acting for a political purpose.

(5) The undertaking or encouragement by the authorities of a State of activities calculated to foment civil strife in another State, or the toleration by the authorities of a State of organised activities calculated to foment civil strife in another State.

(6) The undertaking or encouragement by the authorities of a State of terrorist activities in another State, or the toleration by the authorities of a State of organized activities calculated to carry out terrorist acts in another State.

(7) Acts by the authorities of a State in violation of its obligations under a treaty which is designed to ensure international peace and security by means of restrictions or limitations on armaments, or on military training, or on fortifications, or of other restrictions of the same character.

(8) Acts by the authorities of a State resulting in the annexation, contrary to international law, of territory belonging to another State or of territory under an international regime.

(9) Acts by the authorities of a State or by private individuals, committed with intent to destroy, in whole or in part, a national, ethical, racial or religious group as such, including:

(i) Killing members of the group;

(ii) Causing serious bodily or mental harm to members of the group;

(iii) Deliberately inflicting on the group conditions of life calculated to bring about its physical destruction in whole or in part;

(iv) Imposing measures intended to prevent births within the group;

(v) Forcibly transfering children of the group to another group.

(10) Inhuman acts by the authorities of a State or by private individuals against any civilian population, such as murder, or extermination, or enslavement, or deportation, or persecutions on political, racial, religious or cultural grounds, when such acts are committed in execution of or in connexion with other offences defined in this article.

(11) Acts in violation of the laws or customs of war.

(12) Acts which constitute:

(i) Conspiracy to commit any of the offences defined in the preceeding paragraphs of this Article; or

(ii) Direct incitement to commit any of the offences defined in the preceeding paragraphs of this Article; or

(iii) Attempts to commit any of the offences defined in the preceeding paragraphs of this Article; or

(iv) Complicity in the commission of any of the offences defined in the preceeding paragraphs of this Article.

Article 3.

The fact that a person acted as Head of State or as responsible government official does not relieve him from responsibility for committing any of the offences defined in this Code.

Article 4.

The fact that a person charged with an offence defined in this Code acted pursuant to order of his government or of a superior does not relieve him from responsibility, provided a moral choice was in fact possible to him.

Article 5.

The penalty for any offence defined in this Code shall be determined by the tribunal exercising jurisdiction over the individual accused, taking into account the gravity of the offence.

Though many acts not punishable under the Nuremberg law are in this draft defined as crimes, it will be observed that the Commission has limited the scope of the Code to acts falling under the three categories of Nuremberg, *id est,* Crimes against Peace (Article 2, paragraphs 1–8), War Crimes (Article 2 (11)) and Crimes against Humanity, together with the similar, though not clearer, concept of 'genocide' (Article 2 (9–10)). Article 2 (12), partly enumerates new crimes (conspiracy and direct incitement), partly the forms in which the forementioned crimes can manifest themselves.

Regarding the scope of this draft code, there appears a certain contradiction between its title and the crimes listed. The term 'offences against the peace and security of mankind' is interpreted by the Commission in the introduction to this part of its report as meaning offences which firstly contain a political element and secondly endanger or disturb the maintenance of international peace and security. The second characteristic regards the effect of the offences and limits the first which specifies their nature with a term of doubtful clearness. No doubt, however, can exist concerning the fact that individual acts, as defined under paragraphs 9, 10 and 11, can be committed and will mostly be committed without any danger or disturbing effect on the peace and security of mankind, apart from the fact that this peace and security can never be endangered or disturbed by war crimes, nor probably by crimes against humanity as defined under this code, because their perpetration supposes that the peace is broken.

Though many of the acts enumerated as crimes, notably those defined under paragraphs 2–9, can be committed in full peace, their combination in this code can only be explained in the light of Nuremberg under the law of which only major *war criminals* were tried for acts committed in preparation of, and during war. The question arises whether the two elements mentioned by the I.L.C. must be regarded as limitations on the definitions of the crimes, to the effect that the enumerated acts will only be regarded as criminal when containing a political element and when endangering or disturbing peace and security. As, however, the title of the Draft Code cannot be regarded as a substantial part of it and as the Commission's explanation of the title is not inserted in its text, such an interpretation is not permissible. In its first questionnaire the Commission had opened the possibility that quite different acts from those punished in Nuremberg be included in the draft code. In its reply the Dutch Government submitted a draft code containing many individual acts against heads of State or the interests of another State, concerning, for example public property, passports, currency, publications, etc. [1]).

At its Second Session the Commission decided to limit the draft code in the aforementioned sense, and to exclude from its scope questions concerning conflicts of legislation and jurisdiction in criminal matters, that is, the penal counterpart of private international law. It eliminated also such matters as piracy, traffic in women and children, counterfeiting currency, etc., *id est,* the international crimes with which classic international penal law is concerned, and with regard to which universal jurisdiction is advocated and has in part been established by international custom or treaties [2]).

This limitation had been proposed by Mr Spiropoulos, the special rapporteur of the Commission, in his first report on the Draft Code [3]), on the basis of an analysis of the previous discussions and resolutions on the question of the Draft Code in United Nations organs, especially the Committee on the Progressive Development of International Law and its Codification. In the recommendation of this Committee quoted above [4]), it was suggested that the preparation of a draft code incorporating the Nuremberg principles should not preclude the I.L.C. from drafting "a code of international penal law". In the discussion leading up to this recommendation the distinction made by Prof. Donnedieu de Vabres, member of the Committee, between *crimes interétatiques* and crimes "in which there was an international element", played an important role. The first group, to which the Nuremberg crimes belonged, should be incorporated in a code of offences against the peace and security of mankind, while the second should, together with rules on conflicts of criminal

1) Doc. A/CN. 4/19.
2) Report on Second Session, l.c., p. 17, par. 149. See further Chapter III, section 6 above.
3) L.c., A/CN. 4/25, p. 15.
4) Above, p. 322.

laws and on extradition, be inserted in a code "that would regulate the concerted repression by States of offences bearing an international character"[1]).

If the General Assembly Resolution 95 (I) is interpreted in this way and if the 'draft code' of Resolution 177 (II), which does not speak of an "international penal code", is considered in the same light, it is evident that the I.L.C. correctly limited its task. Yet it remains difficult to see for example the crimes against humanity as *crimes interétatiques, i.e.* crimes characterized by their effect on interstate relations, while on the other hand it is not understandable why acts against heads of foreign States, insults of States or diffusion of evidently false publications likely to endanger the relations with other States were not included in this concept. History more than dogmatics have set the limits to the Draft Code of Offences against the Peace and Security of Mankind.

The Draft Code is remarkable for its shortness. In addition to the first two fundamental Articles, the Draft contains nothing but two particular rules of responsibility, concerning the pleas of 'acts-of-State' and 'superior orders', in conformity with the corresponding Nuremberg principles as formulated by the Commission. Article 5 does not add anything to Article 2 providing that individuals responsible for any of the offences defined shall be punishable. This truism about the task of a tribunal with regard to punishment is the more out of place as the Commission states that it has abstained from drafting an instrument for implementing the Code and as any references to jurisdiction and criminal procedure should be reserved for such an instrument[2]).

Article 1 embodies the fundamental rule of individual criminal responsibility under international law and points towards a general concept of international crimes of which the offences of this code are a specimen. It therefore presupposes the existence of an international criminal law directly binding individuals. The development of this law, though already prepared in theory and envisaged by several pre-war declarations and projects and by the fundamental Charter of London, originates from the Nurem-

1) See First Report on Draft Code, l.c., pp. 12–13.
2) Report on Third Session, l.c., p. 11, par. 58.

berg Trial. Article 1 of the Draft Code now suggests the existence of other crimes under international law, apart from those punished at this trial. This must evidently be understood as a reference to those acts for which in virtue of customary law, like piracy, or in virtue of treaties, like counterfeiting currency [1]), *a universal jurisdiction* exists. The Article therefore assimilates the latter category, of classic 'international crimes', to the Nuremberg crimes and extends accordingly the concept of individual responsibility under international law. It anticipates the international penal code envisaged by Resolution 95 (II).

It is particularly with regard to crimes against peace that the Draft Code includes in comparison to the Nuremberg law a greater number of criminal acts. Under that law only the acts defined in paragraphs 1 and 3 of the Draft Code were criminal and even so within stricter limits, as the Code does not limit its scope to aggressive war but extends it to "any act of aggression including the employment ... of armed force". One great advantage of the draft is that it, finally, does away with the unhappy enumeration of specific activities with regard to war or aggression [2]), that it defines the offence in question as an *act* the authors of which, by no matter what activity they have caused it, are punishable. Conspiracy is mentioned separately under paragraph 12, preparation for aggression is defined as a separate crime and the ambiguous criminality of the 'waging' of an aggressive war is eliminated.

The central crime against peace is henceforward to be considered as the causing of an effect which is the act of aggression committed by a State. The other crimes against peace are defined as acts which cannot be committed by the State as such, but only by an official personally, though doubt may exist with regard to "the threat ... to resort to an act of aggression". Such a threat can be voiced by one official, for example the head of State, but it can only be executed by employment of the State machinery. As all the other acts defined in Article 2 are likewise defined as personal acts, and not as acts which are committed by the State though brought about by individuals, it would have been better

---

1) See Convention on Suppression of Counterfeiting Currency of 1 May 1929, International Legislation, l.c., Vol. IV, pp. 2692 ff..

2) See above, pp. 217 ff. and 304 ff..

from a systematic point of view if the Commission had worded paragraph 1 as it did praagraph 8, where not 'annexation' is defined as criminal but "acts by the authorities of a State *resulting in* the annexation . . .".

This deviation is probably due to the later insertion of 'acts of aggression'. The text of a draft code which the special rapporteur, in his second report on the subject, presented to the Commission at its Third Session, and which was closely followed in the drafting of the final text, did not refer to aggression. In accordance with his opinion that 'the notion aggression' cannot be defined [1]), his proposal mentions as Crime No. 1 the employment or threat of employment by the authorities of a State of armed force, etc. (see Article 2, paragraph 1 of Draft Code above) [2]). He supported this text by a reference to Article 2 (4) of the U.N. Charter.

Though, as has been related before, the Commission could not agree on a definition of aggression [3]), it reconsidered the matter, at the request of Professor Scelle, in connection with the preparation of the Draft Code. It then decided on the present text of paragraphs 1 and 2 of Article 2, where the employment of armed force is subsumed under the concept of act of aggression, and where the threat to resort to such acts is defined as a separate crime.

This decision is open to serious criticism. To define aggression as the employment, or threat of employment, of armed force without further qualifying the nature of the armed force used or the purport of its employment by other than the negative criteria of the draft, is already to give to the concept a dangerous extension [4]). But to suggest that acts of aggression can be committed without any element of armed force is to allow any tribunal applying this Code to punish persons for all sorts of unfriendly international acts which are qualified as economic or ideological aggression.

It is for this reason that the inclusion of a strictly limited definition of aggression in paragraph 1 imposes itself. Without such a limitation all the careful definitions of crimes against peace in

---

1) First Report on Draft Code, l.c., p. 24.
2) Second Report on Draft Code, l.c., p. 40.
3) See Report on Third Session, Chapter III, pp. 8—10, and above, p. 100.
4) See above, pp. 99 ff..

the subsequent paragraphs become superfluous and senseless, as all the acts defined and innumerable others excluded by the Commission can be, and are, called acts of aggression, in current political terminology.

In Chapter II a distinction was drawn between a political and a penal concept of aggression in view of the different consequences of a determination of aggression by the States or the security organ, and of such a determination by the criminal judge. In the first case self-defence and collective measures may follow, in the second case individual punishment. For acts with grave political consequences may not be criminal, while acts not having such consequences may be. But once the latter category, that is, of crimes against peace which do not give the right of self-defence to the offended State, receives separate specification in a criminal code, the use of the term aggression in such a code must be restricted to the classic, political concept of aggression, as opposed to that of military action by way of self-defence. For a definition of that concept reference may be made to the text suggested in Chapter II above [1]).

If the concept of aggression is, however, used in paragraph 1, the second paragraph becomes more or less superfluous. For according to general opinion, expressed notably in the discussion on aggression in the I.L.C., also the threat of employment of armed force is to be considered as aggression, at least the direct, actual threat of such employment, often combined with acts of indirect aggression [2]). Especially because aggression in its most dangerous – and most up to date – form, will in fact often appear as such a complex of acts, it seems desirable to incorporate the current conception of aggression, including the threat of force, in the Draft Code. But it goes too far to define the threat of such aggression as a criminal act, if such a threat is at all imaginable.

Other acts defined as crimes against peace, notably in paragraphs 5 and 6, could also be considered as elements of aggression. "Fomenting civil strife in the interest of a foreign Power" was declared to constitute aggression in Resolution 380 (V) of the General Assembly. But it is doubtful whether the States would

---

1) See p. 113.

2) Report on Third Session, l.c., p. 9, pars. 47–48; see above, pp. 111 ff..

in consequence permit the use of armed force in self-defence against the Power committing such subversive action. The case is anyway not so clear as that concerning the threat of force, so that separate definition of this crime seems justified. In conformity with the foregoing observations on paragraph 1, paragraph 3 could be given a shorter formulation as "the preparation of aggression by the authorities of a State".

In general it may be said that present-day state-practice seems to justify the consideration of the acts enumerated in paragraphs 1 to 8 as crimes under international law. Pending the discussion on the Draft Code in the General Assembly, however, no definite conclusion to this effect can be drawn. As the discussions on the definition of aggression and on the formulation of the Nuremberg principles show, the continous tendency to extend the range of 'crimes' and to perfect their definition is mostly not matched by an equal preparedness of States to accept the consequences of these views, to take positive action in view of their implementation and to limit their 'sovereign rights' of immunity and exclusive jurisdiction accordingly.

Attention must still be paid to paragraph 12 of Article 2. In its comments on the different paragraphs considered above the I.L.C. stated that, as the definitions indicate, these crimes can only be committed by the authorities of a State, but that criminal responsibility of private individuals under international law may arise under the provisions of paragraph 12. The opposite is, naturally, true for paragraph 4. It must be added that this crime by the members of armed bands can only become dangerous for the offended State, and for peace and security, when the activity of these bands is supported or tolerated, notwithstanding protests, by the authorities of a State. In this form, as a State activity, the support of these bands, or the refusal to take action against them, by the State on whose territory they were formed, was considered a case of aggression in the definition of 1933. It would perhaps have been preferable and more in harmony with the concept underlying the Draft Code, if the I.L.C. had followed this definition. The latter would also be preferable in view of a possible situation in which the State from whose territory the armed bands operate is not able to repress their activity.

Of the four subparagraphs of paragraph 12 only two – those

concerning direct incitement and complicity – can give rise to a criminal responsibility of private individuals for the other crimes against peace. For conspiracy and attempts to commit offences which are perpetrated by authorities of a State can only be made by such authorities. Doubt may exist as to conspiracy, but the very limited construction which the Nuremberg Tribunal put upon this concept, suspiciously regarded by all those foreign to Anglo-Saxon law, leads to the conclusion that only the highest State officials can become guilty of this crime. For the same reason criminal conspiracy should be limited to conspiracy to commit the principal crime against peace: aggression. Conspiracy to commit any of the acts defined in paragraphs 3, 7 and 8 either has aggression as its final object or cannot have serious enough a character to deserve the qualification of crime under international law. Conspiracy to commit the acts of paragraphs 5 and 6 seems excluded because of the definition of these crimes themselves; undertaking contains an element of planning.

For exactly the same reasons attempts to commit crimes against peace do not deserve the term crime or are excluded by the very definition of such crimes. As moreover the activities amounting to attempts to commit acts of aggression are covered by the separate definition of preparation, subparagraph (iii) of paragraph 12 cannot possibly apply to the first eight paragraphs.

Direct incitement to commit crimes against peace is an act which can be committed both by authorities and by private individuals, by the latter notably through press campaigns. But here also it may be suggested that, in view of the difference in gravity between aggression and the other crimes against peace, criminality under international law be restricted to direct incitement to commit the crime of crimes.

There remains the question of the criminality of complicity in the committing of crimes against peace. In the foregoing section the incorporation of this criminality among the Nuremberg principles has been criticized because of the unjust and unprecedented extension it gave to individual responsibility for crimes against peace [1]). As, however, the term 'waging of a war' has been eliminated from the definition of the crime of aggression, the

---

1) See above, p. 334.

situation is different under the Draft Code. Making complicity in aggression a crime would be shocking if it led to the consequence that common soldiers or civil servants fulfilling their duties in a war would become punishable for crimes against peace. But it would be regrettable and unjust if especially private persons like industrialists, voluntarily supporting and even encouraging the civil and military policymakers in the execution of their aggressive plans, would be able to escape punishment [1]).

According to the present draft, however, all those participating in 'acts of aggression' which themselves can only be committed by a State, would become liable to punishment. In its comment on paragraph 12 the Commission certainly makes a restriction so as to exclude from responsibility "all those contributing, in the normal exercise of their duties, to the perpetration of offences against the peace and security of mankind", but again the question arises why this limitation is not introduced into the Code itself. But if, as was suggested before, the text of the first paragraph is changed so as to read: "acts by the authorities of a State resulting in any act of aggression . . .", no objection can be made to the criminality of complicity in the committing of this crime. What is necessary is that the accomplice had a necessary part in bringing about the accomplishment of the act [2]); that he had criminal intent, that is, that he was aware of the criminal character of the object pursued, and that he had freedom of action. The latter requirement can never be presumed in the case of subordinate officials or employees, while at the same time only high ranking persons can be said to have had a necessary part in the commission of the act.

These limitations follow from general rules of criminal law, which, just like, for example, the rule excluding punishment in case of irresponsibility, are not formulated in the Code but necessarily govern international criminal law. Within these limits the rules of complicity can be applied to all crimes listed in

1) See A. Sottile, Un peu plus de justice S.V.P., R.D.I., 1948, pp. 372—385, pp. 379—381; N. Veicopoulos, Les Responsabilités des individuels dans la préparation de la guerre, ibidem, pp. 53—62. Cf. above, p. 231.

2) See the judgment in the von Weiszaecker case, quoted above, pp. 233 and 306.

the Code. Their application is necessary to bring also private individuals, acting out of free will, under the scope of the Code. The crimes against peace are perpetrated by the authorities of a State, which term must be understood to include only the highest-ranking officials. A definition to this effect might be useful. Other officials, whether military or civil, can hardly have certainty as to the criminal character of the object of the work demanded from them. The same applies to those employed by private individuals.

What has been said of the Nuremberg Judgement to the effect that the accused were found guilty of the crime of aggressive war in function of a criminal plan [1]), must remain true of all crimes against peace. The fact that these crimes are committed through abuse of the state-organisation involves a great number of people in their execution but makes it at the same time extremely difficult to prove the criminal intent of any individual having a function in the organisation. The fact that this knowledge of the crime must be proved remains the best guarantee against an undesirable and unjust extension of criminal responsibility.

In conclusion it may be suggested that in paragraph 12 a distinction be made between the crimes against peace and the other crimes of this Code which are defined as individual acts. Only complicity should be retained as applying to all the crimes, while attempts to commit crimes against peace should be excluded, and conspiracy and direct incitement to commit acts of aggression should be incorporated as separate crimes against peace.

It is evident that the preparation of a draft code by the I.L.C. was a task completely different from its formulation of the Nuremberg principles. While the latter was a codification of existing law, unhappily not expressly recognized as such by the Commission, the drafting of the Code is an elaboration of new law. The codification of the Nuremberg law has now been left as it is and does not need any further enactment. Open to criticism and neither adopted nor rejected by the General Assembly, it remains what it is: a pronouncement by an authoritative international legal body on the bearing of the essential rules of the Nuremberg law, which in themselves already formed part

---

1) See above, pp. 251–2.

of the body of positive international law. Such a pronouncement will no doubt have a great influence on any future application of this law.

That the elaboration of the Draft Code is a matter of 'progressive development of international law', as opposed to codification, has been recognized by the I.L.C. since its First Session. The opinion is sometimes expressed that the Draft Code could, in virtue of the authority of the Commission, gradually obtain recognition and so become positive law, without any positive enactment in the form of a multilateral convention or of a statute. In addition to the Nuremberg principles, already valid by precedent, and to war crimes and genocide defined by special Conventions, the Draft Code contains a number of crimes for the greater part *de jure constituendo.* These can only become crimes *de jure constituto* through recognition as such by the States or through recognition in law-making judicial decisions. A resolution of the General Assembly cannot amount to such a recognition as this organ has no legislative competence. For the moment it depends on the General Assembly as to what action will be taken in order to give the Code binding force.

In the present international atmosphere no great expectations can be cherished with respect to such action. The hope may anyway be entertained that reasons of political expediency will not again prevent a serious consideration of the Draft Code by the delegates. The fact that the question of the definition of aggression also appears on the provisional agenda for the Seventh Session of the Assembly will perhaps lead to the inclusion of such a definition in the Code. While the Code has a number of deficiencies, mainly from a systematic point of view, the absence of a strict definition of aggression is its main default and overthrows the whole structure of the Code in its present wording.

SECTION 4. JURISDICTION OVER OFFENCES AGAINST THE PEACE AND SECURITY OF MANKIND

With regard to the implementation of the Code, the I.L.C. concluded at its Second Session that, pending the establishment of a competent international criminal court, such implementation had to be achieved through the enactment by the States adopting the Code of the necessary legislation for the trial and punishment of persons charged with offences under the Code [1]). The special rapporteur, in his second report, proposed a code containing in Article III a special undertaking to this effect on the part of the States adopting the Code [2]). When drafting its final text, however, the Commission decided to abstain from proposing methods by which a code may be given binding force, but it suggested the adoption of a "transitional measure . . . providing for the application of the Code by national courts" [3]).

It is not clear what kind of measure is referred to unless it is the internal measures of the States which would have accepted the Code. Once the present Code is in due form adopted by the States, the crimes defined in it will constitute crimes under international law and the States will have the duty to ensure that these crimes are punished by their courts. Whether accomplishing this duty involves the enactment of legislation for the incorporation of these crimes in municipal law is a constitutional question. If it does not involve such legislation the only measure needed would be the internal designation of the courts competent to take cognizance of acts alleged to constitute a crime under the Code. Each State is free in the choice of measures – if any have to be taken – for ensuring the application of the Code.

The question can be asked whether the recognition of the acts listed in the Code as crimes under international law involves the recognition of universal jurisdiction over these crimes. Such jurisdiction does, according to many legislations, exist with regard to such acts as piracy, counterfeiting currency and slave-trade [4]), to which – as argued before – Article 1 of the Code assimilates the acts defined in Article 2. The thesis of universal jurisdiction over war crimes is, moreover, defended by several authors [5]) and different drafts and projects have proposed such jurisdiction with regard to many other crimes of international concern [6]).

1) Report on Second Session, l.c., p. 17, par. 156.
2) Second Report on Draft Code, l.c., p. 45.
3) Report on Third Session, l.c., p. 11, par. 58.
4) See Oppenheim-Lauterpacht, Vol. I, p. 307.
5) See Cowles, Universality of Jurisdiction over War Crimes, l.c., and Janèckzek, o.c., pp. 59 ff..
6) See on those efforts the Memorandum concerning a Draft Code of Offences against the Peace and Security of Mankind, by V. V. Pella, U. N. General, A/CN. 4/39 (24 November 1950).

As the positive attribution of universal jurisdiction is a matter of municipal law, the question should rather be put in the negative form: whether there exists a rule of international law prohibiting States to punish the crimes defined in the Code on seizure of the criminals [1]). In a general way the Permanent Court of International Justice expressed its opinion that there exists no rule of international law which prohibits a State from exercising jurisdiction over a foreigner in respect of an offence committed outside its territory [2]). This opinion is by no means universally accepted and conflicts with prevailing state-practice. In view, however, of the universal interest in preventing and repressing crimes against peace, far more dangerous than acts like piracy and slave trade, a good case can be made for the proposition that international law permits the States to bring before their courts any perpetrators of such crimes of whom they might secure custody, no matter of what nationality they are and no matter where their crimes have been committed. Positive support for this thesis can be found in Article 2 (6) of the U.N. Charter which recognizes the paramount interest of the international community in the maintenance of peace and security.

In his second report Spiropoulos had proposed articles to the effect that the offences defined in the Code should not be considered as political crimes for the purpose of extradition, that the States adopting the Code should undertake to grant extradition in accordance with their laws and treaties in force, and that disputes regarding the interpretation or application of the provisions of the Code might be brought before the International Court of Justice by any party to the dispute [3]).

Regarding the last matter, disputes relating to the interpretation of a treaty or a question of international law can be brought before the International Court if both parties to the dispute have signed the optional clause [4]). Secondly, if a State which has adopted the Code should fail to prosecute persons who had committed an offence defined in the Code and directed against

---

1) Cf. Oppenheim-Lauterpacht, Vol. I, p. 298.

2) See Judgment in the *Lotus* case of 1927, Hudson, World Court Reports, Vol. I, pp. 191—206.

3) Second Report on Draft Code, l.c., p. 46.

4) See Statute of the International Court of Justice, Art. 36.

another State, on its territory, this omission could give rise to international responsibility of the first State, and the offended State could bring the question before the International Court provided again that the States in question had signed the optional clause. If such an omission should amount to a toleration of the offences committed, even criminal responsibility of the authorities concerned would exist under several definitions of the Draft Code.

Express stipulation of all the rights and obligations assumed by the States in adopting the Code, as incorporated in the Convention on the Prevention and Punishment of the Crime of Genocide [1]), is very desirable and even necessary with regard to the acceptance of the International Court and of the obligations of extradition. But as has been argued in the foregoing paragraphs, a number of rights and obligations of States – relating to the punishment by their national courts of the crimes defined in the Code and to the competence of the International Court in disputes concerning the application of the Code – follow from the very adoption and ratification of the present Draft Code in treaty form.

However, especially in the case of crimes against peace, the implementation of the Code by municipal courts remains largely theoretical. These crimes are necessarily committed by the authorities of a State, roughly said by the State itself, and their trial before municipal courts of their own country is virtually impossible [2]). Only in the exceptional circumstances of a warlike government being overthrown by a pacific one, could such a trial follow, if public opinion and national feeling would tolerate it. The other – more likely – possibility is that after an unsuccesful aggression the perpetrators would be brought to trial before a court of the original victim of the aggression. It would, however, be very difficult to accord such a trial the

1) See Gen. Ass. Resolution 260 (III) of 9 December 1948, artt. 5, 6 and 9.

2) The holding of such trials has sometimes been made a condition of a peace-settlement. The history of the Leipzig Trials after the First World War only stresses the difficulties of such municipal trials of war criminals, while the trial of former President Ryti c.s. held in Helsinki in 1946, in fulfilment of the obligation contained in Article 9, paragraph I (a), of the Peace Treaty with Finland of 1947, was rather a doubtful case (the documents of this trial have been published by Hj. H. Procopé, Fällande Dom Som Friar, Stockholm 1946).

conditions for an impartial administration of justice.

It may therefore be said that only if an international criminal jurisdiction existed, crimes against peace could really be repressed with the necessary guarantees of jusice and impartiality. The disadvantages of the establishment of an *ad hoc* international tribunal have been convincingly shown in Nuremberg and Tokyo, though after the adoption of the Code objections could no longer be made on the ground of the maxim *nulla poena sine lege*. Thus, only the establishment of a permanent international criminal tribunal could give a fair and effective implementation to the Draft Code and, notably, make possible the punishment of authorities of a State and their accomplices for acts of aggression or other crimes against peace.

In his first report the special rapporteur of the I.L.C., while suggesting the establishment of such a permanent tribunal, stated "that it would be very unrealistic to envisage seriously the possibility of having persons responsible for international crimes brought before an international criminal court with the rare exception of cases of crimes committed against the will of the governments". He bases this opinion on "the present organisation of the international community, which does not possess *executive organs* for the arrest, against the will of the governments, of perpetrators of international crimes" [1]).

This applies, indeed, to the majority of crimes defined in the Code. Arrest of criminal authorities of a State supposes war or collective action resulting in the defeat of that State by the only 'executive organs' existing at the moment – the other States. War will not easily be waged, nor collective action undertaken, for the capturing of those guilty of genocide or any of the lesser crimes against peace. But aggression will mostly entail war or collective action, and so it becomes evident once again that aggression occupies the central place in international criminal law. Only as a result of the occurrence of war or aggression, can the perpetrators of other international crimes, either war crimes and crimes against humanity or lesser crimes against peace, be brought before an international tribunal, together with those responsible for the aggression. The close

---

1) First Report on Draft Code, l.c., p. 60.

link between international criminal law and war is not only established by the precedent of Nuremberg but also, and even more, by the peculiar condition of prosecuting power in the international community. Only after a war can persons be brought before a court against the will of the States whose nationals they are. Those who speak of victor's justice overlook the fact that only the victor can ensure that law takes its course against criminals within a government or protected by it.

But the establishment of a permanent international tribunal would be a safeguard against unfair trials and the possible arbitrariness of *ad hoc* tribunals, and the existence of a 'neutral' court for such situations would enhance the prestige of a war crimes trial, among victors, vanquished and neutrals alike. The I.L.C. had, in virtue of Assembly Resolution 260 B (III), "to study the desirability and possibility of establishing an international judicial organ for the trial of persons charged with genocide or other crimes with respect to which jurisdiction will be conferred upon that organ by international conventions". After having considered the two opposite views expressed on this question by the special rapporteurs, Alfaro and Sandström, the I.L.C. answered the questions put to it in the affirmative [1]). The establishment of such a judicial organ was deemed both desirable and possible. The Commission did not however recommend the suggestion of the Assembly to establish a criminal chamber of the International Court of Justice. The consideration that the International Court has a great established authority which might be jeopardized by such a close link to the yet uncertain development of international criminal justice, surrounded by strong doubts and succeptibilities, has certainly exercised a great influence on this decision.

In the subsequent discussion of the Sixth Committee [2]), some members expressed the opinion that the establishment of an international criminal court would be "contrary to the sovereign rights of States", as the punishment of crimes committed in the territory of a State was a matter within the jurisdiction of that State. Other delegates deemed the project unpractical as there was no international police force to bring the accused before the

1) Report on Second Session, l.c., Part. IV.
2) Report of Sixth Committee, l.c., pp. 15—18.

court and to execute its sentences. Those favouring the project considered the creation of an international penal court vested with power to try and to punish persons who disturbed international public order as "an effective contribution to the peace and security of the world." In so far as this was a reference to the preventive effect of the establishment of an international criminal court, the argument indeed holds good.

The majority of delegates felt, however, that they could not take a position on this question except on the basis of concrete proposals. The final resolution, 489 (V), recommended, therefore, the establishment of a committee composed of representatives of seventeen Member States who should meet at a special conference "for the purpose of preparing one or more preliminary draft conventions and proposals relating to the establishment and the statute of an international court".

This conference met in Geneva between the first and the thirty first of August 1951 [1]). On the basis of the draft prepared by the Secretary-General, the Committee on International Criminal Jurisdiction elaborated a draft statute for an international criminal court which it submitted in a report to the General Assembly. Like the Draft Code, this item also was removed from the agenda of the Sixth Session of the Assembly but it figures again on the provisional agenda of the Seventh which has begun in New York in October 1952.

The most important provisions of the proposed statute will here be briefly examined. In considering the Draft, mention must be made of the fact that as the memorandum of the Secretary-General was received by the governments concerned but a few days before the opening of the conference, most delegates were without instruction from their governments. The president of the conference therefore proceeded on the understanding that no speaker was committing his Government unless he specifically said so, and the Draft Statute must therefore be regarded as the result of a commission of experts rather than as the decision of an intergovernmental committee [2]). No attention

---

1) See Report to the General Assembly of the Session held 1 August—31 August 1951 of the Committee on International Criminal Jurisdiction, A/AC. 48/4.

2) A/AC. 48/4, p. 8.

can be paid here to the strictly technical provisions of the Draft Statute on the organisation of the court and on its procedure [1]).

The main characteristic of the Draft is that it provides for the establishment of a court without attributing it jurisdiction. In fact it appears that the starting point of the Draft is the assumption of exclusive criminal jurisdiction of States as a sovereign right, which was in the Assembly the thesis of the opponents to the establishment of a court. The relevant provisions of the Draft read as follows:

Article 1.

Purpose of the Court.

There is established an International Criminal Court to try persons accused of crimes under international law as may be provided in conventions or special agreements among States parties to the present Statute.

Article 2.

The Law to be applied by the Court.

The Court shall apply international law, including international criminal law, and, where appropriate, national law.

(and under Chapter III, Competence of the Court)

Article 25.

Jurisdiction as to persons.

The Court shall be competent to judge natural persons only, including persons who acted as Head of State or agent of government.

Article 26.

Attribution of Jurisdiction.

Jurisdiction may be conferred upon the Court, by States parties to the present Statute, by convention or, with respect to a particular case, by special agreement or by unilateral declaration.

---

1) See on the Draft Statute, George A. Finch in A.J.I.L., 1952, (pp. 89—97) who rejects, and Quincy Wright, ibidem (pp. 60—72), who favours the idea of the establishment of an International Criminal Court. See also Röling, Internationale Strafrechterlijke Organisatie, l.c..

Article 27.

Recognition of Jurisdiction

No person shall be tried before the Court unless jurisdiction has been conferred upon the Court by the State or States of which he is a national and by the State or States in which the crime is alleged to have been committed.

Article 28.

Approval of jurisdiction by the United Nations.

No jurisdiction may be conferred upon the Court without the approval of the General Assembly of the United Nations.

Article 29 further provides that the General Assembly, an organisation of States authorized by it and a State party to the Statute which has conferred jurisdiction upon the Court may institute proceedings before it, though the latter only with respect to offences with respect to which it has conferred jurisdiction. Article 30 provides that the jurisdiction of the Court may be challenged by any State referred to in Article 27, and Article 31 provides that only in virtue of an express undertaking of their State will national authorities be obliged to assist the Court on its request in the performance of its duties. To provide for the lack of international executive organs an extremely complicated system has been devised by which a case is to be brought before the Court. Before the Prosecuting Attorney can file an indictment a Committing Authority consisting of nine members elected in the same manner as the judges, must have certified that it is satisfied with the evidence (Articles 34 and 35). A special Board of Clemency is also provided for (Article 54).

It is evident that by the adoption of this Statute no single obligation is undertaken. Pending the attribution of jurisdiction by a State this International Criminal Court is no court at all, a powerless instrument. The cautions and conditions with which the possibility of an international trial are surrounded are so numerous that even the most exaggerated concept of sovereign rights and even the deepest abhorrence of the possibility of international trials in the present international situation cannot lend arguments for a refusal to accept this Statute. Some of these cautions may even be removed without any danger to the sovereign rights; the *exclusive* criminal jurisdiction of States has never been understood to include that over crimes committed on the national territory by foreigners; the consent of the State on whose territory the crime is alleged to have been committed might therefore be dispensed with (Article 27). The attribution of jurisdiction to the Court would then have two consequences for the attributing State: the obligation to consent to a trial of its own nationals and the right to institute proceedings before the Court. From a systematic point of view it would be clearer to define these two consequences now formulated in Article 27 and 29 in Article 26. The obligation to extradite for trial by the Court a national accused of a crime over which jurisdiction has been conferred, now reserved for incorporation in a separate instrument (Article 31), should certainly be included among the consequences of an attribution of jurisdiction.

International criminal law, considered as a part of international law and defined under Article 2 as the law to be applied by the Court, can only comprise the rules of responsibility, as the designation of justiciable crimes has been left to the State conferring jurisdiction upon the Court. In its present wording Article 1 seems even to suggest that insofar as it has not been defined in special conventions [1]) the law applied in Nuremberg is not a part of international criminal law, as the Article refers only to crimes provided in conventions or special agreements and not to those provided in unwritten law. The second part of Article 1 is therefore contrary to the affirmation of the Nuremberg principles by the General Assembly and is, moreover, as a safeguard of the 'sovereign rights' unnecessary, because the designation of justiciable crimes is anyway left to the instruments by which jurisdiction will be conferred.

But even when jurisdiction has been conferred upon the Court by a State the number of obstacles to be overcome before a trial can start is excessive. The General Assembly must approve the conferment of jurisdiction, possible challenges of the jurisdiction

---

1) Like the Hague and Geneva Conventions, containing definitions of war crimes, and the Genocide Convention covering — partly — the crimes against humanity.

by States must first be refuted by the Court, and the Committing Authority must be satisfied with the evidence before the Prosecutor can file the indictment.

Even if safeguards against a rash institution of proceedings are necessary in the interest of peace and security, the procedure could be considerably improved. Instead of the General Assembly a smaller and more responsible body, for example a committee of the Assembly consisting of representatives of the countries having a seat in the Security Council, could approve or reject the conferment of jurisdiction. Instead of the Committing Authority some judges from the Court could briefly examine the evidence.

It has been said above that for the implementation of the Nuremberg principles the establishment of an international criminal jurisdiction over crimes under international law was far more necessary than the elaboration of a Code of offences. The law exists, in virtue of the precedent, but an impartial organ for its application is lacking in the international community. The creation of this organ is the most necessary step to be taken if the world is to fulfill the obligation undertaken at Nuremberg.

It is evident from the foregoing examination that with the adoption of this Draft Statute such a step would not have been taken. The most that can be said in favour of the work done in Geneva is that with the adoption of the Draft Statute an instrument would be created and a procedure fixed which would be ready for use should the States change their present negative attitude towards international criminal law or should the international situation again necessitate a step such as was taken in Nuremberg. In view of the modesty of the Statute which does not impose obligations, nothing could prevent the General Assembly from adopting the Statute and establishing the Court as a subsidiary organ of the United Nations. The prestige of the Court would be greater than if it were established by only a small number of States. The existence of such an instrument under the United Nations might give rise to a movement, perhaps a popular movement, in favour of the attribution of jurisdiction to the Court, which some States might eventually be forced to follow.

POSTSCRIPT

During its Seventh Session the General Assembly has, on the 5th of December 1952, adopted a resolution in virtue of which a new Committee on International Criminal Jurisdiction has been established. This Committee, consisting of the representatives of seventeen Member States to be designated by the President of the General Assembly, shall meet at the Headquarters of the United Nations in 1953, the exact date to be determined by the Secretary-General, with the following terms of reference:

"(a) In the light of the comments and suggestions on the draft statute submitted by governments, as well as of those made during the debates in the Sixth Committee,

(i) To explore the implications and consequences of establishing an international criminal court and of the various manners by which this might be done;

(ii) To study the relationship between such a court and the United Nations and its organs;

(iii) To re-examine the draft statute;

(b) To submit a report to be considered by the General Assembly at its Ninth Session;".

The decision to establish this committee was contained in a Dutch amendment to the draft resolution which the Sixth Commission had adopted on Swedish initiative and which provided merely for a postponement of the discussion on the draft statute till the next session of the Assembly.

Regarding the definition of aggression the Sixth Committee has, after a lengthy discussion on the different aspects of the problem and on the Soviet proposal which has been introduced again this year, adopted a draft resolution to be approved by the Plenary Session of the Assembly. This draft resolution (Doc. A/C. 6/L. 265/Rev. 1) stresses the necessity to continue the efforts to arrive by common action at a generally acceptable definition of aggression, and envisages the creation of a special committee of fifteen members, which is to be invited to submit to the Ninth Session of the Assembly draft definitions of aggression or drafts clarifying the notion of aggression, and to study at the same time a number of specific questions which have arisen during the discussion on the problem. In connection with these questions the draft resolution makes a distinction between, on the one hand, the impact of a definition of agression on the maintenance of peace and security, and its influence on the different U.N. organs in the exercise of their competence, and, on the other, the questions aroused by the insertion of a definition of aggression in the Draft Code of Offences against the Peace and Security of Mankind and by its application in the framework of an international criminal jurisdiction.

BIBLIOGRAPHY

I. *BOOKS AND ARTICLES.*

ANDERSON, C. A., The Utility of the Proposed Trial and Punishment of Enemy Leaders, American Political Science Review, 1943.

ANZILOTTI, D., Corso di Diritto Internazionale, Vol. III, Rome 1915.

—, Cours de Droit International Public, 3me éd. traduit par G. Gidal, Paris, 1929.

AQUINAS, THOMAS, Summa Theologica.

ARONEANU, EUGENE, La guerre internationale d'intervention pour cause d'humanité, Revue Internationale de Droit Pénal, 1948.

BALASZ, A., Die Rechtliche Begründung des Nürnberger Urteils, Friedenswarte, 1946.

BALMER-BASILIUS, H. R., Nürenberg und das Weltgewissen, Friedenswarte, 1946.

BAUER, F., Die Kriegsverbrecher vor Gericht, Zürich—New York, 1945.

BEAUFORT, D., O.F.M., La guerre comme instrument de secours ou de punition, La Haye, 1933.

BELGION, MONTGOMERY, Victor's Justice, London 1948.

BIBO, ETIENNE, Le dogme du bellum justum et la theorie de l'infaillibilité juridique, Revue Internationale de la Théorie du Droit, 1936.

BIDDLE, FRANCIS, Le procès de Nuremberg, Revue Internationale de Droit Pénal, 1948.

BIRKETT, NORMAN, International Legal Theories evolved at Nuremberg, International Affairs, 1947.

BLUNTSCHLI, Le Droit International Codifié, Paris 1895.

BORCHARD, E., Effects of War on Law, A.J.I.L., 1946.

—, International Law and International Organisation, A.J.I.L., 1947.

Budapest Articles of Interpretation of the Kellogg Pact, reproduced in Transactions of the Grotius Society on 1935, London 1940.

BUTLER-MACCOBY, The Development of International Law, London 1928.

CAAMANO MARTÍNEZ, JOSE, Sobre el concepto Schmittiano de la guerra discriminatoria, Revista Espanola de Derecho Internacional, 1948.

CALOYANNI, M., L'Organisation de la Cour Permanente et son avenir, in R.d.C. de l'Academie de Droit International, Vol. 38., 1931, IV.

—, Memorandum on International Criminal Legislation and Peace, Revue International de Droit Pénal, 1946.

CASTRO, BARTHOLOMEO DE, Historia sui Temporis a morte Friderici II, Imperatoris Siciliaeque regis ab anno 1250 ad usque annum 1294 (re-edited in De Principe Templo Panormitano, libri XIII, of P.J.M. Amato, Panormitano e Societate Jesu, Palermo 1728.

Charter and Judgment of the Nuremberg Trial; History and Analysis, A/CN 4/5. (U.N. Publication 1949/V/7).

CHURCHILL, WINSTON, The Second World War, Vol. I, ("The Gathering Storm"), 1948.

COMTESSE, F. H., Betrachtungen zum Nurnberger Prozess, Schweizer Monatshefte, 1946.

COOPER, R. W., The Nuremberg Trial, London 1947.

COWLES, WILLIAM B., Universality of Jurisdiction over War Crimes, California Law Review, 1945.

DESCHEEMAECKER, J., Le Tribunal Militaire International des grands criminals de guerre, R.G.D.I.P., 1946.

DIAMENDESCO, JEAN, Le problème de l'aggression, Paris 1935.

DOMAN, NICHOLAS, Political Consequences of the Nuremberg Trial, Annals of the American Academy of Political and Social Science, 1946.

DONNEDIEU DE VABRES, H., Le procès de Nuremberg devant les principes modernes du Droit Pénal International, R.d.C., Vol. 70, 1947.

——, Le procès de Nuremberg, Revue de Science Criminelle et de Droit Pénal Comparé, 1947.

——, Le jugement de Nuremberg et le principe de la légalité des délits et des peines, Revue de Droit Pénal et de Criminologie, 1946–1947.

EAGLETON, CLYDE, The Attempt to Define Aggression, International Conciliation, No. 264, 1930.

——, The Attempt to Define War, International Conciliation, No. 291, 1933.

——, Punishment of War Criminals, A.J.I.L., 1943.

ECCARD, F., La Signification suprême du procès de Nuremberg, R.D.I., 1946.

ECK, D. VAN, Berechting van Oorlogsmisdadigers en de gronden voor een internationaal strafrecht, Nijmegen 1947.

D'EGLY, MONETHAULT, Histoire des Lois des Deux Siciles, Vol. I, Paris 1741.

EHARD, HANS, The Nuremberg Trial against the Major War Criminals and International Law, A.J.I.L., 1949.

EPPSTEIN, JOHN, The Catholic Tradition of the Law of Nations, London 1935.

Fällande Dom Som Friar, published by Hj. H. Procopé, Stockholm 1946.

FAUCHILLE-BONFILS, Traité de Droit International Public, Tome II, 8me éd., Paris 1921.

FENWICK, C. G., Draft Code of Offences against the Peace and Security of Mankind, A.J.I.L., 1948.

FINCH, G. A., Retribution for War Crimes, A.J.I.L., 1943.

——, The Nuremberg Trial and International Law, A.J.I.L., 1947.

——, Draft Statute of an International Criminal Court, A.J.I.L., 1952.

FISCHER WILLIAMS, JOHN, The Covenant of the League of Nations and War, Cambridge Law Journal, 1933.

FISCHLSCHWEIGER, H., Zum Problem der Kollektiv-haftung, Juristische Blätter, 1951.

FRANÇOIS, J. P. A., Handboek van het Volkenrecht, 2 Vols., 2nd ed., Zwolle 1949–1950.

——, De codificatie van het internationale recht, Economisch-Statistische Berichten, 1949. Nos. 1686–7.

GATHORNE-HARDY, A Short History of International Affairs, 1920–1939, 4th ed., London 1951.

GIRAUD, EMILE, La théorie de la légitime défense, R.d.C., Vol. 49, 1934.

——, La nullité de la politique internationale des grandes démocraties, 1919–1939, Paris 1949.

GLASER, STEFAN, Le principe de la légalité des délits et des peines et les procès des criminels de guerre, Revue de Droit Pénal et de Criminologie, 1947–8.

GLUECK, S., War Criminals, New York 1944.

——, The Nuremberg Trial and Aggressive War, New York 1946.

GOODHART, A. L., Questions and Answers concerning the Nuremberg Trial, International Law Quarterly, 1947.

GOODRICH and HAMBRO, The Charter of the United Nations, 2nd ed., Boston 1949.

GRANT-TEMPERLY, Europe in the Nineteenth and Twentieth Century, 6th ed., London 1952.

GRAVEN, JEAN, De la justice internationale à la paix: les enseignements de Nuremberg, R.D.I., 1946–1947.

GREWE, W. and KÜSTER, O., Nürnberg als Rechtsfrage: Eine Diskussion, Stuttgart, 1947.
GROSS, L., The Criminality of Aggressive War, American Political Science Review, 1947.
GROTIUS, H., De Jure Belli ac Pacis (1625), edited by P. J. Molhuysen, Leiden 1919.
GUGGENHEIM, P., Lehrbuch des Völkerrechts, Basle 1951.
—, Die Schweiz, das alte und das neue Völkerrecht, Schweizer Monatshefte, 1946.
GUTTERIDGE, JOYCE A. C., The Geneva Conventions of 1949, B.Y.I.L., 1949.

HARVARD RESEARCH on Rights and Duties of States in Case of Aggression, A.J.I.L., Supplement 1939.
HANKEY, LORD, Politics, Trials and Errors, Oxford 1950.
HAZAN, EDOUARD TAWFIK, L'Etat de nécessité en droit pénal interétatique et international, Paris 1949.
HERTZ, W. J., Le problème de l'aggression en droit international, Revue Internationale de la Théorie du Droit, 1935.
HERZOG, J. B., La répression des criminels de guerre, Revue Pénale Suisse, 1948.
History of the United War Crimes Commission, and the Developement of the Laws of War, London, His Majesty's Stationery Office, 1948.
HOBBES, T., De Cive, 1642.
—, Leviathan, 1650.
HONIG, F., Nuremberg, Justice or Vengeance? World Affairs, 1947.
HORWITZ, The Tokyo Trial, International Conciliation, No. 465, 1950.
HOWARD, Pacific Blockade, 1908.
HUGUENEY, L., Le procès de Nuremberg devant les principes modernes du droit pénal international, Revue Internationale de Droit Pénal, 1948.

JACKSON, W. E., Putting the Nuremberg Law to Work, Foreign Affairs, 1947.
JANECZEK, E., Nuremberg Judgment in the Light of International Law, Geneva 1949.
JENNINGS, Government in Commission, B.Y.I.L., 1946.
JESSUP, PHILIP C., The Crime of Aggression and the Future of International Law, Political Science Quarterly, 1947.

KANT, I., Perpetual Peace, re-edited after first English translation, New York 1939.
KEEN, F. N., The Preamble of the Pact of Paris, Transactions of the Grotius Society on 1935, London 1940.
KEENAN, J. B. and BROWN, B. F., Crimes against International Law, Washington 1950.
KELSEN, HANS, Collective and Individual responsibility in International Law, California Law Review, 1942–3.
—, The Legal Situation of Germany according to the Declaration of Germany, A.J.I.L. 1945.
—, Will the Judgment in the Nuremberg Trial constitute a Precedent in International Law? International Law Quarterly, 1947.
—, The Law of the United Nations, London 1950.
KENNEY, ROWLAND, The Northern Tangle, London 1946.
KIPP, HEINZ, Moderne Probleme des Kriegsrecht in der Spätscholastik, Paderborn 1935.
KOMARNICKI, T., La question de l'integrité territoriale dans le Pacte de la Société des Nations, 1923.
KOMARNICKI, W., La définition de l'agresseur, R.d.C., Vol. 75, 1949.
KRANZBÜHLER, OTTO, Nürnberg als Rechtsproblem, in Um Recht und Frieden, Festgabe für Erich Kaufmann, Stuttgart-Köln, 1950.

KUNZ, J. L., Individual and Collective Self-defense in Article 51 of the Charter of the United Nations, A.J.I.L., 1947.

LACHS, MANFRED, Le Jugement de Nuremberg, Revue Internationale de Droit Pénal, 1946.
LA PRADELLE, A. DE, Une révolution dans le droit pénal international, Nouvelle Revue de Droit International Privé, 1946.
LARNAUDE, F. and DE LAPRADELLE, A., Examen de la responsabilité de l'Empereur Guillaume II d'Allemagne, Journal de Droit International, 1919.
LAUTERPACHT, H., 'Resort to War' and the Interpretation of the Covenant during the Manchurian Dispute, A.J.I.L., 1934.
—, The Grotian Tradition of International Law, B.Y.I.L., 1946.
LAWRENCE, LORD, The Nuremberg Trial, International Affairs, 1947.
LEVY, A. G. D., The Law and Procedure of War Crime Trials, American Political Science Review, 1934 (Vol. 37).
LISZT, F. VON, Das Völkerrecht, 12th ed., Berlin 1925.
LIVIUS, Historiae Ab Urbe Condita, Teubner ed. T. IV, 1898.

MACHIAVELLI, N., Il Principe (1517).
MANDELSTAM, A. N., L'Interpretation du Pacte Briand-Kellogg par les gouvernements et les parlements des Etats signataires, Paris 1934.
MANNER, G., The Legal Nature and Punishment of Criminal Acts of Violence contrary to the Laws of War, A.J.I.L., 1943.
MAUGHAM, VISCOUNT, U.N.O. and War Crimes, London 1951.
MAYNARD, J. A., Crimes et criminels de guerre, Revue International de Droit Pénal, 1946.
MCNAIR, ARNOLD, The Legal Meaning of War and the Relation of War to Reprisals, Grotius Society Transactions, Vol. II, 1926.
MERLE, M., Le procès de Nuremberg et le châtiment des criminels de guerre, Paris 1949.
MIRKINE-GUETZEVITCH, BORIS, La 'guerre juste' dans le droit constitutionnel français, R.G.D.I.P. 1950.
MOSLER, H., Die Kriegshandlung im rechtswidrigen Krieg, Jahrbuch für Internationales und Ausländisches Offentliches Recht, I, Hamburg 1948.
MOUTON, M. W., Oorlogsmisdrijven en het Internationale Recht, The Hague 1947.

NEPOS, Vitae, Teubner 1874.
NUSSBAUM, A., A Concise History of the Law of Nations, New York 1947.

OPPENHEIM, L., International Law, edited by H. LAUTERPACHT, Vol. I, 7th ed., London 1948. Vol. II, 7th ed., London 1952.
PELLA, V. V., La Criminalité Collective des Etats et le droit pénal de l'avenir, 2nd ed., Bucharest 1926.
—, 'La Nature Criminelle de la Guerre', discutée par l'Union Interparlementaire, et quelques aspets du Pacte Kellogg, Bulletin Interparliamentaire, 1929.
—, La Justice Pénale Internationale, R.D.I., 1945.
—, La guerre-crime et les criminels de guerre, Paris 1946.
—, Fonctions Pacificatrices du droit pénal international et fin du système traditionnel des traités de paix, R.G.D.I.P. 1947.
—, Towards an International Criminal Court, A.J.I.L., 1950.
PHILLIMORE, R., Commentaries upon International Law, Vol. III, London 1885.
PHILLIPSON, COLEMAN, The International Law and Custom of Ancient Greece and Rome, Vol. II, London 1911.
PLUTARCHUS, Vitae Parallelae, T. II, Teubner 1874.
POLITIS, N., The New Aspects of International Law, Washington 1928.

POMPE, C. A., Toepassing van multilaterale verdragen op derde staten, Rechtsgeleerd Magazijn 'Themis', 1951.
POMPE, W. P. J., Handboek van het Nederlandse Strafrecht, 3rd ed., Zwolle 1950.
—–, Enige aspecten van het politieke strafrecht, Utrecht 1947.
—–, Les trois degrés du droit pénal, Revue de Droit Pénal et de Criminologie, 1950.

RADIN, MAX, Justice at Nuremberg, Foreign Affairs, 1946.
REDSLOB, R., Histoire des Grands Principes du Droit des Gens, Paris 1923.
REGOUT, R., S. J., La doctrine de la Guerre Juste de Saint Augustin à nos jours d'après les théologiens et les canonistes Catholiques, Paris 1934.
RENOUVIN, PIERRE, La Crise Européene et la Grand Guerre, Paris 1904–1918.
RÖLING, B. V. A., Strafbaarheid van de agressieve oorlog, Groningen 1950.
—–, Over Psychologische Aspecten van het proces tegen de Japanse Major War Criminals, Publication No. 32 of the Psychiatrisch-Juridisch Gezelschap, Amsterdam 1950.
—–, Stand en Ontwikkeling van het Internationaal Strafrecht, Tijdschrift voor Strafrecht, 1951.
—–, Internationaal Strafrechterlijke Organisatie, Tijdschrift voor Strafrecht. 1952.
ROUX, J. A., A propos de la non-rectroactivité de la loi pénale, R.D.I., 1947.
RUTGERS, V. J., Strafbaarstelling van de aanvalsoorlog, Amsterdam 1928.

SALDANA, Q., La Justice pénale internationale. R.d.C., Vol. 10, 1925.
SALVIOLI, G., Le concept de la guerre juste chez les écrivains antérieurs à Grotius, trad. fr. 1918.
SCELLE, G., Cours de Droit International Public, 3me ed., Paris 1946–1947.
—–, Manuel de droit international public, Paris 1948.
SCHICK, F. B., The Nuremberg Trial and the International Law of the Future, A.J.I.L., 1947.
SCHMITT, CARL, Die Wendung zum diskriminierden Kriegsbegriffs, Schriften der Akademie für Deutsches Recht, Munich 1938.
SCHWARZENBERGER, GEORG, International Law and Totalitarian Lawlessness, 1943.
—–, Jus Pacis ac Belli, A.J.I.L., 1943.
—–, A forerunner of Nuremberg, The Breisach War Crime Trial of 1474, Manchester Guardian, 28 Sept. 1946.
—–, The Judgment of Nuremberg, Tulane Law Review, 1946–7.
—–, Power Politics, 2nd ed., London 1951.
SERRA, ENRICO, L'Aggressione Internazionale, Milan 1946.
SHOTWELL, JAMES T., 'War as an Instrument of National Policy', and its Renunciation in the Pact of Paris, New York 1929.
SOTTILE, A., Les criminels de guerre et le nouveau droit pénal international, seul moyen pour assurer la paix du monde, R.D.I., 1945.
—–, Un peu plus de justice S.V.P., R.D.I., 1948.
STALIN, J., Sur la grande guerre de l'Union Soviétique pour le salut de la patrie, 5th ed., Editions in foreign languages, Moscow 1946.
STEINLEIN, W., Der Begriff des nicht herausgeforderten Angriffs in Bündnisverträgen seit 1870 und inbesondere im Locarnovertrag, dissertation Frankfurt, Leipzig 1927.
STIMSON, HENRY L., The Nuremberg Trial, Landmark in Law, Foreign Affairs 1947.
STRATMANN, F., O.P., Weltkirche und Weltfriede, Augsburg 1924.
STRUPP, KARL, Elements de Droit International Public, Paris 1927.
—–, Der Kellogg Pact im Rahmen des Kriegsvorbeugungsrechts, Leipzig 1928.
—–, Documents pour servir à l'Histoire du Droit des Gens, 2nd Edition of German edition. Vol. I. Berlin 1933.

SUAREZ, FRANCISCUS, Selection from Three Works, The Classics of International Law, Carnegie Endowment for International Peace, No. 20, Oxford 1944.
SUTTON, D. N., The Trial of Tojo, American Bar Association Journal, Feb. 1950.

TAUBE, M. DE, Etudes sur le développement historique du droit international dans l'Europe Orientale, R.d.C. 1926, Vol. II.
TAYLOR, TELFORD, The Nuremberg War Crimes Trials, International Conciliation, No. 450, 1949.
TELDERS, B. M., De juridieke waardering van de oorlog, Leiden 1931.
TEITGEN, M., Le Jugement de Nuremberg, R.D.I., 1946.
THIEL, J. H., Het probleem van de natuurlijke vijandschap in het Romeinse oorlogsrecht, Amsterdam 1946.
TRAININ, A. N., Hitlerite Responsibility under Criminal Law, edited by A. Y. Vishinsky, London 1945.

ULLMAN, W., The Medieval Idea of Law, a Study of Lucas de Penna, London 1946.

VANDERPOL, A., La doctrine scolastique du droit de guerre, Paris 1919.
VEICOPOULOS, N., Les responsabilités des individuels dans la préparation de la guerre, R.D.I., 1948.
VERZIJL, J. H. W., Le Droit des Prises, Leiden 1924.
—, De aanwijzing van den aanvaller bij internationale conflicten, Weekblad voor het Recht, 1933, Nos. 12644 and 12645.
VIGNOL, RENE, La Définition de l'aggresseur dans la guerre, Paris 1933.
VITORIA, FRANCISCUS, De Indis recenter inventis and De Iure Belli (1539) edited in the Classics of International Law, Carnegie Endowment for International Peace, No. 7, Washington 1917.
VOLLE, H., Definition des Angreifers und Beistandsverpflichtungen in den Europaïschen Verträgen des Nachkriegszeit, Europa-Archiv, 1949.
VOLLENHOVEN, Grotius and Geneva, Bibliotheca Visscheriana, vol. VI, Leiden 1926.
—, Grotius and Geneva, Tijdschrift voor Strafrecht, 1926. Vol. XXXVI.

WECHSLER, HERBERT, The Issues of the Nuremberg Trial, Political Science Quarterly, 1947.
WEHBERG, HANS, The Outlawry of War. New York 1931.
WESTLAKE, J., International Law, Vol. II, 2nd ed., 1913.
WHEATON'S International Law, Vol. II, 7th English ed., London 1944.
WOOLSEY, L. H., The Chaco Dispute, A.J.I.L., 1934.
World Court Reports, ed. by Manley O. Hudson, Vol. I, Carnegie Endowment, Washington 1934.
WRIGHT, QUINCY, Changes in the Concept of War, A.J.I.L., 1924.
—, When does War Exist?, A.J.I.L., 1932.
—, The Concept of Aggression in International Law, A.J.I.L., 1935.
—, A Study of War, 2 Vols, Chicago 1944.
—, The Law of the Nuremberg Trial, A.J.I.L. 1947.
—, Legal Positivism and the Nuremberg Judgment, A.J.I.L., 1948.
—, Proposal for an International Criminal Court, A.J.I.L., 1952.
WRIGHT, LORD, War Crimes under International Law, Law Quaterly Review, 1946.
WU, AITCHEN K., China and the Soviet Union, London 1950.

ZIMMERMAN, JOHN L., A Note on the Occupation of Iceland by American Forces, Political Science Quarterly, 1947.

II. *DOCUMENTS (principal documents and official publications referred to in this study).*

General

INTERNATIONAL LEGISLATION, a collection of the texts of multipartite international instruments of general interest, edited by MANLEY O. HUDSON (Washington, Carnegie Endowment for International Peace, 1931–).

WORLD COURT REPORTS, a collection of the judgments, orders and opinions of the Permanent Court of International Justice, edited by MANLEY O. HUDSON (Washington, Carnegie Endowment for International Peace, 1934–).

COLLIARD, C. A., Droit International et Histoire Diplomatique, Documents, Paris 1950.

The Hague Conventions of 1899 and 1907, edited by J. B. SCOTT, 3rd ed., 1918.

Peace Conference of Versailles

Commission des responsabilités des auteurs de la guerre, Documentation Internationale. La Paix de Versailles, No. 3, Paris 1930.

League of Nations

Report of the League of Nations Commission on the Chaco dispute between Bolivia and Paraguay. A.J.I.L., 1934, Supplement.

Report of the Belgian Delegate, DE BROUCKERE, for the Preparatory Commission of the Disarmament Conference, Doc. C. 740, M. 279, 1926. Series IX.

Memorandum on Articles 10, 11 and 16 of the Covenant by V. RUTGERS, L.o.N., Documents of the Preparatory Commission for the Disarmament Conference, C. 165, M. 50, 1928, Series VI.

Report on the Definition of Aggression (POLITIS Report, 1933), Doc. DC/CG 108.

United Nations

U.N.C.I.O., U.N. Conference on International Organisation, Commission III, Committee 3 (on Enforcement Measures). Doc. 881, III/3/3, May 9th, 1945.

Fifth Session of General Assembly.
- Question of the duties of States in the event of the outbreak of hostilities.
  - First Committee Meetings, 4th–10th November 1950, U.N. Doc. A/C. I/SR. 384–390.
- Question of Code of Offences.
  - Sixth Committee, U.N. Docs. A/C 6/SR. 233–239. A/C. 6/SR. 235.
  - Report of 6th Committee on Report of I.L.C., A/1639.

Sixth Session of General Assembly.
- Question of the Definition of Aggression.
  - First Committee Meetings, 5th–23rd January 1952, U.N. Doc. A/C. 6/SR 278–295.
  - Report to the General Assembly of the Session held 1st–31st Aug. 1951, of the Committee on International Criminal Jurisdiction.
  - Observations of Governments on the Draft Code of Offences against the Peace and Security of Mankind and on the Question of the Definition of Aggression, A/2162 (1952).
  - Question de la définition de l'agression, Rapport du secrétaire Général, A/2211 (3 October 1952).

NUREMBERG

International Conference on Military Trials, Report of ROBERT H. JACKSON, State Dept. Publication No. 3080, Washington 1949.
Trial of the Major War Criminals before the International Military Tribunal, Nuremberg, 14th Nov. 1945–1st Oct. 1946, published at Nuremberg, Germany, 33 Vols..

TOKYO

Charter, Indictment and Opening Statement, published in Trial of the Japanese War Criminals, Dept. of State Publication, no. 2613, Far Eastern Series 12. (Washington 1946).
Judgment of the International Military Tribunal for the Far East, in mimeographed Records of the Proceedings of the I.M.T. for the Far East, pp. 48445–49858.
Dissenting Opinions:
JUSTICE PAL, Separate Transcript.
JUSTICE BERNARD, Separate Transcript.
JUSTICE RÖLING, Separate Transcript.

OTHER POST WAR TRIALS

Law Reports of Trials of War Criminals, selected and prepared by the U.N.W.C.C., 15 Vols..
Judgment in the I. G. Farben Trial, Law Reports, Vol. X.
Statement of Defence on Breach of Peace and its Culpability. Transcript.
Judgment in the Krupp Trial, Law Reports, Vol. X.
Judgment in the German High Command Trial, Law Reports, Vol. XII.
Digest of Laws and Cases, Law Reports, Vol. XV.
Judgment in the Weiszaecker Case ('Ministries' Case), Transcript, and Dissenting Opinion of Justice Powers, Transcript.

INTERNATIONAL LAW COMMISSION

Report on First Session, U.N. Doc. A/925.
Report on Second Session, U.N. Doc. A/1316.
Report on Third Session, Doc. A/1858.
First Report on the Draft Code of Offences against the Peace and Security of Mankind (by J. SPIROPOULOS). Doc. A/CN 4/25.
Second Report on the Draft Code of Offences against the Peace and Security of Mankind (by SPIROPOULOS) A/CN. 4/44.
Memorandum concerning a Draft Code of Offences against the Peace and Security of Mankind (by PROF. PELLA), I.L.C. 2nd Session, U.N. Doc. A/CN 4/39.
Report on the Formulation of the Nuremberg Principles (by J. SPIROPOULOS) I.L.C. 2nd Session, U.N. Doc. A/CN 4/22.

INDEX

(In this Index no authors after 1800 have been included.)